About the Author

David Leeming (photo by Leopold Quarles)

David Leeming received his B.A. in English from Princeton University and his Ph.D. in Comparative Literature from New York University. He spent eight years teaching at Robert College in Istanbul and twenty-six years at the University of Connecticut in Storrs, where he is an emeritus professor of English and Comparative Literature. He has traveled widely, studying world myths and traditions. His books include a biography of James Baldwin and many books on mythology, including *Myth: A Biography of Belief* (Oxford, 2002), *Jealous Gods and Chosen People: The Mythology of the Middle East* (Oxford 2004), *The Oxford Companion to World Mythology* (Oxford, 2005), *Creation Myths of the World* (ABC-CLIO, 2010), *Medusa: In the Mirror of Time* (Reaktion, 2013), and a revised edition of *The World of Myth* (Oxford, 2014). He is also editor in chief of *The Encyclopedia of Psychology and Religion* (second edition, Springer, 2014).

Also from Visible Ink Press

Please visit the "Handy" series website at www.handyanswers.com.

THE
HANDY
MYTHOLOGY
ANSWER
BOOK

David A. Leeming PhD

Detroit

THE HANDY MYTHOLOGY ANSWER BOOK

Visible Ink Press®
43311 Joy Rd., #414
Canton, MI 48187–2075

Visible Ink Press is a registered trademark of Visible Ink Press LLC.

Most Visible Ink Press books are available at special quantity discounts when purchased in bulk by corporations, organizations, or groups. Customized printings, special imprints, messages, and excerpts can be produced to meet your needs. For more information, contact Special Markets Director, Visible Ink Press, www.visibleink.com, or 734–667–3211.

Managing Editor: Kevin S. Hile
Art Director: Mary Claire Krzewinski
Typesetting: Marco Di Vita
Proofreaders: Dorothy Smith and Aarti Stephens
Indexer: Shoshana Hurwitz

Cover images: Ulysses and the Sirens courtesy The Art History Archive. All other images courtesy Shutterstock.

ISBN: 978–1–57859–475–7 (paperback)
ISBN: 978–1–57859–521–1 (pdf ebook)
ISBN: 978–1–57859–523–5 (Kindle ebook)
ISBN: 978–1–57859–522–8 (ePub ebook)

10 9 8 7 6 5 4

Library of Congress Cataloging–in–Publication Data

Leeming, David Adams, 1937–
The handy mythology answer book / by David A. Leeming Ph.D.
   pages cm
  ISBN 978–1–57859–475–7 (paperback)
1. Mythology–Miscellanea. I. Title.
BL312.L435 2014
201'.3–dc23   2014013298

Contents

Photo Credits *ix*

Introduction *xi*

DEFINITIONS AND ORIGINS ... 1
Definitions (1) ... Prehistoric Mythology (2) ... Myth-Makers (3) ... Mythographers and Mythologists (4) ... Types of Myths: Creation, Gods, and Heroes ... Philosophy and Psychological Myths (7)

MIDDLE EASTERN MYTHOLOGIES ... 11
Sumerian Gods and Heroes (13) ... Inanna's Descent (16) ... The Semites (18) ... Mythology of Babylon (19) ... The Gilgamesh Epic (21) ... The Hebrews and Canaanites (25) ... The Bible and Judaism (27) ... The Arabs and Islam (28) ... Muhammad (29) ... The Christian Story (31) ... Iran: Zoroastrianism and Mithraism (32) ... The Phrygians (33)

EGYPTIAN MYTHOLOGY ... 35
Egyptian Religion and Mythology (36) ... The Egyptian Pantheons (40) ... Egyptian Creation Myths (42) ... The Myth of Isis, Osiris, and Horus (44) ... Other Egyptian Myths and Influences (47)

CYCLADIC, MINOAN, MYCENAEAN, AND ARCHAIC GREEK MYTHOLOGY ... 49
The Cyclades and Crete (49) ... Daedalus, Icarus, and Theseus and the Minotaur (51) ... Minoan Religion and Mythology (53) ... The Mycenaeans and Homer (54) ... The Trojan War and the *Iliad* (57) ... The *Odyssey* (58) ... Hesiod, the Greek Creation Myth, Wars among the Gods (63)

CLASSICAL GREEK MYTHOLOGY ... 69
The Greek Pantheon and the Olympians (71) ... The Greek Gods and Human Life (76) ... Origins of the Greek Gods (78) ... The Greek Mystery Cults and Hero Sagas (79) ... Herakles and the Twelve Labors (81) ... Theseus (83) ... Perseus and Medusa (85) ...

Jason and the Golden Fleece (87) … The Meaning of the Greek Hero Myths (89) … The Dramas of Ancient Athens (90) … Aeschylus and the *Oresteia* (93) … Sophocles and the Oedipus Cycle (96) … Euripedes, Medea, and Dionysus (100) … Orpheus, Orphism, and Philosophical Myths (103)

ROMAN MYTHOLOGY … 107

Indo-Europeans (108) … Latins, Etruscans, and Archaic Rome (109) … Romulus and Remus (111) … Mythology of the Roman Republic (112) … Aeneus and Virgil's *Aeneid* (114) … Ovid and the *Metamorphoses* (118) … The Emperor-God and Foreign Borrowings (122)

CELTIC MYTHOLOGY … 125

The Insular Celts: Ireland and Wales (127) … The Tuatha de Danaan (129) … Cuchulainn and the *Tain* (131) … Fionn and the Fenian Cycle (133) … Welsh Mythology (134) … The Welsh Pantheon (136) … Heroes of Wales (138) … King Arthur (140)

NORSE MYTHOLOGY … 143

Snorri and the *Eddas* (143) … The Norse Pantheon (146) … The Norse Creation Myth and Wars in Heaven (147) … The Hanging of Odin and Ragnarok (152) … The Norse Hero Sagas: The Volsungs (153) … Norse Mythology and the World (155)

INDIAN MYTHOLOGY … 157

The Indo-Iranians and the Indus Valley Culture (158) … Vedic Culture (159) … Post-Vedic Hinduism (161) … The Indian Creation (163) … The Hindu Pantheon (165) …

Vishnu (167) … Krishna (168) … The *Mahabharata* (170) … The *Rāmāyana* (172) … Shiva (173) … Devi: The Great Goddess (174) … Buddhism (175)

EAST ASIAN MYTHOLOGY: CHINA AND JAPAN … 179

Sources of Chinese Mythology (179) … The Chinese Pantheon (180) … The Chinese War in Heaven, Creation, and Flood (182) … Chinese Heroes (184) … Historizing Chinese Myths; Confucism and Taoism (187) … Buddhism, Shamanism, and Chinese Mythology (188) … The Japanese (189) … Sources of Japanese Mythology (189) … The Creation: Izanagi and Izanami (191) … Amaterasu: The Great Goddess (192) … The Japanese Buddhist and Shinto Pantheons (193)

CENTRAL ASIAN MYTHOLOGY … 197

Central Asian Themes and Gods (198) … Master Spirits and Shamans (199) … Central Asian Creation and Devil-Tricksters (200) … Central Asian Heroes (203)

OCEANIC MYTHOLOGIES: AUSTRALIAN ABORIGINE AND POLYNESIAN … 205

Australian Aborigines and the Dreaming (205) … Australian Creations and Floods (207) … The Polynesians: From New Zealand to Hawaii (209) … Polynesian Pantheons (210) … Polynesian Creation and Flood Myths (211) … Maui, the Hero and Trickster (212)

AFRICAN MYTHOLOGIES … 215

The African Supreme Being and Creation (216) … African Goddesses and Tricksters (219) … Legba and Ananse (220) … African Heroes (222)

MESOAMERICAN AND SOUTH AMERICAN MYTHOLOGIES: MAYA, AZTEC, INCA ... 225

Mesoamerica (225) ... The Maya and the *Popol Vuh* (226) ... The Mayan Gods and Heroes (227) ... Monte Alban and Teotihuacan (229) ... The Toltec and Aztec (230) ... Huitzilopochtli and Quetzalcoatl (232) ... The South Americans (234) ... The Inca (235)

NATIVE NORTH AMERICAN MYTHOLOGIES ... 239

Native American Spirits and Creators (240) ... The Native American Great Goddess (242) ... Native American Tricksters (246) ... Earth Divers and Emergers (249) ... Native American Hero Myths (252)

MODERN MYTHS ... 257

Modern Attempts to Explain Existence (257) ... Psychology and Myth (259) ... The Heroic Monomyth and Modern Gods (261)

THE WORLD MYTH ... 265

Principal Components of the World Myth (265) ... The Supreme Being and Great Goddess (266) ... Fertility and Animal Gods (268) ... Tricksters (269) ... War in Heaven and the Creation (270) ... The Flood (275) ... The Hero (276) ... The World Myth (282)

APPENDIX 1: PARALLEL MYTHOLOGY

Chart of Universal Mythological Types and Themes ... 283

APPENDIX 2: SELECTED MYTHOLOGICAL TEXTS ... 305

The Descent of Inanna (Ishtar) into the Lower World (305) ... The Epic of Gilgamesh, Tablet XI, The Story of the Flood (309) ... Noah's Flood (318) ... The Egyptian Book of the Dead: The Papyrus of Ani (320) ... The Odyssey (324) ... Metamorphoses (329) ... The Words of Odin the High One (334)

CHARACTERS IN MYTHOLOGY   *341*

GLOSSARY   *371*

BIBLIOGRAPHY   *377*

INDEX   *385*

Photo Credits

Thomas Aleto: p. 230.

Jim Anzalone: p.79.

W.V. Bailey: p. 251.

Vijay Bandari: p. 171.

Guillaume Blanchard: p. 45.

Andreas F. Borchert: p. 134.

Bryan Brandenburg: p. 258.

Bruno Comby: p. 259.

Massimo Finizio: p. 64.

Dr. Andreas Hugentobler: p. 199.

George Lazenby: p. 273.

Alan Levine: p. 241.

David Liam Moran: p. 77.

Marie-Lan Nguyen: p. 97.

Non-European collection of the Castello Sforzesco: p. 218.

Okkisafire: p. 186.

Oosoom: p. 136.

Mike Peel: p. 17

Shannon Prickett: p. 211.

Lauren Raine: p. 243.

Steve Ridgway: p. 135.

Kris Roderburg: p. 73.

Sardaka: p. 206.

Steve Swayne: p. 75.

Tetraktys: p. 81.

Tropenmuseum: p. 221.

UNESCO/Michel Ravassard: p. 5 (image of Claude Lévi-Strauss)

Kurt Wichmann: p. 119.

A. Hunter Wright: p. 114.

All other images are in the public domain.

Introduction

In common usage "mythology" used to mean Greek and Roman mythology with perhaps a few Norse stories of Thor and Odin thrown in. The "myths" that made up this mythology had been sufficiently cleaned up by Edith Hamilton and others to make them palatable for even the very young. The stories were fascinating, even if they were obviously untrue. In the western world they formed an important part of "classical education," in which schoolboys, and a few schoolgirls, of a certain class learned their Greek and Latin in part by reading Homer, Virgil, and even some sanitized Ovid. The myths themselves were a vehicle for the learning of language, for an appreciation of literature, and perhaps for some slight understanding of "pagan" culture.

It was not until the advent of such thinkers as Sigmund Freud, Carl Jung, Mircea Eliade, and, most specifically, Joseph Campbell with his *Hero with a Thousand Faces,* published in 1949, that it began to become fashionable to think of myths as in some sense "true" and relevant to the lives of all of us. In this new way of thinking, myths could be considered psychological metaphors, through which "primitive" societies expressed themselves, just as each of us expresses the "inner self" through the bizarre narratives of our dreams. If it was important to look for the meanings behind—the "truth" within—our dreams, why was it not just as important to look for the truth within the "cultural dreams" we call myths? And just as Americans and Western Europeans had dreams, so obviously did Chinese, Afghans, and Polynesians, for instance. Sir James Frazer, in his *Golden Bough,* and other pioneers of anthropology have long reported that these "pagans" had folktales just as worthy of being called "myths" as those of the Greeks. And perhaps not only people of the "dead" religions had myths. Students of world religions were well aware of the strange—obviously "untrue"—stories that were so important to Hindus, Shinto believers, and other non-monotheists whose religions are still practiced.

Inevitably, scholars began to make further comparisons. How did the creation stories of Native Americans or Bantus compare to creation stories of the Hindus or the Australian Aborigines? As communication between races and beliefs have increased in the gradually emerging "global village" another idea has become current. If monotheists think of stories from the Indian *Vedas* or the Japanese *Nihongi* as "myths," is it not just as likely that Hindus and Buddhists and Zoroastrians think of stories such as the parting of the Red Sea for the ancient Hebrews or the Resurrection of Jesus for Christians as, from their perspectives, "myths," as well? Seas, after all, do not part, and people do not rise from the dead any more than goddesses are born from a god's head or than the first people emerged from a hole in the earth.

All of these questions, thoughts, and comparisons have led to a much more important question. If humans all over the world have created religions based on dreamlike, untrue stories, is there any real value to these stories—these "myths"—or might we better conclude simply that all humans are deluded? Once again, the great contribution of the comparatists has been to insist that rather than assuming universal delusion, we compare the myths of the world to make some sense of what the human species as a whole is trying to say with its strange tales of creations, gods, and heroes. In short, it has become no longer possible to relegate the study of myths to the study of "dead" languages or religions. Instead, we have recognized that myths somehow have to do with us and with the way we live our lives here and now, whatever our cultural and religious traditions and beliefs.

Comparative mythology as a subject has revealed many common human thought patterns. Remembering as we always must that myths are cultural, that to emerge into form they must wear the "clothes" of particular cultures and reflect the concerns, climates, traditions, and needs of those cultures, it is also inevitable that we notice the universal patterns or archetypal forms that are revealed when myths of the world are compared.

Many important thinkers of the twentieth and twenty-first centuries have accepted the challenge of such comparison. Their names have themselves taken on a mythic aura among those who study mythology. Carl Jung and Heinrich Zimmer applied the comparative method to Indian mythology. The great French anthropologist Claude Lévi-Strauss used myth to argue, in such seminal works as *The Raw and the Cooked* and *The Naked Man,* that the so-called "primitive" or "savage" mind possessed the same mythic structures as the so-called "civilized" mind of the West. Paul Radin used Native North American mythology to trace the meaning of the universal trickster character. Eric Neumann looked for and found the Great Goddess archetype wearing many cultural clothes. Charles Long did the same thing with creation myths, and Alan Dundes did it with the flood motif. Samuel Noah Kramer exposed and explained the universal reality of the extraordinary mythology of ancient Mesopotamia. Northrop Frye applied the archetypes of mythology to a new approach to literary criticism in his iconic *Anatomy of Criticism*. More contemporary comparative approaches include those of William Doty in his comprehensive study, *Mythography: A Study of Myths and Rituals,* the ground-breaking work of Bruce Lincoln on the question of the powerful and sometimes dangerous use of myth as ideological narrative, and the studies by Mary Douglas on the role of the human body in a given society's mythic symbolism. Feminist critics such as Hélène Cixous have shed new light on such ancient myths as that of Medusa, in effect changing a monster into a symbol of powerful womanhood.

The understanding of the importance of comparing and discovering the unifying power of the great stories of world religion and mythology did not, of course, begin in the twentieth century. As early as the thirteenth century, the great Islamic Sufi, Celaladin Rumi—the founder of the "Whirling Dervishes"—reminded us that all religious rituals and stories are but paths to the same "truth." The crucial point was not to become so attached to one's own story, one's own path, as to fail to understand the validity of other stories and paths.

The comparative mythologist is not concerned with individual belief so much as universal consciousness. When the mythologist speaks of the "myths" of Judaism, Christianity, and Islam, for instance, the purpose is not to denigrate the beliefs of these religions or to label them as "untrue." It is rather to help the reader to see that the sacred stories of the world all point as metaphors to certain universal human concerns. Literal or fundamentalist belief is one thing; a consideration of human collectivity is another.

In this book I have attempted to present a comprehensive picture of world mythology in some of its most highly developed forms. Many mythologies have, of course, been left out. Inasmuch as every culture, past and present, has its own cultural dreams, to include every mythology the world has ever known would be a task well beyond the scope of the present project. After beginning with a chapter on general questions about myth and the origins of mythology in prehistoric times—that is, before the invention of the means to preserve narrative—I have taken up what I have judged to be some of the most revelatory mythic traditions. The chapters that follow cover mythologies from the Middle East, Africa, Europe, Asia, the Americas, Australia, and Polynesian cultures. The penultimate chapter briefly considers modern mythology, a chapter to which readers will want to add their own questions and answers.

Throughout these chapters I have attempted to lead the reader to the recognition of the larger patterns emerging from the discussion of cultural traditions and the retelling of the great myths themselves.

The text ends with a chart of mythological motifs treated by various cultures and a glossary of useful terms for the mythologist. The bibliography includes works referred to or consulted in this study and other works that may be considered a list of suggestions for further study.

DEFINITIONS
AND ORIGINS

DEFINITIONS

What is a myth?

In common usage a myth is a generally held belief that reason tells us is untrue. In all likelihood it is a "myth" that George Washington never told a lie or that eating an apple a day will "keep the doctor away." As limited as this understanding of myth is, it is related to a more sophisticated understanding in which a myth is a story—usually about gods and heroes—that is held by some to be true, but which to others is clearly untrue because it exceeds the possibilities of common experience. Some Native Americans, for instance, tell a complex story about how "in the beginning" they emerged from the earth. Most other people would speak of this story not as a fact but as a myth.

It can be said that a myth is first of all a narrative, a story that is of deep importance to a particular group of people—a family, a clan, a tribe, a religion, a nation. Some see myths as primitive attempts to explain natural phenomena. In this sense, the story of the departure and annual return of the Greek goddess Persephone is an "explanation" of the changing seasons. Many scholars believe that myths are articulations in story form of religious rituals. Thus, the story of the murder and resurrection of the Egyptian god Osiris is related to Egyptian funereal ceremonies. Others see myths as metaphors or allegories that help humans feel related to the universe, or that unite individuals as a group. The Zulu creation myth unites the Zulus as a culture; it gives them a clear identity and source of being. Some analysts see myths as comparable to dreams in that they reflect the inner concerns, neuroses, and priorities—the collective psyche—of the culture that "dreams" them. The Babylonian myth of the female monster Tiamat being killed by the hero Marduk might be said to reflect an ancient Mesopotamian view of the orderly arrangement of society. Ultimately, then, myths can be said to be true stories in that they represent a given group's sense of its relationship

1

with nature, the world, and the unknown. To equate myths with falsehoods is to ignore their power and importance.

Where does the word "myth" come from?

Our word "myth" is derived originally from the Greek root sound *mu*, suggesting a sound made by the mouth. The concept of that sound became, in Greek, *mythos*, or "word." Eventually, in the epic poet Homer's time, mythos became the stylistic arrangement of words as story. Later, the philosopher Plato saw mythos as a metaphorical tale to explain realities beyond the reach of human knowledge, and still later Aristotle equated the term with "plot," the significant arrangement of events that was the most important element of Greek tragedy.

A copy of a second-century B.C.E. Roman bust of the poet Homer.

What is mythology?

First of all, mythology is the study of myths. Another term for this meaning of mythology is "mythography," a term most recently made relevant by the mythographer William G. Doty in his pivotal work, *Mythography: the Study of Myths and Rituals*. Mythographers (or mythologists) study such matters as the nature of myths, the concept of the myth, and the relation of myths to human nature, society, and history. The word "mythology" is also used in connection with collections of myths. Thus, we can speak, for instance, of Greek Mythology, Norse Mythology, Egyptian Mythology, Solar Mythology, World Mythology, or Mythologies of the World.

PREHISTORIC MYTHOLOGY

How and when did myths originate?

Myths originated in prehistoric times, that is, before writing was invented. Without written records it difficult for us to know specifically when or how myths came about. It is only through archeological clues and prehistoric works of art that tentative assumptions about the nature of these early myths can be made. Scholars use burial grounds, figurines, rock carvings, and cave paintings, for instance, as the basis of such assumptions. There are extensive materials of this sort dating back to the Late Stone Age, known as the Upper Paleolithic. By this time our own species, *Homo sapiens*, had long since emerged from Africa and settled in other parts of the world, sometimes mingling with or confronting an earlier subspecies known as Neanderthals. American anthropologist and mythologist Joseph

Campbell has suggested that European Neanderthal sites containing bear skulls in cave niches are possible evidence of an early bear cult and probable accompanying mythology even before the rise of *H sapiens* in that region.

Most scholars agree that *H sapiens* of the Upper Paleolithic in Europe had developed a religious sensibility and mythology. This agreement is based on apparently ritualized burial sites and especially on stone figurines and cave paintings. A statuette of a man with a lion head dating to 40,000 B.C.E. was discovered in a cave in Germany, suggesting a mythological narrative.

On the basis of the discovery of many small figurines of female figures with exaggerated hips, buttocks, and breasts, the most famous of which is the 20,000-year-old Venus of Laussel, anthropologist Marija Gimbutas and others have developed a theory of an early goddess religion in Europe that would almost certainly have made use of myths. The classic sources for theories about Upper Paleolithic mythology are the paintings in the great "cave temples" such as Les Trois Frères and Lascaux in France and the El Castillo in Cantabria, Spain. The animal and human figures in the cave paintings suggest ritual hunts and magical powers. The assumption is that they represent sacrificial rites with mythological implications.

What happened after the Paleolithic Period?

With the development of agriculture in the Middle Stone Age (the Mesolithic, c. 10,000–8000 B.C.E.) and, eventually, established settlements and cities in the New Stone Age, the Neolithic (c. 8000–3000 B.C.E.), the evidence of early mythology becomes more evident. Stonehenge-like apparent temple sites such as Göbekli Tepe in Anatolian Turkey suggest a religious consciousness. It is believed that a new emphasis on agriculture and animal husbandry as opposed to hunting and gathering led naturally to rituals and artifacts related to fertility. We can probably safely assume that such statues as those of an apparently enthroned female figure and a female figure depicted in various stages of life in the seventh millennium B.C.E. site of Çatal Hüyük in Anatolia were of a fertility goddess—a Great Mother—and that accompanying figures of a bull represented her consort, a male divinity, suggesting symbolically the male role in the fertility process.

We also can assume that humans of the Neolithic created myths to accompany these figures: myths of Earth Mothers mating with bull gods; myths of seemingly magical and sacrificial acts by which bodies planted in the earth were resurrected as edible plants; stories of goddesses who passed through stages from maiden to crone, reflecting the seasons of the earth and of human life.

MYTHMAKERS

Are the myth-makers known? Who were they?

Generally, myths grow anonymously and gradually from cultures, but sometimes an actual or legendary name is associated with particular myths. We do not know for sure, for

Are there other "Homers" around the world?

In some instances there are myths about the authorship of myths. In India, the legendary sage Vyasa is said to have dictated the epic events of the great poem, *Mahabharata,* to the elephant-headed god Ganesha, who wrote down the dictated text with one of his tusks. Another "Homer" of India was the legendary Valmiki, who is said to have authored the second great Indian epic, *Rāmāyana.* According to the myth, Valmiki invented poetry when his emotional words expressed his sorrow over a bird being slain by a hunter. In Ireland the mythical poet Amairgen is said to have sung the Irish myth into existence as did his Welsh equivalent, Taliesin.

Historical literary myth-makers such as the Roman poets Virgil and Ovid or the Icelandic-Norse poet-compiler Snorri Sturluson developed traditional myths in such ways as to make them more exciting or palatable to the cultures for which they wrote. Much of what we know of Roman mythology can be attributed to Virgil's literary—that is, carefully composed and written rather than oral—epic, the *Aeneid,* which was meant to answer the nationalistic interests of the Emperor Augustus who wanted a Roman epic that could displace the traditional Greek epics of Homer. Many of what we think of as Greek myths today were actually re-written and altered by Ovid in his *Metamorphoses* to appeal to Roman sexual and moral tastes. And in his *Prose Edda,* Snorri gave new literary life to much earlier Norse myths.

---

instance, where the myth of the Greek hero Odysseus originated, but we attribute the great epic about him—the *Odyssey*—to a traditionally blind poet, Homer, who may or may not have existed. And much of what we know of Greek mythology can be attributed to another eighth-century B.C.E. poet named Hesiod, who told the Greek creation myth, for instance, in his collection of ancient tales known as *Theogony*. A much older epic is the story of the Sumero-Babylonian hero Gilgamesh, and we speak of the Gilgamesh poet as if he or she were a particular person when it is more likely that the story in question is a combination of various narrative strands that gradually emerged from many ancient Mesopotamian settlements.

MYTHOGRAPHERS AND MYTHOLOGISTS

Who are the most influential mythographers?

There have been many highly influential mythographers. A few have achieved what might be called "classical" status. With the development of anthropology and psychology in the late nineteenth and early twentieth centuries, mythology began to be taken seriously. Until that time, more often than not, myths were thought of as mere superstitions or misguided stories of dead religions. People studied Greek and Roman myths in school as literary museum objects that revealed aspects of obviously false ancient beliefs. An important early mythographer was Sir James Frazer (1854–1941), whose multivolume *The Golden Bough* (1890) provided a serious and objective—non-theological—discussion of religion and myths much in the way Darwin approached discussing the natural world. For Frazer, myths were primitive science, attempts to explain nature. The French sociologist Émile Durkheim (1858–1917), in his 1912 *The Elementary Forms of the Religious Life,* compared ancient and modern forms of religion, treating myths seriously as allegorical forms that provided social unity and identity. In Cambridge, England, Jane Ellen Harrison (1850–1928), stood out among a group of scholars generally

Some influential mythographers have been (clockwise from top left) Swiss analyst Carl Jung, French sociologist left): Émile Durkheim, French anthropologist Claude Lévi-Strauss (UNESCO/Michel Ravassard), and Cambridge Ritualist Jane Ellen Harrison.

known as the Cambridge Ritualists, applying archeology and early anthropological techniques to Greek mythology and treating that mythology as the articulation of ritual acts. "Myth," she wrote, "is the spoken correlative of the acted rite." Her major work in this field was 1903, and then frequently revised, *Prolegomena on the Study of Greek Religion.* Among the proponents of the new fields of psychology and psychoanalysis early in the twentieth century, the leading mythographer was the Swiss analyst Carl Jung (1875–1961). Agreeing with Sigmund Freud (1856–1939) that myths could be compared to dreams, Jung went further, suggesting that myth reflected the collective psyche of particular cultures and that archetypal themes—common motifs that transcended cultures—pointed to a collective human psyche or Collective Unconscious. To study myth and common mythic themes such as the descent into the underworld, the flood, and the creation of the world was to study the human mind. Three mythographers of the modern age who generally agree with Jung's universalist approach have been especially influential. These are the Romanian scholar Mircea Eliade, the French anthropologist Claude Lévi-Strauss, and the American mythologist Joseph Campbell.

What is Eliade's approach to mythology?

In his 1959 *The Sacred and the Profane* and many other works, Eliade, like Jung, stresses the importance of archetypes in myth. Furthermore, while finding an essential division between the sacred and the profane, he speaks of the reality of myth as an expression of the sacred and suggests that the profane achieves true value only through

5

the mythical. It is religious behavior that takes the participant back to the sacred—to the mythical time.

What is Lévi-Strauss' approach to mythology?

Claude Lévi-Strauss (1908–2009) is often associated with a point of view known as structuralism. He argues in his 1962 work *The Savage Mind* and in many other works that the human mind in both its "civilized" and "savage" states has created similar mythic structures everywhere and that, therefore, universal laws can be applied to mythological thought.

What is Campbell's approach to mythology?

Joseph Campbell (1904–1987) carries the universalist approach—especially Carl Jung's ideas—forward in a complex analysis of what he sees as a universal hero myth, or "monomyth," with deep psychological implications. The hero's life, he suggests, mirrors or represents our quest for psychological wholeness. More than any other mythologist, Campbell has made mythology a popular subject accessible to general readers, even as he considers the highly complex history of and implications of mythology in influential and important works such as his *The Hero with a Thousand Faces* and his four-volume *The Masks of God*.

TYPES OF MYTHS: CREATION, GODS, AND HEROES

What are the primary myth types?

Three types are found in all mythologies around the world. These are creation myths, deity myths, and hero myths.

What is the nature of creation myths?

Creation myths tell cultures where they came from and how they and their world came into being. Such myths are as important to particular cultures as knowledge of our origins is to us as individuals. For early cultures, creation myths provided essential identity and a sense of and reason for existence in an otherwise chaotic universe. There are several subtypes under the creation myth category. Creation can be *ex nihilo*—from nothing—in which a supreme deity who is alone in a preexisting void consciously creates a world. The creation in the biblical book of Genesis is such a creation. A related form is Creation from Chaos, in which the potential for creation exists in a chaotic state just waiting for something to be done with it. Often the chaos takes the form of primeval waters, as in the Sumerian creation, or primeval air, as in a Chinese creation, or a cosmic egg as in the Dogon creation. In the Creation subtype called the Emergence Creation, people emerge from the earth itself, as in many Native American Pueblo myths. Another popular Native American subtype is the Earth-Diver Creation, in which an animal dives into the primeval waters and brings back a piece of material out of which the world is made.

Often flood myths are attached to creation myths. These floods—as in Genesis or the Gilgamesh epic—usually serve as second creations, which give humans a second chance to behave according to a creator's plans.

What is the nature of deity myths?

All cultures have gods and/or goddesses who in some sense control the universe. Many of these cultures have elaborate pantheons, divine families, or collections of deities with particular attributes and/or responsibilities. In ancient Egypt one such pantheon was made up of eight gods and goddesses known as the Ogdoad ("The Eight"). In Greece the pantheon headed by Zeus was given the name "Olympians" in reference to Mount Olympus, where they were said to have lived. subtypes of deities are many in most pantheons. The creator is ubiquitous. The Great Mother, such as Gaia in pre-Olympian Greek mythology, is important in cultures that stress the dominance of Earth-based power over the might of the deities of the sky. The Trickster, a popular figure who takes many forms especially in Africa and Native North America, is amoral and dangerous, but creative and always capable of changing shapes. Ananse—the Spider—is an African trickster. Raven and Coyote are examples of the Native American form.

What is the nature of hero myths?

As Joseph Campbell, in his *The Hero with a Thousand Faces,* shows us, heroes exist in most mythologies around the world, and they pass though similar stages, making it possible for us to speak of a "hero archetype." Heroes represent whole cultures. They are different from "normal" people. Often they are miraculously conceived and even born of virgins. Almost always they go on important quests. The Greek hero Jason searches for the Golden Fleece, Odysseus searches for home, King Arthur's knights search for the Holy Grail. Culture heroes are heroes who aid the creator in creating particular cultures and who, in some sense, teach those cultures how to live properly. The Native American Corn Mother is such a hero. Campbell uses the term "monomyth" to represent a universal or archetypal hero life that includes many common motifs such as the miraculous conception, the quest, and the descent into the Underworld.

PHILOSOPHY AND PSYCHOLOGY OF MYTHS

What is an archetype?

As explicated by the Swiss psychoanalyst and mythographer Carl Jung, archetypes are the psychic equivalent of instincts. They are primal images and tendencies toward such im-

Both myths and dreams are narratives that often transcend the "real world" restrictions of time, space, and identity. Both myths and dreams contain bizarre situations and also the possibility of metaphorical or symbolic information about the dreamer or the culture. The psychoanalyst sees the dream as a potential revelation of the dreamer's psyche, unimpeded by the defensive mechanism we all employ in our waking lives. Mythographers such as Carl Jung and Joseph Campbell see myths as cultural dreams reflecting the psyches of the given cultures that "dream" them and the archetypal workings of a collective unconscious when myths of many cultures are compared.

ages inherited by what Jung called the "collective unconscious" as opposed to the personal unconscious. These images take specific form in different cultures, creating a set of universal motifs in cultural "clothes." Thus, we have a hero archetype that explains the similarities in the lives of the Greek Theseus and the German Siegfried, for example, or a Great Mother archetype that relates the Phrygian Cybele to the Native American Corn Mother. In myth and literature studies and in psychology, we often use the term "archetype" simply to mean the universal motifs that emerge in literature, dreams, and myths.

Can myths be factually based?

There have always been attempts to tie myths to historical events. Flood myths particularly have been linked to actual floods such as those of the Nile in Egypt and the Tigris and Euphrates in Mesopotamia (Iraq). Heroes, too, are sometimes linked to historical figures. Some scholars have linked the Greek tragic hero Oedipus with the actual Egyptian king, Akhenaten. Certain culture heroes are, in fact, apparently based at least to some extent in fact. There may well have been a King Gilgamesh in ancient Sumer, for instance, or even a Prince Hector in Troy. Attempts to link myth to history, however, tend to ignore the metaphorical or religious importance of myths themselves. It seems likely that myths, like dreams, make use of factual experiences of individuals and cultures, but have power and meaning that transcend such factual experiences.

Are myths religious?

For the most part it is fair to say that myths are religious in that they are narratives that cultures use to illustrate or correlate to their religious rituals and theologies. This is particularly true of Creation myths and deity myths, less so of hero myths. Creation myths and deity myths are metaphorical attempts to establish a link between humans and the unknown. They provide some sort of divine justification for cultures and individuals. Hero myths, when the hero actually represents a religious tradition such as

Buddhism or Christianity or the ancient Irish-Celtic religion, are clearly religious. Heroes such as the Greek Oedipus and Odysseus are at least peripherally religious in that their actions and predicaments reflect a sense of the ambiguous relationship between humans and gods. When that relationship is not evident, hero myths move closer to the world of secular folklore. Many mythical heroes simply reflect cultural pride or secular human desires for power. Paul Bunyan is such a hero as is Siegfried in the Germanic tradition. Some such heroes are clearly factually based and then mythologized for secular purposes; George Washington in the cherry tree story is such a hero.

An illustration of Paul Bunyan and his blue ox Babe, heroes of American folklore.

Finally, it must be said that some myths are clearly told in the folktale tradition primarily to entertain. This is particularly true of some trickster myths, such as those of the Native American Coyote, which emphasize his sexual exploits, or even some Greco-Roman myths of gods and goddesses such as Aphrodite (Venus) and her lover Ares (Mars), who became the laughing stock of Mount Olympus when they were trapped together in a net created by Aphrodite's wronged husband.

Do the great religions of today have myths?

Most religions have oral or written narratives that are central to belief. More often than not these narratives transcend the barrier between actual human experience and the supernatural and are, therefore, "mythic" in nature. Hindus, Buddhists, Jews, Christians, Muslims, and practitioners of Taoism and Shinto, for example, all have "scriptures" containing such narratives. Religions such as many of those in Africa and the Americas have oral traditions with the same kind of stories. A central belief in Christianity derives from the story of Jesus rising from the dead, even though in our actual experience people do not rise from the dead. Jews believe that the Red Sea (or the Sea of Reeds) parted to allow the escape of the Hebrews from the Egyptians, even though seas do not part for such reasons. Some Buddhists believe that Queen Māyā conceived the Buddha in a dream by way of a white elephant, although we know that conception in such a manner is outside the possibilities recognized by our experience and common sense. For fundamentalists, stories such as those above can be believed literally; for others, such stories are considered symbolic or metaphorical. However they are received, one tradition's sacred narrative is a myth to other traditions. We can, of course, recognize another's "myth" as a beautiful and even profound attempt to understand reality.

9

Are myths a burden or a boon?

When a myth helps us to accept a meaningful place in the world or leads us to positive ethical behavior, it can be a boon. When a myth inspires great art and beautiful ritual, it is a boon. Joseph Campbell rightly calls the collective hero myth "the wonderful song of the soul's high adventure." But myths can be extremely dangerous and burdensome when they lead us to a belief in our own cultural and personal importance to the exclusion of others. In this sense myths have often been the justification for some of humanity's most brutal acts.

Why do humans tell myths?

A contemporary philosopher once suggested that the role of humans is "to make creation conscious of itself." We do exactly that by telling stories, and myths are our collective primal cultural stories. They are a celebration of characteristics which, as far as we know, only humans among earth's species possess. Humans are constantly conscious of what Aristotle called "plot" or "mythos." Aristotle defined plot as narrative that has a beginning, a middle, and an end. Unlike other creatures, we are aware of beginnings, middles, and ends. We see ourselves as characters in personal stories and ultimately in the great collective story of the "road of life." We think of our past (our beginnings), our lives now (our present), and our final future (our end). Our myths are our cultural reflections of this thought in its most basic form. What we think of as literature later expands on this basic thought and gives it complex author-inspired details and experiences, reflecting real periods and places and histories. Humans tell stories because consciousness revealed in the telling of stories is what defines us as a species. Ancient myths are our earliest cultural stories. We tell myths because we have to, because we are born storytellers.

MIDDLE EASTERN MYTHOLOGIES

What do we mean by the Middle East?

The term has taken on various meanings over the centuries. With varying degrees of accuracy it has been used synonymously with "the Near East," "the Levant," and "the Fertile Crescent." In colonial times the British meant the Balkans and Asia Minor (Anatolian Turkey) when they spoke of the "Near East." The Fertile Crescent is the fertile land that arches around the Syrian steppes and stretches from the eastern Mediterranean coastal regions, beginning with Egypt in the west, southern Anatolia (Asian Turkey) in the north, and Mesopotamia (Iraq)—a term which means "between the rivers" (that is, the Tigris and the Euphrates)—in the east. "The Levant" is a term that Europeans once used to refer to the countries bordering the eastern Mediterranean. "Levant" is derived from the French word meaning "rising" and refers to the rising of the sun in the east, or the "Orient." In modern times "Middle East" has come to refer, in the geo-political context, to all the places included in the terms discussed above, as well as having been expanded somewhat. It refers generally, then, to the areas of Asia, Africa, and Europe that include present-day Turkey, Israel, the Arab countries (including Egypt), and usually Iran.

Were there prehistoric mythologies in the Middle East?

The figurines and temples at Anatolian sites such as Çatal Hüyük, discussed earlier, indicate a mythological consciousness before writing developed. Figures appearing to be an enthroned Mother Goddess and a Bull God are clear indications of mythology—perhaps associated with fertility and developing agriculture. Graves in Egypt, Palestine, and Mesopotamia suggest ritual burying, perhaps pointing to a belief in an afterlife. Mesolithic (Middle Stone Age, c. 10,000–c. 8000 B.C.E.) sites belonging to a culture known as the Natufian in Syria and Palestine contain figurines of embracing couples, suggesting a sacred marriage.

11

We refer to the mythologies of the ancient Sumerians and the Semitic peoples who followed them in Mesopotamia (the Akkadians, the Babylonians, and the Assyrians); the Anatolian peoples such as the Hittites and the Phrygians; the Western Semitic peoples living in the lands called at various times Canaan, Palestine, Phoenicia, Aram, Israel, Judah, and Samaria and in the Arab countries. We can include the sacred narratives of Judaism, Christianity, and Islam as outgrowths of Western Semitic traditions. In Middle Eastern mythology we also include the Indo-Iranian culture that evolved in Iran into Zoroastrianism. It would be natural to include ancient Egyptian mythology as a Middle Eastern phenomenon, but it is at once so radically different from the other Middle Eastern mythologies as to demand separate treatment.

Natufian grave pits in conjunction with grain storage pits possibly indicate a fertility cult associated with early agriculture. Pre-Sumerian Ubaid sites in Mesopotamia contain ruins of what appear to be religious structures, the precursors of the famous Sumerian and Babylonian temple-ziggurats.

It is not surprising that as nomadic hunting-gathering lifestyles were supplemented or replaced by settlements dominated by agriculture and animal husbandry, cults devoted to fertility with accompanying explanatory stories would have emerged. Prehistoric mythology can only be surmised, however. "History," in the strictest sense of the word the preserved narration of events, by definition, begins with writing.

How and where did mythology begin in the historical period in the Middle East?

If the beginning of the historical period is marked by the invention of writing, mythology in the historical period probably began in Mesopotamia in the Sumerian culture. This is not to say that orally transmitted myths did not exist before they were captured in writing.

Scholars generally believe that the Sumerians invented writing in the mid- to late-fourth-millennium B.C.E. The system used—called cuneiform script—involved the carving of pictographs and later phonemes into clay tablets. Lists of Sumerian gods and fragments of the great Gilgamesh epic have been found on such tablets. According to the Sumerians, a semi-divine hero-king named Enmerkar invented writing when, at war, he found that a messenger—"his mouth heavy"—could not repeat a complicated message exactly. His only recourse was to create picture words on a tablet.

SUMERIAN GODS AND HEROES

Who were the Sumerians?

The Sumerians, as they were called later by their Semitic conquerors, were people of Kengir, now southern Iraq, in Mesopotamia. Their origins are somewhat of a mystery. One theory holds that these non-Semitic people migrated to Mesopotamia from Central Asia in the fourth millennium B.C.E. and mixed with other non-Semitic people, the Ubaids, who had established protocities along the marshlands in the area and had been there at least since the fifth millennium B.C.E. These settlements would evolve into the famous Sumerian cities of Ur, Eridu, Unug (Uruk) and Nippur. These were city-states with a linguistic, legal, religious, political, and architectural basis that would influence the area—including its mythology—long after the Sumerians were conquered by the Semitic Akkadians led by Sargon I late in the third millennium B.C.E. and, after a resurgence, by the Semitic Babylonians in the second millennium B.C.E.

What deities made up the Sumerian pantheon?

The gods and goddesses of the Sumerians represented the elements of nature and the cosmos. In the beginning, the goddess Nammu, the primordial waters, produced An, the original sky god, and Ki, the original earth goddess. An and Ki mated to produce the primary pantheon, the Anunnaki (literally the result of An + Ki). There are many versions of the specific parentage of the members of the Sumerian pantheon. Each city-state had its point of view, as particular deities were patrons of particular cities. Essentially, however, the following deities are the descendants of the An-Ki union and some of the most important of six thousand or so deities:

Enlil—the god of Air (*Lil* = air). He was the chief god, the Odin or Zeus of the Sumerians, responsible for order in the cosmos and in earthly civilization.

Ninlil—the goddess of Air. She and Enlil produced the sun god Utu and the greatest of the Sumerian goddesses, Inanna. An amusing myth tells how Ninlil first fell in love with Enlil but did not know how to attract his attention. It is her mother who tells her to "wash

The Great Ziggurat, originally constructed four thousand years ago in the Sumerian city of Ur (now in southern Iraq), was dedicated to the moon god Nanna.

13

yourself in the pure river" and then to walk in the area where Enlil lived, thus attracting his attention. The flirting worked and Enlil "kissed" the maid who would become his wife.

Nanna—the Moon god. Some say it was Nanna who fathered Inanna with his wife Ningal.

Inanna—goddess of Love and Fertility, "queen of Heaven and Earth." Inanna's mate was Dumuzi. Both play important roles in Inanna's central myth, that of her descent into the Underworld.

Ereshkigal—goddess of the Underworld, the sister of Inanna. Ereshkigal represents the infertile opposite of the fertile Inanna.

Enki—a sometimes trickster god, god of male fertility and holder of the *me*, the essential laws and offices of civilization stemming from Nammu, the original great mother herself. The *me* include such aspects of life as kingship, power, marriage, sexuality, and writing. During a drinking bout Inanna tricks Enki into releasing control of the *me* to her.

Ninhursag—goddess of the Earth. Ninhursag was a sister of Enlil.

What did Sumerian mythology say about the creation of the world?

Some Sumerian tablet fragments suggest that when An (Heaven) and Ki (Earth) joined to form Anki (the universe), it was necessary, as expressed in many of the world's creation myths, to separate them so that the creation of the world could take place in the space between them. It was Enlil who took his mother down away from An. Now the gods and goddesses married and began the work of farming, but the work was difficult and the gods began to complain, especially as the wise and crafty god Enki spent most of his time sleeping while they labored. It was Nammu, (the primordial waters), who woke up her son and suggested that he create humans to work for the gods. This he did by taking clay from the marshes, provided by his mother, and shaping the clay into humans. The humans were set to work, and the gods could relax. The work was supervised, appropriately, by the earth goddess Ninhursag. It is said by some that it was Enki who reordered the primordial waters into the Tigris and Euphrates Rivers, organized cities and the domestication of animals and planting, and stocked the marshland waters with fish. Enki's phallus, we are told, filled the ditches with his semen (that is, water) and wanted to fill the maiden goddess Uttu (Vegetation) with the same fluid, but the goddess's mother advised her daughter to resist unless Enki would bring her apples, cucumbers, and grapes. Enki agreed to the conditions and poured his "water" into Uttu's womb only after he had presented her with these gifts. Eight new plants were created from the excess semen left on the young goddess's body.

Why are the Sumerian myths often so explicitly sexual?

To modern sensibilities the presence of so much sexuality might appear to be pornographic. The Sumerians clearly had a different view of sex. In fact, it seems likely that they saw it in a religious context having to do with the relationship of the activities of the gods to fertility, the essential element in a culture based in agriculture, animal husbandry, and the necessary propagation of the human species. Among the earliest written hymns are those to the goddess Inanna, the goddess of love and fertility, songs celebrating even her most intimate parts.

What is an example of an important Sumerian deity myth?

The deity myth that has attracted most attention among modern scholars is a cycle based on the deeds of the goddess Inanna, particularly the story of her descent into the Underworld. Among all Mesopotamian myths only the Gilgamesh story rivals the Inanna cycle in attention paid to it.

The first part of the Inanna story, recorded in tablets about the Huluppu Tree, in fact, involves Gilgamesh. Soon after the creation, the young Inanna took a tree from the Euphrates and carried it to her city, Uruk, hoping it would grow into her throne. But a serpent made a nest in the roots of the tree and the dark Lilith made a home in its trunk. It is inevitable that we think of other mythological trees here, including those of the Bible's book of Genesis and the Norse Yggdrassil story.

Inanna asked the hero of Uruk, Gilgamesh, to help rid her tree of the invaders. This he did and carved a throne and a bed out of its trunk for his "holy sister."

In a crucial meeting with the wise trickster god Enki, in which the two deities drink a great deal, Inanna succeeds in tricking her older relative into giving her the sacred *me.* Before Enki has time to regret his mistake, Inanna pushes away from her host's dock in the "Boat of Heaven," and escapes with the *me,* now as a deity at least equal in power to Enki. In the next segment of the cycle, which cannot help but remind us of the biblical *Song of Songs,* Inanna searches as the goddess of fertility for a husband to "plow" her "wet ground." The husband will be the shepherd Dumuzi, who will fertilize the embodiment of female fertility itself, and Inanna's "field" will provide the riches of grain and other plants.

But Inanna is not satisfied to be queen of Uruk. In order to realize her full potential as a great deity, she must understand the reality of her dark sister Ereshkigal. To do this she must descend into the world of death. Thus begins this most ancient of the archetypal descent myths. It is a story of losing the self to find the self, of dying to be reborn. It contains elements we associate with better-known descent myths such

A wall carving of the Sumerian trickster god Enki. In art, Enki is often shown with symbols of a bird, a goat, and water.

15

as those of the Greek Persephone, the Egyptian Osiris, and even Jesus. It involves sacrifice and apparent death and culminates in resurrection and return.

INANNA'S DESCENT

What is the story of Inanna's descent?

To prepare for her journey to the "dark side," Inanna abandons her city and temples, turning the rule of Uruk over to her husband Dumuzi. She takes seven of the sacred *me* and wears them transformed as jewels and magnificent clothing. Informed of her illustrious visitor, Ereshkigal is not pleased. She instructs her servant to allow Inanna into her realm only if she leaves one of the *me* at each of the seven locked gates of the Underworld. So it is that when Inanna arrives at her sister's throne she is naked and stripped of all her power and trappings of authority. In death, after all, such powers and trappings are useless. Inanna attempts to usurp her sister's throne but learns the lesson of humility when the Underworld gods hang her up on the wall like a piece of meat.

Meanwhile, back in Uruk, three days have passed and the people and temples all go into deep mourning. Inanna's faithful servant asks Enlil and Nanna for their help in retrieving Inanna, but they refuse. Enki, however agrees to do his best. Living as he does in the *absu*, the underground waters of the marshes, he can hear what goes on in the Underworld. Enki understands how important the goddess of love and fertility is for the welfare of the world. To save his relative and sometimes rival, Enki employs his power as a trickster. He creates two creatures from the mud under his fingernails. Lacking sexuality and gender, these creatures, he rightly believes, will not offend the barren and fruitless Ereshkigal who is continually screaming in the pangs of endless childbirth. To Ereshkigal, unlike to her ripe and fertile sister, sexuality and gender are anathema. Enki gives his mud creatures the plant of life and the water of life and instructs them to proceed to the Underworld and to offer the queen these gifts as a means of easing her pains. Ereshkigal gladly accepts the gifts and, as Enki knew she would, offers his creatures gifts in return. As instructed, they request the release of Inanna. Ereshkigal has no choice and agrees to release her sister. But the Underworld gods insist on a price. Inanna must send a sacrificial substitute to the Underworld in order to remember her own dark side, her abandoned older sister Ereshkigal. Inanna takes up her *me* and her queenly robes and returns to Uruk where she finds Dumuzi reveling in his kingship, apparently unaffected by the loss of his wife. Furious, Inanna names him as her substitute. Dumuzi's sister, however, agrees to spend six months of each year as her brother's substitute in the Underworld, during which time Dumuzi can come home. Dumuzi, too, then, becomes one of the first of many "dying gods" in world mythology

Why was Inanna such an important mythological figure?

Inanna is important because she represents at least the remnants of a time when goddess figures—specifically those representing fertility such as the prehistoric goddess of

Çatal Hüyük—were probably central to mythologies. The sense of the earth's fertility would have been ubiquitous in the Fertile Crescent, especially in the marshlands of Sumer in what is now southern Iraq. Furthermore, Inanna's "death" and resurrection are beautiful metaphorical representations of the essential pattern of agriculture, in which the descent of planting results in the emergence of new life. Finally, then, Inanna is a symbol of the power of civilization to negate the power of death.

How does Sumerian mythology represent real life in Sumer?

Real life in Sumer, as in the marshlands of Iraq today, centered on the relationship of salt and fresh waters, the relationship between sky and earth, the presence of the sun, and, above all, given the complex agricultural society created by the Sumerians, on fertility and established "civilized" rules. The latter are represented in mythology by the *me*. The gods themselves, as we have seen, are personifications of natural elements of most concern in the marshlands, beginning with An (Heaven) and Ki (Earth) and Nammu (the primordial waters).

Was there a flood in Sumerian mythology?

We know that there was a Sumerian flood myth on which the Babylonian flood story contained in the Gilgamesh epic was based. The Sumerian fragments tell us that the gods punished humans by sending a flood. Only the good king Ziusudra and, presumably, some followers, were spared. Having been told by Enki how to construct a ship to ride out the storm, Ziusudra survives the flood in his ark.

Who were the heroes of Sumerian mythology?

The Sumerian mythology that we know of deals primarily with deities rather than with human heroes. The best known of the Sumerian hero figures are Gilgamesh and his friend Enkidu. Sumerian fragments tell us of Gilgamesh's heroic assistance to Inanna in the Huluppu Tree tale. With his heavy armor and giant axe as described in that myth, he has been seen as a forerunner of the Herakles (Hercules) type. A tenderer Gilgamesh appears in the fragment about Enkidu and the Underworld. It seems that Inanna had given Gilgamesh two presents made out of the Huluppu Tree as a reward for his help. These were a *pukku* and a *mikku* (the Sumerian scholar

This cuneiform tablet, housed at the British Museum, is the eleventh in the Gilgamesh epic. It describes a flood much like the one Noah survives in the Bible.

17

Samuel Noah Kramer suggests that these were probably a drum and a drumstick). Somehow Gilgamesh loses his gifts in a hole in the ground and they fall out of his reach into the netherworld. Gilgamesh weeps by the hole in despair. His friend Enkidu volunteers to descend below to retrieve the gifts, but once there is unable to return. Again in despair, Gilgamesh turns to the great god Enlil for help in retrieving his friend, but Enlil refuses. Enki is more helpful, arranging for Enkidu's shade to return. Gilgamesh questions the ghost of his friend about the Underworld, receiving ambiguous answers.

What happened to the Sumerian mythological traditions?

The Sumerian mytho-religious traditions were to a great extent absorbed by their Semitic neighbors and then conquerors—especially the Akkadians, the Assyrians, and the Babylonians.

THE SEMITES

Who were and are the Semites?

The Semites were various groups who spoke versions of a non-Indo-European Semitic language system. The Akkadians, Amorites, Arameans, Canaanites (including the Phoenicians), Assyrians, Babylonians, ancient Israelites or Hebrews, and Arabs were all Semites, as are present-day Jews and Arabs, whose Semitic mother tongues are Hebrew and Arabic, respectively. Tradition has it that Semites descended from Shem (Sem), Noah's first son in the Genesis story.

Who were the Akkadians ?

King Sargon I of Akkad (now a lost city perhaps not far from present-day Baghdad) conquered most of Mesopotamia between 2390 and 2330 B.C.E. Sargon was later mythologized as a archetypal hero: it was said that he had been born of a virgin, hidden in a basket, released into the river, and adopted by a menial.

The Akkadians adapted their own Semitic language to the Sumerian cuneiform script and that language became the *lingua franca* of the whole region.

Who were the Assyrians?

The Assyrians were a Mesopotamian Semitic people with a capital at Ashur, named after the head of the Assyrian pantheon. At various times beginning in the twenty-fourth century B.C.E. the Assyrians were a major power in the Middle East, conquering large regions, including, for instance, Israel. The Assyrians, as did the Akkadians and Babylonians, followed the Old Sumerian religion with a few adaptations, such as Ashur. It was not until the fourth century C.E. that the remnants of the old Assyrian civilization adopted Christianity, which the Eastern Rite Assyrian Church practices in Syria and Iraq to this day.

MYTHOLOGY OF BABYLON

Who were the Babylonians?

In the second millennium B.C.E., Semites known as Amorites established a capital in Babylon—perhaps on the ruins of Akkad. The most famous of the kings of what is now called Old Babylon was Hammurabi (c. 1792–1750 B.C.E.), who was famous for creating a series of unifying laws for the mixture of races living in his kingdom. During this period the Old Sumerian-Akkadian language was used for religious purposes, somewhat as Latin would later be used in the Roman Catholic Church. This was the period of the Babylonian version of the *Gilgamesh Epic* and the great creation epic known as the *Enuma Elish*. The Old Sumerian deities were retained with Semitic names, their stories changed somewhat to reflect the priorities of the Babylonian state. Old Babylon was itself conquered by non-Semitic Indo-Europeans, the Hittites, in 1600 B.C.E. Later, in 1225 B.C.E., the region would be taken by the Assyrians. At the end of the millennium, King Nebuchadnezzar I reestablished Babylonian rule and the old Sumerian-based religion and mythology. The wars with the Assyrians and others continued, however, until the Babylonians successfully established what is now called the Neo-Babylonian civilization, of which the most famous king was Nebuchadnezzar II (605–162 B.C.E.). This was the period of the famous Hanging Gardens, the ziggurat which in the Bible became the Tower of Babel (Babylon), and the Babylonian Exile, or Captivity of the Israelites which followed Nebuchadnezzar's destruction of the Jewish Temple in Jerusalem. The Neo-Babylonians continued to worship the old gods. Much of the mythology surrounding these gods—especially the flood myth—strongly influenced the emergence of biblical narratives.

Who were the Babylonian deities?

The Babylonian pantheon is modeled on the old Sumero-Akkadian pantheon with some significant modifications in terms of names and certain narrative traditions.

In Babylon, Apsu (Sumerian Abzu), the fresh waters, mated with Tiamat (Nammu), the salt waters, to form the first great deities. The most important of these deities and their offspring were Anu (An), the sky god; Ea (Enki), the god of wisdom and water; Sin (Nanna), the moon god; Ellil (Enlil), the storm god; Shamash (Utu), the sun god; and Ishtar (Inanna), goddess of love and fertility. Ishtar's husband was Tammuz (Dumuzi). Her Underworld sister remained Ereshkigal. The new leader of the pantheon was Marduk, the city god of Babylon, the son of Ea, and the hero of the *Enuma Elish*.

What is the *Enuma Elish*?

The *Enuma Elish* ("When Above"), composed in the twelfth century B.C.E., is one of the earliest epics of the historical period. It is the creation story of the Babylonians, one intended to establish the Babylonian patron god, Marduk, as the dominant power in the pantheon (in Assyria Ashur was substituted in the epic for Marduk).

The epic opens with the beginning of time ("When the skies above were still unnamed") and describes the creation of the gods through the union of Apsu and Tiamat. The new gods made so much noise that father Apsu determined to get rid of them. Mother Tiamat, however, objected to the destruction of her children. Much later, in Greece, the mother goddesses Gaia and Rhea will struggle with their mates, Uranos and Kronos, on similar grounds. It is Ea who plays the role of Zeus here, using his magic powers to enchant Apsu, then sending him to sleep forever in the underground waters where Ea, with his earth goddess wife Damkina (Sumerian Damgalnuna) produces Marduk. The new god had four heads and made a great deal of noise and disturbance. Anu with his winds added to the noise and Tiamat decided she had to do something. So she formed an army of monsters led by her son Kingu (Qingu) to attempt to eliminate Marduk and the noise. The gods became

The Babylonian god Marduk, shown with his dragon, is illustrated on this ancient seal.

afraid and called on Ea and Anu to fight Tiamat, now a dragon-like monster herself, but they refused. Ea suggested that Marduk fight her, and he agreed to do so if the old gods would recognize him as their new king. The gods agreed to Marduk's terms.

How did Marduk Defeat Tiamat?

Marduk approached Tiamat and filled her gaping mouth with wind so that she could not devour him. He then shot an arrow into her great belly and threw her body onto the ground. Out of Tiamat's body he created the world. He divided her body into two parts, setting up one half as the sky, the other as earth. Her head became a mountain, her eyes the Tigris and Euphrates, her breasts the hills of Babylon. Marduk instructs Ea to make humans out of the dead Kingu's blood. The humans would do the work that the gods would otherwise have to do.

Finally, Marduk established Babylon and its temples as the seat of the gods. His temple—perhaps the Tower of Babel—would be the most important one.

Were there primary Babylonian human heroes?

Two heroes stand out in Akkadian-Babylonian-Assyrian mythology. The first is Etana and the second and most important one is Gilgamesh.

> ## What is the significance of the Tiamat and Marduk myth?
>
> In the *Enuma Elish,* Tiamat, who as Nammu in Sumer had represented the essential feminine birthing power of the universe, becomes a female monster to be destroyed.
>
> Her defeat and the rise of Marduk signals a basic change in the mythology of Mesopotamia and the view of reality it represented. From a system based on the necessity of fertility and female power, the balance moves to a sense of necessary patriarchal order and power centered in one city and its all-powerful deity.

Etana, reminding us of the Hebrew hero David, was said to have been a shepherd (like the Sumerian Dumuzi) and to have been appointed king of Kish by the gods. Epic fragments tell how when Etana and his wife were unable to produce an heir, the sun god Shamash sent him to find an eagle that had been captured by a serpent and then to ride the eagle to Heaven, where Ishtar ruled as queen. Etana was to petition Ishtar for the Plant of Birth. Etana did as he was instructed and a baby was born to his wife.

The Gilgamesh myth is contained in the great Babylonian epic about the hero that had gained wide popularity in Mesopotamia by the middle of the second millennium B.C.E. As we have seen, Gilgamesh had been well known since the Sumerian period and in all likelihood a Sumerian epic preceded the Babylonian version. There also were Hittite and Assyrian versions.

Gilgamesh was, in fact, a Sumerian king of Unug (Uruk) in the middle of the third millennium B.C.E. He was associated closely with the sun god Utu (Shamash) and, as was Etana, with Dumuzi (Tammuz). A later story, perhaps based on an earlier Sumerian one, tells how a king's daughter becomes pregnant and a court prophet predicts that the child will become king. This causes the king (who as did Herod in the Jesus story and so many other kings in hero myths) to feel threatened, and he has the child thrown off a tower. The child is saved in midflight by an eagle (suggesting a connection with the Etana myth) and adopted by a humble shepherd until later he becomes king, joining David and Etana and Dumuzi as a shepherd-king.

The world knows Gilgamesh best as possibly the world's first *bona fide* hero, in what is the earliest-known epic poem.

THE GILGAMESH EPIC

What is the plot of the Gilgamesh Epic?

The epic opens with an introduction to King Gilgamesh of Uruk, known for having built the city's famous walls and for having written tales of his many adventure on tablets. Although Gilgamesh is praised, a major flaw becomes evident even within the first tablet when we learn that the king displays great human arrogance by tyrannizing his people, even demanding conjugal rights to brides. The people petition Anu, who instructs Aruru, a mother goddess, to find a way of tempering Gilgamesh's power. She creates the bestial Enkidu, who eats plants of the fields and frees animals caught in hunters' traps. When Gilgamesh is informed of Enkidu's presence, he sends out a beautiful prostitute, Samhat, to tame Enkidu. Enkidu is somewhat humanized and, in effect, tamed after six days and seven nights of lovemaking. In Uruk, Gilgamesh has strange dreams involving Enkidu. Ninsun, Gilgamesh's mother, explains to the king that the dreams are about the man who will become his closest friend.

In the second tablet of the epic, Gilgamesh and Enkidu have a wrestling match, which is won with great difficulty by the king. But Gilgamesh is so impressed by Enkidu's courage and strength that he takes him on as his primary companion. In the three tablets that follow, the deeds of the two heroes in the Cedar Forest of Enlil, guarded by Humbaba (the Sumerian Hawawa) whom they kill, are described.

In Tablet 6, we find the story of Gilgamesh's refusal of Ishtar (Sumerian Inanna). Having returned to Uruk after his monster-killing adventure, Gilgamesh is now, in effect, a new man, cleansed of his tyrannical ways. He is approached by Ishtar, who suggests love and marriage and, by extension, fertility for himself, his city, and its agriculture and animals. Using the excuse of the tragic ends of so many of the goddess's former lovers, Gilgamesh arrogantly refuses the great goddess. Ishtar, never having been treated in this way, has Anu send the Bull of Heaven (the natural companion of the fertility and love goddess) to attack Gilamesh and Enkidu and the people of Uruk. Hundreds are killed (perhaps a metaphor for a plague) before the two heroes manage to kill the Bull of Heaven. In an ultimate insult, Gilgamesh flings a thigh of the beast at Ishtar.

The rejection of Ishtar is strange, especially since she was the patron and city goddess of Uruk. The rites of the sacred marriage of kings and goddesses had been a foundation of Mesopotamian culture at least since the Old Sumerian period. The incident seems to suggest the same kind of movement away from a strong goddess-based religion that we have also found in the defeat of Tiamat in the Babylonian *Enuma Elish*.

In Tablet 7, Anu, Ea, and Shamash decide that either Enkidu or Gilgamesh must pay with his life for the killing of Humbaba and the Bull of Heaven.

In Tablet 8, Enkidu dies and is mourned emotionally by Gilgamesh.

Tablet 9 contains the first part of what is, in effect, an archetypal heroic descent into the Underworld. This is a journey marked by Gilgamesh's fear of death and by a danger-filled journey. First, Gilgamesh must convince the horrible scorpion people to allow him passage through a long, dark tunnel. Then he has a relationship with the beautiful Siduri in her jeweled garden, reminding us of later dalliances in Homer's *Odyssey* between the Greek hero and Calypso and Circe, and of the Roman Aeneas's love affair in the *Aeneid* with Dido. These are all seen by their epic authors as temptations by women who, through sex, would undermine the necessary mission of a patriarchal hero. Like Ishtar, Siduri is a force that must be overcome. Reluctantly, again like Circe in the *Odyssey*, Siduri finally helps Gilgamesh on his way.

Tablet 10 finds Gilgamesh being ferried by Urshanabi across the Waters of Death to the ancient Mesopotamian Noah figure, Utnapishtim (Sumerian Ziusudra). Gilgamesh is in search of eternal life and, perhaps, of new life for Enkidu. Utnapishtim reminds his visitor that only the gods control life and death.

Tablet 11 contains the flood myth, which, as many scholars have noted, is remarkably similar to Noah's flood described in the book of Genesis in the Bible. When Gilgamesh asks Utnapishtim to explain how he has achieved eternal life, the old flood hero answers by reciting the story of the deluge.

Ea had come to Utnapishtim and his wife in Shuruppak to warn them that a flood was about to destroy humanity. If they built a boat, for which Ea provided the measurements, Utnapishtim and his family would be spared. Utnapishtim did as he was instructed and filled the boat with valuables, his own family, and representatives of all species. A huge storm ensued and waters flooded the earth. When after seven days, the storm finally abated, the ship came aground on Mount Nisir. After another week had passed, Utnapishtim released a dove, hoping it would find land, but it returned, unsuccessful, to the ship. The same scenario followed a swallow's release. When a raven was sent out, however, it did not come back, and Utnapishtim realized that the flood was over. He gave thanks to the gods and made offerings. The mother goddess promised him care and Enlil granted him the ultimate gift of eternal life.

Gilgamesh, too, longs for eternal life, but Utnapishtim tests his ability to achieve it by setting a test. He challenges the hero to avoid sleep for six days and seven nights. The exhausted Gilgamesh agrees to the test but immediately falls asleep. Utnapishtim's wife bakes a loaf of bread each day that Gilgamesh remains asleep. When the hero wakes up, he finds the now-moldy bread and accepts his limitations. As a human he has human frailties. He cannot

An 1876 drawing reproducing a depiction of the Babylonian hero Gilgamesh.

Why is the biblical flood story so like the Babylonian flood myth?

We do not know for sure why this is so. Scholars argue that the compilers of Genesis were directly influenced in the story of Noah and the flood by stories of the flood told by the Sumerians and retold and developed by the Assyrians and the Babylonians. The influence could have come during the so-called Babylonian Captivity or Exile in the sixth century B.C.E. or, perhaps more likely, during an earlier Assyrian captivity in the period around 700 B.C.E., or even still earlier from contact between the Israelites and the Canaanites, who might well have known the story.

expect eternal life. But before Gilgamesh takes his leave of Utnapishtim, the old man, at the urging of his wife, tells Gilgamesh about an underwater plant that can at least preserve youth. On his way back across the Waters of Death with the ferry man Urshanabi, the hero dives for the plant and succeeds in retrieving it, but once again, he falls asleep, and a serpent steals the plant. This is why serpents can slough off and replace old skin. In despair, Gilgamesh weeps, but he and Urshanabi go back to Uruk together. There Gilgamesh, chastened, nevertheless proudly asks the ferryman to inspect his great wall and his fine city. In a sense, the hero accepts his humanity.

A twelfth and final tablet often included is present only in an Assyrian version of the epic and is essentially a retelling of Gilgamesh, Enkidu, and the Underworld story found in the earlier Sumerian Gilgamesh cycle.

How is the epic of Gilgamesh similar to later epics?

It can be argued that there are two basic types of epic, the war epic and the quest epic. The Gilgamesh epic and Homer's *Odyssey,* for instance, are primarily quest epics; the *Iliad* is primarily a war epic. Virgil's *Aeneid,* consciously building on the two Homeric epics, is both. It is possible that the Homeric poet or poets in the eighth century B.C.E. would have heard of the Mesopotamian epic, but there is no proof that this was the case. In any case, there are many similarities between the Gilgamesh story and the *Odyssey.* Both Gilgamesh and Odysseus are forced to leave home to pursue quests to the very ends of the earth and even to the Underworld. Both are true heroes in that they are humans with direct divine guidance. There are some similarities between Gilgamesh and Achilles in the *Iliad* as well. Each has a divine parent. Each has a more than ordinary love for a male friend and takes his most significant action in reaction to the death of that friend.

Whether there is direct influence or not—and there probably is not—the Gilgamesh epic establishes what is, in effect, an archetypal form of narrative involving the mysterious and far-reaching wanderings of a hero in search of a universal goal such as eternal life or even "home."

THE HEBREWS AND CANAANITES

Who were the Hebrews, or Israelites?

The Hebrews—people who spoke a Semitic language (Hebrew)—began to establish themselves in Canaan (present-day Israel, Palestine, Lebanon, and parts of western Syria and Jordan) in the 1200s B.C.E. Once they achieved a land of their own—Israel—they became known as Israelites, perhaps taking the name which the Torah (first part of the Old Testament of the Bible) tells us was given to the prophet Abraham's grandson Jacob. The term "Hebrew" might be related to an Egyptian term *Habiru,* referring to several non-Egyptian tribes residing in Egypt during the time of the pharaoh Merneptah (1213–1203 B.C.E.) The Hebrews who arrived in Canaan would have been semi-nomadic tribes of herders and occasional farmers. In Canaan they would have mingled and sometimes fought with Canaanites already living there—Semitic peoples such as Edomites, Midianites, Moabites, and Jebusites (the inhabitants of Jebus, which later became Jerusalem under King David). The Hebrews also absorbed some of Canaanite culture. Canaanite religion was attractive to some; they took on the Yahweh religion—perhaps learned from the Midianites—which would be the basis for the later development of Judaism. What eventually unified the Hebrews/Israelites was struggles for settlement land against the Canaanites and the non-Semitic Philistines (the people of Goliath in the David and Goliath story).

Who were the Canaanites?

As noted above, the Canaanites were various tribes living in the land the Bible calls Canaan after a son of Ham, the son of Noah cursed for having seen his father's genitals. The land of Canaan is sometimes used synonymously with Phoenicia, the land of ancient Semitic peoples along the coast of what is today Lebanon. It was the Phoenicians who invented the alphabet in about 1500 B.C.E. The Phoenicians had trade and cultural contact with the civilizations of Mycenaean Greece, Mesopotamia, and Egypt. Canaan—especially as the term relates to discovered mythological texts—is also associated with the city of Ugarit (Ras Shamra in modern Syria).

What was the nature of Canaanite mythology?

Although there were many local versions of the Canaanite pantheon, a generally consistent series of deities and deity types emerges from these versions. First of all, there is a concept of a high god who takes precedence over all others. He is a storm god associated with weather and fertility and creation. He is a somewhat distant figure. A Semitic word for "god" is *el* or *il*. Thus, we have the Hebrew *Elohim* and the Arabic *al-ilah* or *Allah.* Deity lists in Ugarit dating from the second millennium B.C.E. refer to El and to Elib (Ilib), the "father god." The Greeks associated El with Kronos, the father of Zeus. Another term for the high god was Dagan (Dagon). His name refers to grain and he is directly related to the concept of fertility.

25

Goddesses were important among the Canaanites. They were typically the means by which the nature of their male counterparts were actualized. Thus, the Phoenician Ashtart, or Astarte, as the Greeks called her, was "the name of Baal." Athirat (Asherah), the consort of El, is "the Mother of Gods."

But the most popular and significant concept of the high god was Baal in his many forms: son of El, storm and weather god, dying god whose death means draught and whose return means renewed fertility. Baal was strong enough even to rival the concept of Yahweh among many of the Israelites in Canaan. His complex mythology is contained in a cycle that dominated Canaanite mythology.

What is the Baal Cycle?

The Baal Cycle is to the Baal religion what the New Testament is to Christians or the *Enuma Elish* to the Babylonians. It begins with the demand of the old water god Yamm—perhaps a male equivalent of the Babylonian Tiamat—that Baal accept him as the supreme deity. Strangely, the high god El supports Yamm against his son and rival. A parallel exists in Hittite mythology when the god Kumarbi commissions Ullikummi to fight against Tesub, his son and rival for kingship. Baal defeats Yamm as Marduk had defeated Tiamat, and the goddess Ashtart hails him as the new king and conqueror. El now allows a magnificent temple to be built in Baal's honor, a metaphor in itself, like Yahweh's temple in Jerusalem, of a new creation based on new principles.

An argument develops during the building of the temple between the architect, who wanted a window in the building, and Baal who, believing in the old superstition that death enters a home through a window, did not want one. Only much later, after many military victories does Baal agree to the window, and, of course, Death (Mot) enters.

The final and most important part of the cycle narrates the struggle between Baal and Mot (Life and Death). Baal cannot refuse Mot's invitation to visit the Underworld. After celebrating his fertility aspect by mating eighty-eight times with a young cow, the *de facto* Bull of Heaven, taking his children and storm/weather god

A bronze figurine of the Babylonian god Baal that was buried in ancient Ugarit in what is now Syria.

powers with him, enters the Underworld and, in effect, dies to the world. Deprived of fertility, the world dries up. It is Baal's sister and sometimes consort Anat who confronts Mot, who says he has chopped up Baal and "sowed" him in the fields. Anat wins her struggle with Mot and, reflecting the mystery of fertility and agriculture itself, the dying god returns as new life, and the world is renewed. Every seven years, however, the war between Mot and Baal-Anat resumes.

THE BIBLE AND JUDAISM

Is there an Israelite or Jewish mythology?

Many of the familiar sacred narratives of the Jews are contained in the first five books of the Bible—the Pentateuch or the Torah—traditionally attributed to Moses, the hero who, according to the story of Exodus, led the Hebrews out of Egypt through a miraculously parted sea to Canaan, the land promised to Abram (Abraham), a promise reaffirmed with Isaac and Jacob (Israel). The first book of the Torah, Genesis describes among many other miraculous events, the creation of the world by Yahweh, the sin of Adam and Eve, their expulsion from the Garden of Eden, and Noah's flood. All of these Genesis events, like those of Exodus, can be considered mythology, since they are narratives which go beyond what we know of real-life experience but have important metaphorical or spiritual meanings.

The Torah was composed in various stages between about 950 and c. 400 B.C.E., influenced, as we have seen, by contact with other cultures, such as the one experienced in Mesopotamia during periods of exile. Much of the mythology the Torah contains serves to justify the conquest of the "Promised Land" by the Israelites, the people "chosen" by the one-and-only god, Yahweh.

The monotheistic concept was also central to Christianity (which evolved from Judaism), and later to Islam, which was deeply influenced by Jewish and Christian beliefs as well as by indigenous Arabic mythology. All three religions worship the same God and trace their beginnings to the prophet Abraham.

Who was Abraham?

Abraham (at first Abram; Ibrahim in Arabic), the founding hero of the three major monotheistic religions, was the son of a man named Terah in the ancient city of Ur in Mesopotamia. His role as a *bona fide* mythological hero in the monotheistic context becomes clear when as a child he destroys the idols his father makes as a profession. Later Abram begins his heroic quest, when, as he and his family travel toward Canaan, Yahweh appears to him, urges him on, and promises him eventual greatness: "I shall make you into a great nation."After a time in Egypt during a famine, Abram and his wife Sarai returned to Canaan and Abram built altars to Yahweh in Hebron. Yahweh again appeared to him and promised the whole land of Canaan after a four-hundred-year period.

As Sarai was barren, Abram took a slave, Hagar, as a mistress, and in time she gave birth to Ishmael (Ismail in Arabic).

When Abram was ninety-nine, Yahweh renamed him Abraham, "Father of Many Nations," and he renamed Sarai, "Princess," having established a sacred covenant with Abraham. As a sign of his covenant with his people, Yahweh ordered that all males following Abraham be circumcised. This was a symbolic rite of sacrifice and obedience to God. Abraham and Ishmael immediately had themselves circumcised, and Jews and Muslims—believing themselves to be descendants of Abraham and benefactors of the covenant—have practiced the rite of circumcision ever since. For Christians, circumcision has been considered unnecessary because Jesus is believed to have sacrificed himself for all people.

Yahweh said that Sarah, in spite of her barrenness and old age, would produce a child, Isaac. This she did, and afterwards sent Hagar and Ishmael away. The new child, Isaac, would be Abraham's heir, but Yahweh promised that Ishmael would father a great nation. This would be the nation of Islam.

Isaac was only a boy when Yahweh tested Abraham's loyalty by demanding that the boy be sacrificed to him. The ever-dutiful prophet agreed to sacrifice his son and was about to complete the act when a lamb was miraculously substituted for the boy. Some have associated this act of obedience and sacrifice with the rite of circumcision.

Sarah died in Hebron at the age of 127. Abraham died there at 175.

Their son Isaac, along with Isaac's son Jacob, would carry on the heroic quest for the Promised Land. Ishmael (as Ismail) would become the center of an Islamic myth in Arabia.

THE ARABS AND ISLAM

Was there a pre-Islamic mythology in Arabia?

Yes. Various tribes had cult centers marked by holy stones (*baetyls*), sacred trees, or temples. The tribe of the Prophet Muhammad, the Quraysh, for example, worshipped a great tree called the Dhat Anwat on the road between two of the settlements that would become holy to Muslims: Mecca and Medina. Before it became the center of Islamic worship, the Kabah, with its mysterious Black Stone, was a stone cult center. In fact, it was a pilgrimage center and sanctuary with some 360 idols. There are, however, some indications that even before the time of Muhammad some Meccans were moving toward a vision of a single divinity, *al-ilah* (the god), who stood behind such tribal gods who were worshipped, as the Qur'an tells us, in the time of Nuh (Noah).

Goddesses, too, played a part in pre-Islamic Arabian cultures. Manat, Allat (*al-Lat,* "the goddess"), and al-Uzzá are all mentioned in the Qur'an. Manat was particularly associated with pilgrimages to the Kabah. Allat was called "Mother of the Gods," reminding us of the Canaanite Athirat. As for Al-Uzzá, she was the Inanna of the pre-Islamic Arabs—a goddess of love. Later Muhammad would forbid the worshipping of the goddesses, and, like the Hebrew prophets who spoke against the worship of Asherah and other Canaanite goddesses, he experienced some significant resistance from his countrymen.

Who were the Arabs?

The Arabs were Semitic peoples of the Arabian Peninsula whose language was closely related to those of other Semites in the Middle East, including the Hebrews. Like that of the other Semites, Arab culture, traced back as early as 1200 B.C.E., would have been centered on kinship, tribes, and clans. An indication of contact between Arabs and Israelites is indicated by the story of the visit of the queen of Saba (or Sheba) to King Solomon in Jerusalem early in the first millennium B.C.E.

Is there an Islamic mythology?

Like Judaism and Christianity, Islam is a living religion, so many Muslims, Christians, and Jews object to the term "myth" in relation to stories sacred to their religions. However, if we use the word simply to refer to stories that are beyond ordinary human experience, stories that people outside of the religions in question do not take literally, we may reasonably speak of Jewish, Christian, and Islamic myths.

With relatively minor variations, Muslims adhere to the Genesis creation and flood stories. Yahweh is Allah, Satan is Iblis, Adam is Adam, Eve is Haiwa. Noah is Nuh. Moses, as Musa, is important as the revealer of the Torah, itself recognized as a sacred text. The New Testament is important, too, as it contains the story of Isa (Jesus), the penultimate prophet, who was born miraculously of Maryam (Mary).

The story of Abraham (Ibrahim) is particularly essential to Muslims. Islam means "Obedience" or "Submission" to the will of Allah. In his *submission* to God's command that he sacrifice his son, Ibrahim was, in a sense, the first Muslim. In the Islamic tradition it is usually Ismail (Ishmael), rather than Iaaac, who is set up for sacrifice. As the willing victim he is the symbol of the perfect Muslim child, and Muhammad is said by some to have descended from him.

As the son of Abraham by the slave Hagar, Ismail was Abraham's firstborn. According to the Islamic story, Ibrahim felt guilty when, at Sarah's bidding after she gave birth to Isaac (Ishak), he expelled Hagar and Ismail. He went in search of the pair and found them at the well of Zamzam in the place now called Mecca. It was the water of this well, opened for them by the angel Jibril (Gabriel) that had saved their lives in the desert. With Ismail, Abraham built the Kabah.

MUHAMMAD

Who is the primary Islamic hero?

By far, the most important human hero in the Islamic narrative is Muhammad. He is the final Prophet, the ultimate messenger of Allah. Over the years many myths emerged

29

about Muhammad's life. Two stories can be called canonical. These are the receiving by Muhammad of the Qur'an, the true "word of God," and the Night Journey to Jerusalem and Ascension from there to Heaven (al-isra'wa miraj).

How did Muhammad receive the Qur'an?

When Muhammad was forty years old he retreated for meditation to a cave on Mount Hira and on the seventeenth day of the fasting period called *Ramadan*, he was overpowered by the presence of divinity as represented by the angel Jibril (Gabriel). The angel taught Muhammad the proper prayer rituals, recognized him as Allah's Messenger (*rasul*) and commanded him to "say" (*iqra*), the words of Allah which would be the holy book of Islam, the Qur'an. The Prophet would receive segments over the next twenty-three years.

What is the Story of the Night Journey to Jerusalem and Muhammad's Ascent?

The Night Journey to Jerusalem story is full of marvels, and it is found in various versions. It usually begins with Muhammad having gone in the middle of the night to the Kabah to worship. There he fell asleep only to be awakened by Jibril and two other angels, who washed his heart with the waters of the well Zamzam. The winged horse, al-Buraq,

A 1514 illustration from the *Bustan of Sa'di* at the Metropolitan Museum of Art shows a scene from the Night Journey of Muhammad.

arrived and was instructed by Jibril to carry the Prophet to "the Farthest Mosque" Isda, usually thought to be the al-Aqsa in Jerusalem. Once in Jerusalem, Muhammad prayed at the temple-mosque of the Rock, where he was recognized by Ibrahim, Musa, and Isa (Abraham, Moses, and Jesus) as their superior. When presented with a choice of wine or milk he chose the latter and was praised by Jibril for having chosen the "true religion." Now, with Jibril, Muhammad made the steep and difficult climb up the ladder (*miraj*) leading through seven heavens, at each stage learning something more about true Islam, until finally he reached the place of divinity, where he either saw Allah or signs of Allah.

There are many auxiliary stories associated with the Night Journey to Jerusalem. Some say al-Buraq took Muhammad to Mount Sinai, where God had spoken to Musa, and to the birthplace of Isa. In most versions Muhammad passes through symbolic visions representing the sinfulness of humanity as well as the serenity of the faithful. An amusing tale has it that Allah ordered Muslims to pray fifty times a day and that when Muhammad reported this to Musa, Musa urged the Prophet to return to God to request something less onerous. God agreed to five times.

The myths about Muhammad and the words of God, the Night Journey to Jersulam, and the Ascent tie the Prophet firmly to those world heroes like Gilgamesh, Buddha, and Jesus, who all embark on significant quests for the truth about the nature of existence.

THE CHRISTIAN STORY

Is the Christian story a Middle Eastern myth?

The Christian story emerges from the prophecies of the Hebrew tradition, the Jewish hope for a Messiah, and the narratives of the life of the man Jesus, a Jew whose whole life was spent in the Middle East. It is also true, however, that Christianity was deeply affected by interpretations and emphases that can be traced to church leaders and popular culture, both in the Middle East and elsewhere.

What are the primary myths of Christianity?

Christians accept the Hebrew mythology of the Hebrew Bible—the creation, the expulsion from the Garden of Eden, Noah's Flood, the God of Abraham, the experiences of Moses, the prophets and the Israelites—as vehicles of truth. Even more central to Christianity, however, are the words and deeds of, and the events surrounding, the reported life of Jesus. Many of these deeds and life events, while believed literally by some Christians or metaphorically by others, are clearly out of the ordinary. To non-Christians and even to many Christians, then, they are clearly myths, however beautiful or psychologically revealing they might be.

Jesus is a figure who expresses fully the heroic monomyth. He is miraculously conceived by a human woman by way of God. This places him in a fellowship that includes the Buddha, Perseus, and Herakles, to mention only a few great heroes. Like the Iranian Zoroaster, the infant Moses, and many other heroes, he is threatened in childhood by a wicked tyrant representing the non-heroic status quo. His life is dominated by a quest involving temptations and miracles, a search for the father, and even, in one version, a descent into the Underworld (Hell) to confront the epitome of evil. And in the ultimate act of heroism, he overcomes death itself.

It is that death and the resurrection from it on which Christianity is built. The story of Jesus' death and resurrection is known as the Passion. It is told with only minor variations by the four evangelists, Matthew, Mark, Luke, and John—the biographers of Jesus in the Christian part of the Bible, the New Testament (as opposed to the Jewish part, the Old Testament). To the gentiles who later became Christians, Jesus was the long-awaited Messiah.

31

What are the central events around the Passion of Jesus?

In the last days of his life of teaching, Jesus was said to have entered the holy city of Jerusalem, riding on an ass, signifying his new message of humility. But his followers threw down palms in his path, signifying his "kingship" as Messiah. After a Jewish Passover Seder, which would become the basis for a central Christian ritual, the sacred meal, or Holy Communion, Jesus stirred up the Jewish religious and Roman political authorities with what they saw as disruptive words and actions, and he was put on trial, convicted by the Roman authorities and sentenced to die by crucifixion. He was taunted by his captors as the supposed Messiah, the "King of the Jews," and was dressed accordingly and ironically in a purple robe and a crown of thorns.

For Christians, the crucifixion is a new version of the Jewish Day of Atonement (*Yom Kippur*), in which the sacrificed hero atones for the sins of all, dying as a scapegoat, with the sins of everyone on his back. He is the new lamb substituted for Abraham's Isaac.

What happened after Jesus' death?

According to one tradition, after death Jesus descended into Hell to "harrow" it and to symbolically redeem the original sinners, Adam and Eve. Jesus is one of many mythological heroes, including, for instance, the Greeks Odysseus, Herakles, and Theseus, who descend into the Underworld. But it is what happens next that is most important for Christians. It is said by Matthew, Mark, Luke, and John, and by later followers such as Paul of Tarsus (Saint Paul), that after three days Jesus emerged from his tomb and forty days later ascended into Heaven on a cloud. It is this resurrection myth that signifies to Christians the possibility that belief in Jesus can lead to eternal life.

IRAN:
ZOROASTRIANISM AND MITHRAISM

Are there earlier Middle Eastern mythologies or religions besides Judaism and Islam that may be compared usefully with Christianity?

Elements of the ancient Iranian religion, Zoroastrianism, and its mythology have often been compared with Christianity. The same is true of Indian and Iranian myths surrounding the god Mitra/Mithra. The Phrygian myth concerning the man-god Attis possesses elements that make it comparable to Christianity.

What is Zoroastrianism and what are its mythological roots?

Zoroastrianism emerged as a religious and mythological system from the reformation of the ancient Indo-Iranian religion in Iran by the prophet and sage Zoroaster (Zarathustra) in the late second millennium B.C.E. The Indo-Iranian religion—that is, the Iranian version of the religion and mythology of the so-called Aryan invaders of Iran and India early in the second millennium—is sometimes called Mazdaism, in reference to the god Ahura Mazda. The supreme deity of the pre-Zoroastrian religion as well as of Zoroastrianism itself, Ahura Mazda was one of the great gods known as *ahuras* in Iran (Persia) and *asuras* in the related culture and religion in Vedic (pre-Hindu) India. His Indian equivalents are Varuna and Indra.

Central to Zoroaster's reformation was a basic dualism that places the good Ahura Mazda and his heavenly followers, the other *asuras*, against the evil Angra Mainyu and his followers, the *daevas,* demons committed to war and destruction.

Along with this essential dualism, various aspects of Zoroastrianism make it so compatible with Christianity that many scholars suggest it was only chance that Zoroastrianism did not become the primary

Devotional art dedicated to Zoroaster (Zarathustra).

religion of the West. These elements include an afterlife, a last judgment, an apocalypse, the resurrection of the bodies of the good when evil is finally defeated, and, most important, a savior or series of saviors. These Messiah figures are named Saoshyants. In one story, a Saoshyant's virgin mother miraculously conceives him by way of the seed of the first Saoshyant, Zoroaster himself, the seed having been saved and guarded by spirits in Lake Kansaoya. The final Saoshyant, Astvat-Ereta, will ultimately destroy the forces of evil.

What is Mithraism? Who was Mithra/Mitra?

Originally a pre-Zoroastrian Iranian god, whose Indian equivalent was Mitra, Mithra was a solar deity diminished in stature by the Zoroastrian reforms. He became popular in the Roman Empire in the early centuries of the Common Era as the center of the cult of Mithraism. Like many monomythic heroes, he was said to have been conceived miraculously. Born from a rock, he went on to search for and to slay the primal bull, a symbol of sin and disorder. Mithraism, with its rituals of sacrifice, rivaled early Christianity in Rome.

THE PHRYGIANS

Who were the Phrygians?

The Phrygians were an Indo-European people who migrated to Anatolia (Asia Minor, in present-day Turkey) in the eighth century B.C.E. Later they would be conquered by the   33

Persians, by Alexander the Great, and still later by the Romans. The Phrygian capital was Gordium, so named in honor of King Gordias, who was said to have arrived in the city in an ox-cart. Gordias had a famous son, Midas. The story says that in return for having done a good deed for the Greek god Dionysos (Dionysus), Midas—then himself king of Phrygia—was promised anything he wanted. Foolishly, he asked that everything he touched be turned to gold. When even his food became gold, he realized his mistake. As a much younger man, Midas had honored his father Gordias by tying a famous knot to attach his father's ox-cart to a post in the center of Gordium. No one could untie this "Gordian Knot," a term which to this day symbolizes an insoluble problem. When Alexander conquered Phrygia, he solved the problem by slicing the knot with his sword.

What is the story of Attis?

The man-god Attis and the Great Mother, Cybele, were the central figures in the most important Phrygian myth cycle. This cycle has come down to us in several sometimes confusing versions. The most common version says that the Great Goddess in the form of the Virgin Nana, placed a pomegranate on her lap, causing one of its seeds to enter her and to make her pregnant. She then gave birth to Attis at the winter solstice. Attis grew into a beautiful boy who was much loved by the Great Goddess, as Cybele. He was also loved, however, in a sexual way by the evil Agdistis, who had himself been miraculously conceived by Cybele when semen from the sky god Pappas fell on her lap as she slept on the Agdos Rock. Attis, not wishing to be unfaithful to Cybele, refused Agdistis's advances. The conflict between Attis and Agdistis—good and evil—culminated in Attis's sacrificing himself by castration on or near a sacred tree. It was said that he came back to life at the vernal equinox. In Rome, ceremonies recognizing the resurrected Attis as a fertility god of vegetation, were held at the equinox on a day known as the *Hilaria* (Day of Joy). A sacred meal was part of the celebration.

Many elements—the virgin birth at the winter solstice, his struggle against evil, his death on a tree, his resurrection in the spring—associate Attis with other dying hero/gods such as Osiris in Egypt, Adonis in Greece and Rome, and, of course, Jesus, whose rival for recognition he became for a time in the early years of Christianity in the Roman Empire.

EGYPTIAN MYTHOLOGY

Who were the ancient Egyptians?

By the fifth millennium B.C.E., the so-called Pre-Dynastic period of Egyptian history, people with tool-making ability, rudimentary shipping, crafts, and agricultural settlements lived along the Nile River. Much controversy surrounds studies of the ethnic makeup of these people. We know that at the end of this period Egypt was known as a country of "Two Lands." Most scholars agree that the people of the north (Lower Egypt) developed from a culture known as the Merimde, with ties to the Eastern Mediterranean, while people in the south emerged from the Naqada and Badarian cultures with sources in Nubia and northeast Africa. At the beginning of the First Dynasty, about 3100 B.C.E., King Narmer or his son Aha joined the two lands, forming the world's first great nation-state. Collectively known as Menes, it had a captial at Memphis, near present-day Cairo. After that Egypt underwent periods of great power and artistic achievement, as well as periods of division between the two lands. Egyptian history is generally divided into dynasties and intermediary time periods: the Old Kingdom (beginning c. 2780 B.C.E.) and the first Intermediate Period of disruption (beginning c. 2250 B.C.E.); the Middle Kingdom (beginning c. 2050 B.C.E.) and the second Intermediate Period, during which Egypt was overpowered by invaders known as the Hyksos; and the New Kingdom (beginning c. 1580 B.C.E.) and late periods culminating in the rule of the Greek Ptolemy pharaohs, the most famous of whom was Cleopatra. Roman rule, after the defeat of Marc Antony and Cleopatra, began in 30 B.C.E.

What language did the ancient Egyptians speak?

It is generally believed that the early ancient Egyptian language was an Afro-Asiatic one, once called Hamito-Semitic. This language developed, as in most cultures, over the centuries into a middle and then late form, with the earlier form being used, as Latin was in Europe and Ancient Sumerian was in Mesopotamia, for religious and other formal purposes. A demotic form of Egyptian became known as Coptic and is used today only in the liturgies of the Christian-Coptic church, Arabic having displaced Egyptian as the language of the people.

What is the Rosetta Stone?

The Rosetta Stone was carved in 196 B.C.E. in Memphis during the reign of Ptolemy V. It contained a decree in three languages: Ancient Egyptian hieroglyphic, Demotic Egyptian, and Ancient Greek, the latter providing a translation and clear key for deciphering the old Egyptian language. The stone was used in medieval times as building material in a fort, was discovered by a French soldier in 1799 and was taken by the British when they defeated the French in Egypt soon after that. It is now in London in the British Museum.

The Rosetta Stone, housed at the British Museum, was a valuable key in deciphering hieroglyphs because the inscription, which has to do with a decree passed by a council of priests, is written in several languages.

When was writing developed in Egypt and what was its significance for mythology?

Writing in the form of hieroglyphs on pottery and other objects developed at the end of the Pre-Dynastic era, probably not long after writing was invented in Sumer. It first appeared on pottery and other functional objects. Hieroglyphic symbols were both ideograms (signifying ideas) and phonograms (signifying phonetics). It was believed that writing was invented by the god Thoth, and the word *hieroglyphic* is the Greek form of the Egyptian, meaning essentially "God's Words" (*hieros* = sacred, *glypho* = inscription).

Our knowledge of Egyptian mythology before writing can only be surmised archeologically—that is, from depictions on objects. Once hieroglyphics were understood by scholars after the discovery of the Rosetta Stone, a direct route to Egyptian gods and their stories was opened.

EGYPTIAN RELIGION AND MYTHOLOGY

What factors dominated Egyptian religion and its mythology?

Sacred kingship was central to Egyptian religion. Every king (pharaoh) was considered to be the son of the creator sun god and the direct representative of Horus, the son of the great king-god Osiris. The connection with Horus is significant, because the primary responsibility of the king was to preserve divine order (*maat*). In mythology, Horus, representing that order, was in a continual struggle against his uncle, Seth, who represented the opposite.

The connection of the pharaoh to the sun god is important because the daily rising of the sun represented creation itself and the victory of light over darkness.

The most evident aspect of Egyptian religion and mythology is a concern with the afterlife. Anyone who visits the Egyptian wing of a museum is inevitably struck by the presence of mummies, elaborately preserved bodies of ancient kings and noblemen who had been placed—sometimes in pyramids, sometimes in underground tombs—with valuable objects and even sacrificed servants meant to ease the deceased's passage through the Underworld. The visitor to Egypt is drawn especially to the great pyramid tombs of Giza (near Cairo) with the mysterious Sphinx nearby. The emphasis on death and the afterlife was almost certainly related to a natural phenomenon that was ever present in Egyptian life, the annual flooding of the Nile that brought death and then re-birth to the fertile land along the river.

What were the pyramids?

Pyramids were elaborate tombs for powerful kings. One scholar referred to them as "res-urrection machines"—places grand enough to assure the resurrection of kings into the other world. The shape of the pyramids has to do with a common belief that the earth emerged originally from a primeval mound. The pyramids were, in a sense, then, mod-els of the cosmos. With a point reaching up to the sun, they recall the great sun god, and their gradually expanding sides represented the rays of the life-sustaining sun on earth.

The first pyramid, the step pyramid at Saqqara, was built in about 2750 B.C.E. by King Djoser. More pyramids were built somewhat later during the reigns of Sneferu and Khafra. The great pyramid of Khufu (Cheops), built in about 2650 B.C.E.–one of the won-ders of the ancient world—stands out above all the others.

What was the Sphinx?

The huge sphinx that looms over the desert at Giza, probably built in about 2400 B.C.E., is another wonder. This sphinx is one of many sphinxes in ancient Egypt—all with bod-ies of lions and heads of other creatures, sometimes the kings themselves. No one knows for sure what the Great Sphinx signifies. But as the lion was traditionally associated with the sun and solar gods in the Near East, it is possible that the lion body and human head signified the union of the sun god with his "son," the pharaoh.

How have we learned about Egyptian mythology of the Dynastic periods?

We have learned the complex details of Egyptian mythology by way of decorations and hieroglyphs on pottery and especially on tomb and temple walls, as well as in various fu-nerary texts, including works we know today as the *Pyramid Texts*, the *Coffin Texts* and the *Book of the Dead*.

What are the *Pyramid Texts*?

The *Pyramid Texts* are a collection of "spells" or instructions regarding the afterlife of a pharaoh. Written during the Old Kingdom, in about 2400 B.C.E., on the walls of the pyramid tomb of King Weni (Unas) and several other kings and queens in Saqqara, these texts were concerned with the protection of the given pharaoh's remains, the means by which his body could be brought back to life after death in order to ascend to the gods above. The spells are specific, explaining how the king would use certain ladders and ramps and how he would fly to Heaven.

Written in Old Egyptian, the *Pyramid Texts*, along with Sumerian hymns to Inanna, are among the oldest religious writings known to us. They are an important beginning place for an understanding of Egyptian mythology. While the *Texts* do not include detailed mythological narratives, they do touch on major mythological themes such as the creation, the resurrection of a god named Osiris, the struggle between Seth and Horus, and the daily journey of the sun god in his solar boat. The *Texts* mention some two hundred deities, including many of the gods and goddesses now included on touristic and scholarly lists of Egyptian gods: Ra, Atum, Geb and Nut, Osiris, Isis, Horus, Seth, Nephtys, Anubis, Thoth, and the ancient creator goddess Neith, to name only a few. A better understanding of the identities and the symbolism of these gods emerges when we study the specific pantheons of particular religious centers in ancient Egypt and texts that developed later, during the New Kingdom.

What are the *Coffin Texts*?

The *Coffin Texts* are funerary writings found on coffins and tomb walls of the Middle Kingdom—that is, between c. 2055 and 1550 B.C.E. Written in Middle Egyptian and in a later literary or hieratic script, the *Coffin Texts*, like the *Pyramid Texts*, are concerned with the passage of the dead king's life after death. Although there are no complete mythological narratives in the *Coffin Texts*, there is more information about specific myths than exists in the *Pyramid Texts*. There is, for instance, a spell which gives instructions on how to navigate the solar barque of Ra. In a section of the writings known as the *Book of Two Ways*, there are maps of the passage through the afterlife, including the land of Rosetau, where Osiris's body lay in flames and through which the dead person must pass in order to reach the heavenly paradise. More information on creation is given, including an explanation of the dualism represented by the struggle between the creator god Atum-Ra, the representative of divine order, and Apophis, the monstrous representative of Chaos. Many of the same gods mentioned in the *Pyramid Texts* appear. Thoth is important, as are Horus and Seth and Osiris, the resurrection god with whom the dead pharaoh was identified.

What was the *Book of the Dead*?

The collection known to us as *The Book of the Dead* was titled by the ancients themselves as *Spells for Going Forth by Day*. The importance of this text, really a relatively minor collection of spells regarding passage through the afterlife, has been greatly exaggerated. For students of mythology, however, *The Book of the Dead* is important because it contains information about two major gods, Ra, the sun god, and Osiris, the Lord of the Underworld. In one of the spells, involving the judgment of the dead by Osiris, the deceased's heart is placed on one side of a scale and weighed against a feather representing the goddess Maat, herself embodying the sacred concept of *maat* (divine order).

Where were the main religious centers of Egypt?

Several religious, cultural, and political centers achieved relative importance or dominance at particular times in Egyptian history. Although Egyptian religion and mythology have a certain consistency that transcends the various centers, each center did emphasize particular deities and stories.

The most ancient center was Memphis, so named later by the Greeks. Memphis was the capital city of the province of Aneb-Hetch. In about 3000 B.C.E. it became the capital of the newly united Upper and Lower Egypt under the First Dynasty king, Menes. The ruins of Memphis are in the present-day town of Mit Rahina, near Cairo in Lower Egypt. The primary god and creator of Memphis was Ptah, who created with his heart and tongue. He wore a beard and a craftsman's cap; his consort was the lion-headed Sekhmet. Ptah was a great craftsman—a *deus faber*— a craft deity who, like Hephaistos (Vulcan) in Greece, could make beautiful objects, including new bodies for the dead. The temple of Ptah—Het ka Ptah—became "Aigyptos" in Greek and "Egypt" in English.

Thebes was the Greek name of Waset (modern day Luxor). Founded in about 3200 B.C.E., Thebes was the major city of Upper Egypt and at various times was the capital of all of Egypt. The great temple of Karnak is situated near the city. The chief god and creator here was Amun, the "Hidden One," sometimes depicted with a ram's head. He represented sexual power and was associated with a partner, "God's Hand," who used that hand to arouse Amun so that he could create. Later he would be associated with the sun god Ra as Amun-Ra. His queen was Mut, and their son was the moon god Khonsu.

In Dendera, north of Thebes, Hathor, the ancient cow goddess whose headdress combined a solar disk and a pair of cow's horns, was the "Eye of Ra"—the solar disk of Heaven itself. She was also associated with another Horus, her son, who was especially celebrated at nearby Behdet (Edfu).

This statue at Italy's Turin Museum is an image of the Egyptian god Ptah, the primary god and creator of Memphis.

The town of Khmun (Hermopolis) in Middle Egypt was named Hermopolis by the Greeks, after their god Hermes, whom they believed to be the same as the Egyptian god Thoth, a god of wisdom and hidden knowledge and the inventor of writing. The town was originally known as Eight-Town because of a group of eight gods—the Ogdoad (The Eight)—worshipped there. These primeval gods represented the original matter of the world. The Ogdoad consisted of four male and female pairings. Nun and Naunet were the primordial waters. Amun and Amunet were air—the source of life. Kek and Keket were darkness. Heh and Hehet were chaos, or infinity.

The town of Hnes in Lower Egypt, south of Memphis, was called Herakleopolis by the Greeks, after their hero Herakles, whose identity they associated with the ram god Heryshef, the chief god of the city. Heryshef was sometimes thought to be a form of the god Osiris.

By far, the most influential cult center in ancient Egypt was the city of Iunu, named Heliopolis (City of the Sun) by the Greeks because of the predominance there of the great sun god Ra (Re).

THE EGYPTIAN PANTHEONS

What was the pantheon of Heliopolis?

In Greek, the pantheon of Heliopolis was named the Ennead (the Group of Nine). Unlike some other Egyptian pantheons, the Heliopolis pantheon is a family with a specific biography, much as is the case with the Olympian Greek pantheon. The creator god was Atum, who was associated with the great sun god Ra (Re) as Atum-Ra. The offspring of Atum were Shu (Air) and Tefnut (Moisture). Shu and Tefnut produced the earth god Geb and his sister-wife, the sky goddess Nut, who was often depicted as a nude woman whose body arched over the reclining and sometimes sexually aroused Geb. Geb and Nut were the parents of arguably the most important family in Egyptian mythology: Osiris and his sister-wife Isis (the parents of the child Horus) and Seth and his sister-wife Nephtys. Osiris is depicted as a mummy wearing a kind of crown and carrying a crook; Isis wears a throne symbol on her head. Seth's head is often that of a mysterious ferocious animal.

Usually mythologies have Earth Mother goddesses and Sky Father gods. Why in Egyptian mythology is the god Geb depicted on the ground while the goddess Nut arches over him as the sky?

Nut is always called a protectress. She protects the sun god Ra; she protects those who have died and are entering the heavenly world; she protects the dead and resurrected Osiris, her son. Sometimes she is depicted as a cow—like another great goddess, Hathor—or as a sow with udders toward which those below reach up for nourishment, making her position above the hungry earth logical. One can assume that Nut is an ancient goddess representing a religion in which goddesses were not subservient to gods. This tendency in religion is reflected in the relatively strong position of women in Egyptian society and in a movement during various periods toward matrilinealism.

Who were the other most important Egyptian deities?

Anubis, depicted with a jackal or dog head, was, from the Old Kingdom on, the primary funerary god. He assisted in judging the dead in the Underworld, and he was involved in the process of mummification. It is said that he invented mummification primarily to preserve the body of the god-king Osiris. The later Greek writer Plutarch and others told a story that Anubis was the son of Osiris, the result of Osiris's having been somehow tricked into sleeping with his brother's wife, Nephtys.

Another important god was Thoth, the inventor of writing and of human languages. As the magician and wise one among the gods, he had mysterious healing powers. Thoth was usually depicted as a baboon or as a man with the head of an ibis.

Horus, with the falcon head, was an important god from early dynastic times. He represented the sacred kingship. This Horus is usually differentiated from the boy Horus, the son of Isis and Osiris. The older Horus was said by some to have been responsible for initiating creation in primeval times. He was god of the sky with enormous wings and eyes that represented the sun and the moon.

Are there Egyptian versions of the Great Goddess?

There are many Egyptian Great Goddess figures in addition to those who made up almost half of the Ennead. The lion-headed Sekhmet, the great cow goddess Hathor, the "Eye of Ra," and Mut, the consort of Amun-Ra, are all examples of the archetype.

In some cult centers, especially in the Egyptian Delta in the north of the country, the creator was the goddess Neith, who wore the crown of Lower Egypt and was represented by a beetle. Sometimes she had a crocodile head. Some said she was the mother of the great sun god Ra.

Why do Egyptian gods sometimes have animal heads?

The Egyptians probably saw their gods not as literal physical beings, but as symbolic representations of aspects of nature and life in general. Animals have always been given sym-

Why is there so much incest in Egyptian mythology?

Incest among the gods reflects the presence of incest in ancient Egyptian society, especially within royal families. Many reasons have been suggested for this practice. As in many societies, incest was a means in Egypt of keeping power and riches within the family.

bolic value based on certain characteristics. The owl appears to be wise, the fox sly. In Egypt, animal heads signified certain characteristics of particular deities. Sekhmet was part lioness because, in the flood myth, for instance, she is ferocious and destructive. Amun is a creator god associated with fertility; he is depicted with a ram's head because rams are associated with fertility. Hathor has a bovine attributes because she is a nurturer of children and of mothers in childbirth, and cows provide the sustenance of milk. It is also possible that certain animals were totems associated with particular cult centers or temples and would naturally have been connected with the gods of these centers and temples.

EGYPTIAN CREATION MYTHS

What were the Egyptian creation myths?

The creator gods in the various Egyptian traditions emerged as the first light, the first consciousness, out of the primeval mound in the original dark, watery chaos, the *Nun*. Creation required differentiation—between light and dark, male and female, high and low. The creator in some myths contains these opposites: that is, is originally both male and female. In the Memphite theology, the god Ptah created by "heart and tongue"—by thinking reality and speaking it ("In the beginning was the word"). Or, as Khnum, he shaped creation on a potter's wheel, acting as a *deus faber*.

Atum, the creator in the dominant mythology of Egypt, who was also the sun god Ra as Atum-Ra, created the first gods, and, therefore, life itself, *ex nihilo*—that is, from nothing, or, in other words, not from previously existing material but from within himself. The *Pyramid Texts* report that Atum produced Shu and Tefnut (air and moisture—necessities for life) through an act of masturbation. Theologically speaking, this is a logical understanding of how things began, since the only mate available to the creator was himself. One ancient papyrus description is still more explicit and even more logical. It reveals that Atum, at the culmination of the masturbatory act, took his penis into his mouth and received the seed of life with himself. Here the mouth becomes the womb of creation. The *Pyramid Texts* also say that Atum, as Atum Khepri (another name for the creator) eventually spat out Shu and Tefnut. The *Coffin Texts* report that Shu emerged from Atum's nose. Myths from Memphis agree with this but emphasize that it was Atum's thought that changed his seed into Shu and Tefnut. In any case, only when Shu and Tefnut were born did Atum become differentiated as a male and a father. In a later development, The Hand of Atum used in the creative act of masturbation was personified as a goddess—usually as Hathor.

In the *Coffin Texts* Shu was also seen as life itself and Tefnut as *maat* (divine order). Tefnut as maat was the essential principle of creation and, by extension, of life on earth, at the center of which was Egypt. When Shu and Tefnut became independent of their father, they came together in the universe's first sexual act between male and female entities. The result was the birth of Geb and Nut (Earth and Sky).

Is there a myth of the forced separation of world parents in Egypt?

As in the Sumerian system, Earth and Sky were continually together in an apparently endless act of intercourse. But, as in the case of An and Ki (Sky and Earth) in the Sumerian system, they had to be separated to make room between them for the created world. Logically enough, it was to Shu (Air) that the responsibility of separating his children fell. Thus, we find many depictions of Shu standing on Geb, often still sexually aroused, and pushing Nut up to form the arched sky full of stars and other heavenly bodies.

A circa thirteenth-century B.C.E. artwork found in the tomb of Queen Nefertari, depicting the sun god Ra (right) and Imentet (left), a goddess who represented the necropoleis west of the Nile River.

Now there was space in which the creator could arise as the sun god Ra, bringing light and warmth to the world as he rode his solar barque across the sky. And children could be born to Geb and Nut. These children were the great man-god Osiris, his sister and wife Isis, their sister Nephtys, and her evil brother-husband Seth, all principals in the myth cycle that would dominate Egyptian religion and mythology from about 2480 B.C.E.

What was the Solar Barque myth?

The solar barque, or Sun Boat, the "Boat of Millions," was used by Atum-Ra to sail across the sky each day bringing light to the world and through the Underworld each night. Spirits of the dead could travel on the Sun Boat, and Ra himself used the boat to return to the sky in his old age, leaving Osiris as the dominant god.

There are many variations of this myth depending on the spiritual or theological message the given spell in which it occurred was intended to convey. In one version, the sun itself was said to be born of the goddess Nut. The Sun's childhood was morning. At noon the sun was the great falcon god, and by evening he was old—perhaps the tired Ra who wished to remove himself from the solar cycle. Whatever the version, the solar barque, carrying the sun god and his *ka* (soul) enters the Underworld at night bringing new life to its population and emphasizing the concept that death was necessary to life. In some versions of the myth the solar barque is replaced at night by a lunar boat, which hauled the sun god over the chaotic sands of the Underworld. During this time the sun god and his companions, the worthy dead and certain gods, would struggle against chaos, represented by terrible monsters led by the daily slaughtered and reviving serpent Apophis, who forever threatened the divine order represented by the solar cycle. One

43

myth has it that Apophis, 120 yards long, was a product of the spit of the goddess Neith early in creation. Apophis was the closest Egyptian mythology came to envisioning an ultimate devil or Satan figure.

In the days of the early dynasties it was said that Nut devoured the sun god each evening, leaving star gods in his place. In the morning the revived sun god ate the star gods, their blood creating what we see as the sunrise.

The Solar Barque myth may be said to have reflected the reality of death and resurrection acted out in the annual flood of the Nile as well as in the story of the death and resurrection of Osiris.

How was humanity created according to Egyptian myth?

The Egyptian religion paid relatively little attention to humans or human heroes. The primary concern of all the Egyptian cult centers was deities. There are, however, fragments of myths about the creation of humans. In the *Coffin Texts* we are told by Atum that human beings were the product of "the tears of my eye," "my eye" being the Single Eye personified as a goddess—for instance, Hathor or Sekhmet—sent out by Atum-Ra to bring his children Shu and Tefnut back to him in the early stages of the creation. The Eye of Ra, then, represents the drive for order in creation, because without Shu and Tefnut—air and water—placed between the bodies of Geb and Nut—Earth and Sky—there would be no room for life. The reason for the Eye's tears is unclear, but the most likely reason stems from her anger and disappointment when she returns with Shu and Tefnut to discover that the high god had substituted a new Eye—the solar Eye—the sun, for her. To placate the first Eye, Atum makes her into the cobra, the symbol of which was placed on the crown of Egyptian kings.

One of the creator's gifts to humans was the Nile, with its annual flood and the possibility of humans joining him after death in his solar barque.

THE MYTH OF ISIS, OSIRIS, AND HORUS

What was the cult of Isis and Osiris and Horus?

After Ra's withdrawal from daily concerns with earth, his son Geb became the ruler of earth. Eventually Geb ceded his position to his son Osiris. More than any other deities, Osiris, his wife Isis, and their son Horus played out their mythological roles on earth rather than in heaven. Osiris and Isis, acting as culture heroes, were associated with humanity, teaching the people agriculture and the art of civilization in general. Their human aspect made Osiris and Isis and Horus eligible to play jointly the mythological role of the monomythic hero. In their story we find the theme of the miraculous conception and birth, the threat to the hero's life, the death of the hero, and the hero's resurrection and return. The Osiris/Isis/Horus cult was the central one in Egyptian religion for many centuries. It was the myth that most directly connected the people to the gods.

All kings died as Osiris and were crowned as Horus (Osiris resurrected).

The Osiris/Isis/Horus myth is told in various versions in the *Pyramid Text* and the *Coffin Texts*, in the *Book of the Dead*, and in the writings of the first century C.E. Greek historian and biographer Plutarch in his *Moralia*. A combination of the stories related in these sources reveals what has become the canonical (generally accepted, official) myth.

What was the myth behind the Osiris/Isis/Horus cult?

The reign of Osiris and his sister-wife Isis was a golden age. The primary companions of the king and queen were their brother Seth (Set or Typhon) and their sister Nephtys, Seth's wife. Whether because of jealousy over the reported accidental affair between Osiris and Nephtys, or simple envy, Seth turned against his brother and killed him. Some say he trampled Osiris to death. Some say he caused him to drown. The most popular version—the one containing the most devious act—was reported by Plutarch. In this version, Seth secretly obtains his brother's exact measurements and then builds a beautiful coffin-like chest according to those measurements. He promises the chest to anyone who can fit into it exactly. No one fits the chest until Seth encourages Osiris to try and, of course, the fit is exact. Now Seth and some of his followers quickly close the lid of the chest containing the king and they seal it and cast it into the Nile, and it floats out into the sea.

The Egyptian god Osiris (middle) is flanked by his wife, Isis (left), and their son, Horus (right). The Osiris/Isis/Horus cult was the central one in Egyptian religion for many centuries.

Isis, upon learning of her husband's disappearance and death, searches the world for him, finally making her way to Byblos, in what is now Lebanon. Apparently the coffin had become a great tree, which the king of Byblos had incorporated into a column of his palace. Isis asks for the column, and the king gives it to her. Isis extracts the coffin and takes it back to Egypt. But, not to be deterred in his wish to rid the world of his rival, Seth discovers the returned body and cuts it into many parts, which he scatters or throws into the Nile. Again Isis embarks on a search and succeeds in finding all her husband's body parts but for his penis, which a fish has swallowed. With the help of her sister Nephtys, Isis reconnects the dismembered parts of her husband's body. She makes models of the lost penis and some say she buries such models in all the provinces of Egypt and that these burials result in grain production. This aspect of the story relates Osiris to dying gods in other cultures whose resurrections are sources of nourishment

45

for the people. Dionysos in Greece is such a god and he produces the grape. Jesus' death results for Christians in new spiritual food.

What happened to Osiris after his death?

Isis and Nephtys watch over the body of Osiris and, by way of ritual lamentations and spells, restore him to life sufficiently to make it possible for him to impregnate Isis as she flutters over him in bird form. This is the miraculous conception of Horus. Scholars have pointed out that Isis' role in restoring Osiris' virility is analogous to the Hand Goddess of Atum who brought the creator god to orgasm and thus instigated creation itself.

What is the significance of the "resurrection" of Osiris?

The fact that the dead Osiris is restored to wholeness and fertility suggests that he is the first mummy—the representation of the possibility of overcoming death by certain rituals and procedures. It also becomes a metaphor for the receding of the Nile after the annual flood and the resulting fertility of the land.

In keeping with his role as the first mummy, Osiris' body is protected by the magic and the power of Anubis and Thoth, and he becomes King in the Underworld. So it is that the Osiris myth provides the theology behind mummification. So it is also that the divine aspect behind all pharaohs is eternally preserved: the pharaoh dies as Osiris and his successor is enthroned as Horus. In the myth as in real life, the Pharaoh-Horus must continue the eternal struggle between divine order and the chaos represented by Seth.

What was the war between Horus and Seth?

The divine child Horus was born to Isis in the fertile Egyptian Delta. As are so many representatives of the mythological archetype of the divine child—Jesus and Zoroaster are examples—he is threatened by the forces of chaos, represented here by Seth. When Isis was forced away, the child was hidden in the Delta marshes, where he was fed by a wet nurse, the great cow goddess Hathor. Poisoned by a snake sent by Seth, Horus is healed by gods sent by Atum-Ra. As a child, Horus fights off many agents of Seth—evil reptiles and other animals—sent to destroy him. The goal of what is, in effect, a heroic quest, is always to avenge his father's murder and to take the throne of Egypt away from Seth.

A central part of the story of the Seth-Horus conflict is unusual sexuality. Horus complains to his mother that Seth admires him sexually. Isis advises her son to give in to Seth, but in the process to steal some of his magical power. Horus agrees, and in the course of sex he catches the evil king's semen in his hand. When Horus brings the semen to his mother, she cuts off her son's polluted hand, throws it into the Nile, and makes him a new hand. Then she arouses Horus with her own hand and brings him to orgasm, again acting out the original creative role of the Hand Goddess in creation. Isis captures Horus's semen and spreads it on the plants in Seth's garden. When Seth eats the plants, he becomes pregnant and gives birth to a sun disk that Thoth gives to Horus as a sign that he is the true "son" of the sun god creator Atum-Ra.

In what becomes physical combat between Seth and Horus, Seth tears out the boy's eyes, but Horus castrates Seth. The struggle becomes so violent that the gods intervene with a divine tribunal. In most versions of the story, Seth is awarded Upper Egypt—the desert land—and Horus becomes lord of Lower Egypt. Eventually, however, Horus is acclaimed king of all of Egypt.

The Seth-Horus struggle, then, reflects the actual pattern of division followed by unity between Upper and Lower Egypt over the centuries.

In fact, humanity in Egypt was so prone to struggle and antagonism that the high god resorted at least once to universal punishment that culminated in a flood of sorts.

What was the Egyptian flood myth?

Like the Mesopotamian and Genesis flood stories, the Egyptian flood myth begins with the anger of the high god against the ungrateful evil of the human race. A late third millennium B.C.E. myth tells how humanity had gone so far as to plot against Ra himself and that Ra called the gods into council to decide what to do with these "children" of his Eye. Humans had been born of the tears of his Eye, represented by a goddess. In this case the Eye is Sekhmet, the lioness goddess—perhaps as the fiery sun—who, bent on the destruction of her miscreant children, descends upon humans and their world and unleashes all of her violent fury on them. The destruction is so terrible that Ra relents and decides he must put a stop to the terror wrought by his Eye. He creates beer from barley and red ochre and floods all of the fields of Egypt with it. Sekhmet is herself attracted by the beer and drinks so much of it that she becomes intoxicated and forgets about her destructive mission. A few humans are thus saved and are able to begin a new life.

OTHER EGYPTIAN MYTHS
AND INFLUENCES

Were there ever challenges in Egypt to the prevailing religious system and the dominance of the old sun god creator?

In the fourth century B.C.E. a real-life event occurred that might be said to coincide with the myth of the insult to Ra that led to the flood story. The pharaoh Amenhotep IV, whose capital was at Thebes (Luxor), decided to challenge the dominance of the old sun god—Amun-Ra in Thebes. The king proclaimed Aten, a lesser known solar deity, as "the one unequaled god," and he changed his own name to Akhenaten ("Disciple of Aten"). Akhenaten built a new capital named Akhetaten (Tell el-Amarna today) in the god's honor. Although Akhenaten's worship of Aten has led some religious scholars to call him the first monotheist, it is more likely that Aten was seen in this new theology simply as the first among gods or perhaps the only important god. In any case, the king forbade the worship of Amun-Ra, and the worship of other gods was discouraged. Even

47

the old idea of the dead passing into the Underworld was denied. At the center of the new theology was Akhenaten himself and his main queen, Nefertiti, through whom the rays of Aten penetrated the world.

With Akhenaten's death, however, Amun-Ra had his vengeance as his priests and the people rose up against Aten dominance, destroyed the dead king's new capital, and restored the old theology. The son of Akhenaten and Nefertiti was Tutankhaten (c.1348–1339 B.C.E.), the boy king known to the world as King Tut, who after his father's death changed his own name to Tutankamun, honoring Amun-Ra.

What was the cult of Isis?

Some ancient Greeks saw goddesses such as Demeter and Aphrodite as incarnations of Isis, and during the Roman Empire Isis became an important cult figure, a mother goddess and protector of children, whose tears after the death of her husband caused the flooding of the Nile. A temple for Isis existed in Rome, and some have suggested that popular depictions of Isis nursing the boy Horus influenced similar depictions in the Christian era of Mary nursing the baby Jesus.

CYCLADIC, MINOAN, MYCENAEAN, AND ARCHAIC GREEK MYTHOLOGY

THE CYCLADES AND CRETE

Who were the Cycladic and Minoan peoples and what was their history?

The southern Aegean islands known as the Cyclades—perhaps after some nymphs the sea god Poseidon was said to have turned into stones—were inhabited from at least 7500 B.C.E. and its inhabitants almost certainly had contact with Egyptian civilization during the Bronze Age. By 3200 B.C.E. the Cycladic civilization had developed a sophisticated artistic tradition and presumably a mythological one. Its palace-based culture resembled that of the Minoans, with whom they had significant interrelations. The Minoans were a Bronze Age people living on the island of Crete in the Eastern Mediterranean. Their immediate ancestors were Neolithic farmers and fishermen living on the island from at least as early as 6000 B.C.E. The Bronze Age Minoan civilization existed from about 2700 B.C.E. The Minoans were not Indo-Europeans and were not related to the Greeks or to the pre-Greek peoples of Greece and Anatolia, but were active traders with the Mesopotamians, Egyptians, and the inhabitants of the Greek mainland, the islands of the Aegean, and Anatolia. They were known for their architecture, pottery, and other arts and crafts. We do not know what they called themselves. The British archeologist Sir Arthur Evans (1851–1941), who unearthed the great palace at Knossos, called them "Minoans" after the king known in Greek mythology as Minos.

The first Minoan palaces, built between 1900 and 1700 B.C.E., were destroyed in about 1700 B.C.E., either by an invasion or, more likely, an earthquake. They were quickly rebuilt in grander style; palaces such as the famous one at Knossos represented the pinnacle of the Minoan civilization. We have come to think of this palace as the home of King Minos. In Greek mythology Minos' palace is associated, in turn, with the stories of the Minotaur, Theseus, and the Labyrinth. In about 1425 B.C.E. Crete was taken over by the Mycenaean Greeks—the people of whom Homer writes in his *Iliad* and *Odyssey* epics about the Trojan War and the return of the hero Odysseus.

What language did the Minoans speak and write?

We know little of the Minoan language. It was not in any sense a written language until the development of hieroglyphs, perhaps as early as the ninth century B.C.E. The hieroglyphs, possibly influenced by systems in Mesopotamia and Egypt, were essentially pictograms used for lists and commerce. Very soon after the development of hieroglyphs, the Minoans developed a script based on arranged lines representing symbols, sounds, objects, and ideas. Scholars call this script Linear A, and to this day it remains indecipherable. Later the Linear A system would be used by Mycenaean Greeks, beginning in about 1400 B.C.E., to write their own language. This writing was decoded in the early 1950s by Michael Ventris and John Chadwick and labeled Linear B. Linear B was a language like Linear A, used primarily for lists and commercial records. The Minoan language itself eventually died out, being replaced by Greek.

What was the nature of the Minoan cultural contact with Mesopotamia and/or Egypt?

As mentioned earlier, the Minoans traded widely and their writing systems were perhaps influenced by those of the Mesopotamians and Egyptians. There is also evidence that the Egyptians were impressed by Minoan ceramics, as many examples have been found in Egyptian archeological sites. We know, too, that the Minoans imported papyrus from Egypt and that their palaces and paintings were influenced by the art and architectural styles of Egypt. The Mesopotamian connection would seem to be based more on mythic or religious ideas. Both the ancient Sumerians and the prehistoric cultures that preceded them in Mesopotamia and Anatolia placed an emphasis on bull-human combinations, on the double axe, and on powerful goddesses. All these elements are evident in what we know of Minoan mythology.

What was the nature of Minoan cultural contacts with Greece?

The Minoan contact with the Greeks and pre-Greeks (sometimes called Pelasgians) of the mainland and Anatolia were more frequent and more direct. The Greek language would eventually become the language of Crete, and Crete would become important in Greek mythology. The Mycenaean Greeks would bring their version of the Greek pantheon to Crete and were themselves influenced by certain aspects of Minoan religion and mythology. The Greeks, in fact, had a fascination with Crete and its palaces—especially the great one at Knossos—and developed a whole mythology with the island as the setting. That mythology, particularly the stories related to Theseus, the Labyrinth, and the Minotaur, and the familiar stories of Daedalus and Icarus may have had some connection with the history of rivalry and warfare between the Mycenaeans and the Minoans.

DAEDALUS, ICARUS, AND
THESEUS AND THE MINOTAUR

Who was Daedalus?

The myth of Daedalus was told and retold and often revised by various Greek and Roman writers, most notably Apollodorus and Ovid. The first mention we find is in Homer's *Iliad*, where a passing reference indicates that Homer expected his eighth century B.C.E. listeners to know of the story. Homer clearly places Daedalus in the Minoan context, mentioning him as the creator of the dancing ground for the princess Ariadne, the "Lady of the Labyrinth."

Daedalus was, above all, a master craftsman. It was said, however, that in Athens, when his nephew-apprentice Perdix became almost as adept at building, the jealous Daedalus murdered him, making a flight to Crete necessary. In Crete, Daedalus became an employee of King Minos, who immediately set him to work on various famous projects, most notably the famed Labyrinth. If the Labyrinth was originally a dancing ground for Ariadne, in later myth it became associated with the infamous bull-man, the Minotaur, the son of Queen Pasiphae.

According to the Roman poet Ovid, Daedalus became tired of King Minos' demands on his time and decided to escape Crete by making wings for himself and his son Icarus. After attaching the wings to their bodies with wax, Daedalus warned his son not to fly too close to the sun. Icarus, thrilled by flying, ignored his father's warning. He flew up toward the sun, the wax melted, and his wings fell off, and he fell to his death in the sea. Daedalus flew on to Sicily.

Who was the Minotaur and how was he produced?

A strange and even shocking tale leads to the birth of the Minotaur. Minos, according to some sources, was the son of Zeus and the mortal woman Europa. In order to have his way with Europa, Zeus had taken the form of a bull and carried her off over the sea to Crete, where Minos was born. In time, Minos proclaimed himself king of Crete, justifying his proclamation by his divine heritage and claiming the gods would give him anything he asked for. When he asked Poseidon for a special bull to be sacrificed, the god sent him a beautiful white bull. But Minos so admired the

A frescoe on the wall of the Casa dei Vetti in Pompeii depicts the tragic hero Daedalus.

51

bull that he placed it with his own herd and substituted an ordinary bull for the sacrifice. Poseidon was understandably angered by this duplicity and planned a terrible revenge. Minos had married the beautiful Pasiphae and made her his queen. Poseidon caused Pasiphae to fall in love with the great white bull. She so lusted after the bull that she begged Daedalus for help. Daedalus, always clever, built a model of a beautiful cow to attract the white bull. Pasiphae positioned her body inside the model in such a way as to make herself available for intercourse with the deceived bull. The result of this unholy liaison was the half-bull, half-man monster, the Minotaur.

Minos housed Pasiphae's terrifying offspring in the Labyrinth built by Daedalus, really more of a maze than a true labyrinth.

What was the myth of Theseus, the Labyrinth, and the Minotaur?

Theseus was a Greek hero, particularly important to Athens. He had all the characteristics of the archetypal monomythic hero, including a miraculous conception, a search for his father, a quest, and a descent into the Underworld. His connections with Crete and the Minoans are central to his heroic successes. According to some sources he caught and sacrificed the great white bull which had been captured by the hero Herakles and had made its way to Marathon.

A quarrel developed between Theseus' father Aegeus and Minos, and in a war that ensued Minos triumphed and demanded that every seven (some say nine) years seven Athenian boys and seven girls be sent to Crete as a tribute and, according to many sources, as food for the Minotaur. Theseus volunteered to take the place of one of the boys and determined to kill the Minotaur so as to save his fellow Athenians. While in Crete he attracted the attention of the king's daughter Ariadne, who fell madly in love with him. Ariadne led Theseus to the Labyrinth. Having been advised by Daedalus, who

had no love for Minos and knew the Labyrinth well, because he had designed it, she gave the young hero a ball of thread and instructed him to tie one end to the door post and the other to himself so that a path back out of the Labyrinth would be marked for him if he succeeded in finding and defeating the Minotaur. Theseus did find the Minotaur and, after a terrible struggle, killed him, and followed the string back to the Labyrinth entrance. Soon afterward he escaped Crete with the Athenian boys and girls and with the king's daughters Ariadne and Phaedra.

Marble sculpture (1862) by Étienne-Jules Ramey depicting Theseus fighting the Minotaur.

MINOAN RELIGION AND MYTHOLOGY

What was the nature of Minoan religion?

What we know of Minoan religion and mythology before the Mycenaean domination in Crete is based on assumptions derived from archeological material such as frescoes and other objects found in the ruins of palaces such as the one at Knossos. There is evidence from these materials of a kind of ceremony involving youths leaping over bulls. The bull seems to be an object of worship, a fact perhaps confirmed by similar worship in ancient Mesopotamia, Anatolia, and by the prominence of bulls in later myths already discussed concerning Crete. In Egypt, for instance, Hathor was a moon goddess who was also a cow, and the pharaoh was a sacred bull. Much later, in the Irish epic the *Tain*, a connection exists between a great bull and a queen. The doubleheaded axe also is prominent in Minoan art, suggesting a religious function. The later Greek word for the doubleheaded axe is *labrys,* which suggests a connection to the Labyrinth. Was the doubleheaded axe a symbol of the sacred bull? Prominent among Minoan archeology and artifacts is a goddess figure. Many scholars have suggested that Minoan culture was goddess- rather than god-centered. Some claim that Minos means "Moon Man" and refers to a ritual marriage of a priest king with a moon priestess who represented the Great Goddess of Crete. A sacred marriage of this sort existed in connection with the Inanna cult in Mesopotamia. But all of this is mere speculation, colored to some extent by later Greek myths such as the one about Pasiphae and the Great White Bull of Poseidon. What we do know is that a Minoan goddess figure—depicted with bare breasts and often with a pubic area marked by a stylized triangle—appears in many places in Crete. The goddess holds up snakes, familiar goddess companions in many parts of the world. It is probably fair to assume that this figure—especially in connection with a bull god—probably represented fertility. Sometimes a youthful male figure accompanies the goddess. The later Greeks associated this figure with the boy Zeus or with Zeus's son Dionysos, who, in the myth of Theseus and the Labyrinth, marries Ariadne after Theseus abandons her on his way home from Crete.

Some have suggested that the youth was a dying god figure, a mythical representative of youths sacrificed in fertility rituals. There is, in fact, some indication of human sacrifice in Minoan Crete, a fact given mythological form in the later story about the Athenian boys and girls sent as sacrificial tributes to King Minos.

Was there a Minoan pantheon?

It is difficult to establish a specific Minoan pantheon. But what can be surmised from Linear B records that followed the Mycenaean conquest of Crete is the influence of Minoan ideas on the later pantheon of the Mycenaeans and other Greeks. In the Linear B tablets we find a hierarchy in which Diwe (Zeus) seems to reign supreme. Era (Hera) is also there, as are Posedaone (Poseidon), Atana Potinija (Athene), Pajawone (Apollo), Atemito (Artemis), Emaa (Hermes), Are or Enuwarijo (Ares), Apaitioji (Hephaistos), Diwonusojo (Dionysos), and perhaps a form of Demeter, whose name, Da-mater, means "Earth Mother" and who, with her daughter might be associated with the inscription Potniai (Ladies), the descendants of the earlier Great Mother, of Crete and the Neolithic tradition. Aphrodite is missing here; she is probably a post-Mycenaean arrival in Greece from Phoenicia via Cyprus, whose many Semitic goddess relatives (e.g., Astarte and Asherah) themselves look back to the ancient Sumerian goddess of love and fertility Inanna (Ishtar).

Because this list emerges from Minoan script adapted to the Mycenaean Greek, we can best call it a Minoan-Mycenaean pantheon, with the emphasis on Mycenaean.

THE MYCENAENS AND HOMER

Who were the Mycenaeans?

The Mycenaeans were a Greek-speaking people who arrived in Greece sometime around 2000 B.C.E. and whose major centers are known to us primarily through the epics of Homer. Most important of these cities was Mycenae, the city of the quasi-legendary King Agamemnon, the leader of the Greeks—also called Achaeans or Danaans—in the Trojan War described by Homer in the *Iliad*. The Mycenaeans, unlike the Minoans, were a warlike people with castle towns dominated by princely aristocrats. They did have advanced jewelry, architecture, and other arts and crafts, however, and were influenced in these pursuits, as in their religion and mythology, by the Minoans, whom they conquered in about 1400 B.C.E.

Other than the list of deities listed above, little is really known about Mycenaean religion and mythology. Linear B was not conducive to literary practices. Stories and myths would have been told orally and passed down through the generations that way. As the Minoan-Mycenaean deity list indicates, we can say, however, that many of the Olympian gods whom we associate with the mythology of classical Greece were already known and presumably worshipped in Mycenae.

The Mycenaean civilization had fully deteriorated by 1100 B.C.E. for reasons that are unclear but that perhaps can be attributed to the invasion of another Greek-speaking people, the Dorians. In any case, the end of the Mycenaean civilization marked the beginning of the so-called Dark Ages in Greece, a period of social and cultural stagnation that lasted until the emergence of a new writing system in the late eighth century B.C.E., a system in which an alphabet devised by the Phoenicians was adapted to Greek. The end of the Dark Ages and the beginning of the so-called Archaic Age was also marked by the two poets, known to us as Homer and Hesiod, who probably composed orally sometime in the eighth century B.C.E.

Our view of the Mycenaeans is derived in great part not only from archeological ruins, but from Homer's description of them in his epics. It should be remembered, however, that Homer had no written historical records on which to build; he would have depended for his sources on a word-of-mouth transmission of stories that spanned a period of 350 to 400 years.

Who was Homer?

Over the centuries, the two great Greek epics, the *Iliad* and the *Odyssey,* have been attributed to a single author named Homer, who has been claimed as a native of various locales in Asia Minor and the Greek mainland. In fact, the epics were probably the works of more than one person, composed in various stages between 900 and 700 B.C.E. The existence or nonexistence of Homer is the subject of what scholars have long called the "Homeric question." Whether or not there was a

A circa 500 B.C.E. piece of pottery is decorated with a scene from the Trojan War in which the hero Achilles assists the wounded Patroclus.

Homer, the epics in question have been used in schools since ancient times to teach language and Greek values. And the *Iliad* and the *Odyssey* have provided us with a major source for Greek mythology, especially as it applies to human heroes. Whoever or whatever Homer was, he has himself been mythologized as a blind bard who more than makes up for physical sight with powers of insight and subtle understandings of the ways of humans and their all-powerful but fickle gods. In the eighth book of the *Odyssey,* the blind minstrel-poet Demodokos of Phaiakia, who, like the "Homer" of the *Iliad*, sings the story of the Trojan War, provides what some would call a self-portrait. In that book, the hero Odysseus serves as an instrument for the praising of the kind of poet Homer or the several Homers would have been. In so doing he gives life to a tradition that has intrigued humans for more than two thousand years:

> Now came the court crier, leading the
> favored bard, the singer loved by the Muse,
> who gave him good and evil—the power of song
> and the absence of sight. When his thirst was quenched
> and his hunger fed, he sang through the Muse a song of
> heroes, a song known by all, far and wide. Carving a piece
> from his chine of boar, Odysseus called out to the blind poet's
> guide, 'Pray give this meat to Demodokos, and grant him
> peace from unhappy me. Much honor is owed to the bards,
> men loved by the Muse who gives them song.' The guide
> took the meat, and gave it to the bard, whose heart was full
> of joy.

Whether there was one Homer or two Homers—one the composer of the *Iliad* and one the author of the *Odyssey*—or a fellowship of bards known as the Homeridae ("Sons

What are the *Homeric Hymns*?

The *Homeric Hymns* is an important source for our knowledge of Greek mythology. Composed in the Archaic period—the seventh and sixth centuries B.C.E.—the "*Hymns*" is a collection of stories in verse generally attributed to the school of poets known as the Homeridae ("Sons of Homer"). In the collection we find important myths such as those of Demeter and Persephone, Artemis, Apollo, Athene, Dionysos, and Aphrodite.

of Homer"), to whom another important source of Greek mythology, the *Homeric Hymns,* is sometimes attributed, Homer does represent an ancient poetic tradition that has taken form in many parts of the world. Scholars Milman Parry and Albert Lord in their studies of epic poetry found that frequently repeated words or phrases—especially descriptive tags and similes—suggest a method of recited oral poetry in which singing minstrel-poets (*rhapsodes*) used such stock elements as rest breaks to give them time to remember or to create subsequent events. It seems likely that the events Homer describes in his epics—especially in the *Odyssey*—are based on traditional folk tales well known before the composition of the epics. As has already been noted, Homer's reference to Daedalus, for instance, was made in a manner that clearly assumed his eighth-century B.C.E. audience already knew the story of the mythical craftsman.

The Homeric epics as we know them now, written down and divided into "books," which are perhaps related to the length of singing sessions by minstrels in town squares or the houses of the relatively wealthy, were compiled in the sixth century B.C.E., probably in Athens.

How did Homer use the Mycenaean world?

Homer's (for the sake of convenience, he is referred to here as one person) setting for both his great epics was the world of the Mycenaeans because traditions of that world had been passed down over the centuries during the Dark Ages. Obviously Homer did not know that world by direct experience, and in his attempts to depict it, there are, understandably, elements of his own world—tools, foods, clothing, myths, traditions—that would not have existed in the time of the Mycenaean heroes Agamemnon and Odysseus. Although at least the basic outlines of the stories he tells about the Mycenaeans would have, in all likelihood, been familiar to his audience, it was Homer's job to bring them to life in his own age. In telling the story of the *Iliad*, for instance, Homer gave life to a central myth of the Mycenaean period, the war that was said to have taken place between the city of Troy and an alliance of the Mycenaean Greeks. Whether such a war actually took place is open to conjecture. It would not have been unlikely for various groups to attempt to challenge Troy's dominance over the entrance to the straits known as the Dardanelles in what is today western Turkey. That the war was caused by the abduction of King Menelaus's wife Helen is an example of Mycenaean-Archaic Greek mythology. In the *Odyssey*, Homer tells of the return of the Mycenaean hero Odysseus from Troy to Ithaca, describing a period of difficulty and disillusionment that often follows wars and perhaps reflecting the end of the Mycenaean age itself. The highly fanciful, fairytale-like aspects of the poem belong, as do elements of the *Iliad*, to the world of Mycenaean-Archaic myth.

THE TROJAN WAR AND THE *ILIAD*

What is the background of the myth of the Trojan War narrated in the *Iliad*?

The *Iliad* tells a story about the war in Ilium (Troy), waged by the Greeks, or Hellenes (called by Homer Achaeans, Argives, and Danaans), led by King Agamemnon of Mycenae against the people of Troy and their allies (Ionians and Aiolians), under King Priam. The beautiful Helen, wife of Agamemnon's brother, Menelaus, the king of Sparta, had been seduced and abducted by Paris, a Trojan prince, and an alliance of Greeks had come to take her back and to punish Troy for harboring her.

How does the *Iliad* begin?

The epic begins in the tenth year of the indecisive war with a domestic dispute among the Greeks. Agamemnon has been forced to return his war-prize mistress, the beautiful Chryseis, to her father, a priest of Apollo, in order to bring an end to a pestilence sent by the god to infect the Greek camp. Agamemnon agrees, but only after demanding, for his own use, Briseis, the war-prize mistress of his most powerful soldier, Achilles. Angered and humiliated by this arbitrary and arrogant act, Achilles pulls himself and his troops out of the war.

Throughout the epic, the gods and lesser deities take sides and even physically join in the battle, sometimes causing one side to prevail, sometimes the other. The head god Zeus, for instance, almost succeeds, through trickery, in getting the Greeks to go home, but Athene helps Odysseus to convince them to remain to fight. When, in Book III, Menelaus is about to kill his rival, Paris, Aphrodite (the goddess of love, an admirer of Paris) extricates the Trojan from danger. Zeus claims victory for the Greeks because Menelaus has defeated Paris, but Zeus's wife Hera urges him to allow the war to go on. In Book V, the gods actually join in the fighting. Later, after a touching farewell scene between the greatest of the Trojan warriors, Hector, and his wife Andromache and tiny son Astyanax, Hector leads the Trojans out to battle. The Trojans are successful for a while and Agamemnon tries to get Achilles to return to the war, but the still-angry hero refuses. Meanwhile, on Mount Olympus, the home of the gods, Hera seduces her husband Zeus and during the great god's sleep after lovemaking, Poseidon, encouraged by Hera, urges the Greeks on until Zeus wakes up and Poseidon has to withdraw. Once again the Trojans appear to be winning. Now Achilles' close friend and companion Patroclus convinces the

57

great hero to allow him to wear his armor and to enter the battle, thus causing the Trojans to believe that Achilles has returned to the war. The Trojans, thinking Achilles is back, retreat in terror, and Patroclus fights furiously until, with Apollo's meddling help, Hector kills him. Distraught over his friend's death, Achilles rejoins the battle after the blacksmith god Hephaistos makes him special armor. The gods join in and Achilles fights as no one had ever fought before, slaughtering any Trojan in his way. Eventually, with Athene's help, he kills Hector and insults his body and the Trojans as a nation by dragging his victim's body around the city walls. After the victory, the Greeks hold funeral games in honor of Patroclus, and in the final book, King Priam, in a deeply moving scene, comes to the Greek camp and begs Achilles to give him his son's body. Achilles takes pity on the old man and releases the body. A twelve-day truce follows.

What happened after the truce?

We learn what happened after the truce, not in the *Iliad* itself, but in the *Odyssey* from tales told by the minstrel Demodokos, by Helen, and by Odysseus, as well as in the great tragic plays of the fifth century B.C.E. and in a seventh-century poetic compilation of unknown authorship known as the *Little Iliad*.

According to these sources, Achilles is killed by an arrow shot by Paris that penetrates his heel—his one vulnerable spot. The Greeks trick the Trojans into accepting the famous wooden horse into their city as a gift, but the horse is full of Greek warriors, who emerge during the night to sack Troy and thus bring an end to the war. Many of the heroes will return home. Some, like Odysseus, will have difficulty doing so; some will do so with tragic consequences. Agamemnon, for instance, will be murdered by his wife, Clytemnestra, and her lover.

THE *ODYSSEY*

What is the background of the *Odyssey*?

The *Odyssey,* the second of the two great epics ascribed to the legendary Homer, tells the story of the Mycenaean-Greek hero Odysseus. Specifically, it describes Odysseus's ten-year-long adventure-filled voyage from Troy to his home in Ithaca following the Trojan War. Known for his wiliness, Odysseus was a particular favorite of Athene, the goddess of wisdom. Odysseus had once advised the father of Helen (later Helen of Troy) to demand that all the suitors to his daughter abide by the family's eventual choice of a husband by pledging an oath of allegiance to that man. So it was that the Mycenaean princes unified to make war on Troy after the Trojan prince Paris had abducted Helen from the palace of her husband, Menelaus. Meanwhile, Odysseus had married Helen's cousin, Penelope, who had produced a son, Telemachos. When the emissaries of Menelaus arrived to draft Odysseus into the alliance against Troy, the wily Odysseus, citing his responsibilities as a king, a husband, and a father, pretended to be insane and thus useless to the cause. But when his pretense was discovered, he bowed to the terms of the alliance and left for Troy and the war. It is of interest to note that the great Achilles, too, attempted to avoid the draft. He did so by hiding in women's clothing in the harem of his family's palace, but was discovered when he made one of the young girls there pregnant.

During the war, as described in the *Iliad*, the *Odyssey*, and in other works, Odysseus gained fame as a warrior and, primarily, as a strategist. His most famous act was the devising of the wooden horse full of Greek soldiers that the Trojans foolishly allowed into their city.

Like the *Iliad*, the *Odyssey* was in all likelihood based on earlier folktales and myths and was "fixed" in writing in its present book-based form in sixth century B.C.E. Athens. It is generally assumed that "Homer" composed the *Odyssey* some time later than the *Iliad*.

What is the plot of the *Odyssey*?

The first four books are known as the *Telemachia*. They narrate the adventures of Odysseus's son Telemachos as he goes on the hero's archetypal search for his father. Odysseus has been away for some twenty years, and in his palace at Ithaca unruly suitors are demanding marriage with his supposed "widow," Penelope. The suitors are eating their way through Telemachos's inheritance, leaving the boy in a state of depression until the goddess Athene urges him to act as his "father's son" against the intruders.

From the very beginning of the epic the dominance of the gods over humans—heroes and menials alike—is established. The king of the gods, Zeus, acts as a mediator between his daughter Athene, always an admirer of Odysseus, who wants the hero to be allowed to return home, and his brother Poseidon, who holds a grudge against Odysseus and wants to prevent his return. Zeus takes Athene's side, and sends the messenger god Hermes to the island of Ogygia commanding the nymph Calypso to free Odysseus, who has been trapped there as a kind of love slave. Meanwhile, Athene travels to Ithaca, disguised as Odysseus's old friend Mentor, and as such helps Telemachos to leave Ithaca in search of his father. The boy stops at Pylos, where he is greeted warmly by his father's old friend, another famous Trojan War hero, Nestor. Nestor sends Telemachos to Sparta to see Menelaus and his forgiven wife, the beautiful Helen. Menelaus and the once notorious, now gentle and wise, Helen tell the young traveler about the great deeds of his father. Most importantly, they report that Odysseus is said to be still alive. Homer now returns the scene to Ithaca, where the suitors plan to kill Telemachos when he returns home.

It is only in Book V that we finally meet Odysseus, and the man we see could not be more different from the hero we observed in the *Iliad*. He sits on the island's shore weeping and sighing, hopelessly longing for home. Although reluctant to give up the hero, since she greatly enjoys their lovemaking, Calypso has no choice but to bow to the demands of Zeus via Hermes. So she helps Odysseus to depart on a raft. But Poseidon is still angry, and he destroys the raft at sea. Once again, however, Odysseus is helped by Athene and a sea nymph, and, in a bedraggled state, he is thrown onto the island of Scheria, the home of the Phaiakians. Odysseus is discovered by the gentle teenaged

Nausikaa, the daughter of the king, who is doing laundry with friends near the shore. This is one of the more touching scenes in the epic: the naked and battered Odysseus juxtaposed against the innocent and unblemished Nausikaa, who nevertheless summons the courage to help the stranger, leading him to her father, Alcinous.

The king receives Odysseus without knowing who he is. Then, at a feast, the blind minstrel Demodokos appears and answers the mysterious stranger's request for a story about the Trojan War. The saga affects the hero emotionally, and the king notices the stranger's tears and demands that he reveal his identity. Odysseus now does reveal himself and is asked to tell his own story. In this story within a story, contained in Books 9 through 12, Odysseus tells of his fairytale-like adventures leading up to Calypso's island. There is the tale of the Land of the Lotus Eaters, where unwary visitors forget their homeland. The story of the confrontation with Poseidon's monstrous one-eyed son, the Cyclops Polyphemos, is next. It is the fact that Odysseus escapes from the monster by tricking and blinding him that has so turned the god of the sea against the hero. In Book 10 Odysseus tells how the wind god Aeolus gave him the bag of winds which if kept closed would prevent errant winds from blocking the passage to Ithaca. When Odysseus's suspicious companions open the bag, the winds escape, and the ship is blown off course. Giant cannibals, called the Laestrygonians, devour some of Odysseus's crew. Then, on the island of Aeaea, the witch Circe turns the men into swine. Only Odysseus, with Hermes' help, is able to withstand Circe's power, and the witch and the hero become lovers. After some time,

Odysseus and his crew are seduced by the Sirens on this piece of pottery circa 475 B.C.E.

Odysseus and his restored men obtain Circe's help in continuing their journey. Following her instructions, Odysseus visits the Land of the Dead to seek his destiny from the prophet Tiresias. There he meets Achilles and other dead heroes and learns from Tiresias that he will return to Ithaca, but that his entire crew will perish on the way. In a moving scene, Odysseus meets his mother's shade, who informs him of conditions at home.

As they make their way toward Ithaca, Odysseus and his crew must face the Sirens, the terrible *femmes fatales* who lure sailors to their death. To avoid this fate Odysseus places wax in the ears of his crew and has himself tied to his mast so that he alone can hear the famous siren songs without being able to leap to his death. After also surviving the boat-swallowing monsters Scylla and Charybdis, Odysseus arrives at the land of the sun god Helios, where, against his orders, his men eat the god's sacred cattle. Zeus punishes the entire crew but Odysseus by killing them with a thunderbolt, and Odysseus alone makes his way to Calypso's island and then to Phaiakia. So it is that Odysseus, in the role of a bard himself, brings his story up to date, leaving Homer to tell what happens next.

The second half of the epic is devoted to the hero's return home. After the Phaiakians sail him to Ithaca, Odysseus, on Athene's advice, takes on the disguise of a beggar. He is received well by his old faithful swineherd, Eumaeos. Telamachos now arrives, too, fresh from his stay with Menelaus and Helen. Only when Athene magically restores Odysseus to his youthful state does Telemachos recognize his father. After an emotional reunion, the group makes plans. Again disguised as a beggar, Odysseus, with Telemachos and Eumaeos, descends upon his own palace to find that Penelope is still desperately holding off the suitors. The suitors taunt the beggar, but Penelope, even though she does not recognize him, is kind to him and listens with joy as he tells her a soothsayer has told him Odysseus is still alive. It is Odysseus's faithful old nurse, Eurycleia, who first recognizes him when, while bathing him, she notices a tell-tale scar. Odysseus swears the nurse to secrecy. He watches with great interest when Penelope announces that she will marry the man who can string Odysseus's great bow and use it to shoot an arrow through iron axe-helve sockets. After all the the suitors fail, Odysseus, who has now revealed himself to the swineherd and another faithful servant, asks for a turn. Even though the suitors mock the lowly beggar, Penelope insists that he be allowed the bow. Odysseus, still unrecognized by Penelope, strings the bow with ease, shoots an arrow through the axe-helves, and now joined by the two loyal servants and his son, attacks and kills all the suitors as well as the maids who have given them sexual favors.

Book 23 reveals the tender reunion between Penelope and Odysseus, who have been made young and attractive by Athene. In the final book, Odysseus meets with his grieving father, Laertes. After that meeting Athene ends the potential blood feud between Odysseus and the families of the dead suitors, and peace returns to Ithaca.

What happened to Odysseus after the events of the *Odyssey*?

Many stories were commonly told about Odysseus after his return to Ithaca. One story held that, to regain the favor of the offended Poseidon, he traveled inland with a Poseidian trident until the trident was no longer recognized. In this way Odysseus became a *de facto* missionary of the great sea god who had caused him so much pain.

How can someone be called a hero if the gods control what he does?

In the *Iliad* and the *Odyssey* it seems that everything the heroes do is controlled by the gods. A god helps one hero to escape death or makes sure another one dies during the battles in front of Troy. Odysseus is saved by Athene, who seems to be constantly at his side. In the Greek view of things, it was the presence of the gods in the hero's life that indicated his heroic status. The gods are concerned with heroes in more specific ways than they are with lesser humans. The presence of the gods does not make Odysseus any less heroic. In our age a person might say, "the devil made me do it" and still be punished for his actions, or "it was God's will" and still be honored for his successes.

How and why are the *Odyssey* and the *Iliad* so different from each other?

The most obvious answer to the "why" part of this question would be that the two epics were written by different people, as suggested in our discussion of the Homeric question. Robert Graves, a somewhat controversial poet and mythologist, and other scholars have argued that the *Odyssey* might have been written by a woman. Their argument is supported, for instance, by the notable presence of strong women in the later epic. In the *Telemachia* segment we are introduced to a wise and noble Helen, who is nothing like the somewhat flighty Helen of Troy we meet in the *Iliad*. In Phaiakia, Queen Arete and her daughter Nausikaa are impressively independent, and in Ithaca, the faithful and clever Penelope, who has the power at the end of the epic to challenge even her long-lost husband, is a true heroine in an adamantly patriarchal society. Even among the gods, it is Athene who dominates in the *Odyssey*.

In any case, the differences between the *Iliad* and the *Odyssey* are striking. The *Iliad* is a male-dominated epic of war. It glorifies the pride and prowess of warriors, even when they act in morally questionable ways. The main characters—Achilles, Agamemnon, Paris, Helen, and even Hector—often behave in immature ways, risking the lives of thousands to protect their own sexual or material interests and their prideful self-esteem. The argument between Achilles and Agamemnon, on which much of the epic is built, is particularly childish and is detrimental to the common war effort, the war itself having been triggered by an impulsive violation of strict hospitality mores and marriage traditions by Paris.

Even the gods in the *Iliad* are fickle and childish in their squabbling and their ruthless treatment of humans. Homer would have had little knowledge of Mycenaean religion, so it is likely that this depiction of the gods—an almost comic treatment, certainly not a respectful one—reflects attitudes of Homer's time at the end of the Dark Ages rather than those of the Mycenaeans.

Although elements of all these characteristic exist to some extent in the *Odyssey*, the story of Odysseus is more somber. The first time we see the hero, he is not breaking through the walls of Troy in glory; he is weeping, the prisoner of a nymph on a deserted island. This is an epic of the post-war period, of post-war disillusionment and alienation. Odysseus just wants to get home to a domestic life—to his wife and son. He has no more interest in representing a larger Greek cause. The gods remain in place, but they, too, are somehow more serious, involved in a protracted struggle over the fate of an individual who is both worthy and guilty of transgressions.

The attitude toward heroism has evolved in this post-war age as well. Achilles lived by his abilities as a warrior; Odysseus must depend on his wits.

What is the popular appeal of the *Odyssey*?

As a work meant to entertain a general listening audience in an age no longer dominated by an aristocratic warrior class, the *Odyssey,* with its emphasis on the suitors, on Penelope, on the wronged son, and the love affairs of the hero, is more of a soap opera than the *Iliad* and also, with such figures as the Cyclops and the Sirens, more of a fairytale. There is also the sequel element that always appeals. Listeners must have been thrilled to find the notorious Helen early in the second epic and to meet familiar characters when Odysseus speaks with the dead Achilles and the dead Agamemnon and learns of their terrible fates.

One thing that characterizes both epics is the centrality of human beings, their foibles, their beauty, and their feelings. Few scenes in literature are more moving than the one in the *Iliad* between Hector and his wife and baby as he is about to enter his final battle, or the scene in the *Odyssey* when Nausikaa discovers the forlorn and naked Odysseus as she is doing her laundry. The gods are always present in both epics, but our interest is with our fellow humans who are so much at their mercy.

The writer of the Archaic period who has most to tell us about the world of the gods is the poet Hesiod.

HESIOD, THE GREEK CREATION MYTH, WARS AMONG THE GODS

Who was Hesiod?

Hesiod (Hesiodos) was a farmer-poet who probably lived only a bit later than Homer—sometime between 750 and 650 B.C.E. Hesiod probably wrote or had his poems written down by others. Hesiod, like Homer, probably did not invent stories so much as retell and elaborate on stories passed down during the Dark Ages and the Archaic period. With Homer and the composers of the *Homeric Hymns*, he is a major source for what we know of Greek mythology. He is especially known for his *Theogony* ("birth of the gods"), in which we find the generally accepted creation myth of the Greeks and the story of the war between old and new gods that established the Olympian dynasty of Zeus. He also wrote *Works and Days,* in which we find the famous Pandora myth. He is said by some to have been the author of the *Shield of Herakles,* about a confrontation between Herakles and a son of the god Ares.

What was Hesiod's creation myth?

Hesiod tells how the first activity in what was a chaos-based creation was the emergence of nothingness itself—Chaos (the Void). Out of Chaos came "wide-bosomed Earth," known to us as the great goddess Gaia.

The beautiful Eros (Desire) came next, the necessary element in a process that would lead to the procreation of the universe and the gods. Eros, says Hesiod, can undermine the more controlled intentions of the mind, a phenomenon with which most of us are familiar. Darkness and Night also came out of the Void. Then followed the first mating: Darkness was drawn in love to Night and the result was Night's giving birth to Light and Day. Now Gaia produced Sky (Uranos) out of herself, large enough to "cover her" completely in the act of constant procreation that reminds us of the joining of An and Ki in Mesopotamia and Geb and Nut in Egypt. Out of this joining— "without the urging of love"—Gaia gave birth to the mountains, the places loved by the gods, the rivers and lakes and the oceans (Oceanos). The next set of offspring was made up of the Earth goddess Rhea, Themis (Law), Mnemosyne (Memory), Tethys (sea goddess), Phoebe (Moon), and finally, Kronos and several monstrous figures such as the Cyclops. These children of Gaia and Uranos were known as the Titans, the first generation of gods.

Gaia had no love for Uranos or his violent treatment of her children. As each one was born, Uranos forced it back into Mother Earth, causing her great pain. As in the case of the Sumerian and Egyptian copulating creation deities, it became clear that separation was necessary if creation itself was to be realized. It was Gaia herself who devised the solution. She created a huge sickle and challenged her children to use it on their father. Only Kronos was bold enough to take up the task and to listen to his mother's plan. When night came and Sky as usual covered Earth, Kronos was waiting with the sickle, and he sliced off his father's genitals and hurled them into the sea. Gaia absorbed the drops of blood that came from the wound and through them gave birth to the Furies (Erinyes) and the Giants. Out of the genitals flowing in the oceans came a foam-like fluid, out of which sprang a beautiful girl, the Goddess of Love, Aphrodite.

Meanwhile Destruction, Death, Blame, Grief, Retribution, Old Age, and other horrors were born of Night.

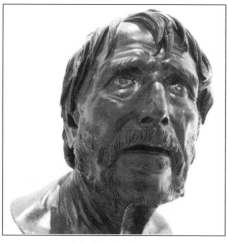
A bronze bust portays the Greek poet Hesiod.

After mating with the Sea, Gaia gave birth to many strange beings, including Phorcys and Keto. They, in turn, produced the monstrous Gorgons. Among these sisters was Medusa, whose hair was to become a nest of snakes.

Gaia's daughter Rhea mated with Kronos and gave birth to several famous offspring, including Hestia, Demeter, Hera, Hades, Poseidon, and Zeus, who would later be known, with some of Zeus's children, as the Olympians, because they would live on Mount Olympus. But Kronos had inherited his father Uranos's evil ways, and fearing that, as prophesied by Gaia and Uranos, one of his own children might displace him as king, he swallowed each one as it was born. And, as did her mother, Rhea undermined her husband's wicked policy. Helped by Gaia and Uranos, she fled to Crete, where she gave birth to Zeus and hid him in a cave deep in her mother, Earth. She swaddled a huge stone and presented the false baby to Kronos, who immediately swallowed it. When Kronos vomited the stone, Zeus came to free his brothers and sisters. He also freed the brothers of Kronos, whom Uranos had imprisoned in Mother Earth. These uncles gave Zeus the gift of the thunderbolt, which solidified his ultimate power over men and gods.

What is the significance of the struggle between the ancient father gods and their wives and children?

Sigmund Freud would see in the father-son struggle—the son being aided by his mother—a metaphor for what he saw as the Oedipus complex, in which any son is naturally jealous of the father, secretly wishing to kill him and becoming the mother's primary love. Whether or not we accept the Freudian view, we can say that the Uranos-Gaia-Kronos struggle has many mythological antecedents—in Egypt and Sumer, for instance, but also in the Anatolian Hittite culture—in which Earth and Sky, the World Parents, must be separated so that creation may take place between them. There is also the fact that the passage from Uranos to Kronos to Zeus represented for the Greeks a passage from a primitive and brutal reality to the somewhat more ordered universe of Zeus and his fellow Olympians, a gradual process of creation. The role of Gaia and Rhea, both personifications of Earth, in working with favored sons against the arbitrary and selfish tyranny of the original father gods, suggests a natural alliance between the world we live in and the possibility of life itself. Without Mother Earth's power and intelligence, creation itself would be swallowed.

The conflict between the primitive reality represented by the early deities and the more ordered reality represented by the Olympians is finally resolved in a great war in heaven.

What was Hesiod's story of the war in heaven?

For a long time, Hesiod tells us, there had been warfare between the Olympians—the children of Kronos and Rhea—and the earlier generations of gods and monsters known as the Titans. The Titans stood on Mount Othrys while the Olympians stood against them on Mount Olympus. Bad blood had long existed between the two sides. Zeus had been angered by the Titan Prometheus, who had stolen fire and given it to humans, and by the powerful and violent Atlas. Zeus had condemned Atlas to hold up the world and had tied Prometheus to a rock where his liver would be eaten by an eagle. Gaia sided with the Olympians, predicting their ultimate victory. The Olympians also recruited the giants known as Hundred-Arms and fed them the food and drink of the gods—nectar and ambrosia—so that they would be especially strong. Now the final stages of the war began. The Hundred-Arms and the Olympians attacked, led by Zeus with his powerful thunderbolts. Against this alliance the Titans had no chance. Soundly defeated and exiled from heaven and earth, their new and eternal home was Tartarus, a gloomy underworld, where they were confined in chains.

Gaia, Mother Earth, now advised the Olympians to proclaim Zeus king.

An 1875 painting by Anselm Feuerbach portraying the great goddess Gaia.

According to Hesiod, what did Zeus do with his new power after the war?

Zeus first assigned duties and areas of control to his brothers and sisters. Poseidon was assigned the Sea, for instance, and Hades the Underworld. The next stage of creation involved the production of the second generation of the Olympians and the elements that would provide order to the universe. Zeus mated with Metis (Wisdom), but Hesiod says that Zeus swallowed Metis (as his father would have swallowed him) to prevent the birth of a god who might displace him. Locked within Zeus, she is responsible for his wisdom and his knowledge of good and evil. According to Hesiod's version of the story, Zeus then slept with Themis (Law), who gave birth to the elements of ordered society, such as Justice and Peace, as well as to the Fates. The king's next mate was Eurynome, the daughter of the ancient Oceanus. The three beautiful Graces—Pageantry, Joy, and Festivity—were their daughters. After Zeus made love to his sister Demeter, she gave birth to the beautiful Persephone, who would be taken away by dark Hades as a wife. Still not satisfied, Zeus embraced the beautiful Mnemosyne (Memory) and thus produced the nine Muses, who were responsible for beauty in the arts. Leto was next, and her mating with Zeus produced two of the king's greatest children, Apollo and Artemis. Finally Zeus took up with the woman who was to be his eternal consort, his sister Hera, who gave birth to Ares and several lesser children. On his own Zeus now gave birth from his head to Athene, whose pre-birth mother had been Metis, imprisoned in the king's stomach. A jealous Hera repaid her husband for this arrogant act by producing the rough smith god Hephaistos miraculously without the seed of her husband. Zeus, in his drive to make a family, slept with Maia, the daughter of the Titan Atlas. Their child was the clever Hermes. With the mortal Semele he produced the mysterious Dionysos. With another mortal, Alkmene, he produced the great hero Herakles, and now the world was ready for the rich body of stories about the twelve Olympians (who were really as many as fourteen or even fifteen, depending on various interpretations). They consisted of the first generation (Zeus, Hera, Poseidon, Hades, Demeter, Hestia, and Aphrodite) and the second generation (Athene, Apollo, Artemis, Ares, Hermes, Hephaistos, and Dionysos).

The family of gods and the elements of creation were now fully established by Hesiod, and in the Classical period that followed the Archaic period, what we think of as Greek Mythology would achieve full development.

What myths did Hesiod tell about human life?

In his *Works and Days* Hesiod reminds us that Zeus had little love for human beings, partly because of their association with Prometheus, who had tricked him and stolen fire for them. Zeus decreed that a punishment must be sent to humans. In spite of Prometheus's warning to his brother Epimetheus not to accept gifts from the gods, Epimetheus accepted the first woman, Pandora, who had been modelled out of clay by Hephaistos. In spite of warnings, Pandora opened the famous box containing all the world's evil and pain that Zeus had given her as a wedding present. The evil spread quickly. Only Hope remained in the box.

Hesiod tells how the life of humans has been marked by five ages. In the time of the rule of Kronos among the gods, a Golden Age prevailed on earth, an age of long life and ease. It was followed by a Silver Age, in which there was some suffering, wars, and a neglect of the gods. A warlike Bronze Age came next and was followed by the Heroic Age of noble wars such as the one in Troy. Heroes who died in war went to the Isle of the Blessed, a kind of paradise. Hesiod's own age was the Iron Age, a time of work and pain.

We know now that Hesiod's age would eventually be followed by what we call the Classical Age of Greece, an age that would influence the world in ways that Hesiod and Homer could not have imagined.

CLASSICAL GREEK MYTHOLOGY

What do we mean by Classical Greece as opposed to Mycenaean or Archaic Greece?

Typically, when people speak of Classical Greece, they refer to a period of the cultural dominance of the city-state of Athens, beginning with the end of a tyrant-based political system in 510 B.C.E. and ending with the death of Alexander the Great in 323 B.C.E. In 507 B.C.E. a new system of government was established in Athens called *demokratia* (democracy), in which all male citizens of eighteen years and older could participate in a governing assembly. One of the first concerns of the Athenians under the new system was a series of wars with Persia, which finally ended with a victory for Athens and allied Greek city-states in 479 B.C.E. The Athenians then led and dominated an alliance called the Delian League beginning in 478 B.C.E. In many ways Athens took unfair advantage of its leadership position, using tribute monies for its own aggrandizement, thus arousing the enmity of Sparta and other city-states. In the 450s, Pericles, the elected general and leader of Athens, used these funds to build up and encourage the cultural activities and monuments that we associate with Greek civilization. During his period of influence the Parthenon on the Acropolis was built in honor of the city's patron deity, Athene. Many other temples were constructed. Historians such as Herodotus and Thucydides wrote. The great Socrates spoke out on philosophical and ethical issues. Medicine developed under Hippocrates, the "father of western medicine." Doctors to this day swear allegiance to a version of the "Hippocratic Oath," concerned with the proper moral approach to medicine. Sculptors, led by Phidias (593–130 B.C.E.) literally redecorated Athens with statues of the Olympian gods. The religious dramatic festival in honor of Dionysos—the City Dionysia—founded earlier by the enlightened tyrant Pisistratus (600–527 B.C.E.), flourished with the work of the great playwrights Aeschylus, Sophocles, and Euripides. The fifth century B.C.E. and part of the fourth was the Golden Age of Athens and of Greece. In addition to the creative geniuses noted above, a survey of Classical Greece would include the post-Periclean philosophers Plato (424–347 B.C.E.) and

Aristotle (384–322 B.C.E.), the sculptor Praxiteles (400–330 B.C.E.), and many others who have deeply influenced western culture.

As successful as Periclean Athens was, its arrogant treatment of allied city-states led to not only the eventual breakup of the Delian League but to a long series of wars among the city-states—especially between Sparta and Athens. The so-called Peloponnesian War (431–404 B.C.E.) ended with a victory for Sparta. Nonetheless, Athens reigned supreme and its cultural influence lasted well into the fourth century B.C.E., when Philip II of Macedonia in 345 B.C.E. established nominal control over the city. He was followed by his son Alexander in whose empire Athens was included. Alexander died in Babylon in 323 B.C.E. After years of rebellion and confusion, Athens and Greece as a whole came under Roman rule.

What role did mythology play in the Classical Greek period?

The inhabitants of Athens or any other Greek city-state during the Classical period would have been literally surrounded by images of and writings about Greek mythology, much as citizens of most European and North and South American cities today are constantly made aware of Christian stories, which are frequently quoted from the Bible and depicted in churches and museum paintings. Stories of Greek mythology were, to the Greeks, religious stories explaining the origin of life and the relationship between humanity and the divine.

By the end of the Archaic period, perhaps thanks to Pisistratus, the Homeric epics and Hesiod's works had been written down and collated in essentially their present form so that they became more widely available. By the fifth century B.C.E. the *Iliad* and the *Odyssey* were considered national epics and were taught in schools. The creation story in the *Theogony* of Hesiod had, by the sixth century B.C.E., been accorded as much reverence as the biblical book of Genesis is accorded by Jews, Christians, and Muslims today. From the Archaic period on, vase paintings were dominated by scenes from famous myths, statues of gods by Phidias and, later, Praxiteles and many other artists were present everywhere, as were the great temples to various deities. Herms, small rectangular posts topped with the head of and sometimes the phallus of the god Hermes, were ubiquitous as boundary markers. The temples, such as the Parthenon in Athens, were decorated with elaborate friezes depicting scenes from Greek myths. Some students would have been lucky enough to attend and participate in serious and sometimes skeptical discussions of the gods with the great Socrates or later with Plato and Aristotle. Poetry readers would have encountered stories of the gods in lyrics by Pindar (522–443 B.C.E.) and Bacchylides (c.518–128 B.C.E.), and by Simonides (556–468 B.C.E.). For some time, the poems of the sixth-century poet Sappho of Lesbos (c.630–570 B.C.E.) had been available. More famous now for her poems about the love between women, Sappho had compiled retellings of many of the Homeric stories. People interested in historical understandings of myth could have read Herodotus's comparisons of Greek and Egyptian deities or the somewhat more skeptical comments of Thucydides on Homer. For citizens of Athens, the annual festival of the City Dionysia, featuring elaborate processions centered on

Dionysos and made famous by the plays of such geniuses as Aeschylus, Sophocles, Euripides, and Aristophanes, would have been impossible to ignore. In short, it is as difficult to separate life in Classical Greece from what we think of as Greek mythology as it would be to separate life in Jerusalem from Jewish, Christian, and Islamic stories.

Who compiled or augmented the Greek myths during the Classical period?

As noted above, the Homeric epics, Hesiod's works, and the *Homeric Hymns* were standardized from the sixth century B.C.E. There were poets such as Pindar, who, in the transition between the Archaic and Classical ages, somewhat revised the Homeric and Hesiodic versions of the gods as sometimes selfish, fickle, and arbitrary. In some of his odes, Pindar is much more respectful of the gods, seeing them as concerned with human welfare. The poets who added most significantly to the body of Greek mythology as it has come down to us were the great dramatists. In the third century B.C.E. a major contribution was made by Apollonius of Rhodes in his epic, *Argonautica*, about the hero Jason's quest for the golden fleece. There were several collators of Greek mythology after the Classical age, the most important of whom were Apollodorus of Athens (180–120 B.C.E.), whose *Bibliotheca* (The Library), much of which was actually written by a later author, contains complete versions of many of the myths, and the Roman poet Publius Ovidius Naso, better known as Ovid (43 B.C.E.–c. 17 C.E.), whose *Metamorphoses* remains a popular sourcebook for myths which, though greatly embellished, were originally Greek.

THE GREEK PANTHEON
AND THE OLYMPIANS

What was the makeup of the Classical Greek pantheon?

The Olympian gods were the pantheon of the Classical period. Whereas the first generation of gods described by Hesiod tended to be personifications of aspects of nature—Uranos as Sky, Gaia as Earth—the Olympians were depicted as essentially an elite family with infinite power. Under the clear leadership of the high god Zeus, each family member had a responsibility for a geographical area of the universe or for an element of the psycho-emotional life of humans.

What was Zeus's role?

Zeus was king of the gods. Wielder of the all-powerful thunderbolt, his particular realm was the skies, which he ruled from the summit of Mount Olympus. His sign as king of heaven was the eagle. Zeus was the guarantor of oaths and sanctuaries. Given his infinite power, he could do whatever he wanted to do, though his actions were sometimes undermined by his ever-watchful and often-jealous wife, Hera. Zeus was a famous philanderer. He was particularly fond of mortal women. In an attempt to hide his infidelities from his wife, he often took the form of an animal in his extramarital escapades.

When he kidnapped the beautiful Europa and swam away with her, he was a bull. When he assaulted Leda, the queen of Sparta, as she strolled by a lake, he was a swan. Almost all of Zeus's sexual relations with mortals resulted in famous children. Europa gave birth to Minos of Crete, Leda to Helen of Troy and to Agamemnon's treacherous wife, Clytemnestra. Sometimes Zeus took other forms to satisfy his lust. He broke through the prison walls of the beautiful Danaë as a shower of gold and she conceived the hero Perseus, slayer of the Gorgon Medusa.

What was Hera's role?

Zeus's wife and sister, Hera, was responsible for marriage, fertility, and childbirth. She was best known for her angry reaction to her husband's infidelities, and the targets of her sometimes violent retributions were more often Zeus's victims than Zeus himself. When Zeus had relations with

A 1597 copper engraving of Zeus, king of the gods in the Greek pantheon.

Hera's priestess, Princess Io of Argos, he tried to protect her from Hera's wrath by disguising her as a beautiful white cow. Hera saw through the trick and sent a gadfly to chase the poor cow around the world. Io crossed the sea, which was later named the Ionian Sea after her. She also crossed the straits between Europe and Asia, causing them to be named the Bosphorus (Cow's Crossing).

What was Poseidon's role?

To his powerful brother Poseidon, Zeus assigned the sea. Poseidon was vengeful and violent; he created earthquakes and terrible storms at sea. It was Poseidon who, in a pique, kept poor Odysseus away from home for so long. Poseidon carried the three-pronged long-handled fork, the trident. His other symbols were the bull and the horse. Like his brother, Zeus, Poseidon had a strong sexual appetite. Ovid says that he raped Medusa in a temple of his rival and niece, Athene, causing the goddess to turn Medusa into a monstrous Gorgon. It was believed by many that he fathered the hero Theseus by taking advantage of Princess Aethra of Troezen while her husband was drunk and asleep.

What was Hades's role?

To his dark brother Hades, Zeus gave the Underworld and the riches hidden there. Usually he is not officially counted as an Olympian because he was rarely if ever on Mount

Olympus. He preferred Hades, the place named for him. Hades shared the violent tendencies and appetites of his brothers. In his most famous escapade he burst out of his realm to capture Persephone, the beautiful young daughter of his sister Demeter, while she played among flowers.

What was Demeter's role, and what happened to Persephone?

Persephone's mother, Demeter, "Mother Earth," was responsible for the earth's fertility and was, therefore, like Hades, rarely on Mount Olympus. Distraught over the kidnapping of her daughter, Demeter allowed the earth to dry up in infertility. Zeus was not pleased by this and when Demeter demanded his help he sent Hermes to negotiate with Hades for the release of Persephone. Hades pointed out that Persephone—now his "wife"—had eaten of the fruit of the Underworld, making Hades her true home. She could return to her mother, but only for part of each year. Winter was the time of year when Persephone lived in the Underworld. During this time each year Demeter withdrew her fertility from the earth.

Who was Hestia?

Hestia was a quiet, older sister of Zeus, Hera, Poseidon, Hades, and Demeter. A virgin, she was responsible for the hearth, that is, for domestic life and order. Unlike her siblings, she was nonviolent and passive, perhaps a model for a patriarchal society's ideal woman.

Poseidon (Neptune) is a popular subject for fountains across Europe, such as the Driemond fountain in Frankendaal, the Netherlands.

What was Aphrodite's role, and who was Ares?

An ancient goddess, not born of Kronos and Rhea, but of the castrated genitals of the original sky god Uranos, was the goddess of love, Aphrodite. Sometimes she was referred to as Zeus's daughter, but if this was the case she can best be called an adopted daughter.

Aphrodite was responsible for the strange power of love, represented sometimes by Eros (Desire), her frequent companion and possibly her son. Aphrodite could cloud minds, leading people to unwise decisions. Married to the lame and least attractive god, the smithy Hephaistos, she had many lovers, including the handsome young mortal Adonis. She also caused turmoil among the Olympian family. By Hermes she produced Hermaphroditus, and by another god—it could have been Dionysos—she mothered the ugly, constantly sexually aroused fertility figure, Priapus.

Aphrodite's most famous sexual exploit was with the god Ares, the god of war. Ares was, understandably, warlike and driven. When War and Love came together, their lovemaking was disturbing to the goddess's husband, Hephaistos, so he trapped them in the course of intercourse in a net and held them up to the ridicule of the other Olympians.

Who was Hephaistos?

Hephaistos had been born ugly and lame. Disgusted by him, his mother, Hera, had flung him out of Olympus into the ocean below, where he learned the crafts for which he became known. Hephaestus fell to earth, landing in the sea near the Island of Lemnos. He had the good fortune to be rescued and nursed back to health by a group of sea nymphs and Titan goddesses. They went to great lengths to keep him hidden from his parents, hiding him in their underwater cave. Some writers say that it was the fall from Olympus that made Hephaistos lame.

In any case, he tricked his mother into allowing him to return to Olympus by sending her a throne which, when she sat on it, tied her down with invisible cords. Hephaistos released her only when she acceded to his desire to marry the beautiful Aphrodite.

What was Athene's role?

Perhaps the greatest of the goddesses was Athene, who, born of Zeus's head, was associated with intellect and wisdom. Her sign was the owl—the wisest of birds. Athene helped heroes such as Jason, Herakles, and Perseus. Although a virgin goddess, she had "crushes," as is most evident in her relationship with Odysseus in the *Odyssey*. Athene was chosen as the patron deity of the city-state of Athens over her uncle and constant rival, Poseidon, because she offered the Athenians the olive tree whereas Poseidon gave them only a salty spring. The Parthenon was built in her honor.

What was Apollo's role?

The only serious rival to Zeus in importance was the great god Apollo. Sometimes known as Phoebus (Brilliant Light), Apollo was associated with the sun, with light, with music and medicine, and with reason and self-knowledge. His centers were in Delos, where he

The famous Parthenon in Athens, Greece, was constructed to honor the goddess Athene.

was said to have been born, and Delphi, the navel of the world in the Greek view of things, and a place of prophecy sacred to him. It was near Delphi, at the foot of Mount Parnassos, that Apollo killed Python, the great serpent that guarded the sanctuary, which was sacred to the ancient earth goddess Gaia. By killing the dragon-like Python, Apollo became the dominant figure in Delphi.

Who was Artemis?

Apollo's twin sister was Artemis, goddess of the hunt and childbirth. She was fiercely protective of her sacred virginity. The story is told of how the young hunter Actaeon happened upon the goddess in the woods, where she was bathing in a pond. Artemis was so furious at having been seen naked that she turned the boy into a stag and set his own hounds on him to tear him apart.

Who was Hermes?

Hermes was a popular god among the Greeks. He was the messenger of the gods and the escort of souls to the Underworld. Hermes carried a magic wand, the *caduceus,* and wore sandals with wings. He was responsible for travelers and for business transactions. He was also a trickster who was fond of lies and deceptions. On the day of his birth he stole the cattle of Apollo.

Who was Dionysos?

The latest member of the Olympian hierarch was Dionysos (Dionysus), an ancient god known to the Minoans and Mycenaeans, but unlike all the others. His mother, Semele, was said by most writers to have been a human, which is perhaps why Dionysos was the only one of the gods to die. According to one story, he was cooked and eaten by the Titans. As did other dying gods he returned to life, however, and became the center of an earth-based rather than Olympus-based cult associated with wine, sexuality, and ecstasy. It was said that Zeus had recovered the unborn Dionysos from the dead Semele and sewed him into his thigh, from which he was born again.

How did the gods reflect actual human life?

The myths of a culture tend to reflect the values, mores, traditions, and concerns of that culture. Ancient Greek culture from the Mycenaean Age to the Classical period of Athenian hegemony was one ruled by aristocratic male warriors and tyrants. Even in fifth-century Athens, the "cradle of democracy," the culture remained strongly patriarchal. Women and slaves were not allowed to participate in legislative assemblies or many public rites. The Olympian Gods reflect the pre-Athenian aristocratic system and the patriarchal outlook of Greek culture in general. Zeus is an aristocratic and often arbitrary husband, father, and king. He does whatever he wishes to do. He can be vindictive and cruel and he is a notorious philanderer, using his position of power to seduce mortal women and even boys, such as the Trojan Ganymede, whom he loved and whom he abducted and made the cupbearer of the gods. Naturally, we can assume that the wives of such men, although ultimately unable to prevent the escapades of their husbands, could complain mightily about them and even attempt to thwart their activities. Hera is the epitome of the unhappy "nagging" wife, an example of the use of comic stereotypes in myth. She also represents the power of sex to influence even such a "player" as Zeus. Homer tells us that during the Trojan War she seduced her husband to keep him occupied so that he could not influence the battle in a way that went against her wishes. There are powerful women in the Olympian family—Athene and Artemis, for instance—but they tend to be unusually masculinized women—virgins dedicated to the hunt and even to war. Other goddesses fulfill more typical roles. Aphrodite represents the dangerous mind-changing power of female sexuality. Hestia represents the values of the passive hearth and home protector. In all families, of course, including those of ancient Greece, there would have been infighting. We see this on Mount Olympus in the interactions between the children of Zeus's generation—between Apollo and Hermes over the cattle theft incident, between Ares and Aphrodite and Hephaistos concerning the adulterous affair exposed in Hephaistos's net.

THE GREEK GODS AND HUMAN LIFE

Did the Greeks see these myths as religion or as entertainment?

For some Greeks, many of the myths of the Olympians had religious significance: the myths contained in the tragic dramas clearly did. But there is the obvious element of soap opera in many myths. Myths served the Greeks as moral instruction in some cases and primarily as entertainment in others. Infidelity, husbands tricked by wives, inap-

The story of Zeus and the young Ganymede reflects the Greek culture in which homosexuality was accepted, especially with regard to a kind of mentor/student relationship (circa 485 B.C.E. pottery on display at the Metropolitan Museum of Art in New York City).

propriate affairs of children, fights between brothers and sisters, political intrigue, and struggles for power, remain to this day staples in the creation of family drama.

The story of Zeus, known for his love of mortal women, abducting Ganymede seems odd. What is the significance of the abduction?

In Greek culture, homosexuality was, at the least, tolerated, and even extolled by some as a higher form of love than that between a man and a woman, especially if the relationship in question was between a young man and a much younger boy and was driven not only by sexual desire but by the older partner's responsibility to teach the boy proper behavior in areas other than sexuality. Mythology simply reflects this point of view. Zeus desired Ganymede just as he had desired Europa or Io or Leda, so he seduced him and then gave him a responsible position on Mount Olympus.

Are there other stories of homosexuality among the gods?

Apollo, a usually restrained god of order and reason, loved a boy named Hyacinth. He was in the process of teaching the boy "manly" athletic arts when the boy was accidentally killed by a discus made to go astray by Zephyrus, the jealous god of the West Wind, who also loved Hyacinth. And there are other stories of "acceptable" homosexual love involving heroes such as Herakles, who loved a youth named Hylas, and Achilles, whose love for Patroclus is seen by some to be homosexual in nature. These stories suggest a general acceptance of the practice of same-sex love within certain parameters.

ORIGINS OF THE GREEK GODS

What are the origins of the Olympian deities?

Most of the Olympians are listed in the Linear B tablets of Crete and Mycenae, indicating existence at least from the eighth century B.C.E. Several of the Olympians likely have origins in cultures that preceded Greek or Minoan culture. The Hurrian-Hittite civilizations of Anatolia dating from as early as the third millennium B.C.E. told a war-in-heaven story that in many ways parallels the war-in-heaven story told by Hesiod. In the Hurrian myth the head god Alulu was defeated by Anu (Sky) and was exiled to the Underworld. Alulu's son Kumarbi then fought Anu and cut off his genitals. Kumarbi himself had a son, Tessup, who defeated his father and became the dominant deity, a storm god of the thunderbolt, like Zeus. Was this story passed down over the centuries and eventually used by Hesiod in the tale of the Uranos (Sky), Kronos, and Zeus successions, or are both stories simply examples of immortals acting out the eternal struggle among animals—including humans, if we believe Freud—between fathers and sons for dominance?

Several deities, such as, for example, Aphrodite, Artemis, Demeter, and Dionysos, have ambiguous origins.

What are Aphrodite's origins?

Most scholars agree that Aphrodite, whose major cult center was in the eastern Mediterranean island of Cyprus, and who was generally not spoken of in myths as an offspring of the Olympian family, was an import to Greece from the East. These scholars have seen Aphrodite as a Greek version of the Middle Eastern fertility goddess named Inanna in Sumer, Ishtar in Babylon, and Astarte in Phoenicia.

What are Artemis's origins?

Artemis, too, originated in the East, probably in Anatolia where the great Temple of Artemis at Ephesus (Selcuk, Turkey), finished in 550 B.C.E., was considered one of the Seven Wonders of the World. The Anatolian Artemis existed long before the completion of that temple and was famously depicted as a fertility goddess with her chest and stomach covered by what have traditionally been identified as breasts but which many modern scholars have decided are bull testicles or gourds.

Whether breasts, testicles, or gourds, the Artemis at Ephesus had been associated mythologically with other Earth mothers, including the Cybele, the great mother of the

Phrygians, also worshiped in Anatolia. When the Greeks included her among their Olympian family, they stripped her of her fertility aspect and made her a virgin huntress and the twin sister of Apollo.

What are Demeter's origins?

Like Dionysos, Demeter was a deity who spent most of her time on earth rather than on Olympus. She is essentially a Greek version of a much more ancient tradition of Earth Mothers, including Cybele in Anatolia and Hathor in Egypt. Demeter and Dionysos were "different" and their mysteries attracted enough people to make followers of the more traditional Olympians wary of them. This was especially true of Dionysos, who was seen as a "foreign" god, which he probably was.

THE GREEK MYSTERY CULTS AND HERO SAGAS

What are the origins of Dionysos?

Dionysos was a late addition to the Olympians and is sometimes not included among the twelve. He was worshipped as early as Minoan times, however, and is listed among the gods in the Linear B tablets. As a dying god he has mythological companions and perhaps ancestors in the Egyptians' Osiris, the Sumerians' Tammuz and Inanna, and in a

Phoenician version of Adonis. Dionysian-type "mystery" ceremonies involving intoxicants and ecstatic freedom of action existed in Greece and probably had sources in similar ceremonies tied to the dying gods Attis in Phrygia and Osiris in Egypt. Like the Eleusinian mysteries associated with the goddess Demeter, the Dionysian mysteries involved a kind of mysticism—even spiritualism—unlike anything else connected with the Olympian religion.

What were the Dionysian mysteries?

The Dionysian mysteries were a ritualized worship of Dionysos and the aspect of life he represented—the freedom from conventional mores and taboos to allow a natural ecstatic expression of the inner self in a ceremonial process. That process involved wine or some other intoxicant, wild

A Roman bust of the god Dionysos, one of the dying gods whose life represented the seasonal cycles of agriculture.

music, and equally wild dancing to overcome ordinary inhibitions. Some say it culminated in orgies. Processions involved in the mysteries included the carrying of a representation of the god's phallus. The source of the mysteries was perhaps the mystery religion of Osiris in Egypt. Both Dionysos and Osiris were dying gods whose life-death-rebirth processes reflected seasonal or agricultural patterns and extended into the sometimes spiritual or even mystical realm of personal or communal renewal. The mysteries were well outside the traditions of the patriarchal Olympian religion and even involved women and slaves, but parts of the mysteries were incorporated more formally into the City Dionysia, the festival that included the production of the plays of Aeschylus, Sophocles, and Euripides in the fifth century B.C.E.

What were the "Eleusinian mysteries"?

Like the Dionysian mysteries, the very popular mysteries of Eleusis were in some sense related to the processes of nature—the planting and harvesting of grain—and by extension, the possibility of life after death. It is thought that the mysteries originated in Minoan Crete or in the stories of Isis and Osiris and Horus in Egypt. Whatever the origins, the mystery cult seems to have existed at least as early as the Early Mycenaean Age. The mystery sanctuary was built in Eleusis, a small city near Athens, in about 1500 B.C.E. Like the Dionysian rites, the secret mysteries, which remain somewhat unknown, apparently involved intoxicants, processions, music, and dancing, and perhaps even the sacrifice of an animal.

The myth behind the mysteries is that of Demeter, particularly the loss of her daughter Persephone (Kore), her search for her daughter, and her daughter's return.

After Persephone was taken by Hades, Demeter separated herself from her Olympian relatives and searched the world for her. At Eleusis she disguised herself as an old woman and became nurse to the infant prince, Demophon. Each night Demeter rubbed the boy with ambrosia, the food of the gods, and set him in a fire to burn away his mortality—all of this to give him eternal life. But when the horrified queen saw her son in the fire, she pulled him out of the flames. Now Demeter revealed who she was and demanded that a temple be built for her in Eleusis where she would teach the people her rites leading to life after death.

Why are the Eleusinian and Dionysian mysteries called "mysteries"?

As is the case with mystery religions or mystery cults in general, they are called "mysteries" because their ritual practices are/were cloaked in secrecy, known only to initiates. To this day the details of Eleusinian and Dionysian ceremonies remain to some extent mysterious.

Who were the most popular of the Greek mythic heroes of the Classical period, and what characteristics define them as true heroes?

Besides the heroes of the Homeric epics, who remained popular in the Classical period, three heroes stand out. These are Herakles, Theseus, and Perseus. These heroes all conform to the characteristics of the archetypal hero outlined by Joseph Campbell when he describes the heroic monomyth. They are all products of miraculous conceptions, "sons of god" in that they were all fathered by gods. Like heroes of most cultures, each was threatened in childhood by people of the status quo who wanted them eliminated. Each entered into a difficult quest involving the killing of monsters, and each descended to the Underworld and returned. In addition to Herakles, Theseus, and Perseus, a more flawed but nevertheless important hero was Jason, the hero of the *Argonautica,* the epic by Apollonius of Rhodes about the search for the Golden Fleece.

HERAKLES AND THE TWELVE LABORS

What is the myth of Herakles?

Herakles's (Roman name, Hercules) conception story makes use of a theme used later by the compilers of the King Arthur myth—conception via lover disguised as husband. As

the story goes, Zeus desired Alkmene, the daughter of the King of Mycenae, who was living in Thebes with her husband Amphitryon. In order to achieve his goal, Zeus disguised himself as Amphitryon while the latter was away on a mission. Zeus and Alkmene spent a night of passionate lovemaking, which the couple enjoyed so much that Zeus extended the one night to the equivalent in length of three. When Amphitryon returned, he, too, slept with Alkmene. In time Alkmene gave birth to twins. Herakles was the son of Zeus, Iphikles the son of Amphitryon. As usual, Zeus's "disguise" was not sufficient to fool his jealous wife Hera, who now dedicated herself to revenge by making life difficult for Herakles. She began by sending serpents to kill him in his cradle when he was eight months old. Herakles demonstrated his heroic qualities for the first time by strangling the serpents—one in each hand. As Herakles grew up he became stronger and stronger and accomplished many heroic deeds and sexual conquests. But Hera's hatred of Zeus's son remained strong. Herakles had married Megara, a princess of

Herakles (sometimes better known as by his Roman name, Hercules) is depicted here in a guilded bronze Roman statue from the second century B.C.E.

Thebes, who gave birth to his three children. Hera caused the hero to go insane and to kill his children and the children of his brother Iphikles. Some say he also killed Megara. Emerging from his madness, Herakles, in despair, sought advice from Apollo's priestess at Delphi, who advised him to move to Tiryns to serve King Eurytheus for twelve years.

It is the "twelve labors" assigned by Eurytheus that made Herakles the greatest of the Greek heroes.

What were the twelve labors of Herakles?

- The first labor was that of killing the Nemean Lion, a monster with an impenetrable hide that was terrorizing the land. Herakles beat the lion to death with his club and thereafter wore the beast's skin to make himself invulnerable.

- The second labor was the killing of the Lernean Hydra, a dragon-like nine-headed monster that grew new heads as the original ones were cut off. As Herakles cut off its heads, his nephew cauterized the wounds to prevent new heads from emerging.

- For his third labor Herakles was sent to capture the Ceryneian Hind, the beast known for its golden horns and bronze hooves. This beast was sacred to Artemis, so Herakles was careful to capture but not kill it. He did wound it slightly, but avoided the wrath of the goddess by blaming the wound on Eurytheus.

- The fourth labor involved the capture of the violent Erymanthian Boar, which the hero netted and brought back to Eurytheus, who was so frightened of it that he hid in a jar.

- For his fifth labor Herakles was sent to clean the Augean Stables, belonging to Augeas, the son of Helios, the Sun. The stables, home to the cattle belonging to Augeas, had never been cleaned. Herakles accomplished the task by diverting rivers to flow through the stable.

- The sixth labor led the hero to the horrible people-eating Stymphalian Birds with their iron claws. Herakles flushed them out of their hiding place in trees with bronze castanets supplied by the helper of heroes, Athene, and shot them one by one with bow and arrow.

The first six labors had taken place in the Peloponnese area of mainland Greece. The final six took Herakles far afield.

- Labor seven took Herakles to Crete, where he was to capture the famous white Cretan Bull of Minos that the king had refused to sacrifice to Poseidon and which had sired the Minotaur on the besotted Queen Pasiphae. Herakles brought the bull to Eurystheus and eventually, after it was released, it found its way to Marathon, where the hero Theseus found it and sacrificed it.

- For labor eight Herakles was sent to Thrace to capture the Mares of Diomedes, which ate the flesh of humans. Herakles killed their owner, King Diomedes, and fed his body to them. He then brought the herd back to Tiryns.

- The ninth labor of Herakles took the hero to Anatolia, where he was told he must find and bring back the Girdle of Hippolyte, Queen of the Amazons. Herakles took the girdle, which had magical powers, after killing the queen.

- Labor ten is that of the Cattle of Geryon. Geryon was a monster with three bodies, living in Hesperides, near Spain. There, helped by the giant Eurytion and a two-headed hound Orthus, he kept a famous herd of red cattle. Herakles was to capture the cattle. He did so by killing Geryon and his helpers and finding his way with the cattle back to Tiryns.

- For the eleventh labor Herakles was once again sent west, this time in search of the Apples of the Hesperides, the three daughters of Night. These golden apples grew on a tree guarded by the serpent Ladon. It was Gaia herself who had given the apples as a wedding present to Hera when she married Zeus. Gaia placed them in the Garden of the Hesperides. There are various versions of how Herakles accomplished this task. The most popular one tells how Herakles, assisted by Athene, held up the world for Atlas while the Titan gathered the apples. Some writers say that on his way to or from the Hesperides he went to the Caucasus Mountains, where he freed Prometheus from the eternal torture Zeus had arranged for him.

- The twelfth labor of Herakles is essentially a descent into the Underworld and a confrontation with death itself—the ultimate heroic adventure. The hero was ordered to capture Cerberus, the three-headed hound of Hades. Herakles required the help of Hermes and Athene to succeed in this, his most difficult labor. After descending to the Underworld through a cave in Laconia, Herakles was informed by Hades that he could take the dog if he could conquer it without weapons. Herakles wrestled with Cerberus and was able to take the hound to Eurytheus. While in the Underworld he released Theseus, who was imprisoned there.

Herakles would eventually die, having been poisoned by a robe dipped in the blood of the centaur Nessus. But even death could not contain this hero. As his body burned in a huge funeral pyre, he ascended to heaven, where he was reconciled with Hera and given her daughter Hebe in marriage.

THESEUS

What is the myth of Theseus?

As is the case with so many heroes, the life of Theseus begins with at least the possibility of a miraculous conception. Theseus's mother was Aethra, a princess in Troezen. When King Aegeus of Athens visited Troezen, the young woman's father made his visitor drunk and gave him Aethra as a bedmate. After spending time with the drunken Aegeus, Aethra waded out to a little island where Poseidon, too, had intercourse with her. Aethra then returned to bed with Aegeus. Poseidon decided that any child born to Aethra in the next few months should be considered to be Aegeus's even if it was his. When Aegeus awoke and found himself with

Aethra, he instructed her not to tell the child who its father was, but if it was a boy, to send him to Athens only after he succeeded in lifting a rock under which Aegeus had left a sword and a pair of sandals. In time a fine boy, Theseus, was born to Aethra and after several years the boy succeeded in removing his legal father's tokens from under the rock. Beginning his search for a father—a common motif in the heroic monomyth—Theseus left for Athens and on the way performed many feats reminiscent of the labors of Herakles. At Epidaurus he killed a famous brigand. Near Corinth he killed a notorious robber. Farther along his route he killed a monster sow and another brigand. At Eleusis he met the terrifying Cercyon, who forced any visitors to wrestle with him to the death. Theseus took up the challenge and defeated the bully. Procrustes, another bully outside of Athens, forced visitors to lie on a bed; if they were too long for the bed he would mutilate them in such a way as to make them fit it. Theseus killed Procrustes and finally reached Athens and the court of Aegeus. There he had to contend with Aegeus's wife, the enchantress Medea, who desperately wanted Medus, her son by Aegeus, to succeed to the throne. As Aegeus had not yet recognized their visitor as his son, but only as a now famous hero who might desire his throne, he allowed Medea to prepare a poison cup for their guest. The poison plot would have worked had Theseus not used his father's sword retrieved from under the rock to cut his meat. Aegeus recognized his sword, knocked the poisoned drink out of his son's hand and embraced Theseus as his heir. Medea and her son were banished.

We have already seen how Theseus volunteered to go to Crete as a tribute hostage and how he killed the Minotaur there before escaping with Minos's daughters, Ariadne and Phaedra. In a poem by the fifth-century B.C.E. poet Bacchylides, the story is told of how Minos challenged Theseus to prove that he was, as he had claimed, the son of Poseidon. Minos threw a ring into Poseidon's sea and said only a son of Poseidon could possibly find it. Theseus dove into the sea and returned with gifts from Poseidon's undersea court.

After the killing of the Minotaur, Theseus and his companions made their way to the island of Naxos. There Theseus deserted Ariadne, who had helped him defeat the Minotaur, but Dionysos took pity on the maiden and married her himself.

What happened to Theseus after the killing of the Minotaur?

Theseus had promised Aegeus to arrive with a white sail if he had been successful in his mission to save the Athenian youths in Crete. But Theseus forgot his promise and sailed by Cape Sounion with his usual black sails. Aegeus, anxiously watching, threw himself off the cliff in despair. The sea into which he leapt is called the Aegean Sea, in his honor, to this day. Theseus now became King of Athens.

Theseus was known as the greatest of Athenian kings. He fought against the Amazons and married the Amazon queen's sister Antiope and with whom he had a son named Hippolytus. A great tragedy would occur later in Theseus's life when his second wife, Phaedra, Ariadne's sister, would attempt to seduce her stepson Hippolytus, and when Hippolytus refused to be corrupted, would falsely accuse him of trying to seduce *her*, thus causing Theseus to banish his own son and bring about his death.

Theseus joined his friend Pirithoüs in a fight against the half-man half-horse beings, the centaurs. He also joined him in an attempt to kidnap Persephone from the Underworld. This adventure failed and Theseus was trapped in Hades until Herakles managed to free him. Thus, like many heroes, Theseus experienced the process of death and the return to life.

PERSEUS AND MEDUSA

What is the myth of Perseus?

Perseus is the primary Greek example of the hero as monster slayer. He is also clearly marked as a hero by the fact that he was a son of Zeus. The myth begins in the Peloponnesus city of Argos, an ancient city founded by Danaus, who came to Greece from Egypt. The inhabitants of Argos were, therefore, called Danaans. Argos was ruled by Acrisius, who, even in his mother's womb, fought with his twin brother Proetus. The fights continued into adulthood when Proetus attempted to take not only his brother's kingdom, but also his daughter Danaë. War broke out between the twins, and Acrisius won. Proetus had to be content with ruling nearby Tiryns. When an oracle told Acrisius that Danaë would give birth to a son who would someday kill him, the king fell victim to the delusion that always affects those warned by oracles; he tried to outsmart fate. To prevent his daughter from having a son, he locked her away in a dungeon. This, of course, was not enough to prevent the always lecherous Zeus from penetrating the dungeon walls and entering Danaë herself in a shower of gold. The result of this miraculous act was the conception of Perseus, marking him from the beginning as a true hero. Acrisius refused to believe that his grandson had been conceived through Zeus and, in any case, he was not about to keep his predicted murderer in his court. Still,

he feared the wrath of the gods if he killed his own daughter and her son, so he locked the mother and child in a chest, which he released into the sea. The chest washed up on the island of Seriphos, where the fisherman Dictys retrieved it and gave it to his brother King Polydektes, to raise Perseus.

Later, when Polydektes attempted to marry Danaë, he and Perseus became enemies.

When Polydektes pretended to be willing to marry another woman and demanded wedding presents, Perseus promised to bring him the monstrous Medusa's head.

An 1895 painting by Frederic Leighton of Perseus on Pegasus on their way to rescue Andromeda.

What is the myth of Perseus and Medusa?

Medusa was a descendant of the ancient family of gods discussed by Hesiod in the *Theogony*. Gaia, the original Earth Mother, was her grandmother. Her parents were Phorkys, the "Old Man of the Sea;" and Keto, a sea monster. Medusa was not their only offspring, but she was the only mortal member of a set of triplets, the Gorgons. Other siblings included another set of triplets, the Graiae, and several monsters, including Thoosa, the mother of Polyphemos, the Cyclops blinded by Odysseus. The Graiae—the Grey Ones—were born with grey hair; they were personifications of the foamy waves, of the rough sea. The Gorgons (*gorgos* = frightening), were terrifying beings from whose belts hung lunging snakes. Of the Gorgon sisters, Medusa was the most famous and most feared. Homer said her head was "a thing of fear and horror." Anyone who looked at her would be turned to stone.

In many ways Medusa was a victim of circumstance. Originally she had been a beautiful priestess of Athene, but she was raped by Poseidon and blamed for the act, as rape victims so often are, making Athene her eternal enemy. Athene turned the beautiful girl into a monster, a figure of horror with snakes for hair. Since Athene was Perseus's half-sister (Zeus was their father) and hated Medusa for her own reasons, she decided to help Perseus on his quest. Athene warned Perseus never to look directly at Medusa lest he be turned to stone. She gave him a polished shield which he could use to see Medusa's reflection without looking at her directly.

Hermes helped too; he gave his half-brother Perseus (Perseus and Hermes were both fathered by Zeus) a sickle with which he was to decapitate Medusa. Furthermore, his divine siblings told Perseus he would need a container called a *kibisis* in which to place the lethal head of Medusa; a helmet belonging to their uncle, Hades, to make him invisible; and winged sandals to make it possible for him to escape the Gorgons after his killing of Medusa. The Stygian nymphs were the guardians of this equipment, but only the mysterious Graiae sisters knew where the nymphs lived. The Graiae lived at the limits of the western world on the edge of night. They shared one eye and one tooth between them, passing the eye and the tooth from one to the other as needed. Perseus found his way to the Graiae home and snatched the eye and the tooth during one such transfer. The Graiae were understandably distraught. Perseus promised to return the tooth and eye if the Graiae would direct him to the nymphs. The sisters told him to go to the land of Hyperborea at the edge of the North Wind. There the nymphs gladly gave the hero the objects he needed and he descended to the end of the ocean, in effect the Underworld, where the terrible Gorgons made their home.

Equipped with the winged sandals, the *kibisis,* and the helmet of Hades, Perseus approached the sisters and found them sleeping. Apollodorus tells us that their heads were "twined about with the scales of dragons," and that they had "great tusks like swine's," but also "golden wings." The bodies of men turned to stone by the sight of Medusa surrounded the sisters. This was truly a Hell. Perseus approached Medusa, being careful not to look directly at her, using Athene's shield as a mirror. Then, his hand guided by Athene herself, he used Hermes' sickle to remove the monstrous head with one swipe. The winged horse Pegasus and the warrior Chrysaor, children of Medusa's liaison with Poseidon, sprang from the Gorgon's head. Pegasus would play a major role in the hero Bellerophon's defeat of another monster, the Chimera. Chrysaor would father the three-headed monster known as Geryon, who played a role in the Herakles myth.

What happened to Perseus after he killed Medusa?

Perseus stuffed the head of Medusa into the *kibisis* and fled her now-awakened and pursuing sisters, using the magic sandals and the helmet of Hades to provide him with the necessary speed and invisibility.

The flying hero was passing over the land of King Cepheus and Queen Cassiopeia when he noticed a young woman tied to a cliff. He flew down to the maiden and immediately fell in love. The girl was Andromeda, the daughter of Cepheus and Cassiopeia. When Cassiopeia had claimed to be more beautiful than the sea nymphs known as the Nereids, she was punished for her arrogance by being required to choose between a devastating flood and the sacrifice of her daughter. She chose the latter, and the girl was left chained to the cliff for a sea monster to feed on. Perseus, however, killed the monster and freed Andromeda in return for her hand in marriage. When courtiers of Cepheus tried to undermine the agreement, Perseus held up Medusa's head for them to see, and they were all turned to stone.

Now with Andromeda, Perseus traveled to Seriphos, where the hero went to the palace of the king and announced that he had brought the promised gift. When the king and his courtiers insulted him, he again held up Medusa's head, turning them all to stone. The circle of stones is still in Seriphos. Perseus now returned the Medusa head to Athene, who placed it on her shield, and he left with his wife and mother for Argos. There the original prophecy of the oracle was fulfilled when during some games, the wind caused Perseus's discus to strike and kill his grandfather, Acrisius. The oracles of the gods do not lie.

JASON AND THE GOLDEN FLEECE

Who was Jason?

Jason was the son of Aeson, the rightful heir to the kingdom of Iolcus, whose brother Pelias had usurped his position. To protect the young Jason, his mother sent him to the hills where he was "home-schooled" by the centaur Chiron. So it was that Jason, like so many heroes, was threatened in childhood by a representative of the status quo. When, after twenty years of exile, Jason returned to claim his rights as heir to Aeson, Pelias agreed to give up the throne if Jason would bring him the famous Golden Fleece.

What is the myth of Jason and the Golden Fleece?

A man named Phrixus had flown on a magical golden ram—a gift from Hermes—to Colchis, the kingdom of Aeëtes at the eastern end of the Black Sea. There he had sacrificed the ram to Zeus and presented its fleece to King Aeëtes. The king had hung it on the branch of an oak tree in a place that was sacred to Ares and had assigned a never-sleeping dragon the job of guarding it.

Jason took up the challenge of obtaining the Fleece. This would be the quest which would establish his position as a true hero in the mode of Perseus, Herakles, and Theseus. First he built a sturdy ship, the *Argo,* and gathered a crew of "Argonauts"that included such powerful figures as Herakles, the greatest of Greek heroes, and Orpheus, the famous musician. Other heroes included in the crew were Peleus, father of Achilles, and Castor and Polydeuces (Pollux)—the twins known as the Dioscuri, literally meaning "sons of god," because they were products with Helen and Clytemnestra of the union between Leda and Zeus (as a swan). The adventures surrounding the quest are related in the *Argonautica* of Apollonius of Rhodes.

What is the plot of the *Argonautica* epic?

The adventures of the Argonauts are reminiscent of those of Odysseus. On their way to Colchis they were received by the husbandless women of the island of Lemnos. There Jason had relations with the queen, Hypsipyle. In Chios they stopped to allow Herakles time to repair a damaged oar. While there, Herakles's beloved, Hylas—a beautiful boy—was seduced by nymphs, and he went away with them. Herakles remained on the island to search for Hylas but never found him.

The Argonauts sailed on into the Black Sea. Their first stop there was at the land of the Bebryces, whose people forced all visitors to box with their king, Amycus, a son of Poseidon. Polydeuces boxed with the king and killed him.

In Salmydessus they met a blind prophet, Phineus, who warned them of perils that awaited them on their journey, especially The Clashing Rocks (the Symplegades), which destroyed ships. With Athene's help, the voyagers outsmarted the rocks. After several other stops, including one during which they were threatened by the Stymphalian birds, which Herakles would later kill, they arrived at Colchis.

At Colchis Jason requested the Golden Fleece. Aeëtes said Jason could have it only if he could accomplish an essentially impossible proof of his worthiness. He was to yoke two fire-breathing bulls that Hep-

Pottery art circa 300 B.C.E. showing the hero Jason presenting the Golden Fleece to Pelias.

haistos had given to Aeëtes. Then he was to use the bulls to plow a field, which he was then to seed with a dragon's teeth. The seeds would sprout as an army of warriors, which Jason would have to fight and kill.

Meanwhile Hera, always a supporter of Jason, and Aphrodite caused the king's daughter, Medea, to fall hopelessly in love with Jason. She was so much in love that she was willing to work against her father to help the visiting hero, rather as Ariadne helped Theseus in Crete. Possessed of magical powers, Medea gave Jason a salve that would protect him from the bulls' flames. When the field was plowed and seeded, Jason threw a stone among the men who sprang up from the earth, and in their confusion the men fought and killed each other. Jason had thus completed the assigned tasks, but Aeëtes still refused to give up the Fleece. Medea, however, used her powers as a sorceress to bewitch the dragon guarding the Fleece. Jason took the Fleece and, accompanied by Medea, escaped Colchis on the *Argo*.

On the way home there would be many more adventures, including a visit to Medea's aunt, the famous Circe, who had been a part of Odysseus's adventures. Medea supported Jason with her magic, often committing deeds such as the murder and dismemberment of her brother, which would come back to haunt her as the Jason-Medea saga continued.

THE MEANING
OF THE GREEK HERO MYTHS

What was the appeal of these hero myths to the ancient Greeks?

For the Greeks of the Classical period, the heroes of the Trojan War—Achilles, Agamemnon, Odysseus, and the others—were essentially historical figures who could represent the "glories" of Greek history and could stand as examples of physical and mental prowess. The fact that these epic heroes had failings—jealousies, exaggerated pride, emotional lapses—made them all the more appealing. At some level these heroes were people like us, with whom we could identify.

Other heroes and the stories surrounding them were more likely seen as metaphorical rather than historical. The events in the *Odyssey,* such as those concerning the Sirens and the Cyclops and the visit with the dead, would probably have been essentially what fairytales and other folktales are for us. They could reflect human curiosity, be used as cautionary tales, and as examples of moral or immoral behavior. Penelope represented fidelity, Odysseus cleverness but also dangerous impulsiveness.

Heroes such as Herakles, Theseus, Perseus, and Jason would almost certainly have been seen by fifth-century B.C.E. Athenians as folklore figures who, nevertheless, like Odysseus, represented certain values and flaws. Theseus was somewhat of an exception as he would probably have been considered a real king of Athens in the distant past. For

89

the most part, however, these hero myths were told for entertainment purposes and for their value as lesson stories.

Is there a deeper meaning to the hero myths?

There is a level—in our post-Freudian age best called "psychological"—at which hero stories would have spoken to the Greeks much as they still speak to us. Many of the great Greek heroes—Achilles, Perseus, Herakles, and Theseus, for example—were miraculously conceived and therefore special. Usually one parent was a deity, but the other was a human being. A miraculous conception would seem to suggest in the Greek hero myths as it does in the hero myths of other cultures—the Jesus story for Christians, the Zoroaster story for Zoroastrians—that although we are human with human failings in sometimes tragic situations, we also contain within us whatever is represented by divinity. The divine aspect of the hero is the potential within us all—the potential to transcend human limitations and problems. The facing of these problems is, in the psychological sense, represented by the hero quest. Heroes like Theseus search for a father—a source of identity. Others, as do Jason and sometimes Herakles, search for an object, which when found becomes a sign of worthiness. Most of our heroes must fight and overcome monsters, which can represent the inner demons that confront all of us in different forms—alcoholism, sex addiction, narcissism—some more extreme than others. When Perseus decapitates Medusa and when Theseus defeats the Minotaur, their actions are, in the psychological sense, metaphors for vanquishing our own demons. The fact that heroes are helped by the gods symbolizes the "divine" potential within us all to overcome those demons.

Did the stories of the heroes enter specifically into the lives of the Greeks in any way?

If the gods were most evident to the Classical Greeks in the great temples such as those on the Acropolis of Athens, the heroes of Greek mythology would have been important in schools as ethical and cultural models, and especially in the famous tragic plays by such writers as Aeschylus, Sophocles, and Euripides and in the comedies of Aristophanes. These plays were the central events, for example, in the great religious festival known as the City Dionysia.

THE DRAMAS OF ANCIENT ATHENS

What was the City Dionysia?

The City Dionysia, probably beginning in the sixth century B.C.E. in Athens, was an annual religious festival in honor of the god of wine, vegetation, and ecstasy. The festival began with processions in which a statute of Dionysos was carried through the streets. As noted above, the central element of the festival was drama.

The playwrights, such as the fifth-century writers of tragedy Aeschylus, Sophocles, and Euripides, competed for the honor of writing the best plays of the year. They each

Painting of the cyclops Polyphemus by Guido Reni (c. 1640). The only complete satyr play we have today is *The Cyclops* by Euripides.

presented a sequence of plays, three tragedies—sometimes related to each other—and a satyr play.

The satyr plays were characterized by bawdy themes celebrating the Dionysian qualities of sex and general madness. They served as a kind of comic relief against the background of the tragedies themselves. The only complete satyr play remaining to us is *The Cyclops,* by Euripides, about the incident in the *Odyssey* in which Odysseus confronts the Cyclops Polyphemos. Satyrs were wild, highly eroticized followers of Dionysos. They had animal tails and hooves and were often depicted with erections. Their female counterparts were known as maenads. These figures reflect or symbolize ancient practices related to Dionysian mysteries in which intoxicant-stimulated men and women participated in Dionysian ritual acts that were outside the usual patterns of behavior considered appropriate in Greek society.

The tragedy competition was preceded by a poem known as the dithyramb, performed by a circular dancing chorus of men and/or boys. The dithyrambs were hymns to Dionysos. Then came the tragedies themselves, plays not *about* Dionysos but *in honor of*

What role did mythology play in the origins of Greek drama?

According to the Greek philosopher Aristotle (384–322 B.C.E.), writing in his great literary work, the *Poetics*, and many later theorists, drama in Greece developed gradually from the worship of Dionysos. It is significant that the dithyrambs—the choral hymns to Dionysos—were an important prelude to the performance of plays in the City Dionysia. It is likely that dithyrambic practices preceded the development of Greek drama itself. According to tradition, it was a man called Thespis in the sixth century B.C.E. who originated drama by instituting dialogue between the dithyrambic chorus and actors. The role of Dionysos is important here because, as the god of intoxication and ecstasy, Dionysos speaks to the cathartic process in Greek tragedy outlined by Aristotle. Of all Greek gods, he was the only one to have experienced death and the catharsis of rebirth.

him and related in some way to the aspects of reality he represented. The characters of the plays were, for the most part, the Greek heroes discussed above. Although gods did not always appear as characters, the struggles between the human needs and desires of the heroes were contrasted with opposing laws and prophecies of the gods. This conflict was the essence of Greek tragedy, a metaphor for what the Greeks saw as an irony of life.

Also part of the City Dionysia was the presentation of comedies, of which the most famous are those of Aristophanes. These plays place the essential irony of life in a comic context.

Finally, the City Dionysia provides a clear indication of the origins of Greek drama and even of what we think of as theater today.

What elements of tragedy did Aristotle emphasize?

Aristotle said that the most important aspect of tragedy was plot (*mythos*)—an appropriate beginning, middle, and end extricated from any given heroic story line. The plot, involving a process by which the hero makes a mistake, endures a major reversal of fortune, and finally participates in some sort of resolution, arouses pity and at the same time fear in the audience, thus providing it, through emotional identification (a kind of Dionysian intoxication) with the hero's plight, with a communal purgation or *catharsis*. An equivalent process would be any religious ceremony in which the audience or congregation participates emotionally and spiritually in the ritualized plot (mythos) of the given religion's hero figure and through that ceremony achieves an ethical understanding and renewal.

How does the myth of Dionysos relate to the myths of the heroes of tragedy?

The movement from pure ritual to drama in Greece involves substituting stories of heroes for the story of Dionysos, so that the plot taken from the long story of Medea or

Agamemnon, for example, becomes a metaphor for the process of intoxication and purgation associated originally with Dionysos. It is in the works of Aeschylus, Sophocles, and Euripides, and to a lesser extent Aristophanes, that we can trace this metaphorical transference and the use of mythology in general in the Greek drama that took place in the City Dionysia.

AESCHYLUS AND *THE ORESTEIA*

Who was Aeschylus and how did he use mythology?

Aeschylus (c. 525–456 B.C.E.) was from a wealthy family in Eleusis and was, in fact, an initiate in the Mysteries of Eleusis. Much of his early life was spent as a soldier in the wars against Persia, but he found time to write a large number of plays and to win prizes for his work at the City Dionysia. The large majority of his plays, of which only a few are extant, are about figures in mythology. His *Seven against Thebes* is about the sons of the unfortunate King Oedipus; *Prometheus Bound* (which some scholars believe was written by another playwright) was about the equally unfortunate Titan. His most famous plays are the three which make up the trilogy, *The Oresteia: Agamemnon, The Libation Bearers*, and *The Eumenides*. In these, as in all his mythic plays, Aeschylus takes a *myth* as it has been passed down over the generations, probably at least from Mycenaean times, and re-interprets it in such a way as to express his sense of the morality or ethical, social, and religious principles it represents —in this case a fifth-century Athenian view as opposed to a view more prevalent in earlier times.

What is the background myth of *The Oresteia*?

In *The Oresteia,* Aeschylus creates three dramatic plots from the long story of the House of Atreus in Mycenae. This is a story which would have been well known to the audience at the City Dionysia. It begins with Tantalus, who, as punishment for feeding the gods the flesh of his own son, is placed in the Underworld, forever "tantalized" as he attempts unsuccessfully to drink from a stream. The House of Atreus is cursed to continue on a path marked by fratricide, cannibalism, suicide, adultery, and sacrilege. As the characters in *The Oresteia* appeared, the audience would automatically have seen them as stained by this horrific history.

What is the plot of *Agamemnon*?

The plot—the *mythos*—of *Agamemnon* begins with a watchman waiting for the return of Agamemnon from the Trojan War. He speaks ominously of the manlike heart of Agamemnon's wife Clytemnestra, and the audience knows that she is angry that, before leaving for the war, the king had agreed to follow an oracular instruction that he sacrifice his daughter Iphigenia. Agamemnon now arrives on the scene with his concubine, Cassandra, the daughter of King Priam. Cassandra is cursed with the ability to see the

An 1817 painting by Pierre-Narcisse Guérin shows Clytemnestra, encouraged by Aighistos at far left, about to kill Agamemnon.

past and the future. Clytemnestra manages to convince Agamemnon to enter his palace by walking on a purple carpet as a conquering hero, an act of extreme pride or *hubris*, a sin which characterizes tragic heroes in Greek drama. Left outside, Cassandra wonders whether to follow. In a soiloquy, she relates some of the horrors of the House of Atreus that she foresees; she realizes what will happen to her and Agamemnon inside the palace. Nevertheless, she enters. Soon there are bloodcurdling cries and the butchered bodies of Agamemnon and Cassandra are displayed to the chorus, representing the people of the polis—the city. Clytemnestra arrives with the bloodied axe used in the execution of her husband. Her lover, Aighistos—the cousin of Agamemnon, whom the king had left to guard his kingdom in his absence—accompanies the queen and speaks with arrogant hubris. The chorus warns of the inevitable return of Agamemnon's son, Orestes, who will certainly act in revenge in the age-old tradition of blood for blood. The mythos of the play involves, in effect, only an hour or so of Agamemnon's complex life. This tiny segment of a life will lead the audience to pity the hero on one hand, but to sit in fear—that is, awe—as it contemplates the horrors of his sin, that of his wife and her lover, and those of the House of Atreus as a whole. The prospect of a neverending blood feud within a family and a society would not have been a prospect with appeal to a law-based city-state such as Athens.

What is the plot of *The Libation Bearers*?

In *The Libation Bearers,* the old blood-for-blood way continues to prevail. Orestes, the son of Agamemnon and Clytemnestra, has arrived at the palace, having been away for some time. He and his cousin Pylades are standing at Agamemnon's grave. They hear someone approaching and hide. Soon Orestes' sister Elektra arrives with a chorus of mourning slaves (the libation bearers) sent by the queen, presumably in hopes of warding off harm to herself as a result of her murderous act.

Orestes and Pylades now reveal themselves and ask why the libation bearers are there performing their ritual. The chorus reveals that Clytemnestra has had a nightmare in which she gave birth to a snake which then sucked a mixture of milk and blood from her breast. Orestes says he is that snake, and brother and sister plan revenge.

Orestes and Pylades pretend to be travelers and request a place to stay at the palace. They tell Clytemnestra that Orestes is dead and, much relieved, she calls for Aighistos. When the usurping king arrives, Orestes kills him and is faced with the central problem of the play. Revenge for the killing of a father and king—fratricide and regicide—is required by the unwritten rules of the old blood-for-blood way. But in this case there is an impossible problem, as the object of revenge must be his mother, meaning Orestes must commit the forbidden sin of matricide. As is so often the case in tragedy, the hero is caught between conflicting demands, and there is no way out. Orestes kills Clytemnestra as he and Pylades, and certainly Elektra—the driving force behind the planned action—believe he must, and as the old law demands. Almost immediately he is set upon by the guardians of the old way, the Furies, known to the Greeks as the Eumenides or Erinyes, who charge the young hero with matricide. Orestes flees in horror, and the chorus says the tragedy of the House of Atreus will continue.

What is the plot of *The Eumenides*?

The audience is now prepared for the third play in the trilogy, *The Eumenides*. Aeschylus has prepared the way in the first two plays for a necessary resolution of some kind. Either Orestes must be punished for matricide, thus preserving the old blood way, or a new, more reasonable set of rules or laws must be established, more in keeping with the reality of the city-state represented by the audience. It must be remembered that the plays of the City Dionysia were cathartic ritual dramas meant to purge the city itself. The heroes on the stage suffer and the audience with them, but order is eventually established and life can go on in a better way.

As *The Eumenides* opens, Orestes is being plagued by the Furies. He flees to Delphi, seeking Apollo's help. Apollo has supported his revenge killings but even he cannot overpower the Furies. He does cast a spell on them, however, causing them to sleep while Orestes continues on to Athens, protected by Hermes. In a terrifying scene, Clytemnestra's ghost appears to the Eumenides and urges them to pursue Orestes. They wake up and search for Orestes' tracks by gathering the scent of the blood of Clytemnestra on his feet. When they find him in Athens, he is holding on to a statue of Athene. As the Furies surround him, Athene intervenes. She calls for a trial. There will be a jury of twelve, of which she will be one. Apollo will represent Orestes, the Eumenides will represent the dead Clytemnestra. In the trial, Apollo argues that in a marriage the man is more important than the woman (Athens was a patriarchal society, so the audience of men would have agreed). In support of the concept of male dominance, he points out that Athene herself had been born of Zeus's head rather than of a mother. Therefore, Clytemnestra's crime is greater than her son's, whose act of vengeance was justified. Athene and five others vote for acquittal, meaning the jury is evenly split. Because Athene at the beginning had stipulated that a tied jury meant acquittal, Orestes is acquitted. The Furies are "furious," but Athene convinces them that a new precedent—a reasonable and wise law of Apollo and Athene—has been established, a law which, of course, reflected Athenian law as opposed to the blood-for-blood law of the old days. The Eumenides are given a new home and are renamed "The Venerable Ones." They will now guarantee the prosperity of Athens, a city based on the understanding that mercy takes precedence over blood revenge.

Not surprisingly, when *The Oresteia* trilogy was performed at the City Dionysia in 458 B.C.E., it won first prize.

SOPHOCLES AND THE OEDIPUS CYCLE

Who was Sophocles, and how did he use use mythology?

As did Aeschylus, Sophocles (c. 497–406 B.C.E.) wrote many plays about heroes long known to the Greeks—heroes such as the epic warrior Ajax, and Elektra of the house of Atreus. Sophocles wrote three plays about the royal family of Thebes: *Oedipus the King (Oedipus Rex)*, *Oedipus at Colonus*, and *Antigone*. These plays were not written as a trilogy but were performed as parts of other trilogies in different years. *Oedipus the King* concerns Oedipus' discovery of his polluted identity. *Oedipus at Colonus* is about the end of the blind Oedipus' life when he is sheltered at a sanctuary outside Athens and protected by King Theseus. *Antigone* tells the tale of Oedipus' heroic and ultimately tragic daughter Antigone. Aristotle held up *Oedipus the King*, performed at the City Dionysia in 429 B.C.E., as the model for Greek tragedy.

What was the background myth of the Oedipus plays?

The plot of *Oedipus the King,* as well as of the other Theban plays, was extracted from the long and complex saga of the House of Thebes, much as Aeschylus' *The Oresteia* was extracted from the story of the House of Atreus. The audience at the City Dionysia would have known the whole story of Oedipus. Homer tells most of it in the *Odyssey*, so it had long been part of the Greek collective memory.

The audience knew that in ancient times the city of Thebes had been founded by Cadmus, famous for killing a dragon sacred to Ares. They also knew that a Theban was famous for having brought homosexuality into Greece. This Theban was Laius, who as a youth had fled Thebes in a dynasty dispute and had been given refuge by King Pelops of a nearby city. Pelops had appointed Laius as a tutor to the king's

A fourth-century B.C.E. bust of the playwright Sophocles.

beautiful young son Chrysippos. The tutor became strongly attracted to the boy and raped him. So it was that the eventual House of Thebes of which Laius later became king was marked at its beginning by a sin.

Laius married Jocasta, the sister of an important Theban, Creon. An oracle told the royal couple that their son would commit the unforgiveable and almost impossible-to-imagine sin of killing his father and marrying his mother. Reacting as anyone in such a position might, the couple tried to rid themselves of their infant son. Laius tied the baby's feet together and Jocasta abandoned her child in the wilds, assuming than an animal would complete the act of infanticide. But the oracle of Apollo is not so easily undermined. A shepherd finds the child—he of the swollen feet (*oedipus*)—and gives him to the childless king and queen of Corinth, who raise him as their son. The young Oedipus, having been told nothing of his early history, believes the Corinthian couple to be his real parents. It is with horror, then, that he hears from an oracle that he will kill his father and marry his mother. Again, understandably, he makes the mistake of attempting to circumvent the oracle by leaving Corinth for good. At a crossroads he meets a party of travelers and becomes involved in a chariot road-rage incident. He kills the leader of the travelers, who happens to be Laius, his father, as well as most of his party and soon arrives at Thebes, where he will request sanctuary. He succeeds in answering a riddle posed by a sphinx who is blocking access to the city and holding it hostage. After killing the monster, as heroes must, Oedipus is received by the Thebans as a savior and is made king. The throne has been vacant, as the old king, Laius, has apparently been killed. It is proposed that Oedipus take the queen, Jocasta, as his wife. This he does and the couple have four children, two boys and two girls. Oedipus, of course, has no idea that he has already killed his father and married his mother. Fate and free will have converged. It must be remembered that the audience knows this whole story but that the characters portrayed on stage do not and that all of these amazing events have taken place before the play, *Oedipus the King,* even begins.

What is the plot of *Oedipus the King*?

What Aristotle sees as the great achievement of the playwright here is the proper choice of the dramatic plot from within that story, a *mythos* that has a clear beginning, middle, and end which will serve as a ritual process for the city's purgation (*catharsis*). The play begins with the city of Thebes suffering from a catastrophic plague. The savior king, Oedipus, is approached by the chorus of elders who ask for salvation from this situation. Oedipus informs them that he has sent his brother-in-law Creon to the oracle of Apollo at Delphi to determine the cause of the plague. Creon returns and announces that the city is under a curse because the murderer of the old king, Laius, has never been found. Oedipus, in a grand gesture vows to find the murderer, whom he curses. One can only admire the effectiveness of this beginning. The audience must have been gripped by the pity and fear described by Aristotle as the murderer, unknown to himself, the source of the town's pollution, vows to destroy himself. This is true tragic irony.

The middle of the play is called the *agon,* from which we derive the word agony, which describes the ordeal of the *protagonist* Oedipus, who is also, unwittingly, the *antagonist* of his own city. The agon involves a struggle between many opposites, but primarily between fate and free will, a struggle inherent in the whole tragic saga of Thebes, and between self-knowledge and the lack of self-knowledge. Thebes cannot return to life, the destructive pollution cannot be removed, until Oedipus can "see" who he is. It is worth remembering here as Sophocles and his audience certainly did, that one of Apollo's mottos was "Know thyself."

Naturally, as clues begin to arrive, Oedipus does all he can to remain "in denial" of himself. One of his weapons will be his own position as king and once the savior of his city. But there is also the overweening pride (*hubris*) derived from that perceived position. He calls on the blind prophet Tiresias for information about the murder, but the prophet refuses to speak. This so infuriates the king that he threatens the old man. In anger Tiresias says, in effect, "You are the murderer." Oedipus more and more loses control. He accuses Creon of conspiring against him with Tiresias. Tiresias leaves saying that the discovered murderer will be a native of Thebes, the killer of his father, the husband of his mother, and the brother and father of his own children. Oedipus threatens Creon, but Jocasta tries to calm him, reminding him that he cannot be the son of Laius or his murderer, as the former king had been killed by others at a crossroad.

Now things begin to emerge in the mind of Oedipus; he begins to accept his identity. He tells Jocasta of his road-rage conflict and of his killings there. A messenger arrives and tells how the baby with the swollen feet had been given to the king of Corinth. A witness to the crossroad killing has survived. Oedipus is revealed for who and what he is.

The resolution at the end of the play is almost inevitable. The sins here, even if committed without knowledge, cannot be forgiven. Pollution, whatever its source, must be removed. Jocasta goes into the palace and hangs herself. Oedipus takes the pins from her dress and blinds himself. Now, like Tiresias, he lacks sight, but has insight. He knows who he is, and Thebes can return to normalcy under the leadership of Creon.

The *mythos* of the play ends, but the story goes on, providing material from which at least two other plots—that of the Colonus play and that of *Antigone*—would be extracted.

What is the plot of *Antigone*?

Antigone is of particular interest because it concerns the travails of a female protagonist, Antigone, the daughter of Oedipus. The play opens with Antigone bemoaning the fact that the king, Creon, has decreed that as a punishment for having fought against the state of Thebes, her brother Polynices is not to be allowed the formal burial required by religion. Polynices' brother, Eteocles, who was just as guilty, has been properly buried. The new decree states that anyone going against it will be killed.

The chorus gives the audience the background of the story that has led to this unjust punishment. The two sons of Oedipus were to have alternately occupied the throne of Thebes, but unsatisfied with this arrangement, they had fought for supremacy, in spite of the obvious harm their war brought to Thebes. Finally the brothers succeeded only in killing each other, and Creon regained the crown he had originally taken after the disgrace of Oedipus. To settle the dispute between the dead brothers, he made a political decision to punish only Polynices.

Now Antigone appears. Distraught over the unburied state of her brother, she asks her sister Ismene to help her bury him secretly, but the more conservative and "law abiding" sister refuses. Antigone determines to act alone, though with the loving moral support of Creon's son, Haemon. Offstage she ritually buries her brother by putting some dirt on his body. Thus, she breaks the law for religious and family reasons. Caught by guards, she is brought before her uncle, Creon, the king, for judgment.

The middle of the play—the *agon*—is thus set up between Antigone as protagonist and Creon as antagonist, but good and evil are ambiguous here. Creon has made his probably wrong decision for good reasons— to preserve the broken state. Antigone has

An 1828 painting by Antoni Brodowski of the blind Oedipus with his daughter Antigone.

acted in the name of traditional family and religious rules and values. But she has broken the law. Both are right, both are wrong, and both are infected with the sin of the tragic hero—pride (*hubris*).

Because she refuses to give in to Creon's pleas that she accept the law, Antigone is walled up and left to die. In her prison she commits suicide. Creon is punished for his pride when his son also commits suicide in support of Antigone.

The whole question of individual conscience versus the state laws is, of course, one that continues to concern and sometimes to bring great pain to human societies, which is perhaps why Antigone remains one of the most performed Greek tragedies in our day.

Why do Sophocles' (and Aeschylus') protagonists suffer the punishment of the guilty when they either have no choice in what they do or know nothing of what they have done?

The simplest answer to this question is to establish that Sophocles, and the other tragic dramatists of the City Dionysia, were not suggesting in their plays that life was "fair." Their attempt was to use the events of myth to express metaphorically the irrationality and arbitrariness that often faces us in life. Certain problems have no obvious solutions. For example, Orestes has no choice but to avenge his father's murder, but to do so he must commit the unforgiveable sin of matricide. Antigone's dilemma pits religious law against state law. As the case of Oedipus reveals, often we suffer even though we have done nothing wrong consciously or even though our actions can be traced psychologically or materially to something abusive done to us long ago. Whatever the reason for a crime, however, society punishes the criminal. The fact that Oedipus did not know that he had killed his father or married his mother, or the fact that others—including his mother and father—ultimately caused his situation by leaving him as a baby to die, does not alter the fact that he is an individual who has committed the unforgiveable sins of regicide, fratricide, and incest. Can we imagine a person burdened with such sins—however unconsciously committed—being allowed to remain as king or being able to live with himself as a "normal" member of society? Life in some cases is decidedly tragic, which is to say, unfair. The injustices that face the tragic hero in the Greek plays is made at least somewhat less painful to the audience by the fact that these heroes all suffer from the very human failing we know as pride.

EURIPIDES, MEDEA, AND DIONYSUS

How did Euripides use mythology?

Euripides (c.480–406 B.C.E.) was a more skeptical playwright than Aeschylus or Sophocles. It is fair to say that he was more "modern" than his two great competitors over the years at the City Dionysia, less directed by traditional religious positions, more by an interest in the inner lives of his mythological subjects. These subjects are treated in a large number of plays. *Alcestis* tells the story of a brave wife willing to be taken to the Underworld in order to save her husband from that fate. *Hecuba* is about the unhappy wife of King Priam of Troy, who tries to dissuade her son Hector from going into battle. *Elektra* takes up the popular theme of the daughter of Agamemnon who was so strident in her desire for revenge against her mother, Clytemnestra. Euripides also wrote plays about Helen of Troy, Orestes, Iphigenia, and Hippolytus. His plays most often studied today are *Medea* and *Bacchae*.

What is the plot of *Medea*?

Medea was first produced at the City Dionysia of 431 B.C.E. It takes up the story of the hero Jason and his sorceress wife after they return to Greece with the Golden Fleece, an ancient myth well known to Euripides' audience. As with Sophocles, Euripides sought to extract a *mythos*, a viable plot for his play from within this long and complex story. The audience knew that in Corinth, where they lived after the Golden Fleece quest, Jason and Medea's marriage had been threatened by Jason's willingness to abandon his wife in order to make a politically advantageous marriage to Glauce, the daughter of the Corinthian king, Creon (not the same as Creon of Thebes in Sophocles' Oedipus plays). The plot as developed by Euripides would focus not so much on Jason as on the inner turmoil of Medea, so, logically, the beginning—to use Aristotle's formula—finds Medea grieving over her impossible position. She is a woman in a world dominated (like fifth-century B.C.E. Athens) by rules and traditions favorable to males, and she is an outsider—a foreign, barbarian enchantress living in a Greek world. And her husband has deserted her. Even a Greek audience would have felt some pity, but the fear Aristotle said was necessary would have been generated by the audience's knowledge of Medea's powers, already demonstrated in the Golden Fleece aspect of the larger story.

In the middle of the plot, the *agon*, as Medea grieves and bemoans the horrors of her position, the king, Creon, arrives and, as does the audience, fearing Medea's powers, announces that she is to go into exile. But Creon agrees to a one-day reprieve when Medea, pretending humility, requests it. At this point the audience, even more aware of Medea's powers than is Creon, would have gasped at Creon's willingness to allow what is, in effect, a time bomb, to remain in his territory even for one day.

Now a famous character, one well known to the Athenian audience, arrives. This is the legendary Athenian king Aegeus, the human father of the hero Theseus. Aegeus is swayed by Medea's sad story and agrees to give her sanctuary in Athens if she can make her way there and if she will help his wife to conceive a child. Once again, knowing the story of Medea in Athens, and her attempt to rid the world of Theseus, the audience must have reacted in disbelief and horror. So far two powerful men have been somewhat outmaneuvered by Medea. The struggle between the protagonist Medea and the antagonist, the patriarchal world, proceeds, as Jason himself arrives. Jason attempts to justify his position, to explain rationally why it is best for him and the children, and even for Medea, to accept his new marriage. Furious, Medea accuses Jason of forgetting that she had left her home for him, that she had made his Golden Fleece quest a success, and that she was, **101** after all, his wife. Jason leaves, and Medea plots revenge. She calls Jason back, apologizes, and pretends to have accepted the new marriage. She sends a poisoned robe to Glauce as a wedding present carried by her two children. Glauce and Creon are both killed by the poison.

The end comes when Jason enters as Medea has killed their children and is being taken away magically by a flying chariot.

Is Euripides faithful to the original myth?

Medea's killing of her children is a radical change made by Euripides to the original myth. In the traditional story the children are left behind in Corinth. By making this change, Euripides emphasizes his particular interest in the myth, the agonizing inner passions of a woman trapped in a patriarchal system such as the one repre-

The hero Jason and his sorceress wife, Medea, shown here in a 1907 painting by John William Waterhouse, are the subject of a play by Euripides.

sented by his audience. But his mythos also centers on a conflict the audience would have felt between whatever sympathy they might have had with Medea and a horror at the acts of what they would have seen as those of an irrational and barbaric foreigner. In short, the audience is left in a quandary without the cathartic social redemption or purgation provided by *The Oresteia* of Aesychlus or *Oedipus the King* of Sophocles.

Perhaps Euripides understood better than the other playwrights the meaning of Dionysos, whose festival, the City Dionysia, was the setting for all their plays. Dionysos was, after all, seen as a foreign god of unknown, probably Eastern origins. His characteristics of passion, ecstasy, and wildness, are decidedly non-Apollonian, really non-Greek. Medea was more Dionysian than Greek, and Euripides' play expresses this fact.

The same can be said of *Bacchae,* which takes its title from Bacchus, another name for Dionysos.

What is the plot of *Bacchae*?

Bacchae is an anomaly among plays performed at the City Dionysia because it portrays the god himself. Athenians would have known that Dionysos was the son of Zeus by the mortal Semele and that he was a different sort of god in that he had experienced death and in that he apparently travelled widely in foreign parts and lived in the world rather than on Mount Olympus. It must have seemed strange, then, when the play began with Dionysos entering to introduce himself and to explain why he had decided to come to Thebes, which is where the events of the play will take place. Thebes, it seems, has refused to officially accept him for the god he is. He tells how Zeus had become enamored of Semele, the daughter of King Cadmus, the founder of Thebes. Disguised, he visited her often and eventually she became pregnant. The jealous Hera convinced Semele to ask Zeus to appear to her as himself. Having promised Semele to do anything she wished him to do, Zeus had no choice but to appear in his true thunderbolt form, which caused Semele's death. Hermes rescued the unborn child, however, and Zeus hid it from Hera by sewing it into his thigh. Later, then, Dionysos was born of Zeus. Dionysos has come to Thebes not only on his own behalf, but to make the Thebans believe Semele's original claim that she had been made pregnant by Zeus.

The middle of the play—the *agon*—involves the conflict between the protagonist Dionysos and the antagonist King Pentheus, representing Thebes. Pentheus, the unbeliever, enters and scolds two familiar mythological figures of Thebes, Cadmus and Tiresias, who as old men, have become interested in the Dionysian rites practiced on Mount Cithaeron by Theban women, including the king's own mother Agave, daughter of Cadmus. The two old men are dressed in the clothes of the Maenads (Bacchantes), the followers of Dionysos and participants in the Bacchanals, the Dionysian mysteries.

Pentheus announces that any Thebans participating in these mysteries will be arrested. The guards bring in the blond stranger, Dionysos, disguised as a priest of the rites. Pentheus, who has begun to come under the same Dionysian spell that has affected Cadmus and Tiresias, and the women of Thebes, questions the stranger about the rites, but the stranger will tell him nothing and is arrested. But Dionysos simply breaks out of prison and punishes Pentheus by causing an earthquake to destroy his palace.

A shepherd arrives to announce that Dionysian rites are taking place on Cithaeron and that the women are tearing apart cows in their ecstatic frenzy. In spite of himself, Pentheus is curious. The blond stranger, Dionysos, dresses the king in women's clothes to disguise him, and Pentheus, now under the god's spell, heads off for the mountain seeing strange visions of Thebes and bulls—the latter being common symbols of Dionysos.

The end or resolution of the play comes when it is reported by a messenger that Dionysos had placed Pentheus in his women's clothes at the top of a tree so that he could watch the revelers. The god had then called his followers to witness the intruder. Led by Pentheus' own mother, they had torn him to pieces, making him a *de facto* sacrifice to Dionysos.

It should be noted that Dionysos himself had suffered dismemberment in the Orphic tradition.

ORPHEUS, ORPHISM, AND PHILOSOPHICAL MYTHS

What was Orphism?

Orphism was a religious system that emerged in the sixth century B.C.E. in Greece. It was part of the mystery religion tradition, as opposed to the more orthodox Olympian religion. As such, it is related to other mystery cults such as the Dionysian and Eleusinian mysteries. Orphism takes its name from Orpheus, the musician whose talent created ecstasy among his followers. When his wife, Eurydice, was killed, Orpheus travelled to the Underworld, hoping to bring her back. There his beautiful music so enchanted even Hades and Persephone that they agreed to allow his wife to follow him back to the upperworld as long as he did not look back at her during their journey. In the passage out of Hades, having almost succeeded, Orpheus cannot resist looking back, causing poor Eurydice to fade back into death.

Many unorthodox myths pervaded the Orphic tradition. The most important one involves Dionysos in his Thracian (northeastern Greece/southern Balkans) form as Zagreus. In this myth, Zeus was the father of Persephone by his sister Demeter. Zeus then seduced his daughter Persephone, taking the form of a snake to do so. The result was the child Zagreus-Dionysos. The jealous Hera convinced the Titans to kill the child, which they did by dismembering him and eating him. In his anger, Zeus turned the Titans into ashes with a strike of his thunderbolt and the mixture of ashes and the bits of the divine Dionysian flesh resulted in the creation of humanity. Thus, humans contain within themselves the possibility of rebirth or resurrection. Zeus recovered the dead child's heart and placed it in Semele, who then gave birth to the resurrected god.

Like the Dionysian and Eleusinian mysteries, then, the Orphic ones celebrated the concept of life beyond death and formed the basis of what was, in effect, a philosophical myth.

What are philosophical myths?

The concept of the philosophical myth, as opposed to the kind of myths told by Homer and Hesiod and others, was developed by the Greek philosopher Plato (428–347 B.C.E.), a student of the philosopher Socrates (469–399 B.C.E.). Plato distinguished between a *mythos* (story) and a *logos* (concept). In effect, he made up stories to teach concepts; that is, he expressed thoughts via narratives, the idea being that humans understand better when ideas are turned into metaphors. It could be argued, of course, that most of the world's myths are metaphors used to convey philosophy, but these traditional myths developed gradually in the folk tradition involving gods and heroes. Philosophical myths are created by an individual for a specific teaching purpose. Generally they do not require gods and heroes. The most famous philosophical myth is Plato's allegory of the cave.

What is Plato's cave myth?

In the sixth book of the *Republic* Plato develops an allegory which has sometimes been called a "myth." He has Socrates ask his listeners to imagine some men who have always lived in an underground place that can only be reached by way of a passage that eventually opens to the light. The men are chained by the neck; they can see only what lies in front of them. A fire creates light above and behind them, and between them and the fire is a track with a wall below it. The wall hides other people behind it, much as puppeteers are hidden in a puppet show. These people manipulate objects that appear on the track above them. The objects are representations of animals, humans, and other figures.

This 1604 engraving attempts to capture the fascinating philosophical situation of the cave myth posited in Plato's *Republic*.

The people chained to the wall cannot see the fire, the opposite wall, or the track; they can see only the shadows projected on the wall in front of them. When the manipulators behind the wall add voices to the objects they move, the prisoners hear only echoes of those voices. Plato, through Socrates, says that the condition of the prisoners stands for our position in relation to reality. As are we, the prisoners are separated from the source of reality and are condemned to see only shadows of being.

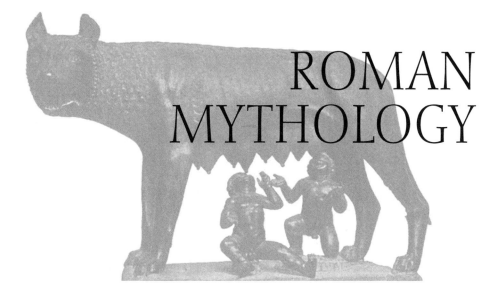

ROMAN MYTHOLOGY

What do we mean by a Roman and Roman mythology?

Today a Roman is simply someone who lives in Rome. To be a Roman once meant to be a citizen of a city-state and republic and then a vast empire, the capital of which was the city of Rome. The language of Rome was Latin, the ancestor of the modern Romance languages. When we speak of Roman mythology, we refer to the mythology of Rome in its various geopolitical stages before the establishment there of Christianity as the dominant religion.

Is it true, as commonly assumed, that Roman mythology was simply Greek mythology translated into Latin?

Greek mythology was only one of many influences on Roman mythology. The people in the eighth century B.C.E. who inhabited the village, or *urb* (*urban, suburban*), on the Tiber River that would become Rome spoke an Italic language as did other inhabitants of Latium, including, for instance, several Latin tribes and the Sabines. The source of their language and their patriarchal and warlike culture was that of the Indo-Europeans who migrated into Italy sometime in the second millennium B.C.E. The early Romans and other Latins interrelated and often fought with the Etruscans in the north and the Greek colonies in the south. These interrelationships had definite influence on the development of Roman religious and mythological traditions. The Etruscans controlled Rome from 750 B.C.E. until Rome gained independence and founded a Republic with a senate in 509 B.C.E. Two hundred fifty years of Etruscan dominance was bound to have a significant effect on Roman religion and mythology. Many years of trade and eventual Roman control of the Greeks in the south in the third century B.C.E. resulted in direct Greek mythological influence as well.

A *de facto* Roman Empire was established in the third century B.C.E. with the conquest of Greece itself and of Carthage by the end of the Punic Wars. The Republic essentially came to an end when Julius Caesar established an effective dictatorship in 40 B.C.E. After the caesar's assassination in 44 B.C.E., a long civil war between Marcus Junius Brutus and Gaius Cassius Longinus on one side and Marcus Antonius and Octavian on the other, and later between Marcus Antonius and Octavian (all of these made famous by Shakespeare in *Julius Caesar* and *Antony and Cleopatra*), resulted in Octavian's victory in 31 B.C.E. and the official establishment of the Roman Empire under Octavian, now Augustus Caesar in 27 B.C.E.

With the gradual expansion of the Roman Empire under Augustus and later emperors, the Romans interacted with the cultures of the peoples under their control and these interactions resulted in the absorption of various mythological traditions from as far away as Persia (Iran) and Anatolia (Turkey). When Christianity became dominant in Rome in the fourth century C.E., Rome adopted the narratives and rituals of that tradition and became the center of what would become Roman Catholicism.

INDO-EUROPEANS

Who were the Indo-Europeans, and what was their mythology?

The Indo-Europeans were peoples who had perhaps once spoken a common language (Proto-Indo-European), and who migrated into India, Iran, Anatolia, and Europe probably during the middle of the third millennium B.C.E. Eventually various languages evolved from the original language. By the seventh century B.C.E. in Italy there is written evidence of an Italic Indo-European language, the ancestor of Latin and later the Romance languages. Various connections between the languages of India and Iran and those of Europe—including Italic and Latin and the Romance languages, as well as the Germanic and Celtic languages—have been discovered by scholars. Connections between gods and themes of Vedic mythology in India and those of Greek and Roman and other European mythologies of people speaking Indo-European languages. This suggests an original Indo-European mythology based on powerful sky gods, warrior heroes, male-subjected but sometimes violent goddesses, and a generally patriarchal warrior-based vision of the world.

What are some of the apparent themes of Indo-European mythology that influenced Roman mythology?

Scholars have proposed the existence of several cultural themes that characterize Indo-European mythologies from India to Iran to Europe—including Rome.

The first of these is tripartization, the dividing of society into three classes: religious, military, and farming and herding. In India these classes are represented by Brahmins (religious caste), Kshatriyas (warrior caste), and Vaishyas (farmer caste). In Rome the same classes were the flamines, the miletes, and the quirites. In Roman mythology sovereign gods were related to priests and kings, warrior gods to warriors, and fertility gods to farmers. An outgrowth of tripartization is the ubiquitous presence of the Indo-European triad of gods representing sovereignty, power, and community: Brahma, Shiva, and Vishnu in Hindu India, and Jupiter (Iuppiter), Mars, and Quirinus in ancient Rome, for example.

Twins are another important aspect of Indo-European mythologies. The Ashvin twins in India had counterparts in Castor and Polydeuces (Pollux) in Greece and in Remus and Romulus in Rome.

The theme of the warrior hero is basic to Indo-European mythology. Arjuna in India, for example, has a Roman relative in Aeneas.

LATINS, ETRUSCANS, AND ARCHAIC ROME

Who were the Latins, and what was the basis of their mythology?

The so-called Latins were several tribes who spoke a form of Latin, an Indo-European language, and lived along the Tiber River in an area known as Old Latium from early in the first millennium B.C.E. The primary god of the Latins was Jupiter Latiaris. Also important was Diana Aricana, who eventually was reduced in stature under the dominance of Jupiter.

Who were the Etruscans, and what was the basis of their mythology?

The Etruscans were non-Indo-European speakers whose civilization was the most advanced on the Italian peninsula before Rome's emergence and dominance there.

Their religion was characterized by haruspicy (the study of entrails of animals sacrificed for prophecy), by other practices of divination, and rituals growing out of a mythic prophet called Tages. Tages was said to have been born in a furrow in a field as a gray-haired child already possessed of the wisdom of a sage. In this respect he resembled other world heroes such as the Buddha, Krishna, and the Irish Cuchulainn, who as very young children possessed adult powers. Another Etruscan-based myth was that of the *Sibylline Books* that contained guidance for difficult times. According to a Roman story, an old woman, actually the great Sybil of Cumae, offered her nine prophetic books for sale to Tarquin, the last of the Etruscan kings of Rome. Tarquin balked at the high price demanded by the woman, and in anger she burned three of the books before offering the remaining six for sale. When Tarquin refused these, she burned three of them. Tarquin accepted her price for the remaining three, and these Sybilline Books remained on the Capitoline Hill as a source of advice for Romans during difficult times for centuries to come.

It was the rape by Tarquin's son of the aristocratic woman Lucretia that was said to have set off the revolution that ended monarchy in Rome and marked the establishment of the Republic in 509 B.C.E.

Who were the Etruscan gods?

The Etruscans, like the Romans, were more than willing to assume that foreign deities were equivalents of their own gods. The Phoenecian Astarte and the Greek Hera, they saw as embodiments of their own great goddess, Uni. Another important goddess was Menrva. Tinia was a powerful god of lightning. Turan was a goddess of love. Many of these deities were directly adopted from the Greeks. Aplu and Artumes, for example, were versions of Apollo and Artemis.

How did the Romans incorporate Etruscan and Latin mythology?

The most important incorporation was of the prophetic traditions symbolized by the Sybilline Books and the traditions of divination that prevailed in Rome throughout its history. As for deities, in some cases it is difficult to know whose gods came first. Did the Romans adopt the Etruscan gods or did the Etruscan gods simply become Roman ones? We know that the Etruscan Uni was the Roman Juno, that Tinia was the Roman high god Jupiter, that Turan was Venus, Nethus was Neptune, and

A bust of Turan, the Etruscan goddess of love, from around the first half of the third century B.C.E.

Turms was Mercury. And did the Roman Jupiter descend from the Latin Jupiter Latiaris and Diana from the Latin Diana Aricana, or did both the Etruscans and the Romans and other Latins take their gods from those of the Greek colonists in the south?

Assuming many influences and common traditions, what was the particular essence of Roman mythology as opposed to Greek, Etruscan, or Latin mythology?

The answer to this question depends very much on the period of Roman history being considered. It is possible to speak of the different mythological emphases among the Archaic Romans, followed by those of the Republican Romans and finally, those of the Imperial Romans.

What was the nature of Archaic Roman mythology?

When we speak of Archaic Rome, we refer to the period which precedes Etruscan dominance. In the ancient Latin settlement later known as Rome—the City (*Urbs*)—the supreme god was Jupiter, or Iuppiter, whose Indo-European root is Iou, or *dyeu*, thus relating the god linguistically to Zeus (dyeus) and the Sanskrit for the sky (*dyaus*). Iuppiter and the other Archaic Roman gods were usually not anthropomorphic. Rather they were expressions of concepts. Iuppiter was the power of the sky, Fides was the goddess of good faith, Ceres was the agricultural fertility goddess, Consus was stored grain, Ops was opulence, Vesta was sacred fire. The goddesses Angerona and Mater Matuta were associated with aspects of the solar year. Most important was a version of the Indo-European triad—Iuppiter (sovereignty), Mars (power), and Quirinus (prosperous community). The importance of the triad is reflected in the Roman foundation myth of Romulus and Remus, which probably emerged in the Archaic period.

ROMULUS AND REMUS

What was the Romulus and Remus myth?

The story of Romulus and Remus was well known in Rome by the fourth century B.C.E. and probably had much earlier folkloric roots. Romulus and Remus were the Roman version of the Indo-European sacred twins. They were the result of the union between Mars and the mortal Rhea Silvia (Earth). In order to prevent her from having children, King Amulius had usurped the throne of Rhea Silvia's father, Numitor, and had forced the girl to become a vestal virgin so that she would not have a child who might seek revenge for his evil act. But, as always happens when kings in mythology attempt to thwart the will of the gods, his plans came to nothing. Rhea Silvia conceived the twins by Mars, and when they were born, Amulius tried, like Perseus's grandfather and Oedipus's parents, to overcome the inevitable by casting the twins away. When the ark in which he had placed them ran aground, a she-wolf found the babies and suckled them. So was born the symbol of Rome to this day.

As young boys the twins were adopted by a shepherd (again, like so many abandoned heroes—Oedipus, for example) and became famous for their unusual strength. But one day Remus was captured by followers of the old king Numitor. When Romulus went to his brother's rescue, their identity as Numitor's grandsons was uncovered and the newly united family made war on and defeated the usurper Amulius. Soon after, Romulus and Remus made their way to the place on the Tiber where they had been suckled by the wolf and founded the city of Rome. Here Romulus killed his brother in a fight over the name of the city. Thus, the city was named Rome after Romulus.

The new city was in desperate need of women. To solve this problem, Romulus invited the neighboring Sabine tribe to a feast, during which the Romans raped the Sabine women.

After a long war between the Romans and Sabines, the women—now Roman wives and mothers—arranged a truce be-

At the Museo Nuovo in the Palazzo dei Conservatori, Rome, Italy, one can see this statue showing Romulus and Remus, the founders of Rome, getting nourishment from a she-wolf.

111

tween the sides. Romulus, like many heroes, was eventually taken up to heaven and made a god. So it was that Roman emperors could later claim precedence for their supposed divinity.

In terms of Indo-European parallels and significance, the killing of Remus by Romulus signifies the sacred sacrifice out of which creation is born. The world of the ancient Indian *Vedas* is born of the body of Yama, the twin brother of Manu. Here Rome is born of the body of Remus, allowing Romulus to become the sacred king, the first man of Rome, the instrument of the sovereignty of Iuppiter, the son of the power which was Mars, and the embodiment of the prosperity which was Quirinus. Romulus and Remus were known as the *geminos quirinos,* the twin *quirini.*

MYTHOLOGY OF THE ROMAN REPUBLIC

What was the nature of Roman mythology during the Roman Republic?

The mythology of Republican Rome was an amalgam of indigenous, Latin, Etruscan, and Greek influences. Lenus, for instance, a god from Gaul, became Mars Lenus and Jupiter Dolichenus took his name from an area in Thessaly in Greece. Aphrodite of Mount Eryx in Sicily, recognized by the Romans during the Punic Wars with Cathage in the third century B.C.E., was given a temple on the Capitoline Hill as Venus Erycina.

The Romans were particularly impressed by Greek culture and eventually attempted to make their pantheon syncretic with that of the Olympians.

What were the Roman "equivalents" of the Greek gods?

The list of Greek-Roman deity equivalents is well known to most school children:

Roman God	Greek God
Jupiter	Zeus
Juno	Hera
Neptune	Poseidon
Pluto	Hades
Ceres	Demeter
Minerva	Athene
Apollo	Apollo
Diana	Artemis
Vesta	Hestia
Venus	Aphrodite
Cupid	Eros
Mars	Ares
Vulcan	Hephaistos
Dionysos	Bacchus

But was Roman Republic mythology, therefore, the same as Greek mythology?

No, as noted above, Republican Roman mythology was essentially a mixture of Latin, Etruscan, and Greek concepts. The Romans did admire the Greeks, however, and did try, as noted above, to make their deities syncretic with those of the Greeks. They even applied the Greek idea of divine families, which had not been an aspect of earlier Roman mythology. Thus, Jupiter was seen as the husband of Juno, for example, just as the Greek god Zeus was married to Hera. Earlier, Juno had been more important, a version of Uni-Astarte, a great goddess of the Middle East, ruling Rome as an equal power with Jupiter and Minerva. Still, even in her married state, Juno was more powerful in Rome than Hera was in Greece.

As tempting as it is to simply equate Roman gods with their Greek counterparts, to do so is to oversimplify the particular significance of the Roman deities. Mars, for example, was equated with the Greek god of war, Ares, but in Rome he was a much more important figure than his counterpart in Greece. Mars was a martial god, but more importantly, he was an agrarian one associated with crops. Diana, although she gradually became less important as she became associated with the Greek Artemis, had long been important on the Italic peninsula and remained a more significant figure than her counterpart did in Greece. The goddess Vesta was associated with the rarely mentioned Hestia in Greece, but was a far more important figure as the embodiment of an ancient Indo-European fire cult in connection with the Vestal Virgins. Venus is a good example of how the Roman deities differed from the Greek ones. Like Aphrodite, the Greek goddess of love (Venus's name derives from the Vedic word for desire), Venus attained a stature in Rome more like that of Athene in Greece. As the mother of the primary Roman mythological hero, Aeneas, she was no longer an erotic vamp. Her role was to keep Aeneas focused on his goal of establishing the new city in a Roman founding myth later made popular in Virgil's epic, *The Aeneid*. The more frivolous aspects of love and desire were associated with Venus's son Cupid, the Roman version of Eros. The Roman equivalent to Athene was Minerva, who in the Etruscan-Roman period had been part of a ruling triumvirate that also included Juno and Jupiter.

How did Roman mythology change in the Imperial period?

As the Roman Empire grew in the period following the ascendency of Octavian—Caesar Augustus—so did the scope of Roman mythology. As the Romans continued to absorb rather than to eradicate the mythologies and religions of the people they conquered, by the end of the Imperial period, Roman mythology was quite different from the "Greco-Roman" mythology outlined in most textbooks. The Imperial myth that stands out above all others is an addition to the Roman founding myth of Romulus and Remus. This was the myth of Aeneas, eventually given full narrative form by the poet Virgil.

AENEUS AND VIRGIL'S *AENEID*

Who was Aeneas, and where did his myth originate?

In the eighth century B.C.E. Homer includes Aeneas in the *Iliad* as a cousin of the great Trojan hero Hector and as the son of the goddess Aphrodite (Venus in Rome). In the *Iliad,* Poseidon says Aeneas is destined to be king of Troy, which the Romans would have seen as the New Troy, Rome. Furthermore, we know that as early as the seventh century B.C.E., parts of an Aeneas story were popular in Old Latium. It had long been a tradition that heroes returning from the Trojan War settled in Italy and Sicily, legendary founders of the Greek colonies that developed there. As Rome gained power on the peninsula and as Romans sought to free themselves from what even they saw as the cultural superiority of Greece, Aeneas became popular as a survivor of the Trojan War who fought against the Greeks. According to the legend, Aeneas managed to escape the burning city and accepted the mission of founding the New Troy, Rome.

Who were the major Roman mythographers?

The two writers of the Imperial period who stand out as mythmakers are known to the English-speaking world as Virgil (Vergil) and Ovid.

Who was Virgil?

Publius Vergilius Maro (70 B.C.E.–19 B.C.E.) was born near Mantua in the Roman province of Gaul. After being educated in various places, including Rome, he decided on poetry as a career and became associated with the circle of the Emperor Augustus. Famous for defeating Marc Antony and thereby ending a long civil war, Augustus was also known as Octavian. Virgil's first major work was a series known as the *Eclogues*. The most famous is the fourth *Eclogue,* called the "Messianic Eclogue" by later Christian commentators because it seemed to them to predict the birth of Jesus. In fact, Christians in the Middle Ages would consider Virgil a prophet of sorts because of this eclogue. Virgil's next important work was the *Georgics,* a series of poems on farming and husbandry that was clearly influenced by Hesiod's *Works and Days* and which retells the myth of Orpheus in the Underworld.

A Roman bust of Virgil that was discovered in Naples, Italy.

What is the background of the *Aeneid*?

An epic poem which tells the story of the founding of Rome based on the legend of the hero Aeneas, the *Aeneid* was commissioned by Augustus himself. The emperor wanted a truly Roman epic that would be comparable to the works of Homer but that would express Roman rather than ancient Greek values and traditions. Augustus had a particular interest in the story of Aeneas as a means of justifying his own reign. It was generally believed that Julius Caesar was a direct descendant of Aeneas. Aeneas's son Ascanius was also called Iulus (Julus). Because he was the nephew and adopted son of Julius Caesar, Augustus saw himself also as a descendent of Aeneas and, therefore, as the rightful leader of Rome. The *Aeneid* would be the story of *his* family's founding of Rome.

But Virgil's poetic reputation rests firmly on his greatest work, the *Aeneid,* which the poet was still editing at the time of his death of fever in Brundisium.

How was the *Aeneid* influenced by Homer, and how did it differ from the Greek poet's epics?

The *Aeneid* is made up of what are, in effect, two parts. The first part describes the travels of Aeneas from the fallen city of Troy to Italy, where the New Troy will be founded. This part of the epic owes a great deal to Homer's *Odyssey*. As does Odysseus, Aeneas faces many extraordinary adventures, including sexual temptation and a descent into the Underworld. Also, as in the case of the Greek hero, Aeneas has a specific goal in mind, the arrival at a particular place. The second part of the *Aeneid* reminds us of the *Iliad*. Like the older epic, it is a story of war and heroic struggle.

The *Aeneid*, however, differs from the Greek epics in significant ways. The Greek epics are primary, oral epics—developed gradually out of a collective folklore and given form orally by the probably collective imagination we call Homer. The *Aeneid* is a secondary or literary epic, created according to a fully conscious form by a known literary artist. Even though it makes use of an ancient Roman legend, it is not a folk epic but rather a literary work written for a particular purpose, the celebration of the founding of Rome by a particular family.

Most important, the whole tone of the *Aeneid* differs from that of the Homeric epics. This is primarily because Aeneas is a Roman hero who would have been distinctly out of place in Greece or the Troy from which we are told he flees. Epics were considered educational in Greece. Augustus required an epic that would educate according to Roman ways. If Achilles and Odysseus and Agamemnon and the other Homeric heroes represented individual heroism, the self-based pride called *hubris,* Aeneas represented Roman values of perseverance, piety, honesty, and subservience to a higher cause—Rome itself. There is no room for *hubris* in Aeneas, whereas there is a great deal of room for it in Agamemnon, Achilles, and Odysseus. As the *Aeneid* progresses, Aeneas becomes increasingly an instrument of the fate that has determined that Rome must be founded.

What is the story of the "Odyssean" half of the *Aeneid*?

As in the *Odyssey,* the gods play a large role in determining the progress of the central figure in Virgil's epic. It was Poseidon's grudge against Odysseus that for many years prevented the hero's return to Ithaca. In the *Aeneid* it is Juno, the wife of Jupiter, who attempts to prevent the hero from achieving his goal. Aeneas is a Trojan warrior, the son of Anchises and the goddess Venus, and a cousin of the great Trojan hero Hector. He has managed to escape Troy after its fall to the Greeks and is on his way to Italy when Juno sends a terrible storm that forces him to land in Libya. Upset at Juno's treatment of her son, Venus begs her father Jupiter to end the hero's suffering.

Jupiter promises Venus that her son will eventually get to Italy and that his descendants, Romulus and Remus, will found Rome, the mightiest of all empires. Thus, Virgil employs his story line as a means of celebrating his nation and, by extension, its emperor.

In Libya Aeneas finds his way to Carthage, ruled by Queen Dido. To assure Aeneas's welcome and to protect him from further interference by Juno, Venus sends Cupid to cause Dido to fall in love with Aeneas.

Dido asks Aeneas to tell the story of his journey from Troy. As does Odysseus at the palace of Phaiakia, Aeneas agrees and becomes the teller of his own tale, one that begins at the fall of Troy.

He tells of the wooden horse that led to the Trojan defeat, of how Hercules (Herakles) came to him in a dream to warn him of the disaster, of how he witnessed the killing of King Priam, of how he blamed Helen for his city's destruction until Venus appeared to him saying it was not Helen's fault. Venus urges Aeneas to flee Troy; the gods have other plans for him. Virgil and his readers know that these plans involve the founding of Rome. Aeneas loses his wife, Creusa, who is killed in the confusion, but does manage to escape with his father Anchises and his son Ascanius (Iulus).

After leaving Troy, Aeneas goes to various places before trying to build a new Troy in Crete. A plague undermines his efforts and the gods tell him he must go to Italy. What follows is a ten-year voyage that parallels Odysseus's long trip home at the same time. Using a popular trick of storytellers, Virgil has his hero meet up with some familiar figures, all known to readers of the *Odyssey* or the *Iliad*. On one island he meets Andromache, the wife of the dead Hector, who warns him against the monsters Scylla and Charybdis. On another he meets stranded followers of Ulysses (Odysseus), who tell him how their leader had blinded the Cyclops. Eventually the Cyclops and his brothers appear and Aeneas is forced to flee to Drepanum, where his father Anchises dies.

As Aeneas's story causes Dido to fall even more in love with him, Juno sees an opportunity for preventing the founding of Rome. In fact, Aeneas and Dido make love and Aeneas would have stayed with her had Jupiter not sent Mercury to remind him of his

This 1560 Italian fresco depicts the hero Odysseus caught between a rock and a hard place; that is, the Scylla and Charibdis.

destiny. Always duty-bound and appropriately stoical, Aeneas leaves Dido to continue his journey, as Odysseus, albeit more willingly, had left Calypso and Circe to continue his. In despair, Dido commits suicide.

Reaching Sicily, Aeneas holds funeral games for his father and Anchises appears to him in a dream saying he must visit him in the Underworld. Book VI is the tale of Aeneas's Underworld experience—one that parallels Odysseus's experience in the *Odyssey*. Aeneas's ships come to Cumae, where Aeneas visits the Sibyl at the temple of Apollo. The

117

Sibyl tells him of the war that he will have to fight in Latium before the founding of Rome. Once again Virgil uses mythology to back up Roman "history." The Sibyl also tells him that before he can travel to Dis (the Underworld) he must find a sacred golden bough. This he does and the Sibyl leads him to the Land of the Dead. There, in a poignant scene, he is snubbed by Dido. Shades of fallen Greek warriors flee from him in terror. Aeneas, who had been an insignificant Trojan in the *Iliad,* has become for Virgil the embodiment of the Roman power to come. Most important, Aeneas receives the blessing of his father, and Anchises foresees the glories of Rome under the descendants of Ascanius.

What is the story of the "Iliadic" section of the *Aeneid*?

The last six books of the *Aeneid,* reminiscent of the *Iliad*, contain the story of war, in this case the war that will establish the power of Aeneas and his followers on the Italian peninsula, specifically in Old Latium.

Aeneas and his followers arrive at the mouth of the Tiber. At first they are welcomed by King Latinus of the Latins, and based on a prophecy that his daughter Lavinia will marry a foreigner, Latinus promises her to Aeneas in spite of the fact that she is betrothed to the Latin hero Turnus. In terms of the parallels with the *Iliad*, Turnus becomes the Hector of this story and Aeneas the Achilles. War, instigated by Juno, breaks out. Evander and the Etruscans come to Aeneas's aid and Venus brings Aeneas a beautiful set of armor made by her husband, Vulcan. As in the *Iliad*, the battles are brutal and many are killed.

During a council in heaven Jupiter announces that Aeneas must prevail, but Juno achieves a compromise whereby the Trojans will establish an Italian-based culture in which the Latins will retain their language and customs and will become with Aeneas and his people not Trojans, but a new and powerful civilization.

Finally a truce is called and it is agreed that the dispute should be settled by single combat between Turnus and Aeneas, a combat which Aeneas wins, paving the way for the founding of Rome.

OVID AND THE *METAMORPHOSES*

Who was Ovid?

Publius Ovidius Naso, was born in 43 B.C.E. in Sulmo (Sulmona). Educated in Rome, he traveled widely in Greece, Asia Minor, and Sicily, where he became particularly interested in Greek mythology. In 8 C.E. he was exiled from Rome by Augustus for reasons which remain unclear. He died in 17 or 18 C.E. Ovid is generally considered to be one of the most important if not "the most" important of the Imperial period poets.

What was the *Metamorphoses*?

Ovid's fifteen books of mythological transformations, the *Metamorphoses,* contains some 250 myths and presents an overview of mythological "history" from the creation to the deification of Julius Caesar. As the Caesar myth indicates, the book is clearly a Roman-inspired work, and Ovid's knowledge of mythology included Italic traditions, especially as contained in the works of Virgil. But his primary sources were myths told earlier by the Greeks, especially Homer, Hesiod, Aeschylus, Sophocles, Euripides, and Apollodorus. Ovid's great contribution is the lively, artful, and innovative retelling and embellishing of the old stories. He arranges them in an epic-like continuous form and in so doing maintains a darkly comic and ironic tone rather than a tragic one.

Why do we speak of Greco-Roman mythology?

Because of Ovid's work and his sometimes free use of his sources, we commonly speak of "Greco-Roman" mythology. When we consider the myth of Zeus and Europa told earlier, are we really considering a Greek or Minoan myth or is it a Greco-Roman myth

This 1887 statue of the Roman poet Ovid by Ettore Ferrari is displayed in the city of Constanta, which was Tomis, the city of Ovid's exile.

because the version we learn in school is usually the one told by Ovid? Is the story of Narcissus a Greek myth or has it become in Ovid's hands—now the story of Narcissus and Echo—a Greco-Roman one? The same question could be asked of most of the myths in the *Metamorphoses,* many of which we have already discussed, including, for example, the myth of the Rape of Europa in Book One and versions of the Perseus and Medusa myth and the story of Hades's abduction of Proserpina (Persephone) in Books Four and Five, and the equally familiar stories in Books Seven and Eight of Jason and Medea, Minos, Theseus and the Minotaur, and Daedalus and Icarus. Other myths we know primarily from Ovid are the Hercules (Herakles) myths in Book Nine, and the Orpheus and Eurydice, Hyacinth and Apollo, and Ganymede and Jupiter myths in Book Ten. Books Eleven and Twelve tell of the death of Orpheus, of King Midas with his golden touch, and the Trojan War.

Ovid tells other familiar myths such as those of the great flood; Tiresias; Narcissus and Echo; Tereus, Procne, and Philomela; Pygmalion, Myrrha, Venus and Adonis; Midas; and Orpheus.

What is Ovid's myth of the great flood?

In Book One of the *Metamorphoses* Ovid includes the story of Deucalion and his wife who were spared in the flood the angry Jupiter sent to punish the wickedness of humans.   119

After the flood Deucalion and Pyrrha are instructed by the goddess Themis to create a new population of humans by casting behind them the bones of their Great Mother. Eventually they understand that the Great Mother is earth and her bones are stones. The stones Deucalion casts are transformed into men; those cast by Pyrrha become women.

What is Ovid's myth of Tiresias, and how does he connect it to the Narcissus and Echo myth?

The ancient seer Tiresias, well known from the Greek tragedy of Oedipus, was called upon to settle an argument between Jupiter (Jove) and his wife Juno over whether men or women gain more pleasure from sex. Tiresias was the perfect person to choose because he had once been transformed into a woman as a punishment for disturbing two copulating snakes and had experienced sex in both of his gender embodiments.

When Tiresias took Jupiter's side, agreeing that women had more pleasure in sex, Juno became angry and blinded him. One day the blind seer was asked whether a beautiful baby, Narcissus, would have a long life. His answer, like those of most soothsayers

Tiresias is turned into a woman after hitting two snakes in the midst of copulating, as shown in this circa 1690 engraving.

was ambiguous: "Only if he does not know himself." Girls fell in love with the boy as he grew. One such girl was the beautiful nymph Echo, who had once helped Jupiter trick Juno so he could be with a lover and as a punishment had been deprived by Juno of her ability to speak. She could only "echo" the last few words of the speech of others. Echo loved Narcissus, but the boy haughtily refused her. Making his way to a pond he caught sight of a face in the water, actually, of course, a reflection—that is, echo—of his own face. Falling in love with that unreachable face he withered away and eventually was transferred into a narcissus flower. For our modern psychologically oriented world, he has become a symbol of a dangerous psychological condition that prevents normal interpersonal communication—that is, narcissism.

What is the myth of Tereus and Procne and Philomela?

In Book Six we find the strange tale of Tereus and Procne, which readers of T.S. Eliot's poem, "The Waste Land," will recognize. Tereus, king of Thrace, has married Procne, daughter of the king of Athens. After five years of marriage, Procne begs Tereus for permission to see her much-loved sister Philomela, and Tereus agrees to go to Athens to fetch her. Once he sees her, however, he desires her, brings her back to Thrace, hides her, and rapes her. To prevent the revelation of his crime, he cuts out Philomela's tongue so that she cannot speak. Philomela, however, weaves a depiction of the rape and sends it to her sister. For revenge, Procne serves a special dinner to Tereus. The meal is their son, whom Procne has killed and cooked. After dinner she tells Tereus what she has done and she and Philomela are turned into birds to escape his wrath.

What is the myth of Pygmalion, Myrrha, Venus, and Adonis?

Book Ten contains the myth of Venus and Adonis, Ovid's embellished version of an earlier Greek Adonis myth. Leading up to the Adonis myth is a complex background. A man named Pygmalion is disgusted by the immorality of women, so he decides to make his own perfect woman in the form of a statue. He falls in love with the statue and begs the gods to bring it to life for him. The gods comply and the result is a beautiful son, Cinyras. Cinyras eventually has a daughter, Myrrha, who unfortunately falls in love with him and tricks him into several nights of incestuous love. When her father discovers the trick he tries to kill Myrrha, but the gods turn her into a tree to save her. As she had been pregnant, her child, Adonis, is born from the tree.

This complex tale of uncontrollable love then continues when Cupid inadvertently pierces his mother, Venus, with one of his arrows, causing her to fall desperately in love with Adonis. When Adonis is killed by a wild boar while hunting, Venus mourns her loss. She sprinkles his blood with nectar and a blood-red flower emerges from the earth.

How does Ovid make his poem distinctly Roman at the end?

Books Thirteen through Fifteen are filled with myths of particular importance to Rome. Ovid retells the essential events of Virgil's *Aeneid*, and continues the story with that of the apotheosis of Aeneas. His dead body is adorned by his mother Venus with ambrosia

121

and nectar, and the hero is raised up to heaven as a god, thus establishing the principle of the deity of Roman leaders. Ascanius becomes king and later Romulus, who at his death is also raised to heaven as a god. The final apotheosis is that of Julius Caesar, descendant of Aeneas and Ascanius and surrogate father to Augustus, whose future apotheosis as a god Ovid implies.

THE EMPEROR–GOD
AND FOREIGN BORROWINGS

What was the nature of and purpose of the emperor-god cult?

Many Romans believed that the emperor was guided from within by his divine spirit or *genius*. Furthermore, it was believed that a great ruler would achieve apotheosis or full deification in heaven after his death. Julius Caesar was the only Roman emperor deified during his lifetime. He was recognized as a god by the Roman Senate in 44 B.C.E. Augustus was deified by the senate in 14 C.E. after his death. Thirty-five other emperors were deified in the same way until the Christian era when Theodosius ended the practice in 337 C.E. Some emperors—including Augustus—treated the deification idea ambiguously, but Augustus and others realized its importance in establishing a kind of "divine right" to rulership which, in a multicultured empire, was politically useful.

How did the Empire use the mythologies of the people it conquered?

As noted earlier, instead of stamping out the religious traditions and deities of the people in their empire, the Romans tended to absorb them. This, of course, was true only if the peoples in question recognized the official elements of the Roman religion, including the deification of emperors. Some Jews and Christians, for instance, refused to accept what they saw as "pagan" practices and, as a result, these people suffered persecution.

Examples of "foreign" deities who became popular in Rome were Attis and the Great Mother Cybele from Phrygia in Asia Minor, Isis from Egypt, and Mithras from Persia (Iran).

How were the myths of Cybele and Attis, Mithras, and Isis and Osiris used in Imperial Rome?

Cybele had long been exalted in Rome, and Sir James Frazer describes the Roman spring festival of Cybele's son Attis during the Imperial period. During the festival a pine tree trunk was brought into the sanctuary of Cybele and wrapped in cloth as if it were a corpse. It was then decorated with flowers and an effigy of the dying god Attis was placed on it. Priests of Attis then danced in a frenzy around the tree, splattering the effigy with blood. The effigy was placed in a tomb. In the night, however, the tomb was revealed to be empty.

The mythology of Mithras became particularly important in Roman military circles. Mithrian rituals included communal gatherings, ritual sacrifice, and a shared ritual meal. The Roman emperor Gaius had a temple built to the Egyptian goddess Isis, who was associated with the revival of the dead god Osiris.

All these rituals and imported traditions helped to make Rome fertile ground for the development of the stories and rituals of Christianity.

How did the Christian narrative and tradition fit into and come to dominate the Roman mythological tradition?

In the New Testament Book of Acts (14:11–13), we are told that when Saint Paul and his companion Barnabas were traveling as Christian missionaries performing curings in what was then the

A floor mosaic of the Persian creation god Mithras being born. Mithraism was a popular religion in ancient Rome.

Roman province of Laconia in southern Greece, the people said, "The gods are come down to us in the likeness of men." They called Barnabas Jupiter, and the primary speaker, Paul, they saw as Jupiter's messenger and called him Mercury. The local priest of Jupiter even appeared with the intention of making sacrifices in honor of the two "gods."

As we have seen, myths and rituals of death and resurrection were well known in Rome before the advent of Christianity there, so although early Roman converts to Christianity were persecuted for not accepting Roman religion as a whole, Christianity, with its central emphasis on the death and resurrection of Jesus, believed by Christians to be both human and divine, would not have been a jarring prospect for the Roman mythological mind. In the end, Christianity became more appealing than the myths of other sacrificed man-gods such as Attis and Osiris and Mithras. Perhaps the significant moment leading to the eventual hegemony of the Christian stories and rituals in Rome came in the Battle of the Milvian Bridge in October of 312 C.E., when the emperor Constantine attributed his victory not to Hercules or Mars or Mithras, but to the god of the Christians. By 341, "pagan" sacrifices were prohibited and soon after the temples of the old gods were closed, having been replaced by the churches of the new one.

CELTIC MYTHOLOGY

Who were the Celts?

The origin of Celtic culture is unclear. Some scholars have suggested the existence of a proto-Celtic Indo-European people in central Europe as early as the third millennium B.C.E. Others date the origins to the second millennium B.C.E. More solid claims date the beginnings to the central European Hallstatt culture of the ninth century B.C.E. The aristocratic-warrior La Tène culture of Europe in the fifth century B.C.E. is generally considered to have been Celtic. We know from the Greek writers Herodotus and Hecataeus of Miletus that Celtic peoples, speaking related languages, lived in most areas of central and western Europe by 500 B.C.E. Early in the fourth century B.C.E. Celtic tribes, called Celtae or Galli by the Romans, sacked Rome. Not long after that Celts, now called Galatae, moved as far east as Asia Minor, where they founded the city of Galatia. Meanwhile, to the west, Celtic migrations to Brittany in France and the Islands of Great Britain and Ireland took place between the fifth and first centuries B.C.E. Julius Caesar led Roman wars against the Celts in Britain beginning in about 50 B.C.E. and against Celts in the areas of Germany and France known as Gaul somewhat earlier. Caesar never reached Ireland and achieved only minor success in Wales and Scotland. To this day Celtic people of the Gaelic linguistic branch dominate the populations of Ireland and Scotland, while Brythonic Celts live in Wales, Cornwall, and Brittany. The word *British* is derived from the Breton *Bryttas,* a name for Celts living in the British Isles.

How have we learned about the Celts?

More specific knowledge of the Celts, at least from their own perspective, is limited because the Celts lacked a practical writing system; their stories and traditions were passed down orally. The early written history of the Celts, therefore, comes from writers such as Herodotus and, of course, Julius Caesar, who wrote about the Continental Celts—the Gauls—in his famous history of the Gallic wars. When we speak of Celtic history and

125

mythology today, we speak of the "Continental Celts," about whom we have limited knowledge, mostly from their enemies, and the "Insular Celts" of Ireland and Great Britain whose traditions, especially in Ireland and Wales, were well preserved by later writers with a genuine respect for Celtic culture.

How is Celtic culture and mythology related to the culture and mythology of Greece, Rome, and other civilizations?

Celts are part of the large cultural and linguistic Indo-European family. Their languages are related to those of the Greeks, the Romans, and most of the peoples of Europe (including English), Iran, and the Indian subcontinent. As noted earlier, it is generally thought that all these languages have roots in an ancient Proto-Indo-European language. There are indications, as well, of a deeply inherited common culture that includes such mythological themes as the Great Mother, the sacred twins, a warrior father-god, cattle stealing, an almost ritualistic heroic life pattern, the hero as monster slayer, tripartization, and creative sacrifice.

What was the pantheon of the Continental Celts?

Julius Caesar in his *de Bello Gallico* (Gallic Wars) is our major source for Continental Celtic mythology. In the typical Roman fashion of absorbing foreign or conquered gods, Caesar assumes Roman identity for the Celtic gods. Because figures of a god of arts, crafts, and journeys seemed to be everywhere in Gaul, Caesar considers this god to be the most important Celtic deity. Caesar identifies him as Mercury. He also identifies a god who cures disease as Apollo, a god who rules the heavens as Jupiter, a god of war and healing as Mars, and a goddess of arts and crafts as Minerva. The Gaulish Mercury sometimes had three heads, suggesting the Indo-European tripartization. Caesar's Celtic Apollo was, in fact, a composite of several deities, including the solar gods Belenus and Grannus and a thermal god Bormo who was himself associated with Damona, a figure in the Indo-European tradition of the bovine goddess. Caesar's Minerva was really Sulis or Belisama, probably a Great Goddess representing the land itself.

The Roman writer Lucan tells us that "harsh Teutates, "dread Esus," and Taranis

A bronze Gallic figure of Taranis, a god of the Underworld, holding wheel and thunderbolt.

all were gods demanding sacrifice. Taranis was apparently a god of the Underworld, who, according to Caesar, the Celts saw as their ancestor. Some scholars have seen the Teutates-Esus-Taranis combination as a typical Indo-European tripartization, equivalent to the early Roman Jupiter-Mars-Quirinus triad.

THE INSULAR CELTS: IRELAND AND WALES

Who were the Insular Celts?

As noted above, the so-called Insular Celts were the ones who settled in the islands of Ireland and Great Britain. Their descendants inhabit primarily Ireland, Wales, Cornwall, and Scotland. Two major branches of insular mythology have come down to us: the mythology of Ireland and the mythology of Wales.

What are our sources for Irish-Celtic mythology?

Druidic bards, or *filid* (*filidh, fili*), passed on the myths of the Celts from generation to generation in Ireland until well into the age of Christian dominance beginning in the sixth century C.E. The monks who wrote down the old tales at least had a reasonably accurate source from which to work, as the oral tradition was strong and practiced with great care. Many of these early writings, however, were destroyed and only recovered in part; they are included in the compilations of the eleventh and twelfth centuries such as *The Book of the Dun Cow, The Book of Leinster,* and most important, *The Book of Invasions.* Naturally the monks who did the compilations interjected something of their own faith into the old myths. In one version of the creation of Ireland, for instance, it was said that it was Cesair, the granddaughter of Noah, who, with her father, "discovered" Ireland after seven years in an ark during the great flood. Still, there was a sufficient nationalistic and ethnic interest in Ireland to assure at least a reasonable transmission of the old myths, especially since Ireland was not greatly affected by the Roman invasion of Great Britain.

Was there an Irish-Celtic creation myth?

If there was a creation myth, it has been lost. There is the Cesair myth, and there is also the story contained in the *Leabhar Gabhāla* (*The Book of Invasions*), which is more a founding myth of Ireland than a creation myth as such. It features the poet-prophet Amairgen.

Who was Amairgen?

In Irish mythology Amairgen was the Druid *filid* who, as did the great Indian man-god Krishna, contained his world within himself. It can be said that at least one origin myth of Celtic Ireland involves this poet-warrior-prophet's "singing" of his inner self into existence when he sets foot in the land that will be Ireland. This song of Amairgen occurs in *The Book of Invasions.*

127

What is *The Book of Invasions*?

The *Leabhar Gabhála* (*The Book of Invasions*) is to Irish mythology what the *Aeneid* is to Roman mythology or the Bible to Hebrew mythology. In a series of segments, it relates the "history" of the island that will become Ireland. A number of landings there, beginning with Noah's granddaughter and ending with the Celtic Milesians, is the mythological story of the founding of a culture and eventually a nation. The monks who compiled the work long after the periods depicted worked from various oral and written sources and colored the events with their own religious perspective, beginning with the biblical story of the creation and an Exodus-like story of the wanderings of the early Gaels, descendants of one of the builders of the Tower of Babel. These Gaels eventually made their way to Iberia (Spain).

What were the earliest Invasions?

The first "invasion" of Ireland was that of Cesair, the granddaughter of Noah, who, with all her companions, except for her husband Fintan, perished. Fintan turned himself into a salmon to avoid death in the flood and survived into the Christian era as a primary source of knowledge of the past.

Three hundred years later came Partholón, who, with his people, developed social customs that would become part of Irish tradition. The Partholonians also cleared land and fought off the simultaneously arriving Fomorians, a demonic group of one-legged, one-armed beings from under the sea. Unfortunately, the Partholonians all died of a plague. They were quickly followed by the arrival of Nemed and his four chieftans, who also cleared land and established local customs and crafts. After a long war with the Fomorians and the death of Nemed, the Nemedians came under cruel Fomorian rule. Eventually they rebelled, and after a flood, which destroyed most of both populations, the remaining few left for other lands.

Who were the Firbolg?

One story has it that they were so called because they had been made to carry bags of earth during their enslavement. The Firbolg are credited with the division of the island into three, and then five, provinces or *coiceds* and establishing a sacred kingship based on the relationship between the king's integrity and the land's fertility. The provinces would become Ulster in the north, Connaught in the west, Munster in the south, Leinster in the east, and Tara, the place of the king, in the center.

A golden age of the Firbolg lasted only thirty-seven years before the arrival of the Tuatha de Danann, a group of "invaders" who are the pre-Celtic equivalent of a pantheon of Irish mythology.

Some of the Nemedians made their way to Greece, where they were enslaved. After many years, some rebelled and returned to Ireland as the Firbolg, or "bag men."

THE TUATHA DE DANANN

Who were the Tuatha de Danann?

There are indications that the Tuatha de Danann, although technically mortal in *The Book of Invasions*, were in pre-Celtic Ireland considered to be divine. Their name, meaning "People of Danu" indicates a connection with Danu or Ana, a version of an ancient Indo-European mother goddess. We know little about Danu, but assume she would have been primarily a fertility goddess associated with the general well-being of Ireland. *Da Chich Annan* ("Paps of Ana") is the common name of two hills in County Kerry near Killarney.

Descendants of the Nemidians, the Tuatha de Danann, had achieved at least semi-divine status by the time they reached Ireland in *The Book of Invasions*. Having apparently learned druidic magic and achieved extraordinary powers, they arrived in Ireland in a cloud and landed on a mountain in Connaught. The writer of *Invasions* says it was not known whether they were "of heaven or of earth."

Several of the Tuatha had cognates in the pantheon of the Continental Celts. The Irish Lugh was a form of Caesar's Mercury, containing within himself the Indo-European tripartite powers of the arts, of warfare, and of priestliness. Caesar's Apollo here is Aonghus, the trickster-like son of the All-Father Dagda, or simply "the Dagda," the supreme druid, the "Good God." The continental Minerva is Dagda's daughter Brigid, a healer who would later be assimilated as a Christian vestal-virgin-like saint. The Vulcan of Romano-Gaul is Goibhniu in Ireland. The Underworld god, Dis Pater in Gaul, is the mysterious Donn in Ireland. Ogma is a Hercules figure. An important Tuatha

The Irish god Lugh, depicted in this engraving based on a bas-relief found in Paris, was a form of Caesar's Mercury, containing within himself the Indo-European tripartite powers of the arts, of warfare, and of priestliness.

129

healer is the powerful Dian Cecht, who plays a significant role in what are known as the Battles of Mag Tuired.

What were the Battles of Mag Tuired?

The Tuatha established their court at Tara, with Nuada as king. In the first battle of Mag Tuired fought against the Firbolg, Nuada lost an arm and, now imperfect, could no longer serve as king. Dian Cecht replaced Nuada's lost arm with a silver one. Dian Cecht's son Miach would later replace the silver one with a new real one.

In a second battle of Mag Tuired, the Tuatha, led by the repaired Nuada and later by Lugh, fought the Fomorians, who had returned to Ireland. In a terrible struggle, King Nuada and his warrior queen Macha were killed by the monstrous one-eyed Fomorian Balar, whose glance could kill armies. When Lugh pierced the eye with a slingshot, the eye was turned around so that its powers were turned on the Fomorians, destroying them once and for all.

Who were the final Invaders of *The Book of Invasions*?

The final pre-Christian invasion of Ireland was that of the Gaels, the Celts who had long ago fled Ireland for Spain and now returned as the Milesians, the "Sons of Mil," that is, Mil of Spain. A leader of this invasion was the druidic poet-prophet and warrior Amairgen, who uses his powers to push aside the clouds created by the Tuatha to hinder their arrival. Amairgen contains all the elements of creation within his druidic self. "The sea's wind am I," he sings, and with his song Celtic Ireland is born. Moving

---

What books contain the hero stories?

The heroic narratives are contained in several works written by Christian monks in the eleventh and twelfth centuries, based on material from as early as the eighth century C.E. The *Lebor na hUidre* (Book of the Dun Cow) contains part of the *Tain Bo Cuailnge* (The Cattle Raid of Cooley), the most famous of the narratives which make up what is called the Ulster Cycle, or the Red Branch Cycle. Other important works are the *Lebor Laignech* (The Book of Leinster), the so-called Rawlinson manuscript, and several fourth- and fifth-century books, including most importantly the *Leabhar Buide Leacain* (The Yellow Book of Lecan), which contains most of the Ulster Cycle.

A second great heroic cycle is the Fenian, or Ossianic, Cycle, which contains heroic tales from various works, some as early as the eighth century.

Other heroic cycles are the Mythological Cycle containing the stories of the Tuatha de Danann discussed above, and the Historical Cycle, which is made up of the stories of the early Irish kings.

toward Tara, the Milesians meet the triune queens, Banba, Fotla, and Eriu, whose names will be associated with Ireland forever. The three kings at Tara work out a truce with the Milesians. The Milesians will retreat to the sea and "invade" again. The Tuatha send a powerful wind to keep the Milesians at sea, but Amairgen's power is stronger, and the wind is brushed aside, leaving the Milesians free to land and to defeat the Tuatha. In the peace agreement, the Milesians take control of the world above ground and the Tuatha are confined to the land below. The Tuatha remain in *sidh*, underground mounds, and have been referred to ever since as the *sidh*, the "fairies," or "Little People."

Ireland was now ready for the deeds of the early kings and for the heroic events that characterize the mythological sagas of the country.

CUCHULAINN AND THE *TAIN*

Who were the primary Irish mythic heroes?

The primary figure in the Ulster Cycle is Cuchulainn. In the Fenian Cycle it is Fionn mac Cumhail. These heroes interact with several other heroes and heroines in the *Tain Bo Cuailnge* and other works of the Ulster Cycle and in the many fragments which make up the story of Fionn.

What was the *Tain Bo Cuailnge*?

The *Tain Bo Cuailnge* (The Cattle Raid of Cooley) is an epic-like prose work which tells the tale of a war between the province of Connaught, led by Queen Medb and her husband Ailill, and the province of Ulster, represented by the young hero Cuchulainn. The war is the result of Queen Medb's desire to steal the great stud bull of Ulster, Donn Cuailnge, in order to achieve equality with her husband, who owns another great bull, Finnbhenach. In her war, Medb is assisted by Fergus mac Roich, an Ulsterman who has turned against the Ulster king, Conchobar.

In a series of contacts between gods and humans, we are reminded of the divine interference in Homer's war epic, the *Iliad*. When a plague undermines the army of Ulster, it is perhaps caused by the goddess Macha. When the goddess Morrigan, in the form of a beautiful woman, offers to help him, Cuchulainn refuses her, much as Gilgamesh had refused Inanna in the Sumerian epic. Cuchulainn pays for his insult in many ways throughout his life.

The only hope for the ill Ulster forces is the seventeen-year-old Cuchulainn, who fights alone aided by his charioteer Laeg. As hard as he fights, Cuchulainn, who reaches a truce of sorts with Fergus, his foster father, cannot prevent Medb's capturing of Donn Cuailnge. Once again, divine interference is crucial. The god Lugh, revealing himself as Cuchulainn's true father, puts his son to sleep for three days so that his wounds can

131

heal. When Cuchulainn awakens, he becomes a wild monster-like warrior who does serious damage to the Connaught army. Finally, in a series of single combats, Cuchulainn is forced to kill his foster brother Ferdiad. In a parallel battle, the bull of Ulster, Donn Cuailnge, fights and kills the bull of Connaught, Finnbhenach. Donn Cuailnge then roams around Ireland before returning home to die.

What is the rest of the story of Cuchulainn?

Said to have lived in the first century B.C.E., Cuchulainn's life is described in many versions beginning as early as the eighth century C.E. Cuchulainn is what Joseph Campbell called a monomythic hero. Like so many heroes, his life begins miraculously, his childhood reveals extraordinary powers, and his life is a quest marked by battles, monsters, femmes fatales, and a descent into the Underworld.

King Conchobar's sister Dechtire is visited by the sun god Lugh in the form of a fly. Dechtire swallows the fly and the result is the birth of a boy whom Dechtire names Sentata. From the moment of his birth, Sentata is possessed of great power and talents. As a seven-year–old he fights off 150 attackers who hope to overpower the court of Conchobar. At the age of twelve he kills the great watchdog belonging to the smith, Culann, and as a punishment replaces the dog as the smith's protector, changing his name to Cuchulainn (Culann's Hound).

Cuchulainn falls in love with the beautiful Emer, and to win her hand agrees to undergo a series of trials that include confronting monsters and even, as did Odysseus and Aeneas, descending into the Underworld.

The primary figure in the Ulster Cycle is Cuchulainn, depicted here in a 1905 illustration carrying Ferdiad, the foster brother he has mortally wounded.

Cuchulainn's most famous feat is victory in the war against Queen Medb, described in the *Tain Bo Cuailnge,* during which he acquires the enmity of the goddess Morrigan by rejecting her advances when she approaches him in her form as a beautiful *femme fatale.*

Cuchulainn's life is not without tragedy. Aside from having to fight against his foster father and foster brother, he kills his son Conla as a result of mistaken identity, reminding us of Herakles's killing of his wife, and finally he is not able to escape the vengeful power of Morrigan and her allies. With the approval of Morrigan, the young kings of Munster and Leinster, whose fathers Cuchulainn has killed in battle, trap him near the Pillar of Stone. Cuchulainn has arrived at the spot with his horse, Battle Gray, and his charioteer,

Laeg. At the stone he is taunted by three bards, who threaten to defame him. He kills the bards, but the two young kings appear and kill Battle Gray and Leig and wound Cuchulainn. Cuchulainn ties himself to the Pillar of Stone so he can die standing. Morrigan, as a crow, perches defiantly on the hero's shoulder, as Lughaid of Munster cuts off his head. Cuchulainn's falling sword severs the offending arm of Lughaid.

FIONN AND THE FENIAN CYCLE

What is the story of Fionn?

Fionn mac Cumhail (Finn Mac Cool) was the central figure of the Fenian Cycle, sometimes called the Ossianic Cycle after Fionn's son Oisin. Fionn was leader of the Fianna or Fenians, said to have been bodyguards of the Irish high king beginning from c. 300 B.C.E. Some have suggested that the tradition of the Fenians influenced the myths of King Arthur and the fellowship of the Round Table. The source material for the Fenian tales probably dates back to the third century C.E. , based on the tellings of the filidh. But the tales as we know them were written down in the twelfth-century *Acallamh na Senorach* ("The Colloquy of the Ancients") by Christian monks, the influence of whose religion is apparent in the myths. The narrator of the *Acallamh*, Cailte, or sometimes Oisin (thus, Ossianic Cycle), for instance, recounts the Fenian adventures to Saint Patrick.

What is the story of Saint Patrick?

Saint Patrick is said to have arrived in Ireland in 432 C.E. There are many myths associated with Patrick. Most famously, he rid Ireland of snakes. According to one myth, when the infant Patrick was brought to the blind Gornias to be baptized, there was no water to be had, so the old man used the child's hand to make the sign of the cross over the ground and water sprang up. And at the same time Gornias was cured of his blindness. Another myth tells how when Patrick arrived in Ireland at the Feast of Beltene to claim Ireland for his god he did something similar to what Amairgen and the Milesians had done when they proclaimed a Celtic Ireland during the same feast in ancient times. Beltene was the druidic feast of purifying fire.

When Patrick arrived at Tara he set a huge bonfire, thus upstaging the druidic tradition for his own religion. As the Tuatha powers had overcome the Firbolg and Fomorians, and as Amairgen's powers had supplanted those of the Tuatha, the spiritual fire of the Christian "Holy Spirit," the source of Patrick's "magic," would take control of the soul of Ireland.

Named Demna by his druidic parents, the boy hero was so fair that he was re-named Fionn. The druid Finegas gave Fionn the Salmon of Knowledge to cook. The boy burned a finger in the process and, naturally enough, sucked on it to relieve the pain. In so doing he acquired the Salmon's knowledge. In much the same way the Norse hero Sigurd gained certain powers when he sucked on a finger burned while roasting a dragon's heart.

After a series of adventures, Fionn saved the high king, Cormac Mac Art, and was made leader of the Fianna. In a battle known as the Battle of Fionn's Strand, Fionn overcame the mysterious "King of the World." By the goddess Sadb, he fathered Oisin. It seems that Fionn had seen a fawn while hunting and that at night the fawn had become, for a brief time, human and female and had become Fionn's lover. It was the "Dark Druid" who had turned Sadb into a fawn. Later, while looking for Sadb near Ben Bulben, Fionn found a naked fawn boy; this was his son Oisin.

Oisin, too, became a great hero, even taking a journey into the Underworld, where he stayed for three hundred years. It is upon his return that he tells the Fenian tales to Saint Patrick.

It is thought that one day Fionn will return to save Ireland, a "once and future king," like King Arthur.

A stained glass window at the Church of Our Lady, Star of the Sea, and St. Patrick in Goleen, Ireland, pays homage to St. Patrick.

WELSH MYTHOLOGY

Who are the Celts of Wales?

The Welsh are the people of the nation of Wales in the United Kingdom. The Welsh language is a Brythonic (as opposed to Gaelic) Celtic language that developed from the Old British language of the Britons who lived in Wales. By the eleventh century C.E. the Brythonic Celtic language had split into Welsh, Cornish (the language of Cornwall), and Breton (the language of Brittany in France). The Welsh produced a complex mythology that in many ways parallels that of Gaelic Ireland but that has a distinctive character, as seen in in the many Welsh tales of King Arthur.

What are our sources for Welsh mythology?

The Celtic mythology of Wales has been more corrupted by the dominant presence of non-Celtic people (e.g., Romans, Saxons, English) than the Celtic mythology of the more isolated island of Ireland. Two

A monument to Taliesin stands on the shore of Llyn Geirionydd, where legend says the poet-prophet was born.

Latin texts concerned primarily with the Arthurian stories are the early ninth-century *Historia Brittonum* by Nennius and the twelfth-century *Historia Regum Britanniae* by Geoffrey of Monmouth. And there are oral sources, including, traditionally, poems attributed to the almost certainly mythic sixth-century poet-prophet Taliesin, the Welsh equivalent of the Irish Amairgen. The major source for Welsh mythology, however, is a medieval collection of tales known to us as the *Mabinogion* (*Mabinogi*).

Who was Taliesin?

Taliesin (Shining Brow) was the poet-prophet of ancient Wales. According to the *Book of Taliesin*, he was said to have been miraculously conceived by the magician Ceridwen. Gwion Bach, a servant of Ceridwen disguised himself as a grain of wheat and was swallowed by the magician, who soon gave birth to Taliesin. This story cannot help but remind us of the conception of Cuchulainn in Ireland. Like Sigurd, Moses, and other heroes, the baby Taliesin was abandoned—left to float away in a leather bag. He was rescued and adopted by the youth, Elffin. At King Arthur's court, Taliesin would demonstrate his poetic powers by reducing the sounds of the king's bards to "Blerwm, blerwm." His song was powerful enough to liberate Elffin, who had been imprisoned by Arthur.

What was the *Mabinogion*?

The *Mabinogion* comes to us from two fourteenth-century manuscripts, the *White Book of Rhydderch* and the *Red Book of Hergest*. Based on oral narratives, these books took literary form in the eleventh and twelfth centuries. The *Mabinogion* is made up of sections known as the "Four Branches," followed by four "Independent Native Tales" that include the earliest known Welsh Arthurian tale, "Culhwch and Olwen," and by three later Arthurian romances.

THE WELSH PANTHEON

What was the ancient Welsh pantheon revealed in the *Mabinogion*?

The ancient deities of Wales are known as the Family of Don. Don is the earth goddess equivalent of the Irish Danu, from whom the Tuatha de Danann take their name. Don/Danu's roots probably reach back to the Indian Danu.

Don was the daughter of Mathonwy and the sister of Math. Her husband is sometimes believed to be the god of death, Beli. Their children include Gilfaethwy, Gwydion the storyteller, Aranrhod the dawn goddess, Lludd, Gofannon, and Penarddun. Penarddun married Llyr, whose name is said by some to be the source for King Lear's name. Llyr was the father of Bran and Branwen, who are important figures in the "Second Branch" of the *Mabinogion*. Many stories of the Family of Don are also featured in the "Fourth Branch."

What is the story of Bran and Branwen?

Llyr's first wife was Iweriadd, or "Ireland," the mother of the gigantic Bran the blessed, King of Britain and brother to Branwen, the goddess of love. According to others, it was Llyr's wife Penarddun, the daughter of the mother goddess Don, who was Bran and Branwen's mother.

According to the tale, King Matholwych of Ireland arrived in Harlech in Wales to marry Branwen. Efnisien, the strife bringer, angry at not having been consulted about the marriage, does harm to the Irish king's horses, leading Bran to calm his angry brother-in-law by giving him a magic cauldron, the famous Cauldron of Plenty, which has the power to bring the wounded back to life.

In Ireland Branwen gives birth to Gwern, an heir who is to bring lasting peace between Bran and Matholwych, that is, between Wales and Ireland. But because of the evil deeds of Efnisien at the marriage in Wales, Branwen is harshly treated by her husband, being forced to work like a servant in the court kitchens and to bear the blows of the court butcher. Branwen teaches speech to a bird, however, and the bird flies off to Wales with a message to Bran describing his sister's treatment. Furious, Bran invades Ireland, using his gigantic body to make a bridge between the

Sculptor Ivor Robert-Jones created this sculpture showing the deceased hero Gwern being carried on horseback by his uncle, Bendigeidfran.

lands so that his army can easily cross the sea. Matholwych agrees to peace, but Efnisien undermines the truce by throwing Gwern into a fire. In the battle that follows, Efnisien causes the destruction of the magic cauldron that had made possible the endless resuscitation of fallen Irish warriors. Bran is badly wounded, however, and instructs his followers to decapitate him and to take his head back to Britain. On the way home, Bran's head continues talking and even eating. The war leaves Ireland with only five pregnant women alive to repopulate the island. Only a few Welsh, including Branwen and Taliesin, survive to return to Britain. Branwen dies of a broken heart over the war she blames herself for starting. Welsh deities, as did the Irish ones, could die.

What is the story of Blodeuwedd and Lleu?

The married Blodeuwedd has an affair with Gronw Pebyr of Penllyn, and the lovers decide to kill Lleu. Like Delilah in the Bible and other femmes fatales, Blodeuwedd talks her husband into revealing the fact that he can never be killed in a house, on a horse, or on foot outdoors. In fact, he can only be killed only by a special spear. One day when Lleu is taking a bath, he is tricked into standing with one foot on the tub and the other on a goat, a position which negates the restrictions on his death and makes him vulnerable to Gronw's special sword. In death he soars off as an eagle, but Gwydion finds him and brings him back to human life. Lleu then returns, kills Gronw, and his guilty wife is turned into an owl.

What is the "Fourth Branch" story of Math and his family and the birth of Lleu?

Math of Gwynedd, son of Mathonwy, is a god of wealth. He has a strange fixation, requiring that when he is not at war his feet must rest on the lap of a virgin. His nephews Gwydion and Gilfaethwy trick Math in order that Gilfaethwy might have the virgin used by Math. When the ruse is discovered and the virgin found no longer to be a virgin, Math turns his nephews into boars for three years. Gwydion tries to substitute his sister Aranrhod for the stolen footstool maiden, but she gives birth to a boy child, the sea god Dylan, as she steps over Math's sword during her virginity test, making her ineligible to be Math's footstool. And soon after that, an object emerges from her that Gwydion hides away. This is, in

The lovers Blodeuwedd and Gronw are lovers in a Celtic myth about the murder of Lleu, Blodewedd's husband. As with the story of Samson and Delilah, the murder must be conducted using trickery.

fact, Lleu (a cognate for the Irish Lugh), the product of an incestuous relationship between Aranrhod and her brother Gwydion. Ashamed, Aranrhod refuses to name the child. But when Gwydion and the child come to the king's court as shoemakers, Aranrhod inadvertently names her son by exclaiming over his brightness and skill. Thus, he becomes Lleu Llawgyffes ("Fair-haired and skillful of hand"). When Aranrhod declares that the boy will never bear arms not given to him by her, Gwydion uses his magic again to overcome that oath. Math and Gwydion also undermine Aranrhod's determination that Lleu must never marry into a race "now on earth," by creating a wife, Blodeuwedd ("Flower") for him from the blossoms of three plants.

HEROES OF WALES

Who were the Welsh-Celtic heroes?

There are many Welsh heroes featured in the *Mabinogion*. These include, for instance, Pwyll and Pryderi in the "First Branch" and the "Third Branch," and the most famous of all Welsh heroes, King Arthur. Another hero, who is actually a product of Celtic Cornwall, is Tristan, whose name is of Welsh origin.

What is the story of Pwyll?

Pwyll ("Good Judgment"), lord of Dyfed, is out hunting one day when he insults another hunter who is, in fact, King Arawn of the "Otherworld" (Annwn), the land of rebirth from which on October 31/November 1 (Christian All Saints and All Souls Days and later Halloween—derived from All Hallows' Eve, Hallows being "saints") souls can return to the world and take vengeance on offenders. Pwyll drives off Arawn's hounds and substitutes one of his own in pursuit of a stag. Furious, Arawn demands that Pwyll wear his—Arawn's—face for a year and live as king in Annwn for that time. He is to sleep in the Otherworld king's bed, but must promise not to make love with his wife.

When the punishment period is over, Pwyll returns to Dyfed and holds a great feast. Soon after he takes his place on his throne, a beautiful woman rides by on a white horse and Pwyll pursues her, begging her to stop. After a fruitless chase of the woman, Pwyll begs her to stop, which she does. The woman is the goddess Rhiannon, daughter of Arawn; she offers herself as Pwyll's wife. Rhiannon has possible cognates in the Irish goddesses Edain Echraide ("horse riding") and Macha, who outran horses, and in the Continental Celtic horse goddess, Epona. All these figures have roots in earlier Indo-European horse-based myths and rituals. During their wedding feast Pwyll loses his wife to Gwawl ("light") as a result of a foolish granting of a wish. He wins her back, however, at Rhiannon and Gwawl's wedding, by tricking his rival into entering a magic bag given to him by Rhiannon.

What is the story of Pryderi?

Rhiannon gives birth to a boy, Pryderi, and the child is abducted when his care-taking women fall asleep. To save themselves from punishment, the women smear animal blood on Rhi-

Artist Edmund Leighton portrayed the ill-fated Tristan and Iseult in his 1902 painting.

annon so that it will appear to Pwyll that she has killed their son. Pwyll is deceived by this cruel act and punishes Rhiannon harshly. It is not until years later when the child is discovered to be alive and is returned to his parents that Rhiannon is redeemed. The child has been named Gwri, or "Golden Hair," by the people who had found him as a baby and had cared for him. Finally relieved of her worry, Rhiannon renames the child Pryderi ("Care").

In the "Third Branch" of the *Mabinogion,* Pryderi has married Cigfa and has succeeded Pwyll as king of Dyfed. Rhiannon has married Manawydan, a son of Llyr. As is the Irish Manannan mac Lir, Manawydan is associated with rebirth. During a feast at Arbeth, the two couples are sitting in a cloud of mist on the magic throne mound. There is a clap of thunder before the mist clears and the couples find themselves in a totally deserted Dyfed. After two years of wandering, they make their way to Lloegyr (England), where Pryderi and Manawydan take work as saddlers, shoemakers, and shieldmakers.

When the four finally return to Arbeth, Pryderi disregards the warnings of Manawydan and allows himself to be drawn by a boar into a mysterious castle that has a fountain in which a golden bowl sits on a marble slab. Some have considered this to be

139

the Cauldron of Plenty—the pot which supplies endless food—or even the Holy Grail sought by King Arthur's knights. Pryderi loses speech and cannot release his hands when he grasps the cauldron. Rhiannon tries to rescue her son, but she, too, loses speech and is stuck to the cauldron. Mother and son disappear into a mist.

The perpetrator of these enchantments and the abduction of the hero and his mother is Llwyd, an associate or friend of the evil Gwawl. Manawydan and Pryderi's wife Cigfa return to England as shoemakers, but eventually return to Arbeth to grow corn. When mice are discovered carrying the corn away, Manawydan captures the slowest of them and prepares to hang it on the throne mound, when a bishop turns up and reveals that the mouse is actually his wife. The bishop also reveals that he is actually Llwyd, and in return for his wife he puts an end to the terrible curses and spells that had enchanted Pryderi and his family.

What is the story of Tristan and Iseult?

The first Celtic version of the story of these star-crossed lovers is in a Welsh manuscript of the sixteenth century. There is also a later Cornish version and many continental versions. Tristan, a nephew of King Mark of Cornwall, is a warrior, poet, musician, and storyteller. He is assigned the task of traveling to Ireland to bring Mark's bride-to-be, Iseult (Isolde), to Cornwall. On the way to Cornwall, the couple swallow a magic potion that causes them to fall in love with each other. Their love affair is discovered, causing their banishment and tragic death.

KING ARTHUR

Who was King Arthur?

King Arthur is a legendary figure. No one knows for sure who or what he really was. Tradition has it that he was a Celtic British warrior, and perhaps king, who in the early sixth century fought heroically against the Saxons, who eventually drove the Celtic peoples away from England and into Wales and Cornwall. In about 820 C.E. the Welsh monk Nennius, in his *Historia Brittonum,* mentions several important battles led by Arthur. Another cleric, Geoffrey of Monmouth, who may or may not have been Welsh, developed the Arthurian legend in his *Historia Regum Britanniae* (History of the Kings of Britain), written in the 1130s C.E., claiming that his information was based on much earlier Celtic manuscripts. It was not until later in the twelfth century that French writers Maistre Wace and, especially, Chrétien de Troyes added the elements of chivalry and courtly love that we now associate with Arthur's court, the legendary Camelot. Sir Thomas Malory gave us much of the Arthurian legend in the eight stories of his *Le Morte d'Arthur*, written in 1470 and published in 1485. The Arthurian legend as we commonly know it is a compounding of these many sources. The story includes, as it does for many archetypal heroes, an unusual conception, a demonstration of power early in his life, an important quest, a tragic betrayal and death, and a promise of return.

What is the story of King Arthur's birth?

Uther Pendragon, King of Britain, was busy fighting the Saxons with his able general, the Duke of Cornwall, when he fell in love with the duke's wife, Igraine. To keep his wife away from the king, the duke took her away to his castle at Tintagel on the Cornish coast. This did not stop Uther, who enlisted the help of the magician, Merlin. While the duke was away fighting the Saxons, Merlin used his magic to make Uther look like Igraine's husband. In this disguise, the king was able to enter both the castle and Igraine's bed. That very night the Duke of Cornwall was killed in battle, and Uther and Igraine married before the queen gave birth to Arthur, the product of their first night together. When Uther, to test Igraine, asked her who the child's father was, Igraine confessed that she had slept with a stranger who looked exactly like her husband. Uther revealed that he was that stranger. Merlin predicted that Arthur was so special a child that he must be protected by being placed in a household other than the king's. It was for this reason that Arthur spent his childhood in the castle of Sir Ector.

How did the youthful Arthur reveal his power and importance?

When Uther Pendragon died, the kingdom was threatened by disorder. To prevent chaos, Merlin arranged a meeting of nobles at Canterbury to decide who should be king. A sword suddenly appeared in a churchyard stone. On the stone was a statement: "Whoever pulls out this sword is the lawfully born king of Britain." Many knights tried and failed to remove the sword. When Sir Ector was travelling the scene with his son, Sir Kay, with Arthur acting as Kay's squire, Sir Kay asked Arthur to return to their camp to bring him a new sword. Arthur returned without having found the sword, but noticed the sword in the rock and easily pulled it out and took it to Kay. Kay recognized the sword and decided to claim it and the throne, but his father demanded that he replace it in the rock and remove it as proof of his worthiness. Kay failed in his attempt to remove the sword and admitted what he had done. After Arthur again removed the sword from the rock and Merlin revealed his parentage, he was accepted as king.

What quest was central to the Arthurian saga?

The central quest in the Arthurian tales is the search for the Holy Grail, the cup said to have been used by Jesus at the Last Supper and by Joseph of Arimathea to catch the blood of Jesus as he hung on the cross. The tradition was that Joseph, who had provided a tomb for Jesus, had come to Britain with the Grail.

The Grail quest was undertaken in Arthur's name by knights of the king's court, the Round Table fellowship. In the *Later Arthurian Tales* of the *Mabinogion,* for instance, Peredur, Son of Efrawg, the Welsh version of the hero Percival (Parsifal), searches for the Grail. In other versions of the Arthurian romance, questers include Gawain and Galahad. The heroes are always tested during their quests. They face such figures as the Fisher King, the wounded guardian of the Grail, whose wound affects the fertility of the land he rules. If the questing hero does not ask him certain questions, he and his land

A fifteenth-century French manuscript illuminated with a depiction of King Arthur and the Round Table knights.

may be doomed to infertility, and the Grail may not be fully achieved. Or the hero—even Arthur himself—can be tested by a *femme fatale* such as Arthur's half-sister Morgan Le Fay.

How does Arthur's reign end?

Arthur was betrayed by Sir Lancelot, who had a love affair with the king's wife, Guinevere, causing a terrible struggle between Arthur and his old associate, Lancelot. Arthur was said to have been betrayed and killed by his son (or nephew) Mordred (Modred) in the war. But another tradition has it that he was not killed but was taken away by fairy queens, perhaps one of them his half-sister Morgan Le Fay, to the mysterious island of Avalon—the Isle of Women in the old Celtic tradition—from which, one day, he would return to Britain to rule.

How was the Arthurian legend associated with the coming of Christianity?

The Arthurian legend was inevitably associated with the coming of Christianity to Great Britain because of the story of Joseph of Arimathea. According to tradition, Joseph brought to Britain not only the Holy Grail but some of the thorns used to make a mock crown for Jesus before the crucifixion. It is believed by many that the thorn tree still growing in the abbey grounds at Glastonbury, where a grave stone marks what is said to be King Arthur's grave, are from the thorns brought by Joseph.

142

NORSE MYTHOLOGY

Who were the Norse people?

The term *Norse* is commonly applied to pre-Christian northern Germanic peoples living in Scandinavia during the so-called Viking Age. Old Norse gradually developed into the North Germanic languages, including Icelandic, Danish, Norwegian, and Swedish. Bronze Age rock carvings in Scandinavia suggest a Bronze Age origin for the Norse people.

Who were the Vikings?

Vikingr (Viking) is an Old Norse term that refers to a seafaring warrior who goes on some sort of expedition abroad. The word is commonly used to refer to Norsemen of the eighth to the mid-eleventh centuries who traded with, invaded, and/or explored places outside their own territories. Vikings conquered much of the British Isles, expanded their activities to include parts of Spain and southern France, and even found their way to Kiev, Constantinople, and Baghdad, and probably to pre-Columbian North America.

SNORRI AND THE *EDDAS*

Who were the Norse myth-makers?

We do not know who the original Norse myth-makers were. We do know that the Danish historian Saxo Grammaticus (1150–1220 C.E.) was a major redactor of Germanic myths, including the Norse myths. The composers of the thirteenth-century *Volsung Saga* provide us with much of the heroic material of Norse mythology—the story of Sigurd, for example. But the most important redactor of Norse mythology was undoubtedly Snorri Sturluson.

Who was Snorri Sturluson?

Snorri Sturluson (1179–1241 C.E.) was an Icelandic chieftain, landowner, historian, politician, and poet. Brought up in a family steeped in Icelandic traditions and lore, he became an expert on ancient poetry, known as skaldic verse (*skalds* were bards, the *filidh* of the north), and on Norse myths. This expertise is fully revealed in his masterful work, the *Prose Edda*, based on an older work, the *Poetic Edda*. Snorri's goal was to encourage Icelandic poets to remember the myths and poetic methods of skaldic poetry.

What was the *Poetic Edda*?

A thirteenth-century manuscript known as the *Codex Regius* was rediscovered in an old Icelandic farmhouse in 1643 C.E. Scholars believe that the poems of this manuscript are based on stories from the Viking period. The Codex Regius material, along with other discovered material, is now known as the *Poetic Edda* or *Elder Edda,* or sometimes *Saemund's Edda*, after a now-discredited attribution of the compilation to one Saemund Sigfusson. The most famous poems in the collection are the *Voluspa* (the Prophecy of the Seeress), containing the myths of the beginning and end of the world; the *Grimnismal*, in which the high god Odin speaks in his disguise as the "hooded one" (Grimnir); and the *Havamal*, containing the myth of Odin's self-hanging.

What was the *Prose Edda*?

Snorri Sturluson composed the *Prose Edda* in about 1220 C.E. in elegant Icelandic prose. The *Prose Edda* begins with the *Gylfaginning* (the "Deluding of Gylfi"), in which a legendary Swedish king, Gylfi, disguised as a beggar called Gangleri, visits Asgard, the home of the gods, and questions Odin, who is also disguised, and two other mysterious figures, about mythological history. This section owes much to the *Poetic Edda* and its mythological content. The second section is the *Skaldskaparmal* ("Poetic Diction"), which supplies rules for traditional poetry and many myths as well. The final section is *Hattatal* ("Verse Form List").

The *Eddas* contain essentially all of what we know about Norse mythology, not only the Norse pantheon, but such myths as the creation, the end of the world (Ragnorak), the hanging of Odin, the death of Baldr, and the world tree (Yggdrasill), to mention only a few.

A 1666 edition of the *Prose Edda*, originally composed in 1220 by Snorri Sturluson.

What was the Norse cosmology?

The mythic universe of the Norse consisted of three levels divided from each other by space. At the top was Asgard, home of the Aesir, the warrior gods led by Odin and Thor.

The great hall in Asgard where slain warriors continued to fight and then be revived was Valhalla. In Valhalla, Odin's maids, the Valkyries, served the warriors pork and mead.

The top level was also the home of the Vanir, the ancient fertility gods who once opposed the Aesir. Elves lived on the top level, too, in a place called Alfheim, and the righteous dead lived there in Gimli.

The middle level of the universe was Midgard, the home of humans. It was surrounded by an ocean in which the world serpent, Jormungand by biting its own tail and forming a kind of belt, held the world together. The terrible giants, who opposed the Aesir, lived on this middle level in a place called Jotunheim. Dwarfs, or Dark Elves, also lived on this level in Nidavellir and Svartalfheim.

In the bottom level of the universe was Niflheim, the home of the evil dead. Here was the citadel of Hel, ruled over by a queen, herself named Hel.

The *axis mundi* (axis of the world) of this universe was the world tree Yggdrasill, the cosmic ash tree with roots leading to Hel and to Midgard. At the foot of the tree were the spring of Uror (Fate) and the well of Mimir (Wisdom).

What is the relationship of Norse culture and mythology to Germanic myth and culture?

Norse mythology is an aspect of Germanic mythology; essentially Norse is the term applied to northern Germanic mythology. It is not surprising that there are significant parallels between Norse mythology and that of the other Germanic peoples—the Anglo Saxons of

Britain, for example, and the Germans themselves. Thus, the equivalent of the Norse god Odin is the German high god Wotan and the Anglo-Saxon Woden, and the Norse Thor had German and Anglo-Saxon cognates in Thunr and Thunor, respectively. Sagas such as the Norse *Volsunga Saga* and the *Nibelungenlied* epic in Germany have much in common, both telling the story of the hero Sigurd (Siegfried in Germany) and his family.

THE NORSE PANTHEON

What was the Norse pantheon?

The Norse pantheon was made up of two sets of deities, the Vanir and the Aesir, who eventually merged and were known collectively as the Aesir.

Who were the Vanir?

Many Norse scholars believe the Vanir were a group of fertility deities who existed in mythology before the original Aesir, perhaps representing an older religious system, much as the Gaia-Uranos family represented an earlier religion in Greece than that of Zeus and the Olympian or as the Irish Firbolg represented an earlier religion than that of the Tuatha de Danaan. The Vanir were fertility gods, more earth-oriented and more concerned with the welfare of humanity than the more warrior-like and patriarchal Aesir. Their most important god was Freyr, the god of fruitfulness and prosperity who descended from the ancient Germanic earth goddess Nerthus. Typically he was depicted with a large phallus, symbolizing human fertility as well as that of nature. His female counterpart and sister was the love goddess Freyja, known for her erotic passions and active sex life. She once sold herself to four dwarfs in exchange for a famous necklace—the necklace of the Brisings.

Freyr and Freyja's father was the oldest of the Vanir, Njord, associated with the winds and the sea. Another important god who was probably originally a member of the Vanir, was Heimdallr, whom some credit with having created the first man and woman.

Who were the original Aesir?

The two leading gods of the Aesir were Odin and Thor. Odin was the All Father and was also credited with the creation of humans. Like his German cognate, Wotan, he was the god of battle. He was also the god of poetry—real passion being needed for both war and poetry. Odin had mysterious magical and shamanic properties and could even extract the wisdom of the dead, as he did when he sacrificed himself on the world tree. Odin had only one eye and always carried his magic spear, Gungnir. Odin's son Thor, by Fjorgyn (Earth) was a very different kind of god; he represented law and order.

With his famous hammer, Mjollnir, Thor fought off the evil giants and even competed with the terrible world serpent, Jormungand. The wheels of his mighty chariot were the source of thunder, a word derived from his name.

Another son of Odin was Tyr. Known for his bravery, he even sacrificed his own hand in the necessary binding of the dangerous giant wolf Fenrir, who threatened not only the gods but the whole world.

The first among the goddesses of the Aesir was Odin's consort, Frigg, who could predict the future. Odin and Frigg produced the gentle and wise Baldr, who was killed accidentally by his brother Hod.

A highly ambiguous god was the trickster Loki, who brought mischief, serious damage, and creativity into Asgard and the whole world.

THE NORSE CREATION MYTH AND WARS IN HEAVEN

What was the Norse creation myth?

Snorri Sturluson used the tenth-century eddic poem, the *Voluspa,* as his source for the telling of a Norse creation myth. According to this myth, creation occurred between two entities that were already there—Muspell in the south and Niflheim in the north. In Muspell, Black Surt waited with his sword of flames for a chance to destroy any world that might be created. In Niflheim, a place of ice and snow, was Hvergelmir, a spring from which eleven rivers flowed. Between Muspell and Niflheim was Ginnungagap, the void into which the rivers flowed, leaving desolate iciness in the north and desolate volcanic moltenness in the south. Where the two climates met in the middle of Ginnungagap, there was a temperate area where melting ice became the evil frost giant Ymir. A man and a woman emerged from under the left armpit of the melting giant. From his legs came a family of frost giants. And out of the melting center of Ginnungagap came the cow, Audumla. Ymir drank the four rivers of milk that poured from her.

Audumla licked the ice until Buri came forth. Buri had a son, Bor, who married the frost giant Bestla, and Bestla gave birth to the gods Odin, Vili, and Ve. These gods hated Ymir and the other frost giants, so they killed Ymir. They used his body to form the world. They used his blood to form lakes, rivers, the seas, and a wide ocean surrounding the world. They made the sky from the giant's skull and established four directions by setting a dwarf in each corner. From the sparks of Muspell's fires the gods made the sun and moon and the stars. They made the walls of Midgard out of Ymir's eyebrows and clouds out of his brains. Out of a fallen ash tree and a fallen elm they made Ask and Embla, the first man and woman and gave them Midgard as a home. The gods made dwarves out of the maggots crawling about in Ymir's flesh. Finally, the gods made Asgard for themselves. This myth must remind us of the Babylonian myth in which Marduk uses the body of Tiamat to form a world. Similar myths exist in India, Native North America, and elsewhere.

In Germanic mythology, the world emerges from the giant Ymir after he suckles from the udder of the cow Audumla, as illustrated in this 1790 artwork by Nicolai Abraham Abildgaard.

Was there a Norse flood myth?

After the first gods killed the great frost giant Ymir and made the world out of him, his spilled blood drowned all the other frost giants except for Bergelmir and his wife, who used a boat made out of a hollowed tree trunk to escape the deluge. The similarity of parts of this flood myth to those of other cultures, such as the Sumerians and the Hebrews, suggests a possible common source.

What was the Norse war in heaven?

As in the case of so many Indo-European-based mythologies, Norse mythology has its war in heaven between two sets of deities. In Celtic Ireland it was the Firbolg against the Tuatha de Danaan. In Greece it was the old Kronos alliance against the Zeus-led Olympians. In the Norse world it was the Vanir against the Aesir.

One day the Vanir Gullveig, who was possibly really the goddess Freyja, came for a visit to the Aesir in Odin's hall. When she spoke at length about her love of and lust for riches, the angry Aesir threw her into the fire. This happened three times, but each time

Gullveig (now Heid—the shining one), being a true enchantress, emerged whole from the fire. When the Vanir heard of the violent treatment of their Gullveig, they decided to make war on the Aesir. The Aesir, too, prepared themselves for war and Odin started things by hurling a spear into the midst of the Vanir. The Vanir used their magic spells to destroy the walls of Asgard, and the Aesir destroyed much of the Vanir home, Vanaheim. The war became stalemated, and finally the two sides decided on a truce and, in the Norse manner, exchanged leading members as a guarantee of good intentions. Njord, Freyr, and Freyja went to the Aesir. The Aesir sent the wise god Mimir and the god of long legs, Honir, to the Vanir. Thinking the Aesir had somehow tricked them, the Vanir decapitated Mimir and sent his head back to the Aesir, but Odin, using his trickster powers, revived the head so that it could speak to him and become the source of his wisdom. We are reminded here of Bran's talking head in the Welsh myth. Eventually the Aesir and Vanir merged and became the new Aesir.

What role do tricksters play in Norse mythology?

Tricksters of all cultures tend to have several characteristics in common. They can change shapes, they have access to the dead, they possess magical powers and can cast spells, they have large appetites of all kinds, they are amoral, and they are both creative and destructive. In Mesopotamia Enki has trickster qualities, as does the Celtic Aonghus. In Norse mythology the primary trickster is Loki, but Odin, the All Father himself, has trickster qualities. Odin can change his shape and his gender. As we have seen, he can revive the head of Mimir. He tempts death itself hanging on the world tree, learning the mystery of the ancient runes. Loki's trickster qualities are employed for more evil purposes. It is he who causes the death of the gentle god Baldr, and it is he who fathers the monstrous wolf Fenrir, the horrible goddess Hel, and the world serpent, Jormungand. And, although he sometimes helps the gods out of difficulties, Loki becomes so dangerous that he has to be restrained by them, much as his son Fenrir would have to be restrained.

What is the myth of the death of Baldr?

Baldr the Beautiful, as he was often called, was the gentle son of the All Father, Odin. When he had dreams foreshadowing his destruction, the gods tried to help him. His mother, Frigg, arranged for every living thing on earth to promise never to harm her son. Only the tiny mistletoe was missed. Now that Baldr was apparently safe, the gods began throwing things at him for fun. But the trickster Loki entered the game without fun on his mind. Disguised as a female, he learned from Frigg about the overlooked mistletoe. He then picked the plant and gave it to Baldr's brother, Hodr, and urged him to throw it. As Hodr was blind, Loki guided his hand, and the mistletoe hit Baldr in the heart, causing his instant death. The gods were bitterly sad at the loss of so wonderful a companion, and Odin realized that Baldr's death foreshadowed the death of all the gods and the end of the world. Frigg begged for a volunteer to travel to the land of Hel to retrieve her beloved son. Hermod, one of her other sons, traveled

Odin rides his eight-legged horse Slepnir into Hel in this illustration from a 1908 edition of the *Poetic Edda*.

to Hel, where he discovered Baldr and was told that the god could return to Asgard only if all things animate and inanimate would mourn him by weeping. As soon as he was informed of this requirement, Odin ordered a universal weeping, and everything did weep—all things, that is, except for a giantess, who was in reality the disguised Loki. Instead of tears, the Loki-giantess pronounced what was, in effect, a curse: "Let Hel keep what is hers." And so the gentle Baldr had to remain in the land of the dead, making the end of the world—Ragnarok—unavoidable. But a belief emerged that one day the earth would revive from its destruction and that Baldr would lead some of the gods back, as a kind of "once and future king" like the Welsh King Arthur. And Loki would pay for his betrayal of Baldr.

What is the source of the Baldr myth?

There are scholars who have suggested that Baldr originates with Middle Eastern fertility gods such as Attis, Baal, Adonis, and Osiris, who died in the old year and then revived with the plants of the new year. Baldr's plant was the mistletoe, which typically is found on the oak tree, a tree sacred to the Norse, to the Celts, and to Indo-Europeans in general. In Christian times, northern Europeans would see the Baldr myth as a prophecy pointing to the story of their own god, who after his death was said to have harrowed hell and returned with a host of the dead now freed from the torments of hell. It is certainly possible that the Baldr myth was itself affected in its retelling by Christians, as was probably the case of the strange myth of Odin's hanging on the world tree.

What is the myth of the binding of Loki?

Realizing how angry the gods were over his role in the death of the much-loved Baldr, Loki realized he must go into hiding, away from Asgard. Hiding in a deserted area of Midgard, Loki's fear of being found by the gods grew day by day until he decided to use his trickster shape-shifting talents to turn himself into a salmon. But Odin could see all things from his position as All Father in Asgard, and he sent a party of gods to capture the renegade. The gods made many attempts to capture the Loki-salmon in a net they had made for the purpose, but eventually it was Thor who grasped the fish as he flew upstream over the net. Then the gods bound the trickster to three slabs of rock with the entrails of his own son and placed a snake over his face so that its venom would drip on his face until the end of the world.

The trickster god Loki is punished by the gods of Asgard in this 1900 engraving by Louis Huard.

What is the myth of the binding of Fenrir?

Fenrir was the terrifying and dangerous wolf born to the evil Loki and the giantess Angrboda. The wolf's siblings were Jormungand, the world serpent, and Hel, the ghastly mistress of Hel itself. Fenrir lived in Asgard, where the gods could keep an eye on him, but only Tyr dared to feed him. The wolf swallowed his meat, bones and all, in huge hunks. Finally, the gods decided that Fenrir must be removed from Asgard. To remove him they would have to bind him. The gods realized they would have to do this surreptitiously by pretending to hold a contest which would appeal to Fenrir's vanity. In so doing, they challenged him to break whatever bonds they could devise. With no trouble, the beast broke the first two sets of bindings. But the gods enlisted the dwarfs to make ropes of magical power. The dwarf-made ropes were made of the noise made by a moving cat, a woman's beard, a fish's breath, a bird's spit, and other unlikely ingredients. Fenrir now agreed to be bound by these ropes only if a god would place his arm in his mouth as a sign of good faith; Tyr agreed to what was, in effect, a noble act of self-sacrifice. After Fenrir struggled unsuccessfully to break the binds of the dwarfs' ropes and failed, he bit off Tyr's arm. The gods nevertheless gagged the wolf with a sword through its jaws. But Fenrir and his father, Loki, would continue to oppose the gods even in the events of Ragnarok at the end of the world.

THE HANGING OF
ODIN AND RAGNAROK

What is the myth of Odin's hanging on Yggdrasill?

The strange myth of Odin's sacrifice is another Norse myth sometimes seen as related to the Christian story. The source for this myth is a section of the *Elder Edda* known as the *Havamal.* Although the All Father and primary warrior god, Odin also has trickster and shamanic powers and is driven to understand ultimate mysteries, represented by the mysterious runes, some that can only be understood among the dead. It is to understand the wisdom of the dead that Odin sacrifices himself on the world tree, Yggdrasill. Odin's quest for wisdom had already cost him an eye when he achieved wisdom at the spring of the talking head, Mimir, at the foot of Yggdrasill. In the hanging myth, Odin literally mounts his horse—the *drasill*—as "the Terrible One"—*Ygg.* Yggdrasill is "Odin's Horse," a kenning, or compound word, that replaces a usual word, in this case "gallows." Hangings were an important aspect of the Odin cult. Odin hung on the "windswept tree" for nine days and nights. He was pierced by a spear and left by himself to die and so to learn the runic mysteries of the dead—the mysteries of life and death—before returning to continue his rule of Asgard and the world. The myth of Odin's hanging reminds us not only of the Christian story of death and resurrection and the harrowing of Hell, but of the much earlier myth of the Mesopotamian Inanna's descent into the Underworld to learn the mysteries embodied by her sister Erishkigal.

What was the Norse end-of-the-world myth?

Snorri tells the story of the apocalypse, Ragnarok (the "End of the Gods"), in his *Prose Edda,* basing his narrative on the second part of the *Poetic Edda*'s *Voluspa.* According to the myth, a seeress from the dead tells Odin not only how the world was created, but how it will end. There will be wars in Midgard, the land of the humans, she said. Family members will fight each other. The social fabric will deteriorate; incest will be rampant. After a three-year winter, the wolf, Skoll, will consume the sun, and his brother Hati will destroy the moon. Fenrir and Loki will escape and cause havoc. There will be destructive earthquakes. Gullinkambi, the golden cock of Asgard, will awaken the Aesir and the world tree will shiver. The seas will flood the shores, made violent by the approach of Loki's son, the terrible world serpent Jormungand. Loki will guide a ship of the dead from Hel and the giants will form an army. Fenrir will tear apart Asgard and Midgard, and Jormungand will poison all of creation. Fire demons, led by Surt with his flaming sword, which will replace the sun, will cross the Bifrost, destroying the Rainbow Bridge. All the enemies of the Aesir will gather, and the gods, summoned by Heimdall's mighty horn, will march through Valhalla against them. Odin, wielding the sword Gungnir, will challenge Fenrir, and Thor will attack Jormungand, will kill him, but will die of the serpent's venom. Freyr will fall to Surt. Tyr and Garm the Hound will kill each other, as will Loki and Heimdall. The awful Fenrir will swallow the All Father, but Odin's son Vidar will take revenge by destroying the jaws of the wolf. Finally, Surt will set fire to all the universe, and all will die.

But as in the passing of the ages in ancient India, a new world will be born of Ragnarok. A new sun will be born, and gods, led by the gentle Baldr, will return to Asgard. Because two humans, Lif and Lifthrasir, will have hidden themselves in Yggdrasill and so escaped the fire of Surt, a new race of humans will be born as well.

THE NORSE HERO SAGAS: THE VOLSUNGS

Are there human heroes in Norse mythology?

It is in the sagas such as the *Volsunga Saga* that the myths of heroes such as Sigmund and Sigurd are told.

What is the *Volsunga Saga*?

A *saga* is literally "something said," that is, a story or history. The *Volsunga Saga* is the story of the legenday or mythological Volsung family, of which the two most important heroes are Sigmund and his son Sigurd (Siegfried in Germany). The *Volsunga Saga* is a thirteenth-century prose epic-like tale based on much older material. Essentially the same tale is told in Germany as the *Nibelungenlied*. Opera lovers will recognize the tale in Richard Wagner's opera cycle known as *Der Ring des Nibelungen* (*The Ring of the Nibelung*).

What is the story of Sigmund?

King Sigmund was a direct descendant of the god Odin. Sigi, a son of Odin, had a son named Rerir, who became King of Hunaland. Rerir's wife became preganant in a miraculous manner, and after a six-year pregnancy produced the hero Volsung. Cut from his mother's dying body, Volsung was born already well grown. He became king and married Hljod, who produced many children, the oldest of whom were Sigmund and his twin sister, Signy. When a visiting king, Siggeir, asked for Signy's hand in marriage, Volsung agreed, in spite of Signy's unwillingness. Volsung had built a fine palace with a great tree named Barnstock at its axis. During Siggeir's visit, a

Illustration by Arthur Rackham of the hero Sigmund, a direct descendant of the Norse god Odin.

hooded old man with one eye—a favored disguise of the one-eyed god Odin—pressed a sword named Gram into the tree, promising it to anyone who could remove it. Of all the would-be heroes at the court of Volsung, only Sigmund was able to remove the sword, thus proving himself to be a true hero in the archetypal sense. This situation, of course, brings to mind the story of King Arthur and of his pulling the sword from the rock. When Siggeir demanded to buy the sword, Sigmund refused his offer, mortally offending the visiting king and beginning a feud, and eventually a war that would decimate the Volsungs. Sigmund and his sister Signy succeeded in avenging the slaughter of most of their family. Before his death, Sigmund married Hjordis, who gave birth to Sigurd. At Sigmund's death, the sword Gram was broken into two pieces.

What is the story of Sigurd?

Sigurd was the greatest of the Norse heroes. In the *Volsunga Saga*, he is the last of the Volsungs, the son of Sigmund. He was brought up in the court of a foster father, Regin (Mimir the smith in some sources). Regin had a brother, Fafnir, who had killed their father and stolen his gold. The gold was cursed, and after the theft, Fafnir had transformed himself into a venomous dragon. From then on he had, as did so many mythic dragons, jealously guarded his treasure in his lair and caused havoc in the surrounding countryside. Meanwhile, Sigurd's foster father Regin taught his charge the lessons of nobility and the mystery of runes. When he thought the boy was ready and strong enough, Regin urged him to confront and kill Fafnir. Sigurd agreed to do so, only if Regin would forge a magnificent sword for him. After two blades were proven to be unsatisfactory, Sigurd instructed the smith to make a blade out of the broken parts of his father's sword, Gram. When Regin refashioned it, it cut easily through the anvil itself. Sigurd now agreed to face Fafnir, once he had avenged his own father's death. This he did and then returned to Regin and prepared to fulfill his promise. On the heath where Fafnir lived, Sigurd and Regin found a track leading from a watering hole to the dragon's lair. Regin instructed Sigurd to dig a trench across this track, and to wait in it until the beast passed over it, allowing Sigurd to thrust his sword into its belly and heart. When Sigurd asked what would happen to him if he became submerged in the dragon's blood, Regin accused him of cowardice and left. Trusting Regin, Sigurd was digging the trench when an old hooded gray-beard appeared and warned him that he would need to dig more than one trench so that the blood could be diverted from him in the main trench. The old man then vanished. Once again the young hero had been helped by his divine ancestor, Odin, much as in the Greek monster-slaying myth of Perseus, the hero had received divine advice. Now Sigurd hid in the main trench and waited. Soon the dragon approached, causing the earth to shake. As the beast passed over him in his hiding place, Sigurd thrust the sword with all his might into his prey. By so doing, Sigurd fulfilled the monster-slaying requirement of so many heroes, from Perseus, to Beowulf, to King George, to mention only a few. When the dying Fafnir asked who had slain him and why, Sigurd foolishly revealed his identity, thus allowing the dragon to pass the curse of the gold on to him. Sigurd did not fear death, however, and so determined to take the gold anyway.

With his evil brother safely put to rest, Regin reappeared and made demands. Sigurd could keep the treasure, but he wanted the dragon's heart. Sigurd agreed to this, and Regin drank some of the serpent's blood and fell into a deep sleep. Meanwhile, Sigurd began roasting the dragon's heart for his foster father. He burned his finger in the process and put his finger into his mouth to ease the pain. When he tasted the dragon's blood he suddenly found himself able to understand the speech of birds, who told him that Regin planned to kill him. So Sigurd drew Gram once more and decapitated Regin.

The rest of the saga describes tragic events surrounding a ring given to the shield-maiden Brynhild by Sigurd and the confused demands of love and treasure that eventually lead to Sigurd's death as well as to the death of Brynhild.

NORSE MYTHOLOGY AND THE WORLD

How is Norse mythology related to other mythologies such as the Greek, Roman, Indian, and Celtic?

The Norse people, like those of Greece, Rome, India, and the Celtic lands, spoke an Indo-European language—one that can be traced to the related peoples who migrated in various stages into India, Iran, and Europe in ancient times. It is not surprising that along with language similarities we find common themes in the mythologies of India, Iran, Greece, Rome, Ireland, and the Norse lands. The Norse war in heaven has counterparts in the war between the Titans and the Olympians in Greece and Rome and that between the Firbolg and Tuatha de Danann in Ireland. The world serpent exists in Norse mythology as Jormungand, who surrounds Midgard, and as the world serpent Sesha on whose back the god Vishnu rests in the creation story of India. Sometimes the serpents become the prey of the hero as monster-slayer, as in the case of Apollo with the Python in Greece, Krishna with the demonic serpent Kaliya in India, and Sigurd with Fafnir the dragon in the Norse saga. The role of Audumla the cow and her milk in Norse mythology surely has something in common with the significant role of cows and milk in Indian myth. And the role of the first being, Buri, has a cognate in the Purusha in Indian mythology. Thor, as a god of Thunder, has a counterpart in Zeus in Greece. The parallels are numerous.

More than any European mythology, Germanic mythology—particularly of the Norse tradition—is in keeping with the ancient Indian sense of life as a part of a huge cycle of creation, preservation, and destruction. Many see this cyclical pattern as a reflection of an essentially pessimistic view, perhaps, reflecting the long dark days of the seemingly endless northern winters. Others see it, as Hindus do, as a natural cosmic history of birth, death, and rebirth.

INDIAN MYTHOLOGY

Who are the Indian people?

The Indian people populate the part of the south Asian subcontinent known as India. The Indian nation is made up of people representing a variety of ethnic and cultural backgrounds and languages who have varying mythological traditions.

What is Hinduism?

Hinduism is the religious system that has developed over the centuries in India and continues to develop. It is difficult to define the beliefs of Hinduism because they vary so significantly from one group to another. One person's religion might center on one god, another's on another god. So rather than speak of oneself as a Hindu, a given individual might establish his or her religious identity by calling himself a worshipper of Shiva, or of Vishnu, or of another deity. There are literally millions of deities or subdeities in Hinduism with a particular few being the dominant foci of worship. There are several aspects which do unify Hindus more generally. Although Hindu narratives or myths have evolved over time, Hindus share common religious texts or scripture, such as the *Vedas*. They all recognize at least the major deities even if they tend to identify

What periods of Indian cultural history contributed to Hindu mythology?

The answer depends very much on the position one takes with regard to whether what evolved into classical Hinduism originated with so-called Indo-European or Aryan invaders into the subcontinent in the second millennium B.C.E. or with the people who were already in India, whether or not the invasions took place.

themselves in connection with particular ones. Hindus also share a general belief in certain ritual processes and an understanding of what can be called the cyclical nature of universal history.

THE INDO–EUROPEANS AND THE INDUS VALLEY CULTURE

Who were the so-called Aryans or Indo-Europeans?

Essentially, in the context of Indian history, the Aryans were those Indo-Europeans who, according to most scholars, came into the subcontinent from the north in about 1500 B.C.E., bringing various traditions with them. Indo-Europeans also came into Europe and the Middle East—particularly Iran and the Hittite lands—and all spoke languages related to the original Proto-Indo-European language. There are scholars who see connections between Semitic and Indo-European languages and cultures as well. The language of the Indo-Europeans in India was Sanskrit, which remains the liturgical and scriptural language of Hinduism. Again, there are scholars who doubt the whole theory of an Indo-European "invasion" of the subcontinent, arguing instead for the development of Indian culture—including Hinduism—from within the continent, beginning as early as 6500 B.C.E.

Who were the people in India before the arrival of the Indo-Europeans?

Whether or not there was an Indo-European invasion, there clearly were people and civilizations that existed in India before 1500 B.C.E., and archeological evidence suggests that the religious traditions of these people deeply influenced the evolution of Hinduism and Hindu mythology. The primary early culture in India has come to be known as the Indus Valley or Harappan culture—after Harappa, one of the main ancient settlements in the Indus Valley. It is also sometimes called Dravidian, after the language spoken by many indigenous Indian peoples.

What was the mythology of the pre-Indo-European period in India?

Because there is no written evidence for pre-Indo-European mythology in India, it is impossible to discover specific myths of the period. It is clear, however, that the Indus Valley culture possessed a mother goddess. In the ruins of a settlement known as Mehrgarh, dating back to 6000 B.C.E., goddess figurines have been discovered, which seem to confirm the importance of goddess power during the ancient period. This powerful female figure would become the various aspects of Devi. It is also evident that a god associated with the practice of a kind of *yoga*, a god who would evolve into the great Hindu god Shiva, was revered. Seals and figurines also indicate that the Indus Valley people worshipped snakes (nagas) and practiced ritual bathing and ritual sacrifice.

VEDIC CULTURE

What were the stages of the development of Hindu mythology?

What we think of now as Hindu mythology, as it emerged from the early Indo-European culture in India, begins with the Vedic, or Samhita, period, which extends from about 1500 B.C.E. to about 900 B.C.E. and is notable for the production of collections (*samhitas*) of sacred scriptures known as the *Vedas*. Next came the Brahmanical and Aranyaka period from about 900 to about 600 B.C.E., during which time the *Brahmanas* ("Commentaries") and *Aranyakas* ("Forest Texts") were developed. Between about 800 and 400 B.C.E., the Upanishadic period, the early *Upanishads* (philosophical additions to the *Vedas*) were composed. The Epic Period extends from about 400 B.C.E. to about 400 C.E. This is the period of the gradual composition of the two great mythological epics, the *Mahabharata*, which, in addition to its primary story, contains the philosophical appendix, the *Bhagavadgita*, and the *Rāmāyana*. The Puranic Period is that of the *Puranas*, sacred texts dating from about 250 C.E. to about 1000 C.E. Hinduism and its mythology continued to develop in the Middle Ages and into modern times, with the emergence of various movements and forms such as Tantra, and various teachings of popular gurus, or swamis.

Hindu mythology can be thought of as a vast collection of complex and sometimes conflicting metaphors that developed over many centuries in an attempt to shed light on the meaning of the universe, the world, and life.

What are the *Vedas*?

The word *veda* itself means "knowledge." The original four *Vedas*— the *Rigveda*, the *Yajurveda,* the *Samaveda,* the *Atharvaveda*—dating in their present form back to the early Indo-European period, 1500 to 1000 B.C.E., are poetic Sanskrit works containing stories, hymns, incantations, and rituals for sacrifice. They were not transmitted in writing because oral transmission by *rishis* (seers, gurus, sages, brahmins) was considered more accurate. Thus, these texts are considered to be particularly sacred, or *sruti* ("heard"), texts as opposed to less sacred, or *smrti* ("remembered"), written texts. It is believed by Hindus that the *Vedas* have always existed and that with the help of a series of beings known as Manus, or with the help of avatars (incarnations of the god Vishnu), the texts re-emerge even after regular dissolutions of the universe. Attached as corollaries to the original *Vedas* are several groups of texts also considered to be *sruti*. These texts—*Brahmanas, Aranyakas*, certain *Upanishads* , *Vedangas,* and *Sutras*—are traditionally included as *Vedas*.

How did the *Vedas* contribute to Hindu mythology?

What we know of early Indo-European mythology in India comes to us more from the *Rigveda* than from anywhere else. The *Rigveda* contains creation myths, a cosmology, and a series of early pantheons governed by triads such as the one in which Varuna,   **159**

Mitra, and Aryaman—all solar deities—dominate, and then by Indra, Agni, and Surya, who replace them, at least in name. Because there are contradictions between mythical elements of the *Rigveda* and those of other sacred and semi-sacred texts and within the *Vedas* itself, it can be assumed that the myths are metaphors relating to various aspect of life rather than stories to be taken literally, even by believers.

What are the *Brahmanas*?

The *Brahmanas* are commentaries associated with the four original *Vedas*. They tend to be particularly concerned with the proper use and performance of rituals, and they tend to be more dogmatic than are the *Vedas*. The dogmatism of the *Brahmanas* is in contrast to the *Rigveda*, for instance, which describes the origins of the universe and other aspects of creation with a note of uncertainty.

How did the *Brahmanas* contribute to Hindu mythology?

In the *Brahmanas,* the tradition of a triad of gods (*devas*) consists of Agni the fire god, Indra the monster slayer, and Surya the sun god. In the *Rigveda,* Indra and Surya had been the most important of these. Indra was the god king, son of Dyaus Pitar (Heaven) and Prithvi Mata (Earth) and the slayer of the monstrous demon Vritra. Surya, as the sun, was the creator, the sustainer of life. In the *Brahmanas,* Indra and Surya, in effect, are demoted in favor of Agni, who is specifically related to a tradition of fire sacrifice.

What are the *Upanishads*?

The *Upanishads*, also known as *Vedanta* (*anta* = last + Veda = last of the *vedas*), are a series of philosophical discussions, often between a sage and his or her followers. Thus, the literal meaning of the Sanskrit term, "sitting near." The *Upanishads* form the philosophical basis of Hindu theology. The term Vedanta also applies to a philosophical school of Hinduism.

The Indian devas (left to right) Surya, Agni, and Indra.

How did the *Upanishads* contribute to Hindu mythology?

Perhaps the primary mythological contribution of the *Upanishads* to Hindu mythology is Brahman, a concept of the Absolute developed by the Vedanta school of the religion. For this school, especially the one known as Advaita Vedanta, Brahman—the gender-neutral form of Brahma in Sanskrit—is the unknowable essence of all reality. Brahman is the universe. The gods are metaphors for Brahman. By discovering the true Self (Atman) within, we discover that we are Brahman.

POST-VEDIC HINDUISM

What are the *Puranas*?

The *Puranas* are religious texts based on *bhakti,* devotion to a particular deity, particularly the post-Vedic Hindu *trimurti* (trinity or triad) of Brahma (not to be confused with Brahman), Vishnu, and Shiva—Creator, Sustainer, Destroyer—in which Devi, the goddess in her many forms, has, in effect, displaced Brahma in importance.

How did the *Puranas* contribute to Hindu mythology?

The *Puranas* include myths of creation and cosmology, in addition to the deeds of the great gods. Examples include the *Bhagavata Purana* and the *Vishnu Purana*, centering on the god Vishnu; the *Shiva, Skanda*, and *Linga Purana* about Shiva; the *Brahma Purana* about Brahma; and the *Brahma Vaivarta Purana*, which tells myths of Devi and of Krishna and the popular elephant-headed god, Ganesha. Gurus, and other sages and priests, use the *Puranas* to popularize the complex concepts of Hinduism by way of stories of the gods. Along with the *Rigveda* and the epics, the *Puranas* are the richest source of Hindu mythology.

Who were the Hindu myth-makers?

Traditionally, the compiler of the *Vedas,* the *Puranas,* and the *Mahabharata* was Vyasa, or Veda Vyasa. As he would have had to live for more than a thousand years to accomplish this task, we can assume that Vyasa is a generic name for all those hearers of *sruti,* the divine texts. In a sense, then, Vyasa is the representative of a whole class of hearers known by various terms: *rishis*, seers, sages, *yogis,* priests, *brahmins*, gurus. Among the best known of the ancient seers were the Seven Sages, the Saptarishis or Maharishis, whose yogic power gave them particular insight. A whole mythology is attached to Vyasa.

Vyasa is said to have been born of the brahmin Parashara and the famous fisherwoman Satyavati. Satyavati had been born of a fish, rejected by a king because of her smell, and impregnated by the Brahmin Parashara. After the lovemaking, the child Vyasa was immediately born and his mother's virginity restored, establishing her as a member of the large group of miraculous birth-givers to mythological heroes. Because his complexion was dark (*krishna*) and he was born on an island (*dvaipa*), he was also known as Vyasa Krishna Dvaipayana. Vyasa was the progenitor of the two families who struggle against each other in the *Mahabharata*. A popular legend has it that Vyasa dictated the events of the epic to the elephant-headed god Ganesha, who wrote it down with one of his tusks.

Whoever Vyasa was, his name can be seen as the collective name for the primary myth-makers of the remarkable cosmology, creation stories, pantheons, and heroes of Hindu mythology.

Another of the "Homers" of Hindu mythology was Valmiki, the legendary author of the epic, the *Rāmāyana*. It is said that Valmiki invented poetry; when deeply moved by the killing of a mating bird by a hunter, he broke into emotional poetic song.

What is the Hindu cosmology?

According to Hindu mythology, Mount Meru—like other Indo-European world mountains or world trees such as the Norse Yggdrasill—is at the center of the universe. It is surrounded by seven continents interspersed with oceans. At the top of the cosmos are the gods; then, moving down, the planets, including earth; then the underworlds, including the twenty-eight hells. The division of sacred space into the cardinal directions is reflected in the laying out of Indian towns and in the practice of rituals. It is the four directions that produced the three *lokas* (worlds)—the *triloka* of the cosmos, which is the earth, the atmosphere or space, and the world of the gods and the sun, moon, and stars. North is the realm of humans. East is that of the gods, who come to humans during the ritual sacrifices. South is the world of death and the ancestors. West is the realm of the animals and other aspects of life that provide sustenance.

1905 depiction of Mount Meru, which, in Indian mythology, is at the center of the universe.

THE INDIAN CREATION

What are the Hindu creation myths?

There are many Hindu creation myths, beginning with those of the *Rigveda*. An early Vedic myth tells of a golden cosmic egg of mysterious origin as the beginning of creation. Another says that Dyaus (the Sky Father) and Prithvi (the Earth Mother) joined to begin things. An important Vedic creation myth is the one in which the god Indra defeats the demon Vritra (Chaos). By defeating Chaos, the gods made the way to creation (order) possible. Still other myths center on the cosmic being, Purusha, whose dismemberment, or sacrifice, formed the basis of creation, much as in Mesopotamia and in the Norse world the dismembered parts of early beings became aspects of the world. An important creator was Prajapati (or several prajapatis), who was replaced in later myths by Brahma. Some say that Brahma created humans by making sons from his mind. Others say he or Prajapati created a woman in his mind and joined with her to create the world. In the Prajapati version of this myth, the creator finds himself alone in the universe, so he creates a man and a woman out of himself. But the woman, fearing incest, flees in the form of various animals, only to be chased and mated with by the man, who takes the male form of these animals. The result is the creation of the animal world. In the mythology of the later *Puranas*, in which particular gods of the Shiva/Vishnu/Devi triad dominate, we find creation myths in which each of these gods, who for their followers are the supreme being, like the Brahman of the *Upanishads*, contains the universe itself and thus is its *de facto* creator. In one Vishnu myth we find the earth-diver form of creation, in which an agent of the god Vishnu dives into the maternal depths to bring up the earth. In a popular Vishnu creation myth, Vishnu and his wife Lakshmi sleep on eternity, which is represented by the thousand-headed world serpent Ananta Shesha. The world exists during that sleep only in the god's mind. It is when Vishnu awakens and meditates on his thought that the re-creation of the world begins. At this point the old creator god Brahma is perched on a lotus blossom, which has grown out of the navel of the much greater god Vishnu, the real creator. Brahma becomes merely the agent of Vishnu's thought.

Still another creation myth involving Vishnu is the one about the churning of the Ocean of Milk. There are various sources for this myth, including the *Mahabharata* and the *Puranas*. According to most versions, it was Vishnu (also called Narayana) who urged the gods (*devas*) and the demons (*asuras*) to churn the primeval waters so as to find the lost *Soma*, the ambrosia that provides the gods with immortality. The gods had the world serpent Ananta (Vasuki or Shesha) uproot the world mountain, Meru (Mandara) and place it on the back of the Vishnu avatar, the Great Tortoise. The mountain became the churning stick and the serpent the churning cord. During the churning process Soma flowed into the sea, making it milk, and with the continued churning, elements of the world emerged.

A consistent theme among the many Hindu creation stories is the concept of ages, the *kalpa,* a period of 8.64 trillion years in human time, or a day and a night in terms of Brahma's time. At the end of each *kalpa,* creation is destroyed, much as in the Norse Ragnarok. And each destruction—like each individual's life—is followed by a new creation.

Vishnu creates Brahma, who is perched on a lotus blossom, during the creation of the universe. In Hindu mythology, Vishnu is a greater god than Brahma, who is only the agent of Vishnu's thoughts.

What is an avatar?

An avatar (*avatara*) in Hindu mythology is an earthly form taken by a deity, especially by the god Vishnu and his consort Lakshmi,. The most famous of the Vishnu avatars are Rama, the hero of the epic the *Rāmāyana,* and Krishna, who preaches the great truths of the universe to the hero Arjuna in the *Bhagavadgita*. Incarnations of Lakshmi include Draupadi, the wife of the Pandava brothers in the *Mahabharata*, and Sita, the wife of Rama in the *Rāmāyana*.

Is there an Indian flood myth?

There are various versions of an Indian flood myth. The *Satapatha Brahmana* and the *Mahabharata* are among the sources for the story, in which the Noah figure is Manu, the progenitor of humanity. Manu is washing his hands in a river when a fish comes to him begging protection from larger fish. Manu protects the fish until he is large enough to survive on his own. The fish is actually Matsya, an incarnation (avatar) of the god Vishnu. Grateful for his protection, Matsya warns Manu of the coming of a great flood to punish humanity for its evil ways. He instructs Manu to build a boat and to fill it with grains and, according to some versions, representatives of all living beings. Matsya ties the boat to himself, and when the waters come, he guides the boat to a mountain top, where it remains until the waters subside and Manu can proceed to repopulate the world.

The Churning of the Ocean of Milk might also be considered a kind of flood myth.

THE HINDU PANTHEON

What is the Hindu pantheon?

The Hindu pantheon changes and develops over time. In the early Vedic tradition, Dyaus (Dyaus Pitar = Father Sky, the Greek Zeus and the Roman Jupiter) and Prithvi (Mother Earth) are, like Uranos and Gaia in Greece, the original deities. They are followed by a second generation of *devas* (deities) led by Indra. Indra, Surya (sometimes Mitra), the sun god, and Agni, the fire and sacrifice god, form the first of the great Hindu triads. Another important early figure is Varuna, sometimes the supreme deity, sometimes a god of the waters, sometimes representing night as opposed to Surya-Mitra's day. Lesser Vedic gods are the Ashvins, the first of the many Indo-European sacred twins; Vayu, the wind god; Ushas, the goddess of Dawn; and Vac, the goddess of speech and "Mother of the *Vedas*" and wife of Indra. Vishnu and Rudra (a pre-Shiva), are only minor figures in the early development of what would become Hinduism.

During the period of the *Upanishads*, complex creative principles become embodied by Prajapati and, in an even more complex manner, by Brahman.

Eventually a second great triad or *trimurti* develops, in which Brahma is the creator, Vishnu the sustainer, and Shiva the necessary destroyer of the universe, which must undergo constant creation and recreation. Brahma's wife is Sarasvati, Vishnu's is Lak-

A Cambodian sculpture of Vishnu (left) from the eleventh or twelfth century; at right, an 1800 illustration of Shiva and Pārvatī.

shmi or Sri, and Shiva's is Pārvatī. Vishnu and Shiva remain dominant in classical Hinduism, but Brahma is essentially replaced in importance by Devi, the great goddess in her many forms, such as Durga, Kali, and Shakti, and in a sense any feminine incarnation such as the wives of the three gods of the *Trimurti*.

In addition to these major figures are a great number of lesser deities, among the most famous of whom are Ganesha (Ganapati), the elephant-headed son of Shiva and Pārvatī, and the many Manus and Prajapatis of various eras.

Was there a war in heaven in Hinduism?

There were wars in heaven in Hindu mythology. Indra's battle against the demonic Vritra was an aspect of such a war, as are the many battles between the "good" deities, the *devas*, and the not-so-good ones, the *asuras*. In the end, the devas, like the Greek Olympians and the Norse Aesir, won over their more primitive enemies.

Who is Indra?

From his position as the great king of gods, the fiery warrior, and establisher of order represented by his defeat of the monstrous and chaotic Vritra, Indra gradually lost importance in favor of Shiva, Vishnu, Brahma, and Devi. First a great king, later he is depicted as a womanizer besotted with Soma, the sacred drink of the gods. He even became an object of jokes and lessons, as in the famous story of Indra and the Parade of Ants.

What is the Parade of Ants?

The *Brahma Vaivarta Purana* tells how Indra, as an overly demanding monarch, commanded the divine architect Vishvakarman to build him the most splendid of palaces. As the architect proceeded with his work, Indra demanded more and more, until finally Vishvakarman appealed for help to the creator god Brahma. Brahma, in turn, appealed to an even higher source, Vishnu. Vishnu agreed that something had to be done about the avaricious Indra, and so came about the parade of ants.

One morning a Brahmin boy came to Indra and said he had heard of the king's plans to build a great palace and wondered how long the project would take to complete. He pointed out that no other Indra had ever succeeded in building the kind of palace envisioned by the king. Indra was shocked. "How many Indras could there have been," he asked. Now the boy revealed himself as a wise and ancient man, an emissary of Brahma and Vishnu, who had witnessed many creations, destructions, and re-creations of the universe, and many Indras. The comings and goings of twenty-eight Indras was the same as a single day of Brahma. Now a seemingly endless parade of ants appeared and the boy revealed that each ant had at one time been an Indra who attached himself to vain and selfish pursuits. So it was that Indra learned about *karman (karma),* the principle that past actions will affect the individual in future incarnations. Life, he learned, is a series of deaths and rebirths determined by past actions.

Who is Surya?

Surya was an important Vedic god, or *adityas*. Sometimes he is called Savitar (the Nourisher). Surya was the sun, the illuminator and creator, who ruled over life itself. Gradually, over the centuries, Surya lost his standing and his qualities were absorbed by other deities. In connection with Agni and Indra, he was the solar fire who ruled the heavens.

Who is Agni?

In the Vedic triad with Surya and Indra, Agni was the fire of the ritual sacrifice. As the spiritual fire in animals, plants, and humans, he was the ruler of Earth. Like Indra and Surya, he lost importance during the gradual emergence of post-Vedic Hinduism.

Who is Brahma?

In the Brahma/Vishnu/Shiva triad of important deities that followed the diminishing importance of the Indra/ Agni/Surya triad, Brahma replaced Prajapati as the creator god. But even in that position he was usually seen as greatly inferior to his triadic brothers and, in effect, his position in the great triad was taken over by the Great Goddess, Devi, one embodiment of whom was Brahma's wife, Sarasvati. Brahma grew four heads facing the four directions so he could always keep his eyes on Sarasvati.

Who is Sarasvati?

Sarasvati has, since Vedic times, been a goddess of knowledge and learning, who in many ways surpasses her husband Brahma in continuing importance. In the *Puranas,* Sarasvati was sometimes seen as the daughter of Brahma for whom he had incestuous desires. For a while she was seen as one of Vishnu's wives, who was given by that god to Brahma in order to stop quarrels between his spouses.

VISHNU

Who is Vishnu?

Vishnu is one of the three most important deities of classical Hinduism, each of whom some Hindus would consider to be embodiments of the unknowable Absolute, Brahman. Vaishnavism is the form of

A sandstone carving of the head of Brahma, which faces four directions so that he can keep an eye on his wife, Sarasvati.

bhakti (devotion) in which Vishnu is seen as the supreme deity. In the early *Vedas*, Vishnu was a minor figure, but in the Brahma/Vishnu/ Shiva triad he is the preserver or sustainer of creation. In the Puranic period, Vishnu became even more powerful, creating Brahma, the creator, from the lotus growing from his navel, and, for his followers, even surpassing Shiva in importance. The power of Vishnu is evident in the myth of the Churning of the Ocean of Milk. Vishnu's skin is dark blue and he has at least four arms. For transportation he rides on the sun eagle Garuda. His primary wives are Sri and Lakshmi, often considered as one (Sri-Lakshmi). He has many earthly incarnations or avatars, the most important of which are Rama and Krishna.

Who is Sri-Lakshmi?

Sri-Lakshmi usually holds a lotus. She represents prosperity, is a form of Shakti, the feminine creative energy of her spouse, and is an aspect of the Great Goddess Devi. In the *Devi Bhagavata Purana,* she is said to have been born miraculously from the supreme being's side. As Vishnu took various incarnations, Lakshmi did, too, becoming, for instance, Sita, Rama's wife in the *Rāmāyana,* and Draupadi, the Pandava wife, in the *Mahabharata.* The *Vishnu Purana* reveals that she took corresponding forms to each of the avatars of Vishnu.

Who are Vishnu's avatars?

The ten avatars of Vishnu are Matsya the fish, Kurma the turtle, Varaha the boar, Narashimba the lion-man, Vamana the dwarf, Parasu-Rama (Rama with the ax), Sri-Rama, Balabhadra-Rama, Krishna, and Kalki, an avatar who will come at the end of the present age, the Kali Yuga. Some count the Buddha as an avatar of Vishnu. Rama and Krishna were by far the most important of the avatars.

KRISHNA

Who is Krishna?

Krishna, the greatest and most popular of Vishnu's avatars, is literally "the black (*krishna*) one," who in the *Bhagavata Purana* is provided with a complex hero-based mythology involving a miraculous conception and birth and the slaying of monsters.

Krishna's parents were Vasudeva and Devaki. From the beginning, Krishna was threatened by Kamsa, his evil uncle. Born with four hands holding the symbols of Vishnu, Krishna immediately revealed his past lives to his father and gave him instructions relating to his present one. He then returned to the form of a human baby and Vasudeva took the baby to another couple to protect him from Kamsa. He returned home with a substitute baby, who was an incarnation of Devi. When Kamsa arrived to kill it, the baby ascended to the sky, announcing that the future killer of Kamsa was already born. In his fury, Kamsa undertook a massacre of innocent babies, so Krishna's foster father took the child away to Gokula, where the boy grew up among the cow herders known as Gopalas. Krishna developed many trickster characteristics, especially in his relationship with the cow-herding girls, the Gopis. One day when the girls went swimming, for instance, he stole their clothes and made them come to him to retrieve them.

In erotic episodes he divided himself into many Krishnas and had relations with the Gopis. His favorite was Radha. The Gopis' lovemaking with him represents religious devotion and total subservience to Krishna.

In one trickster act the boy Krishna swallowed dirt, causing his foster mother to demand that he open his mouth. When he did so and she looked in, she witnessed the whole universe.

In his youth Krishna was also a monster slayer and protector of the people.

In the *Mahabharata,* Krishna is serving as the apparently human charioteer for the Pandava hero Arjuna during an epic battle, when suddenly he reveals himself as the supreme being, the Lord Krishna, incarnation of Vishnu.

A painting of Himalayan origin of Krishna with cows. Krishna developed many trickster characteristics, especially in his relationship with the cow-herding girls, the Gopis.

Eventually Krishna, in his human form, was killed by a poison arrow, which pierced his foot, the only place in his body not protected by a magical potion. At his death he rose up to the heavens and once again became Vishnu.

Readers of the *New Testament* and of the myths of Achilles will be reminded in the Krishna story of King Herod and the massacre of the innocents, of the ascension of Jesus, and of the fatal vulnerability of Achilles' heel.

What is the *Bhagavadgita,* and what is its message?

"The Blessed Lord's Song," the *Bhagavadgita* was composed about two thousand years ago and was inserted into the *Mahabharata.* It is a text frequently consulted for messages of ultimate truth. The poem is made up of seven hundred verses in Sanskrit. The teacher in the *Gita,* as it is often called, is the Lord Krishna, the charioteer of the hero Arjuna, who reveals the ultimate truths of existence itself.

As a great battle rages around him, Arjuna asks the obvious questions about the justification for the senseless killing that is war. Krishna justifies war in the context of duty *(dharma).* As a member of the warrior caste, Arjuna must do his duty without regard for the consequences. In any case, the individual is in actuality immortal, only seeming to control his destiny. The individual is ultimately linked to divine reality. Here Krishna, in effect, reveals himself as Vishnu, the incarnation of the impersonal supreme primal power, what many Hindus would call Brahman. As Vishnu, Krishna is the universal poet who contains within himself the whole epic of existence. The relationship of Arjuna to Krishna is a metaphor for the true connection between the human and the divine.

THE *MAHABHARATA*

What is the background of the *Mahabharata*?

The Indian epic, the *Mahabharata,* is eight times as long as Homer's *Iliad* and *Odyssey* combined. Its authorship is attributed to the Indian "Homer," Vyasa, the famous sage *(rishi),* otherwise known as "Krishna Dvaipayana," suggesting a connection with Krishna and, therefore, Vishnu. As noted earlier, it is said that it was the elephant-headed god Ganesha, a son of Shiva, who dictated the epic to Vyasa.

Another tradition has it that Vyasa was the begetter of the first Indians, the Bharatas, the ancestors of both warring families in the epic. Thus, the title *Maha-bharata* (Great Bharatas). In fact, the creation of the epic was gradual, reaching back to stories of ancient "Aryan" tribal warfare. Much of the epic was transcribed by brahmins in the fifth century B.C.E., and additions were made as late as 500 C.E.

The theological context for the epic is the fact that the goddess in her form as Earth is being oppressed by demons and humans. There is a need for sacrifice in order for prosperity to be restored. Vishnu and other gods play significant roles. Vishnu, as Krishna, befriends the Pandava brothers, who, themselves, are *bona fide* heroes in that they have been fathered by gods. Yudhishthira, the Pandava king, is fathered by the personified Dharma (duty and proper order). Arjuna, the central figure of the Bhagavadgita section of the *Mahabharata,* is fathered by Indra, his brother and fellow warrior hero Bhima by Vayu (Wind). The twins, Nakula and Sahadeva, are fathered by the divine twins, the Ashvins, representing social welfare. The Pandavas share a single wife, Draupadi, an incarnation of Sri-Lakshmi, who is Prosperity. The Pandavas as a whole embody the drive for *dharma*. The epic concerns the struggle between the Pandavas and their hundred Kaurava cousins, led by the particularly arrogant Duryodhana and assisted by Karna, the son of Surya, the sun god. The Kauravas represent the opposite of *dharma,* or *adharma*. The war between the families in the larger theological context will be a cleansing sacrifice that will end one age and usher in a new one. It will relieve Earth's burden. It is this that Krishna, as Arjuna's charioteer, will make clear in the *Bhagavadgita*.

What is the plot line of the *Mahabharata*?

After political struggles, Yudhishthira claims universal kingship, but is challenged by Duryodhana, who challenges him to a decision-making game of dice. Yudhishthira loses, giving up everything he and his brothers own, including Draupadi. In short, he loses Prosperity itself, since Draupadi is an incarnation of Lakshmi. When the winning Kauravas attempt to humiliate Draupadi by disrobing her, Krishna uses his powers to make her sari endless. She and her husbands, nevertheless, go into exile, marking the preparation for the great sacrifice that will come. Later, in a war to end wars, the Pandavas defeat the Kauravas, but almost all the warriors are killed, bringing to an end the current age, the *kaliyuga*. Vishnu, thus, has relieved Earth of her burden in preparation for a new creation.

Who is Ganesha?

Ganesha, or Ganapati, the elephant-headed god, is worshipped by many Hindus, especially Ganapatyas, whose devotion is directed specifically to him as their major deity. The *Brhaddharma Purana* tells the story of Ganesha's birth. Pārvatī, Shiva's wife, wanted a child, but the ascetic-yogi Shiva saw no need of creating descendants. Finally he agreed to his wife's desire for a baby but maintained a distance from the conception process. He instructed her to tear off a piece of her dress and to use that

During the festival of Ganesha, a likeness of the elephant-headed god is carried through the streets of Hyderabad, India.

as the agent of conception. When the baby was born into Pārvatī's hand while she was taking a bath, Shiva became jealous of it and decapitated the child. Later, feeling remorse and giving in to Pārvatī's threats against creation itself, Shiva arranged for a new head to be placed on the boy. The head was that of an elephant. Ganesha is the god who provides wealth and success.

THE *RĀMĀYANA*

Who are Rama and Sita?

Rama, conceived miraculously from divine pudding given to his mother by Vishnu, is the second greatest avatar of that god. As a young man he was forced with his wife Sita and his brother Lakshmana into exile to meet the demands of one of his father's wives. In the forest, a powerful demon fell in love with Rama but was rejected by him, reminding us of Gilgamesh's similar rejection of Inanna in the Mesopotamian tradition and Cuchulainn's rejection of Morrigan in Irish mythology. In spite of complications exposed by the events of the epic of Rama, the *Rāmāyana*, Rama and Sita represent the perfect relationship between husband and wife, and after their deaths they are raised up to heaven into Vishnu and Lakshmi, the deities of whom they had been incarnations on earth.

What is the plot line of the *Rāmāyana*?

Rama had met Sita at her father King Janaka's court during a long struggle with Ravana and his allies. Sita had been born miraculously from a farrow in the earth and was discovered by Janaka as he was plowing his fields. Thus, she is a child of Prithvi (Earth). Rama proves himself worthy of Sita as a true hero when he succeeds in bending the great bow of the god Shiva. He also succeeds in bending the bow of Vishnu. Because of promises made to one of his wives, Janaka has no choice but to accede to the exile of Sita

What is the background of the *Rāmāyana*?

The second of the two great Indian epics, the *Rāmāyana,* is always attributed to Valmiki, the second of the Indian "Homers." In fact, the epic was gradually compiled from various legends and folktales between 500 B.C.E. and 200 C.E. Like the *Mahabharata,* it is not only a story but an allegorical or symbolic record of Hindu ideas. As an avatar of Vishnu, the epic's hero, Rama, embodies *dharma* (duty and order). His wife Sita, an avatar of Vishnu's wife, Lakshmi, is Prosperity. In their exile in the forest, Rama and Sita stand not only for the perfect husband and wife but also for the preparation for the necessary sacred sacrifice that will be necessary to defeat evil in the world, evil represented by the terrible demon Ravana.

and Rama for a period. During the forest exile Ravana kidnaps Sita and imprisons her in his Lanka fortress. Rama must now go on the major quest of his life, the highly symbolic quest for his divine creative energy, his Shakti, which is embodied in Sita. The monkey god Hanuman and his army help Rama to free Sita by building a bridge from India to Lanka (Sri Lanka). Rama kills Ravana, thus fulfilling Vishnu's higher purpose.

Since Sita could theoretically have been defiled by Ravana, even though, in fact, she is innocent, she must undergo a trial by fire. As Rama's wife, she must prove her faithfulness by performing *sati*. That is, she must allow herself to be placed on a funeral pyre. The flames refuse to burn her, so Rama can receive her as the perfect wife. Rama's doubts revive, however, and the sacrifice of Sita continues when she is exiled to the forest. There she gives birth to twins and stays with the poet Valmiki, who composes the *Rāmāyana*. Sita finally returns to Rama but asks her mother, Earth, to take her back as proof of her innocence and fidelity. Earth rises up and takes her child to her lap; the earth regains the Prosperity that had been threatened by Ravana. The necessary sacrifice is complete and Rama reigns as king for a thousand years.

SHIVA

Who is Shiva?

Shaivas, those who practice Shaivism, the devotion (*bhakti*) to Shiva, believe that Shiva is the greatest of the gods, the principle incarnation of ultimate divinity, or Brahman. More specifically, if Brahma is the creator, and Vishnu the preserver, Shiva, in the context of the Brahma/Vishnu/Shiva triad, is the destroyer, he who demands the sacrifice out of which new life can be born. He stands for the fact that life itself, the universe, is a process of death and regeneration. He is the Nataraja, the lord of the cosmic yogic dance, the dance of the universe itself. He is the ultimate guru-yogi, the ascetic who brings release (*moksha*) to those who follow his asceticism, his yoga.

An ancient pre-Indo-European Indus Valley seal depicts a three-faced divinity sitting cross-legged in a yogic style. It is assumed by many that this is a depiction of an early form of Shiva, later known in the *Vedas* as Rudra.

Shiva is often shown in union—sometimes sexual union—with his consort or *Shakti*, his creative energizing power.

Shiva is worshipped by way of his linga (sacred phallus) which reaches endlessly into the heavens. Sometimes his linga is implanted in his consort's yoni (sacred female organ).

What is an example of a Shiva myth?

There are countless myths about Shiva. One famous one tells of the origin of the sacred river Ganga, the Ganges. A certain king wanted the heavenly Ganga to come down to earth to purify the ashes of his dead warrior sons. Eventually a sage went to the Himalayas and convinced the river to come down, but in order to prevent the powerful force of the river from destroying the world, the sage convinced Shiva to allow the water to be diverted through his hair. When Ganga did so, the three great rivers were formed that make up the present Ganges.

Who is Parvatī?

The wife of Shiva, Parvatī, the "Daughter of the Mountain," is an embodiment of the Great Goddess Devi. As her husband's *Shakti,* she is frequently depicted in a sexual embrace with him. As is evident in the story of the birth of Ganesha, she was capable of standing up to him. Devotees of *Shakti—Shaktas*—would say that without his Shakti, deprived of his feminine aspect, Shiva (or any other god) is essentially nothing.

DEVI: THE GREAT GODDESS

Who are Devi and Shakti?

Shakti is divine creative energy, sometimes personified as one manifestation of Devi, the Great Mother goddess.

Shiva, Vishnu, and Brahma all have their Shaktis in the form of their wives, Parvatī, Lakshmi, and Sarasvati, all of whom are also manifestations of Devi. Devi is most often seen in connection with Shiva, as one of his wives— Parvatī, Kali, and Durga. She is also incarnated as Radha, the favorite wife of Krishna, and Draupadi, the Pandava wife, who can also be seen as an avatar of Lakshmi. In fact, Devi is a collective name for all Hindu goddesses. Or she can be worshipped by her particular devotees as Mahadevi (Great Goddess), an equal in the trinity she forms with Shiva and Vishnu. The most popular mythological manifestations of Devi are the terrifying goddesses Kali and Durga.

Who is Kali?

Kali is "the black one," the dark aspect of Mahadevi, the anger of Shiva's wife, Parvatī. Kali thirsts for both wine and the blood of animal sacrifices. She dances wildly on the body of her husband, the apparently dead Shiva, who is nevertheless depicted in union with her.

Kali is the feminine form of the Sanskrit *kala,* meaning "time," the inevitable devouring principle that consumes all things. Whereas Shiva's dance is eternal cosmic time, Kali's dance on Shiva is earthly time, which ends in death. Kali has bloody fangs and sometimes wears human heads around her head as a necklace. As a devourer, Kali is a logical wife, or Shakti, for Shiva the destroyer. Shiva's sexual contact with her suggests fertility and perhaps the idea that death is a necessary part of the cycle of life.

Who is Durga?

In many ways Durga resembles Kali, and the two forms of Devi and Shiva's wife are sometimes treated as a single being. Durga is immensely popular and worshipped widely.

She is the goddess of cosmic illusion and mystery who comes to the world to kill evil in its many forms. Some say she was born of the wax in Vishnu's ear. As a combatant against evil, Durga is herself, like Kali, bloody and terrifying. Her most important feat was the slaying of the frightful Mahisha-asura, the demon who could not be killed by a male. It is said that Mahisha had expelled even Brahma, Vishnu, and Shiva from heaven. In desperation, the gods combined their powers to form a beautiful goddess, Durga, who announced that she would marry anyone who could beat her in combat. Mahisha took the bait, and when he assumed the form of the buffalo demon, Durga cut off his head, thus rescuing heaven for the gods and so restoring cosmic order. Some say that Kali was born of Durga's head.

Arjuna, seen here meeting Krishna, is one of a number of Hindu heroes of mythology.

Who are the Hindu mythic heroes?

The primary mythic heroes of Hinduism—those humans who have characteristics of the monomythic hero such as miraculous conceptions, relatives among the gods, difficult quests, and ascensions to heaven—are avatars such as Krishna, Rama, Sita, and Draupadi; Arjuna and his brothers—the epic heroes—are less perfect, but are heroes in the sense that Homer's epic characters are. They often have divine ancestry, they possess powers much greater than those of other humans, but are also flawed, particularly by a very human tendency toward pride. A different kind of hero emerges from Buddhism, another form of devotion that emerged in ancient India.

BUDDHISM

Where did Buddhism come from?

Buddhism is said by most scholars to have originated in eastern India sometime in the late sixth century B.C.E., although the dates vary from scholar to scholar. The source of Buddhism was the teaching of Siddhartha Gautama, or Shakyamuni (of the royal Shaka family), the man now known as "the Buddha" ("The Enlightened One"), who by no means thought of himself as a deity, but who taught the way to spiritual enlightenment, or *nirvana*. Buddhism took many forms in the centuries that followed and has been widely practiced in the countries of south Asia other than India.

What are the major schools of Buddhism?

The earliest form is known as Hinayana or Theravada. Its monks read texts in Pali, an ancient Indo-European language which, like Sanskrit, is no longer generally spoken. This school was more a philosophy than a religion, stressing the striving for personal nirvana. In the first century C.E. Mahayana (Great Vehicle) Buddhism emerged in Asia. The Buddha became a *de facto* deity and past and future buddhas became a kind of pantheon. The idea of *bodhisattvas,* enlightened ones who postponed personal nirvana to help others and to better the conditions of humanity, developed in Mahayana. This is the most widely practiced form of Buddhism in China and elsewhere in Asia. A third form of Buddhism, called Tantrism or Vajrayana or Tibetan Buddhism, developed in the seventh century C.E. and is most popular in the Himalayan region (Tibet, Nepal). Tibetan Buddhism is an aspect of Mahayana in that it stresses bodhisattvas, but it has a much more complex mythological system, based on bodhisattvas who are clearly seen with their female counterparts as deities.

What is the mythology of the Buddha?

Some of the earliest myths about the Buddha are found in the *Jataka Tales,* many of them dating to the Pali tradition of Theravada. These myths include birth stories of the Buddha and his former incarnations. Other stories have emerged out of the Buddhist folk tradition over the centuries.

Prince Siddhartha, shown here in a 1914 illustration, fulfills his destiny by leaving his home and life of privilege to become a teacher, the Enlightened One called the Buddha.

One myth tells how the Buddha was conceived miraculously by his mother, Queen Maya of the Shakas, during a dream about a white elephant who walked around her three times and touched her right side. In this myth, Maya gave birth in a Lumbini grove. As soon as the boy was born he took several steps and proclaimed, "I am the most honored one in all the world."

Maya died seven days later. The boy, named Siddhartha Gautama, or Shakyamuni, prince of the Shakas, received a princely upbringing and was protected from the world. His father had been told by a prophet that his son would become a great leader if he remained at home or a teacher if he left home. The father preferred the former path and might have succeeded in keeping Siddhartha from the world if, during a ride with his charioteer, the boy had not witnessed an old man, a sick man, a dead man, and a wandering ascetic. Moved by his visions of aging, sickness, death, and asceticism, Siddhartha left his wife and child and the comforts of the palace to confront and understand reality—to seek enlightenment as a wandering ascetic himself. In time he found his way to the Bodhi Tree, under which he sat and began meditation. There he was tempted in many ways by Mara the Fiend. But Siddhartha resisted these temptations and became The Enlightened One, the Buddha. He remained seated for seven days, relishing the bliss of nirvana. The Buddha spent the rest of his life as a bodhisattva, teaching others. When he died, his funeral pyre ignited spontaneously and nothing was left after the fire but a pile of relics.

Are there other mythological figures in Buddhism?

Mahayana and Vajrayana provide many myths to create a post-Pali Buddhist mythology. That mythology is particularly developed in Tibet. Partly influenced by Bon, a pre-Buddhist religion, Tibetans speak of such figures as mountain gods, nature spirits, and evil spirits. But the real contribution of Buddhism to Tibetan mythology is the concept of the bodhisattva. Two Tibetan bodhisattvas who are, in effect, divinities, stand out. These are Avalokiteśvara and his *Shakti,* Tara. Tibetans hold that Avalokiteśvara was their progenitor and that he is reincarnated in each Dalai Lama, who lives as the bodhisattva had on Potola, a mountaintop from which the cries of suffering humanity may be heard. As for his female self, Tara, it is said by some that Tara was born from one of Avalokiteśvara's tears. Another Tibetan myth says that in ancient times Tara took the form of a rock demoness and mated with the bodhisattva in his form as a monkey. She then gave birth to monkeys who became the Tibetans. Avalokiteśvara would take various forms in Chinese and Japanese mythology.

EAST ASIAN MYTHOLOGY: CHINA AND JAPAN

Who are the Chinese people?

Within the boundaries of what today we know as China are some fifty-six ethnic groups, long dominated by one group, the Han.

Is there a unified ethnic-based Chinese mythology?

In China there is no single "authorized" collection of myths equivalent to the sacred texts of the monotheistic traditions, the *Prose Edda* of Iceland, or the *Vedas* and other sacred texts of India. What we think of as Chinese mythology today is made up of many often-fragmented stories, told over the centuries in many traditions and many dynasties and ultimately transmitted primarily by Han scholars and storytellers.

Who invented Chinese writing?

We do not have a factual answer to this question, but there is a mythological answer. The inventor of the Chinese writing characters was said to have been a culture hero, Cangjie, who had four eyes and who could write from the day of his birth. From his precise visualizations of aspects of the natural world around him, Cangjie created the pictograph signs that would become Chinese written characters. The design of feathers, the footprints of various animals—everything in nature—contributed to the characters.

SOURCES OF CHINESE MYTHOLOGY

What are our sources for Chinese mythology?

The best known Chinese myths come to us in various states of completeness in several texts, including *Shanhaijing* (The Classic of Mountains and Seas), *Chuci* (The Songs of Chu), *Huainanzi* (The Scholars of Huainan), and *Soushenji* (Searching for Spirits).

179

What is *Shanhaijing*?

One tradition has it that this ancient and somewhat fanciful survey of the geography of ancient China, which also contains a significant collection of myths, was composed by the flood hero Yu or his assistant Boyi. It is much more likely to have been written by Zhou Dynasty scholars in the fourth century B.C.E. and finalized by Han scholars in the second century B.C.E.

What is *Chuci*?

Written by the famous poet Qu Yuan (343–278 B.C.E.), this long poem includes "Tianw Wn" (Heavenly Questions), in which many of the best-known Chinese myths are told.

What is *Huainanzi*?

It was Liu An, the King of Huainan, himself who was the primary compiler of *Huainanzi* in about 139 B.C.E. It is based on the knowledge of many scholars of Huainan and is the source for many of the stories of Chinese mythology.

What is *Soushenji*?

The scholar Gan Bao (d. 336 C.E.) based this work on interviews and on the examination of ancient mythological writings. The many myths recorded here were affected by the reworkings of a much later Ming Dynasty scholar, Hu Yingling.

THE CHINESE PANTHEON

What is the Chinese pantheon?

A canonical Chinese pantheon is difficult to establish. There is no developed heavenly family such as the ones we find in Norse or Greek mythology. Even the supreme being changes at various stages in Chinese history. In the early Shang period (1600–1300 B.C.E.) the great god was Shang Di. Later, during the Zhou Dynasty, he was Tian (Heaven) Di. The term *tiandi* represents the union of sky and earth. Tian Di was for some the same being as Shang Di, Shang Di being the deity's name, Tian being more of an abstraction. Another supreme deity name is Di Jun of the Yin people in eastern China.

Much later, in the Common Era, the supreme deity was Yu Di, the Jade Emperor. For Daoists the supreme being is T'ai. The root meaning for many of these names is "sky," the place of the gods. Because of conflicts between the many ethnic groups in China, the pantheon was repeatedly rearranged to fit political realities and the dominance of particular groups. When the Shang and Zhou united, Di Ku became the supreme deity and the mothers of the founders of the two groups became his wives. During the so-called Warring States period (475–221 B.C.E.) of the Zhou Dynasty, another attempt was made to create a new pantheon. Zhurong had been the divine founder of the Chu people; his name was changed to Zhuanxu. For some, his son was the more famous Yu, who is sometimes treated more as a human hero-type than as a god. The confusion of heroes with gods is a constant element in the Chinese pantheonic vision, as in the case of several of the grouping known as the Five August Emperors. There are several important goddesses in the Chinese pantheon, the most important of whom are Nuwa and, under Buddhist influence, Guanyin.

Who were the Five August Emperors?

The Five August Emperors are an example of the tendency in Chinese mythology to unite history with myth and heroes with gods. Huang Di, Zhuanxu, Di Ku, Yao, and Shun are the names usually applied to the legendary first five kings of China, who are associated with the cardinal directions (North, South, East, West, and Center) and elements (metal, wood, water, fire, and earth).

Huang Di (Xuanyuan) was the Yellow Emperor, the most important of the five and often seen as the supreme deity or the Thunder god. It was he who put down a serious rebellion—a "war in heaven"—led by Chiyou, a son of the god of war. As an example of the hero rather than deity archetype, Huang Di was conceived miraculously when his mother, Fupao, saw a bolt of lightning circling a star. The lightning apparently impregnated her and after twenty-five weeks she gave birth to Huang Di, who could talk almost at birth and who lived three hundred years. Zhuanxu (Gaoyang), the second August Emperor, was a descendant of Huang Di. It was he who ordered the separation of heaven and earth. He lived as a human for eight hundred years. Di Ku (Gaoxin) was the third of the August Emperors. He could speak his name at birth, and his favorite means of transportation was

Among the first five kings of China was the Yellow Emperor, who is often seen as the greatest, even becoming a supreme deity. (151 C.E. illustration.)

a dragon. One of Di Ku's wives gave birth to eight sons in succession after she dreamed that she had swallowed the sun. Yao, one of these sons, was the next August Emperor. He is known for having ordered the stopping of the great flood. Another son was Qi, the founder of the Shang Dynasty. Qi's birth was miraculous, too. His mother, Jiandi, became pregnant when she consumed a swallow's egg. The fifth of the Five August Emperors was Shun (Yu Shun), who gave up his throne to the great demigod and hero, Yu.

THE CHINESE WAR IN HEAVEN, CREATION, AND FLOOD

What was the Chinese version of the war in heaven?

The Chinese version of the war in heaven is told in many variations over the centuries. It usually involves the rebellion of Chiyou against the first and greatest of the Five August Emperors, the Yellow Emperor and supreme being, Huang Di.

In one variation of this story, the war is one between natural elements. When Chiyou, who according to some sources was a member of the emperor's court, attacked Huang Di, the emperor ordered his flying dragon, Yinglong, to collect all the water in the world. Chiyou ordered the wind and rain gods to release the water in a massive downpour. Huang Di countered by ordering the goddess of drought to dry up everything, and then Huang Di killed Chiyou. Some say that he killed his enemy with the help of the horrific sound made by his thunderous drum made from the hide of a one-legged monster. There was another war in heaven involving the gods Zhuanxu and Gonggong, which led to the collapse of the sky.

Who was Nuwa?

Nuwa is the Great Goddess of Chinese mythology. She had a woman's head and a serpent's body. As was the hero-god Fuxi, the creator of humans, Nuwa was also one of the greatest of the culture heroes. It was she, for instance, who taught men and women to mate in order to have children. When the four pillars that held up the sky fell down because of the war in heaven between Zhuanxu and Gonggong, it was Nuwa who repaired things.

What is the Chinese creation myth?

There are several creation myths in China, just as there are various pantheons. One of the most popular involves the divine first human, Pangu, the Chinese equivalent of the Vedic Purusha. The Pangu myth is at once a cosmic-egg and an animistic world-parent creation story. Born in the unformed chaos of the pre-creation world, Pangu found himself in what was, in effect, a giant cosmic egg, in which he gradually formed the heavens and the earth over an 18,000-year period. Pangu was extremely tall. When the egg finally burst, Pangu uncoiled himself as the heaven rose up and the earth sank below. A later myth relates how when Pangu finally died, his body became the universe. One of his eyes became the sun, the other the moon; his voice became thunder; his blood became rivers; his body hair plants; and so forth. Pangu resembles other world parents whose very bodies animated the universe, figures such as such as Purusha in India, Ymir in Iceland, and several corn mothers in Native North American mythology.

What is the myth of the separation of Heaven and Earth?

A form of the fall from grace archetype in China is the story of the separation of the world parents, Heaven and Earth. The world-parent separation motif occurs in many creation myths around the world, as, for instance, in the myth of Uranos and Gaia in Greece and of Geb and Nut in Egypt. In the Chinese myth, Earth and

Pangu (shown in a 1607 illustration), a creation myth world parent from China who creates the world in a kind of cosmic egg.

Heaven were tightly attached to each other when Chiyou's rebellion caused the people to become corrupt, leaving the supreme being no choice but to instruct the gods Zhong and Li to break the connection between the two worlds. From then on, the people were separated from their gods.

How were humans created?

Some say that humans were born of the spit of deities or that they were transformed from plants or animals. More widespread is the myth of the Great Goddess Nuwa's molding them from clay. It is believed by some that the molding process drained Nuwa's strength and that after she molded the upper classes, she dragged a rope through the mud and then shook it, the droppings off the rope forming the common people.

Is there a Chinese flood myth?

There are several Chinese flood myths. One concerns the water god Gonggong, who, in a rage at being unable to unseat the supreme being, decided to inundate the world by damming all the rivers. Providentially, the resulting flood was overcome by the hero Yu, who created flood channels to divert the waters. Some say it was the goddess Nuwa, who stopped the waters with reed ashes. In any case, Gonggong was killed by the supreme being for his evil acts. A popular myth tells how humans were re-created after the flood by a brother and his sister, the only remaining humans, who married and began the process of repopulation.

CHINESE HEROES

Who are the heroes in Chinese mythology?

It is difficult to distinguish gods from heroes in Chinese mythology. There are culture heroes who taught certain aspects of civilized life to their people: Ling Lun invented music, Cangjie invented writing, Shennong invented agriculture. But there are also hero figures such as Fuxi, Qi, Yi, Gun, and Yu who, although sometimes thought of as gods, are marked by characteristics which in most mythologies we associate with the archetypal hero, the man or demigod who is born miraculously and who possesses qualities that make possible a difficult quest.

Who was Fuxi?

An ancient Chinese god, Fuxi was also a culture hero and human king. His heroic credentials are indicated by his miraculous conception; he was conceived by his mother when she stepped into a large footprint. He was sometimes seen as husband or sister to the Great Goddess Nuwa, and as was she, could be depicted with a serpent body and human head. Together Nuwa and Fuxi created social rules for civilization based on the harmony between *yin* and *yang*. In some texts Fuxi and Nuwa are the brother-sister couple who recreated humanity after the flood. Fuxi is considered the first of the Three Divine Sovereigns, followed by Nuwa and Shennong. As a culture hero, Fuxi is still popular, credited with many inventions, including, for instance, the eight trigrams used in Chinese divination, the rules of marriage, animal husbandry, and metallurgy. He was particularly concerned with the welfare of the people, who often seemed not to have enough to eat. It was he who, watching a spider weave a web, came up with the idea of using nets to catch fish. Fuxi is still worshipped, especially at the Renzu Temple in Huaiyang, where he is said to have been born.

What are yin and yang and T'ai?

In Chinese philosophy *yin* (shadow)and *yang* (brightness)—the male and female, positive and negative principles in the world—must ideally be balanced in all aspects of life, including nature and the human body. Traditional Chinese medicine, for instance, attempts to balance the two principles. In Taoism, *yin* and *yang* are the opposite boundaries of the absolute supreme reality *(T'ai)*. The meditative exercises known as *t'ai chi* represent, in part, the balancing of the two principles in unity with the supreme being.

In a creation-based myth of the second century B.C.E., it is said that in the beginning there was only chaos, containing light and dark. Light, which was the *yang* principle, became the sky and dark, the *yin* principle, became the earth. The sky— *yang*—gave, and the earth— *yin*—received. This is like Indo-European concepts of the original union of sky and earth. In the Chinese myth, when *yin* and *yang* became one—that is, *tiandi*— the elements came into being and humans were created.

Who was Qi?

Qi was the culture hero of the Shang people. He was miraculously conceived, and thus identified for us as a bona fide hero, by Jiandi, Emperor Di Ku's second concubine, when she ate a swallow's egg while taking a bath. Qi assisted Yu in his struggle against the great flood.

Who was Yi, and what was the myth of the shooting of the suns?

Yi (sometimes Houyi) was the culture hero who is best known as the great archer who shot down the unnecessary nine of the ten suns. There are many versions of this myth and sometimes Yi is replaced by other archers. One myth begins with the goddess Xihe, the wife of the supreme being Di Jun, giving birth to ten suns. At first the suns, carried by crows, worked in succession to warm the earth, but somehow a problem arose and the suns shone simultaneously, burning everything. It was the wise king Yao who ordered the hero Yi to shoot down nine of the suns. Yi was also, in the universal heroic pattern, a great monster slayer.

Who were Gun and Yu?

Gun and Yu, father and son, were two of the most important culture heroes of ancient China. Their story is intricately associated with the flood myth. A descendant of the Yellow Emperor, Huang Di, Gun was determined to put an end to the great flood which had inundated the land. To accomplish his mission, he followed in the tradition of several cultural heroes in world mythology—Prometheus in Greece, for example—by stealing a valuable asset. Here, Gun steals from the Supreme Being Tian Di. In the case of Prometheus the asset was fire; here it was the mysterious self-growing soil, Xirang. Gun planned to use the soil to block the flow of the waters. Furious at the theft, the Supreme Being ordered the fire god Zhurong to dispose of Gun.

It was out of the dead Gun's belly that the flood hero Yu sprang, riding on a dragon, the miraculous birth already marking him as a hero. His sacred quest was to fulfill his father's dream of stopping the flood. This time the Supreme Being, or some say the August Emperor, Yao, ordered Yu to continue with Gun's use of Xirang. He also devised a plan by which the waters were diverted into the sea in channels dug by the dragging tail of the dragon Yinglong. It took Yu thirteen years to accomplish his great task. Along the way he followed another typically heroic pattern, the slaying of monsters, including Wuzhiqi, the evil spirit of the raging Huai River. When he was thirty, Yu married Tushanshi (The Tuschan Woman), who helped him with his work. Once, when he was about to dig through a mountain to form a channel to the sea, he instructed his wife to send him food when he beat on a drum. To work faster, Yu changed himself into a bear, and when he accidentally stepped on the drum, the sound attracted his wife, who arrived with food. Horrified by her husband's having become a bear, she fled from the tunnel and changed herself into a rock. When Yu came out of the tunnel he begged the rock to give him the baby with which his wife had been pregnant. In this version of the myth, it was the rock that gave birth miraculously to the hero Qi. Later Yu became emperor, as did his son Qi.

How are Chinese heroes like those in other mythologies?

Like heroes from around the world, Chinese mythological heroes are miraculously conceived and born, indicating their special role—one that transcends the division between Heaven and Earth. They are also marked by the necessity of a quest, the success of which will improve the lot of the people they represent. Commonly, these heroes, like all world heroes, are monster slayers, signifying their ability, perhaps reflected in our own lives and psyches, to destroy the forces that threaten us from both without and within.

What role do dragons play in Chinese mythology?

Dragons are and always have been important in Chinese mythology and folklore. Figures of dragons appear in Chinese archeological sites from as early as the fourth millennium B.C.E., indicating an ancient dragon mythology. Dragons in China are associated particularly with water, divinity, and heroes. They can fly, and their breath creates clouds. Many divine figures and heroes—including especially Fuxi and Nuwa, but also sometimes Z and Huang Di—have human heads and dragon bodies. Dragons such as Yinglong help heroes, for example, Yu, to overcome negative obstacles. In one myth it was a dragon, Zhulong, who created the universe with his body. In another, told by the Miao

The Sanggar Agung Temple in Surabaya, Indonesia, is decorated with enormous dragons. The dragon plays an important role in the mythology of many Asian cultures. Rather than being considered monsters, as they are in Europe, dragons are seen as divine beings.

people in southwest China, we learn that before there were humans on earth there was only a dragon living in a cave. When monkeys came one day to play with the dragon, he turned them into human beings with his breath. Dragons are still much admired in China and, some Chinese even pray to them when rain is needed.

HISTORICIZING CHINESE MYTHS: CONFUCISM AND TAOISM

How have Chinese myths been historicized?

There is a strong tendency in China to rationalize myths and to associate them, as metaphors, with history, or to use them simply as a means of teaching about moral and social order. It has been suggested by many scholars that this is because the Chinese have traditionally been less interested in the supernatural than are many other peoples. Whether or not that is the case, many Chinese intellectuals, dating back to the early first millennium B.C.E., have doubted the factuality of the myths and have treated them accordingly as representative of worldly concerns. To one extent or another, this is true of the great thinkers in all three of the religions or religious philosophies that have dominated in China: Confucianism, Taoism (Daoism), and Buddhism.

How did Confucius affect Chinese mythology?

Many of the myths of pre-Buddhist China are known to us primarily through the work of Confucian scholars, who have placed the old stories in a historical context and used them for their own purposes. Confucius (Kong Qiu, Kongfuzi, 551–479 B.C.E.) himself replied to a question about the four faces of Huang Di by asserting that the four faces referred to the four directions. A good example of Confucius' historicizing tendency is pointed out by the contemporary scholars Lihui Yang and Deming An in their valuable *Handbook of Chinese Mythology* (Oxford, 2005, 33–34) in connection with a myth about Kui, a one-legged monster who lived on Mount Liubo and caused a storm whenever he dove into the sea. The storm made a large thunderous noise. Huang Di caught and killed the monster and made a drum of its skin. As Thunder god, Huang Di used the drum well to demonstrate his dominance. Confucius explained that "one-legged" really meant "one is enough" and that Kui was actually a state official and that because he was so talented it was agreed by all that one such official was enough.

How did Taoism affect Chinese mythology?

The Taoists, too, used the ancient myths according to their own philosophy. The most famous of the Taoist philosophers was Zhuangzi (369–286 B.C.E.). His work is replete with Taoist interpretations of the myths. Lihui Yang and Deming An use the Hundun myth as an example. Hundun was a god with no body orifices. When the gods Shu and Hu tried to chisel holes into Hundun's body, thinking this would be helpful to him,

Hundun died. For Zhuangzi, Shu and Hu represented the artificial realities of time and direction whereas Hundun was the chaos that preceded creation, a chaos which was in reality perfect wholeness. In this case, artificial order destroyed natural harmony and diverted attention from the proper "way," the Tao.

BUDDHISM, SHAMANISM, AND CHINESE MYTHOLOGY

How did Buddhism affect Chinese mythology?

It is unclear as to when exactly Buddhism came to China from India and Nepal. Scholars generally put the date between 200 B.C.E. and 150 C.E. There were Chinese translations of Buddhist scriptures by 148 C.E., and Buddhism gradually gained ground on its rivals, Confucianism and Taoism, after that until by the sixth century Buddhism in the Mahayana form predominated in Chinese religious thought. Buddhism contributed in new ways to Chinese mythology. The gods of Mahayana were associated with government ministries, for instance. A given government minister might have an alter ego among the Ministry of Gods. And, of course, Buddhism brought its own mythology, such as that of the Tibetan bodhisattvas Avalokiteśvara and Tara, a probable combination of which became the well known Guanyin.

Who is Guanyin?

Guanyin is a goddess of compassion. She is almost always female in China, but does appear from time to time in male form. The myths of Guanyin are often mingled with Taoist or earlier Chinese mythologies, as in the case of the story of Guanyin and the Dragon King's son. The Dragon King controlled the sea. His son transformed himself into a fish, was caught by a fisherman, and was about to be sold for food when Guanyin intervened and the fish was returned to the sea to become once again a dragon. It was Guanyin's reminder to the people of the superior importance of compassion that allowed for the release of the fish.

Guanyin also led people to peace after death.

The goddess of compassion, Guanyin, is usually depicted as a woman, as in this circa 1025 statue from the Sung dynasty.

What role did shamanism play in Chinese mythology?

Shamans are people who have the ability to cure because of their ability to communicate with the spirit world. In the process of curing ceremonies, shamans often tell or sing the creation myth of their culture. Shamans, or medicine people, in both Chinese and certain Native North American cultures, memorize and thus preserve the ancient myths.

THE JAPANESE

Who are the Japanese people?

There has been much scholarly discussion and disagreement about the origins of the homogeneous people who make up the current population of the Japanese islands. The dominant theory is that indigenous Jomon people—today's Ainu—lived in Japan for thousands of years before they were joined by Yayoi people between 400 and 300 B.C.E., combining with them to form the present day Japanese.

What was the influence of Chinese culture on Japanese culture?

In terms of political and governmental arrangements and reforms, especially in the seventh and eighth centuries C.E., the Chinese influence on Japan was crucial. These reforms had their source in Chinese Confucianism and replaced older indigenous ideas of government. In terms of language, the Chinese provided the Japanese with a formal "classical" language much as the Romans provided the medieval Europeans with Latin. In religion, the Chinese were responsible for the presence of Buddhism in Japan, and Buddhism would in many ways merge with and change the indigenous Shinto religion. According to Chinese sources, Chinese Buddhist monks arrived in Japan in 467 C.E. By the eighth century Buddhism was firmly established in the country and a compatible relationship with Shinto was eventually established.

SOURCES OF
JAPANESE MYTHOLOGY

What are the sources of pre-Buddhist, or Shinto, mythology?

In the seventh century C.E. the Emperor Temmu ordered that the myths preserved in written fragments and the oral tradition be gathered together to establish aristocratic genealogies. His ultimate purpose, in all likelihood, was to trace the genealogy of the imperial family to the creation of the Japanese islands. The works which emerged eventually from Temmu's orders, the *Kojiki* and the *Nihon shoki,* or *Nihongi,* became the primary sources for Japanese mythology.

What is the *Kojiki*?

The *Kojiki* (Record of Ancient Matters) was composed in 711–712 C.E. by Ono Yasumaro, under the patronage of the Empress Gemmei. It contains myths of the Shinto gods and the creation of Japan and is written in a form of classical Chinese.

What is the *Nihon shoki*?

The *Nihon shoki* (The Chronicles of Japan), or *Nihongi,* is the second of the great collections of Japanese mythology commissioned by the Empress Gemmei. It was compiled by Prince Toneri with the help of Ono Yasumaro in classical Chinese and was completed in 720 C.E.

While not scriptural equivalents of the Bible, the Qur'an, or the *Vedas,* in that they do not pretend to be in any sense the word of the divine, the *Kojiki* and the *Nihon shoki* serve as the primary sources for our knowledge of the Shinto perspective.

What is Shinto?

Shinto, or *kami-no-michi* ("Way of the kami"), is the indigenous religion or spiritual system of Japan. At its center are the *kami,* the spirits who sometimes take individual form as gods and sometimes animate the natural world. The term *Shinto* comes from the Chinese *shén dào* for "spirit path"—that is, *shin* (spirit) *to* (path), thus *shinto*. Shinto is not dogmatic. Its rituals and myths are meant to establish connections between the

The Tōshō-gū Shinto shrine in Tokyo. Shinto is the indigenous religion in Japan.

past—including the ancestors—and the present, especially between the ancient *kamis* and the imperial family.

THE CREATION:
IZANAGI AND IZANAMI

What is the Japanese creation myth?

The *Kojiki* and the *Nihon shoki* tell how the universe existed in a state of chaos or un-differentiated matter with no sound until the spontaneous movement of particles created a huge cloud, the top of which became heaven (Takamagahara), marked by the light, or *yang*, and the bottom of which remained dark (*yin*) and unformed with no terra firma. Three gods (*kami*) emerged spontaneously in heaven and then, from a reed, two more gods emerged. Next, two more gods emerged and then five male-female pairs of gods, including Izanagi and Izanami. The original five gods instructed Izanami and Izanagi to continue the work of creation and gave them a beautiful jeweled spear to help them in their work.

Izanami and Izanagi made their way to the Floating Bridge of Heaven that connected heaven and the unformed earth and gazed at the primal waters below. They thrust the spear into the waters and when they removed it, drops of liquid from it formed the island of Onokoro, to which the two deities descended. There they built the Heavenly August Pillar and a magnificent palace. Izanami noticed that one part of her body remained empty and Izanagi noticed that one part of his had grown excessively. He suggested that by joining his excessive part with her empty one, they might create new land. Izanami agreed and the couple proceeded to carry out a marriage ceremony. They walked in opposite directions around the pillar and when they met, Izanami said, "What a handsome young man," and Izanagi replied, "What a fine young maiden." The result of their union, however, was badly formed offspring, which they abandoned to the primal waters. The five original deities suggested that the problem had arisen from the fact that the woman had spoken first in the pillar ceremony. So the couple repeated the ceremony, this time with Izanagi speaking first, and soon the Japanese islands were born.

What does this creation myth suggest about a Japanese view of the world?

The first thing we notice is that the primary object of creation is not the universe, or the world, but Japan. Izanami and Izanagi are clearly Japanese gods (*kami*) whose interest is only in the Japanese islands. The myth reflects the fact that the Japanese, in the time of the writing of the *Kojiki* and the *Nihon shoki,* wanted little or nothing to do with the world beyond its own shores. The myth of the marriage ceremony between Izanagi and Izanami reflects the Japanese view at the time, of the "proper" secondary status of women in relation to men.

191

What happened to Izanagi and Izanami?

The strange story of the two creator gods continues with their procreation of the many deities who inhabit or personify the various aspects of the natural world. Tragedy struck, however, when, while giving birth to the fire *kami*, Izanami's genitals were so badly burned that she died. In a rage, Izanagi beheaded the fire god, from whose blood more deities sprang. Longing for his lost wife, Izanagi, like Orpheus in Greece, descended to the Underworld, Yomi, in hopes of bringing her back. When he found Izanami in the pitch darkness, she agreed to ask the gods of the Underworld to release her, but meanwhile, Izanagi was not to look at her. After a time Izanagi lit a fire and saw his wife, disfigured and infested with maggots. Ashamed, Izanami chased her husband out of Yomi. Izanagi fled and closed the door to the Underworld with a huge rock. Izanami screamed out that she would kill one thousand people a day in their created islands. In response, Izanagi said he would see that 1500 were born each day. This is why although people die, more are always born.

The twin creator gods Izanagi (right) and Izanami (left) as depicted in a painting by Kobayashi Eitaku.

Izanagi bathed to purify himself after his ordeal in the Underworld and more deities arose from his discarded clothing. The sun goddess Amaterasu was born when Izanagi washed out his left eye. Tsukuyomi, the moon god, was born from Izanagi's right eye. Susanowa, the god of the sea and storms, was born of the creator's nose.

AMATERASU: THE GREAT GODDESS

Is there a Japanese war in heaven?

A war in heaven of sorts developed between the goddess Amaterasu and her brothers, Tsukuyomi and Susanowa. At first Amaterasu became the ruler of the sun and heavens with her husband-brother Tsukuyomi, who ruled the night. The couple shared the sky until Tsukuyomi became disgusted with and killed the goddess of food when she produced food from her nose, mouth, and anus. Angry over this act, Amaterasu separated from her brother, making day and night different realities. Amaterasu never got along well with her brother Susanowa. When Izanagi told him to leave heaven, Susanowa went to his sister, supposedly to say goodbye, and they exchanged "seeds," allowing Susanowa to give birth to five women from his sister's necklace and Amaterasu to give birth to three women from her brother's sword. After a time, and arguments over the ownership of these offspring, Susanowa turned on Amaterasu, destroying her rice fields and attacking her servants. Amaterasu escaped Susanowa's rage by hiding in a cave, thus depriving the world of the sun, until other deities persuaded her to come out by using a mirror, by which she was attracted to her own beauty. Susanowa was banished, but eventually he reconciled with his sister, giving her his sacred sword.

What is the significance of Amaterasu in the Japanese pantheon?

Amaterasu is the most important god in the Japanese Shinto pantheon. She is the goddess of the Rising Sun, the religious basis of the imperial family and, therefore, of the state itself. According to the ancient sources, after Amaterasu became the dominant god in heaven, she sent her grandson, Ninigi-no-Mikoto to rule the earth. With him she sent the sacred regalia, which still mark the authority of the Japanese imperial family, of which Ninigi is said to be the ancestor. The regalia include a jewel, a sword, and a mirror—all elements of importance in the quarrel between Amaterasu and her brother Susanowa and symbols of the sun goddess's power. According to tradition, the first emperor of Japan was Jimmu (660–585 B.C.E.), who claimed direct descent from Ninigi and, therefore, Amaterasu. The royal family's claim of divine ancestry was dropped after World War II.

THE JAPANESE BUDDHIST AND SHINTO PANTHEONS

What is the Japanese Shinto pantheon?

The major deities (*kami*) of Shinto include the following:

- Amaterasu, the Great Goddess of the Sun, the *de facto* primary deity of Shinto due in part to her connection to the emperor
- Uzume, the Heavenly Alarming Female, the Goddess of Dawn and Celebration
- Kami-no-Kaze (Fujin), one of the oldest of gods, God of the Wind
- Hachiman, God of War
- Inari, Goddess of Rice and Fertility
- Izanagi and Izanami, the creator couple
- Ninigi, the first ruler and ancestor of the first emperor of Japan

- Omoikane, God of Wisdom
- Owatatsumi, Dragon God of the Sea
- Raijin, Storm God
- Suijin, God of Water
- Susanowa, Storm God and Sea God and rival and brother of Amaterasu
- Tenjin, God of Learning
- Tsukuyomi, Moon God and brother of Amaterasu

What is the Japanese Buddhist pantheon?

Although Buddhism came to Japan from outside—primarily from China—it has generally coexisted easily with Shinto. In part this is because Buddhists have seen the *kami* of Shinto as embodiments or avatars of various Buddhist bodhisattvas and Buddhas.

There are, however, many Buddhist bodhisattvas, Buddhas, and deities who have achieved high individual status on their own in Japan. These include especially Amida Buddha and the Bodhisattva Kannon. Amida Buddha (Amitabha Buddha of the Indian Pali tradition) is the great Buddha of a form of Buddhism popular in Japan, Pure Land Buddhism. Amida Buddha is a Buddha who still concerns himself with this world and its pain. He acts to bring people to salvation.

An 1891 woodblock of the legendary Japanese emperor Jimmu.

Kannon Bosatsu, who is essentially the Chinese Guanyin, derived from Tibetan Buddhism's bodhisattvas Avalokiteśvara and Tara, in Japan can be either male or female, the *de facto* god or goddess of mercy and compassion. Some see Kannon as an incarnation of Amida Buddha.

Are there Japanese mythic heroes?

As in Chinese mythology, the heroes of Japanese mythology—figures who are not specifically deities but who represent sacred values in their actions—tend to be emperors.

The supernatural sometimes plays a role in the lives of these figures, a fact which establishes their identity as true heroes, backed by the divine powers. Otohime, the grandmother of the first emperor Jimmu, for instance, turns into a dragon after giving birth to the hero's father, and Jimmu, guided by a three-legged crow, succeeds in his battle to rule Japan when he attacks his enemies with the sun—that is, Amaterasu—at his back. Like many heroes in world mythology, Jimmu dies at an unusally old age. In general, however, Japanese mythology is concerned with deities rather than human heroes.

Is mythology alive in Japan today?

Shrines and temples venerating Buddhist and Shinto mythological figures are common in Japan. If the people tend to be secular, they also visit such temples and shrines for cultural or nationalistic purposes and, in some cases to pray for assistance in various passages of life. The Grand Shrine to Amaterasu at Ise, for example, is a much-visited pilgrimage site, and the priestess of the shrine must be a member of the imperial family, that is, for fundamentalist believers, a descendant of the great goddess.

CENTRAL ASIAN MYTHOLOGY

What do we mean by Central Asia?

Central Asia is a somewhat vague term used to indicate, generally, the area of Asia between Turkey, China, Afghanistan, and Russia. There is no "nation" of Central Asia. In terms of modern configurations we are speaking of the area that includes Mongolia, Kazakhstan, Kyrgyzstan, Tajikistan, Uzbekistan, Turkmenistan, and parts of Afghanistan, western China, and Siberia.

Who are the people of Central Asia?

The Central Asian population is composed of a wide variety of people speaking various languages, many of them belonging to the Altaic family. There are, for instance, Samoyeds, Tungus, Ostiaks, and Voguls of the Finni-Ugrian race; Yakut, Tuvin, Buryat, Khakass peoples of the Turko-Mongol race; and the Chukchi, Galyak, Koryak, and Yukaghir people of the Paleo-Siberian race.

To what extent, then, can we speak of Central Asian mythology?

We can only do so carefully, concentrating on the themes that form at least the indication of a common mythology. The search for Central Asian mythology is made more complex by the fact that the peoples of the area have for a very long time been Muslim, and before that Buddhist and Zoroastrian, though some remain shamanistic in some sense. When we speak today of Central Asian mythology, we generally mean the pre-Buddhist and pre-Islamic mythology of an area (and a mythology) that has attracted less attention than, for instance, Japan and China, to say nothing of the cultures of Europe and the Middle East. There are no parthenons, no temples of Ise or Karnak, no *Eddas* to help us. Much of what we know of Central Asian mythology comes through stories passed down as folk legends and or spoken of by present-day shamans, whose tellings have in all likelihood been "corrupted" by the influences of the religions which, over the centuries, have replaced the older mythology.

CENTRAL ASIAN THEMES AND GODS

What common themes do emerge from a study of the region's pre-Buddhist and pre-Islamic mythologies?

There are several themes—nearly all of them associated with creation myths and nearly all of them familiar as aspects of a larger world mythology. There are earth-diver creation stories that eventually migrated with Central Asians across the land bridge between Siberia and North America. There are the familiar primordial waters, and, especially, there is the theme of the trickster who undermines the creator's work and points to an essential duality in the world between the forces of good and those of evil. There are also myths of a Yggdrasill-like axis tree.

Who are the Central Asian deities?

There is always a creator. Sometimes the creator, a personification of the sky, because he was long ago separated from earth, interferes very little in the world. He is a *deus absconditus,* who keeps in contact with the world only via shamans. For the Tungus people he is Buga, for others he is Num, Es, or Turum. A Mongol Earth Mother-creator was Atugan, who sits at the base of the axis tree. Other Earth Mothers were the Yakut goddesses Itchita, the protector of health; Ynakhsyt, the protector of cattle; and Ajyst, the protector of children and of women in childbirth. Some Turko-Mongols and Yakuts were essentially monotheistic. The Turko-Mongol Tengri, the Yakut "White Master Creator," and the Tartar Ulgen flowed smoothly enough into the Muslim concept of Allah. Tengri and creators like him watched over creation and controlled the social order of humans. There were always, however, other gods who were aspects of the high god, much as Shiva and Vishnu in India are seen by some as embodiments of the ultimate reality, Brahman. Odlek was the personification of Time, the goddess Umai was Earth and Fertility. Other

Is there a consistent Central Asian mythic cosmology?

There are several Central Asian visions of the makeup of the universe. One of the most common is the belief in an egg-like structure in three parts: an Underworld; a middle world, where we live; and an upper world. The three worlds are built along the axis tree, at the base of which sits the Great Goddess. The sun and the moon sit at the top of the tree and in its branches are found the souls of the as yet unborn.

aspects of the Supreme Being were gods and godesses of the sun and moon and other aspects of nature. Other Central Asian deities gave an animistic character to the overall mythology. These were master spirits who, like the *kami* of Japan, were extremely powerful and ever present in all aspects of life. Perhaps the most important deities after the Supreme Being in Central Asian mythology were the master spirits and the tricksters.

MASTER SPIRITS AND SHAMANS

What role did the Master Spirits play?

The Master Spirits are the essence of what makes the Central Asian world, like the Japanese, African, and Native American worlds, animistic. Among the Central Asians, any group's territory—its water, its mountains, its animals, its particular places—is watched over by these spirits. The individual is attached to a particular spirit, as well, a spirit called Seveki by some. But when a person dies, he or she goes to live in the Underworld with the spirit associated with the cause of death. The spirits can take on animal or human shapes. In most Central Asian cultures the Master Spirit of Fire tends to be an old woman who presides over a cooking fire. Every home has a Mother Fire who must

A shaman performs a fire ceremony in Tuva, Russia, just north of Mongolia.

be fed and who, in return, protects the herds. The Master Spirit of Water tends to be an old man who lives in the water. The Tungus have territory Mother Spirits who watch over the Tungus world. Other groups have positive Master Spirits of the Underworld; these are the direct ancestors of the shamans, who can travel to that world. Such spirits can be associated with the idea of the soul of the dead person returning to earth as a new clan member. Among the Buryats there are spirits known as the *tengri*. Half of these live with the good god Eseg Malan in the west; the others live as bad spirits with the god of the dead, who, in the case of the Buryats, is sometimes Erlik.

What role do shamans play?

In Siberia and elsewhere in Central Asia, as in parts of Native America, shamans still play a role. The shaman's job is to cure diseases, to perform important hunting, birthing, and other rites, and to serve as a mediator between the spirit world and the human world. Shamans are "called" to their profession by their spirit ancestors in the Underworld. The shaman's soul is sometimes said to have entered the human world in the form of his special totem animal. Shamans have the power to change shapes in order, to, for instance, enter the spirit world during ritual séances. In this shapeshifter aspect of their beings, shamans resemble tricksters. To Native Americans, these shamans became "Medicine Men."

CENTRAL ASIAN CREATION AND DEVIL-TRICKSTERS

What role do the tricksters play in the myths?

Tricksters play an undermining devil-like role in most Central Asian creation myths, always the most important myths for any society. The Central Asian trickster is often a relative of the creator and usually acts as his questionable assistant. As such, the trickster is a close mythological relative of the amoral tricksters we find in Africa and in Native North America.

What are some examples of Central Asian creation myths?

Each Central Asian group has its own creation myth, but the theme of the struggle between the creator and the devil-creator provides a consistency to the various myths of the Central Asian peoples. Also consistent is the theme of the earth-diver creation. The archetypal skeleton behind the Central Asian creation myths is evident, for instance, in a wide variety of cultures that include the Turkic, the Tungus, the Buryat, the Mongolian, and other peoples of Siberia and the Caucasus.

What is an example of a Turkic creation myth?

Before they migrated in the Middle Ages to Iran and Anatolia, the people of the Mongolian plateau practiced a religion sometimes called Tengriism, a name which refers to the Father Sky God Tengri ülgen, who presided with Mother Earth over the world. Tengri, as a great white goose, flew over the primordial waters and, urged on by the Great White Mother, undertook the task of creation. Tengri was lonely as he worked, so he created Er-Kishi to help him. Er-Kishi was evil, however, and interfered with Tengri's creation, so Tengri departed for heaven, sending down sacred animals to guide the people he had created.

We can recognize these animals as personifications of the spirits that were sent to animate the world. In Tengriism, shamans maintained contact between this spirit world and heaven.

What is an example of a Tungus creation myth?

The Tungus, originally from Manchuria, who speak an Altaic language and live in northern China and eastern Siberia, had a shamanic-based religion. They taught that originally there were only the primordial waters until the Sky God sent down fire, which burned away part of the waters and made land. As soon as he came down to that land to begin creating, the Sky God found a devil figure, Buninka, there. Buninka wanted to help with creation, but the Sky God refused, and the devil became so angry that he broke the Sky God's lyre. When the Sky God challenged the devil to make a tree out of the primordial waters, Buninka tried, but his tree was weak. When the Sky God made a tree, it was strong, so Buninka gave up creating.

The tree created by the Sky God in this creation story would seem to be a version of the world tree, the axis of all of creation. The struggle between the Sky God and Buninka is the struggle between shamanism and witchcraft.

What is an example of a Buryat creation myth?

Living in the Lake Baikal region of Siberia, the Buryats are of the Mongolian race. Their creation myth is a classic Central Asian earth-diver story.

In the beginning the Sky God, sometimes named Sombov, looked down on the primordial waters and saw the water bird Anghir. He instructed the bird to dive down into the depths of the maternal waters to find some material for the making of earth. The bird did as he was instructed and emerged with some black earth and some red clay. Sombov made our earth out of the black soil and humans out of the red clay. These first humans were covered in wool and Sombov decided not to make them alive until he could find souls for them. He left a dog—still furless at this stage—to watch over his creation while he went to heaven to find the souls. Now the devil, Shiktur (sometimes Erlik) approached the shivering furless dog and promised him a coat if he would allow him to see Sombov's creations. When the dog gave in, Shiktur undermined the new creations by spitting on them. When the creator returned, he saw what had happened and was furious. The dog, he proclaimed, would always shiver in spite of its new fur coat, and wherever the devil's spit hit the new humans, their wool would be removed. This is why humans—especially women— have hair only in very particular places on their bodies.

This myth is not only a "how the leopard got its spots" type of story, it is an explanation of the imperfection at the basis of creation itself. As in all Central Asian creation myths, the devil figure is the trickster who cannot resist putting his own creative powers to work to undermine the perfection of the creator's intention. He is the Central Asian version of the archetype also realized in figures in other cultures, such as the Satan/serpent of the Bible.

In another Buryat myth it is the devil—here called Shlomo—who offers to dive into the waters to find earth. The creator—here called Burkhan—used the bit of retrieved soil to make the earth, but agreed to give Shlomo some to use as a place to plant his staff. It was the hole made by the devil's staff that allowed all of the evils of the world to emerge.

In an Altaic myth of the Caucasus, the creator sends the devil-trickster into the depths to find earth but the devil hides some in his mouth when he returns. But when the creator causes the mud to expand, the bit in the devil's mouth expands too, forcing him to spit out what he had hidden. This mud becomes the world's wetlands.

What is an example of a Mongolian creation myth?

The Mongol people, living in parts of what are now China and Russia, have this earthdiver myth. Some of the names of the characters in the myth are similar to or the same as names of different characters in other Central Asian myths.

In the beginning Sky Father looked down on the primordial waters. He had two sons, Ulgen Tenger and Erleg Khan, to whom he assigned aspects of creation. Ulgen sent the loon into the depths to find mud for the making of earth, but the loon failed. The duck was sent next and was more successful. She brought up some mud, on which Ulgen immediately fell asleep. Now Ulgen's brother, Erleg, approached and tried to pull the earth out from under his brother, but this only caused the earth to spread out. When Ulgen woke up he created more things. Here the myth becomes very similar to the Buryat myth. Ulgen leaves the dog to watch over his work while he returns to the sky, but his evil brother corrupts the dog, and the results are smelly dogs and all the pains we have in life.

The themes of the diving animals, some of whom fail, and that of the two brothers— one good, one evil—will find homes, as we shall see, in the myths of Native North Americans.

What are some Siberian creation myths?

One Siberian myth has as its creator the god Ulgen, who saw some mud floating on the primordial waters and a human face reflected from the mud onto the waters. So he instilled the face with life, and this was the first human, Erlik. Erlik was, in fact, the devil, who, although expelled to an outer region, always returns to undermine Ulgen's creation. This myth also contains the theme of the betrayal by the dog.

Some Siberian myths are more positive, having been influenced by Buddhism. One myth tells how the creator, Otsirvani, had a good helper, Chagan-Shukuty, a name for the Buddha. It was Chagan-Shukuty who dove into the depths. When he returned, the creator ordered him to sprinkle the mud on the stomach of an upturned frog who had agreed to lie on the primordial waters. When the mud began to spread the gods went to sleep on it. While they were asleep the devil arrived and tried to pull the earth out from under them. This only caused the earth to grow, as in the Mongolian myth.

CENTRAL ASIAN HEROES

Are there mythic heroes in Central Asia?

The Central Asian heroes are usually deified historical figures. The Mongol conqueror Genghis Khan was said to have been conceived by spirit figures, the Blue Wolf and the White Doe. The Turko-Mongol ancestor Alp Kara Aslan (Heroic Black Lion) was born of a woman but was raised by an eagle and eventually adopted by a lion. The Uigur leader Buqu Khan was conceived by the union of two trees and was born of a knothole. All these conception and birth tales combined with historical power indicate the need of the given cultures to create what we recognize as the monomythic hero.

A fourteenth-century drawing of Genghis Khan, the real-life Mongol conqueror who was, according to myth, conceived of the spirit figures the Blue Wolf and the White Doe.

OCEANIC MYTHOLOGIES: AUSTRALIAN ABORIGINE AND POLYNESIAN

What do we mean by Oceanic mythologies?

Oceanic mythologies are those of the indigenous peoples of Australia, New Zealand, and the Pacific islands, including those populated by Micronesians, Melanesians, and Polynesians. The most complex mythologies are those of the Australians and the Polynesians.

AUSTRALIAN ABORIGINES AND THE DREAMING

Who are the indigenous people of Australia?

The Australian natives are generally called Australian Aborigines. Of all the peoples of the world, the Aborigines can claim the longest connection to a particular land after the migration of humans out of Africa. DNA indicates direct connections with the first wave of humans leaving Africa, and although estimates vary, it seems likely that the Aborigines have been in Australia for at least 40,000 years and that, until the arrival of Europeans beginning in the seventh century, their gene pool remained essentially pure.

What is the basis for Australian mythology?

There are, of course, many aboriginal groups in the various parts of Australia and each group has its own mythology. The common thread among these groups is the concept of the Dreaming, or Dreamtime.

What is the Dreaming?

There is no word in English that truly captures the sense of the aboriginal "Dreaming." The Dreaming refers to the "Dreamtime" when spirits or sacred ancestors created the

This painting, found inside Baiame Cave in New South Wales, Australia, is related to Aborigine beliefs in the Dreamtime.

world. "Dreaming" can also refer to a set of beliefs or to the animistic or spiritual basis of a group. Many indigenous Australians also refer to the creation time as "The Dreaming". The Dreamtime established the patterns of life for the aboriginal people. The concept becomes clearer in the aboriginal deity and creation myths.

Is there an Australian pantheon?

As there are many aboriginal groups, there are many groups of gods, but rarely complex family arrangements of gods such as we find in Greece or Egypt, for instance. The following are some of the most important of the aboriginal deities.

The sun is usually personified by male deities but in Australia, as in Japan, the sun is represented by a female goddess. In some areas she is Alinga, in others Wuriupranili. In southeast Australia she is Gnowee, who in Dreamtime, when the world was still dark, lost her son. She lights a torch and climbs the sky each day looking for him. In northern Australia the solar goddess can be Wala, who travels across the sky each day. In the west, Bila is a sun goddess who had cannibal tendencies, roasting humans each day over the fire that provided light for the world. To save humans, Kudnu, the Lizard Man, and Muda, the Gecko man, threw a boomerang at her, injuring her and causing her to turn into a ball of fire, which ran off, leaving the world in darkness. Kudnu threw several more boomerangs and finally caught the fireball in the east, from which direction it returns each day to bring warmth and light to the world.

As in most mythologies, the creator god holds an important place in many aboriginal mythologies. In southeast Australia, Biame is the creator. Among the Bandicoot clan in Aranda, Karora is the creator. In the north, some groups claim a Great Mother, Eingana, as the creator. She is a snake goddess who in Dreamtime created water, animals, and land. In the beginning Eingana had no vagina and became swollen with creation until the god Barraiya relieved her pain by creating a vagina for her with his spear. Like Kali and Durga, expressions of the great goddess in India, Eingana is also a goddess of death; without death, creation could not continue.

There are many other important Dreamtime deities. Anjea in Queensland is a fertility goddess. Julunggul in the north is another fertility goddess; like Eingana, she is a snake.

In northeast Arnhem Land the Djanggawul Sisters are important. Djanggawul was a child of the sun, who had two sisters. The three Djanggawuls traveled about the country in a bark canoe. Djanggawul had a very long, uncircumcised and decorated penis, and his sisters had exaggerated clitorises. On approaching land they performed a walkabout, their dragging genitals leaving sacred marks on the ground, marks still present today. The Djanggawuls also left "dreamings" in the form of stories and ceremonies, including models of the brother's penis as decorated poles. In each place where they stopped, Djanggawul had intercourse with his sisters, and humans were born. As in the Indian *Vedas* and many other mythological sources around the world, incest in the early stages of creation is a common theme among the Australian Aborigines. Some say that to remove some of their over-sized genital equipment Djanggawul and his sisters instituted the tradition of circumcision.

Two sisters—from the north—are the Wawalag Sisters, who also roam the world in Dreamtime, naming creatures and plants. They are swallowed and then regurgitated by the snake deity Yurlunger. Still another creative pair known to the northern Gunwinggu people were Wurugag, the first male, and Waramurungundi, the first female, who was in effect a Great Mother goddess as she gave birth to earth itself.

Trickster figures exist among the Aborigines. In the northern area Bamapana is popular, a trickster who, like tricksters in other parts of the world, is amoral, a sower of discord who uses his creative powers as a kind of anticulture hero, even committing incest. Among the Wurundjeri people, a more helpful trickster is Crow, who in Dreamtime stole fire and enjoys playing tricks on other animals, such as Swamp Hawk and Eagle.

AUSTRALIAN CREATIONS AND FLOODS

Are there specific Australian creation myths?

All Australian Aboriginal deities are concerned in one way or another with the Dreaming and creation. In addition to the myths already identified, there are complex myths of creation such as one involving the Creator Goddess Yhi of the northern Karraur people. Yhi lay sleeping in dark Dreamtime, before the world was created, when a strange whistling sound woke her up. As her eyes opened, the world became full of light. As the sun goddess, she brought prosperity to the world through her light and warmth. Performing the ritual walkabout of the Dreaming, she left plants everywhere she stepped, and soon the world was a plant paradise. Yhi sat down and looked around her. She realized that as the plants could not move from place to place, she needed to create something that could. Now the sun goddess made a descent to the place beneath the earth, much as Inanna did in Mesopotamian mythology. There evil spirits tried to destroy Yhi, but her light and warmth prevailed, and beautiful dancing forms came from that warmth and light—butterflies and other insects—which Yhi led up to the upper world. Then she directed her powers to the caves of ice in the high mountains, and water, full of fish, flowed into the world. Birds and other animals were freed from the caves. Yhi blessed the new creatures and told them she would now return to her own world. As she moved away, darkness came over everything, and the new creatures were afraid. But sleep came and then the dawn, as Yhi climbed across the sky, and the creatures celebrated. This pattern went on through Dreamtime until the creatures became dissatisfied. So once again Yhi came down to earth and asked her creations what was bothering them. The creatures all wanted something they did not have. The bat wanted wings, the seal wanted to swim; everything wanted something new, so Yhi gave them what they wanted and returned to the sky. Now Yhi had created a male human but realized that the male required a woman. So, as the male slept one day, Yhi created a beautiful flower on a grass tree. The male was drawn to the flower bathed in the power of Yhi. The flower became a woman and the first man and woman joined hands.

Are there Australian flood myths?

Most Australian Aboriginal tribes have flood myths. One example comes from the southeast. It seems that the world had become overpopulated with birds, reptiles, and other animals, so a conference was called to decide on a proper solution. The conference took place on Blue Mountain. Tiger Snake began by proposing that birds and animals who could move easily should move to a new country. The next day the lizards, who knew about rainmaking, decided to act. Their desire was to rid the world of the platypuses. They instructed all of their family to perform the rain ceremony just before the new moon. The lizards fled to mountain tops, but a deluge covered the land below, and most of the world was destroyed. The flood finally ended and there were no platypuses. But sometime later the cormorant told the emu that he had seen a platypus beak mark near a river. In fact, the platypuses were hiding from the other creatures. Kangaroo called the animals together and proposed a search party for the platypuses. After some time Carpet Snake discovered the platypus home. Again Kangaroo called the animals together, and the lizard was expelled for his cruelty. And the animals discovered that in one way or another they were related to the platypuses. The platypuses were invited back and treated as ancient dignitaries. Eventually the head platypus married into the Bandicoot family. But platypuses have never been comfortable with other animals.

Who are the mythic heroes of Australia?

As in the case of Chinese mythology, it is difficult to differentiate deities from heroes. The closest we come to *bona fide* human mythic heroes among the Aborigines are culture heroes such as I'wai in Queensland and Warrunna in New South Wales. These figures perform the traditional role of the culture hero in teaching the people how to live by laws and traditions and how to survive. Bunjil in Victoria does all these things, but he is also a creator and, therefore, in some sense a deity. As a human-like culture hero, he once took shelter in a cave in Dreamtime and that cave remains a sacred place today.

THE POLYNESIANS: FROM NEW ZEALAND TO HAWAII

Who are the Polynesians?

The native peoples of the Pacific Islands, such as Tahiti, Samoa, Tonga, Fiji, and Hawaii are Polynesians, as are the Maori, the indigenous people of New Zealand. The term "Polynesian" comes from the Greek, meaning "many islands."

What is the essential nature of Polynesian mythology?

Polynesian mythology, in general, directly reflects a reality involving the sea and the natural environment. Gods reflect aspects of nature and its activities. For the Polynesians, mythology expresses an animistic understanding in which all aspects of life contain spiritual power, or *mana*.

Where did the Polynesians come from?

The origins of the Polynesians has always been a controversial topic. The dominant theory holds that in about 4500 B.C.E. a migration began from south China of people speaking an Austronesian language, the family of which the Polynesian languages are members. It is thought that Taiwan was the first land to be colonized by these people, who eventually moved to what are now New Zealand and the Pacific Islands. Other scholars argue a much longer presence in Papua New Guinea and other islands. Still others suggest a mingling of ancient Melanesian peoples already on the Pacific Islands with the Austronesian settlers, resulting in what today we call Polynesians. Whatever their origins, we know that the Polynesians were skilled seafarers and that their migration from island to island in double-hulled canoes involved that skill. We know that by about 1250 C.E., Polynesian culture dominated in the so-called Polynesian Triangle that includes Hawaii in the north, Easter Island in the east, and New Zealand in the south.

POLYNESIAN PANTHEONS

Are there Polynesian pantheons?

Not surprisingly, given the vast distances between the islands, various Polynesian cultures and mythologies emerged over the centuries. There are, however, distinctive correlations between these mythologies and, especially, their pantheons. The Maori pantheon is ruled by Rangi (Sky Father) and Papa (Earth Mother). In Hawaii, Ao and Po were the equivalents of Rangi and Papa. In Tahiti the supreme male god, the equivalent of Rangi, was Ta'aroa.

Sea gods were important among the Polynesians. For the Maori, this was Tangaroa, a son of Rangi and Papa. Other Polynesians called him Tangaloa. The Hawaiians knew him as Kanaloa. Tawhiri was the Maori storm god, another son of the original Sky-Earth couple. Tu, or Tumatauenga, was the Maori god of War. Tane was the god of the Forest. In Hawaii he was Kane. In Hawaii one of the most popular deities was Pele, a goddess of volcanoes, capable, as was the Indian Kali, of great violence. The most popular of all Polynesian deities was Maui. More detailed pantheonic family structures become clearer in the stories of creation.

What is the myth of Pele?

Pele was a descendant of Sky and Earth. She was rivalled in power only by her older sisters, the goddesses of the sea and of the snow-capped mountains, who worked to curb her natural volcanic fury. Her favorite sister was Hi'iaka', who had been born of an egg kept warm by Pele, under her arm, until the hatching. Pele and Hi'iaka' lived out of the reach of their two threatening sisters in the fiery crater of Kilauea, high above the sea on the Big Island. One day in a dream Pele heard the sound of drum beats and dancing and was so attracted to the sound that she sent her spirit to follow it—all the way to Kauai. There she witnessed wonderful dancing and music and, disguising herself as a beautiful young woman, she joined in. Soon after, she was noticed by a handsome chief named Lohiau, and the two became lovers. But the time came when Pele's spirit needed to return to her sleeping

Wooden carving on a storehouse in New Zealand depicts the Maori gods Rangi (Sky Father) and Papa (Earth Mother).

and dreaming body on the Big Island, or else the fires of her volcano would have died out. So her spirit left Lohiau. But now the lovers longed for each other, so Pele sent her brother Lono to Hi'iaka' to ask her to bring Lohiau to her. Hi'iaka' managed to overcome monsters and other trials and to make her way to Kauai. There she found that Lohiau had died, but she succeeded in reviving him. Some say that Pele became impatient, assuming that Lohiau and Hi'iaka were having an affair, so she attacked them with her fire. In one version of the story, Hi'iaka and Lohiau did, in fact, end up as lovers, even in the face of Pele's rage.

The Polynesian god Pele is associated with the volcano Kilauea on the Big Island of Hawaii.

POLYNESIAN CREATION AND FLOOD MYTHS

What are the Polynesian creation myths?

There are as many Polynesian creation myths as there are individual Polynesian societies. Even within societies there are variants. One creation myth with versions in most of the islands is this Maori myth. According to the myth, it was Rangi and Papa who existed in the beginning. Rangi was the masculine force in the universe, associated with sky and light. His consort Papa was the feminine force of earth and darkness. As in the Greek, Egyptian, and many other creation myths, the first parents were so close together that a separation was called for in order that creation might continue. It fell to the children of Rangi and Papa to do something about the dilemma. Their son Tu (Tumatauenga), god of War, suggested that their parents be killed.

The others disagreed and decided that the parents should be pushed apart. First Rongo, the Cultivated Food god, tried to execute the separation but failed. Next Tangaroa, god of the Sea, with the help of his brother, god of wild food, tried and failed. Finally, it was Tane, god of the Forest, who succeeded. As he lay on his back and separated his parents by pushing upward with his legs, the primal couple screamed in agony. But room now existed for further creation. Room also existed, however, for a "war in heaven" between the children of Rangi and Papa.

In one Hawaiian myth, more credit for creation is given to Kane. It was he who created Rangi (Ao) and Papa (Po) by throwing a calabash into the air, where it broke apart forming Sky and Earth. In some Maori myths the equivalent of Kane was Io, who created Rangi and Papa *ex nihilo*—from nothing. In the Hawaiian version, Kane then assigned various aspects of the natural world to his brothers. Kanaloa, for instance, would control the sea, Ku the forests. The gods then created the first man and woman out of clay.

What was the Polynesian war in heaven?

As in so many mythologies, the creation process of the many Polynesian groups involves a war in heaven. The Maori version of this archetype takes place immediately after the separation of Rangi and Papa. Tawhiri, the storm god, was angry at the separation of his parents, so he left his siblings and went up to join his father in the sky. There, joined by his children, winds and clouds, he attacked the forests of Tane and tore up the seas of Tangaroa. He also attacked his brothers dedicated to cultivated and wild foods. His attacks caused his brothers to fight against each other as well. Finally, it was Tu, the war god, who stood up against Tawhiri and made peace in heaven, heaven being the same as the world, for it was on Papa's earthy being that this war took place.

Are there Polynesian flood myths?

There are many Polynesisan flood myths. In Tahiti the sea god became enraged when a fisherman's fish hooks caught in his hair. He sent a flood to cover the whole world except for the tops of the highest mountains. The Samoans say that a flood occurred when the gods of fire and water fought each other. The Maori tell of Ruatapu, a woman who became angry at the nobility and lured their children into a canoe and then sank the canoe in the ocean. Only a man named Paikea somehow survived. Now Ruatapu got the gods to send a huge flood to destroy the world. Paikea, an archetypal flood hero like Noah, was saved on a mountain top with the help of a goddess.

Who are the Polynesian heroes?

As in the case of the Australian Aborigines and the Chinese, heroes are difficult to differentiate from deities in Polynesian mythology. There are, however, demigods or culture heroes who are sometimes depicted as gods, but sometimes seem to be clearly human. The most famous of these figures is Maui, who belongs to all Polynesians.

MAUI, THE HERO AND TRICKSTER

Who was Maui?

Maui was a trickster, and like the tricksters of Australian Aborigine mythology, he also played the role of culture hero and can best be considered in that context as a demi-god rather than as a god.

What is the story of Maui?

In the many versions of his history, Maui takes on the aspects of the archetypal hero, beginning with a miraculous conception and birth. He is also clearly a culture hero, playing a role in the creation process and the civilizing of his people. And he is just as clearly, like Coyote in North America or Ananse in Africa, a trickster whose acts can cause difficulties in the world, even bringing death to creation. In one myth, Maui is said to have been conceived when a woman looked at the rising sun. The Maori say that when a premature son was born to Maui's mother, she wrapped the child in a lock of hair from her top knot (*tikitiki*) and then threw him into the sea. Rangi, the sun, and presumably his father, rescued him and raised him in heaven, but when grown he emerged from the sea as Maui Ti'itit'i. In Hawaii, the island of Maui was named for him.

Both a hero and a trickster, Maui mischievously snares the Sun in this illustration by Arman Manookian, circa 1927.

Upon his emergence, Maui became a culture hero/trickster. In most Polynesian islands he is credited with helping the people by catching the sun and slowing it down to provide more time for work and with bringing the islands themselves up from the depths, making him a type of earth-diver creator. One of Maui's greatest feats was tricking the goddess of fire into revealing the secret of that element. In Samoa they say that Maui descended to the Underworld—a universal heroic act—to retrieve fire.

Maui died in the act of trying to overcome a female monster and death goddess, Hine-nui-te-po, by entering her vagina and emerging from her mouth. In this case the monster won and Maui was cut in half. By dying, Maui, who had sought immortality for humans, allowed death into the world.

Maui myths, like those of other tricksters, are often highly sexual and focused on genitals. One famous story can be seen as a fertility myth, perhaps reminding us of the ancient story of the Mesopotamian Inanna and her lover, Dumuzi. The beautiful goddess (or, some say human) Hina was living with Tuna the Eel (Te Tuna). Dissatisfied with Te Tuna, Hina went in search of more satisfying love. When she arrived at the land of the Male Principle Clan, she introduced herself as the "shameless pubic patch in search of love." The men were afraid of Te Tuna, however, and sent her on her way. Now even more desperately craving love, Hina came to the land of the Maui Clan, and Maui, acceding to his mother's urging, took Hina as his wife. The two lived together and experienced great passion for some time until some of the people informed Te Tuna of what was happening. When Te Tuna asked the people about Maui, they told him the hero's penis was inferior. The people now warned Maui that Te Tuna was on his way to seek revenge, and Te Tuna approached Maui's land from the sea, revealing a penis so large that it caused a tidal wave. Maui's mother urged her son to reveal his own penis to Te Tuna to stop the wave. This Maui did, raising his member before the oncoming wave. In a great fight, Maui then killed Te Tuna's companions but spared him. For a time the two rivals lived together with Hina, but finally they decided to fight for the sole rights to her. In a sexualized struggle, the rivals entered each other, and finally Maui cut off Te Tuna's head and buried it (some say that Hina performed the burial). Before long a huge tree, known now as the coconut tree, grew from this "planting," and the people have benefitted from the coconut's nourishment to this day.

Is the explicit sexuality of this myth meant to be taken seriously?

It is true that some myths seem to have been created primarily to entertain. This is true, for example, of the Greek myth in which Ares and Aphrodite are exposed by Hephaistos during an adulterous act. Other highly sexualized myths are clearly meant to convey an important cultural belief. Such a myth is the Mesopotamian story in which Inanna uses explicit sexual language to express her longing to fulfill her role as a goddess of fertility. Sexuality is also typically associated with the trickster figure. The Maui myth has humorous aspects, but if we recall that Maui is the son of Rangi, the personification of the masculine principle, it is not altogether surprising that he should use the symbol of that principle, that potency, to hold back the tidal wave. As for the two masculine forces sharing the feminine one represented by Hina and then fighting over her, it is possible that this myth reflects not only a cultural sense of the proper relationship between men and women, but a cultural decision from some time in the past—presumably established by the culture-hero—that two men possessing the same woman was a taboo arrangement, much as most societies prohibit polygamy. The myth also celebrates the particular power of Maui as not only a culture hero, but as a trickster of great prowess.

AFRICAN
MYTHOLOGIES

Is it possible to speak of a single African mythology?

Africa is a continent with an indigenous population made up hundreds of tribes and a huge variety of languages. Each group has its own mythology, and in addition, colonialism, from an anthropological perspective, has "infected" these mythologies with ideas and images derived from foreign-based religions. Still, there are certain general characteristics that can reasonably be associated with the mythologies of Africa. These include, for instance, the withdrawn presence of a creator, with the earth often personified as the creator's wife, the creative but sometimes disruptive actions of culture hero/tricksters, the preponderance of animals, and, most important, the dominance of animism.

What is an example of a myth affected by colonialism?

One example might be the creation myth of the Bulu people of Cameroon. In the beginning, according to this myth, Membe, the creator, sent his son Zambe to earth to create Human, Chimpanzee, Gorilla, and Elephant. Zambe named each of these animals after himself. One of the men he created was white and one was black. Like a good culture hero, he gave the animals good things to provide viable life, including water, tools, fire, and a book. The men stirred the new fire, but the white man was disturbed by the smoke that got into his eyes, so he went off with the book. Chimpanzee and Gorilla ignored Zambe's gifts and went off to eat fruit in the forest. Elephant just stood around. The black man remained to stir the fire, not caring about the book. One day Zambe returned to his new creations and asked its inhabitants what they had done with his gifts. When Chimpanzee and Gorilla and Elephant admitted they had done nothing with them, Zambe gave the first two hairy bodies and big teeth and ordered them to spend their lives foraging. Elephant was sent off in much the same way. When Zambe interviewed the black man, he asked him what he had done with his book, and the black man said he had not read it because he was too busy tending to the fire. Zambe told him

What is animism?

The word *animism* is derived from the Latin *anima* or *animus*, meaning "spirit" or "soul." Animism as a concept assumes that all things are animated by spirits, that there is a direct connection between the physical and spiritual worlds. It assumes that humans have souls; that trees, the sea, the plants, the animals all have spirits. Animism assumes that spirits are everywhere, which is different from the concept of a single god (monotheism) or of many gods controlling various aspects of life (polytheism). Animism in this sense could be called the mother of and the oldest of all religions. Animism is clearly reflected in the mythologies of Japanese Shinto, for instance, with its concept of the ubiquitous *kami* and in Oceanic mythologies in which deities are simply metaphors for a spiritual reality in the elements of nature. Animism is clearly present in the mythologies of the Americas and is especially evident in the mythologies of Africa. It can be said that three major religions and accompanying mythologies now dominate in Africa. These are Islam, Christianity, and Animism. The dominance of animism does not, however, preclude the existence of deities, who themselves become animating forces in creation. Supreme Beings as creators, earth goddesses, and especially tricksters all play important roles in African mythology.

he would have to spend his life working and taking care of others because he had no book knowledge. Zambe finally asked the white man what he had done with the gifts. "I have only read the book," answered the man. "Well," said Zambe, "this is what you shall continue to do; you will learn many things, but you will need the black man to care for you." This is why animals do what they do and why black and white men do what they do. The white man reads a lot; the black man keeps the fire going.

THE AFRICAN SUPREME BEING AND CREATION

Who are some of the African Supreme Beings?

Most African tribes have a creation myth involving a Supreme Being, either male or female. Many of these supreme beings become examples of the *deus otiosus* or *deus absconditus*, the creator who creates and then retires or who simply absents himself from his creation in disgust. The southwestern Nigerian Yoruba creator is Olorun, who left creation to an underling and then remained essentially aloof from humanity, leaving the earth to spirits known as *orishas*.

The Bushman creator, Mantis, lived with his human creations in the beginning, but human foolishness so bothered him that he simply abandoned the world, leaving universal hunger behind. The creator of the Pygmies of the central equatorial region is Khonvum, who once lived on earth as an animal master but who now lives in heaven and concerns himself with the stars and solar system. He deals with humans only through animal spirits. The Kikuyu creator Ngai sent the culture hero Gikuyu to help the people; then he went away. Nyambe, the Malozi creator of Zambia, became so disgusted by the fact that humans ate their fellow animals that he retired to a mountain top. He invited the animals to join him there in safety, but for some reason they decided to stay in the world. The humans constantly try to find the creator, but he stays away.

Other creators are challenged by rivals. The Hottentots, whose language includes the *click* sound, have a creator Tsui-[click]-Goab who fought what, in effect, was a war in heaven against a negative force, [click]-Gaunab. The good god won, but was wounded in the process. The Ijaw of Nigeria have a female creator, Woyengi, who was angered by a woman named Ogboinba, who overstepped the boundaries set by the goddess at creation. The seminomadic Maasai of Kenya and Tanzania say that Enkai created the world in which a black god and a red god struggle with each other for dominance. The West African Ashanti high god Nyame had his creative work undermined by a famous trickster. The same was true of Fidi Mkulla, the southeastern Congo supreme god of the Baluba and Basonge.

A more overtly animistic creator is the Zulu Unkulunkulu, who created everything and, somewhat like the Indian Brahman, *is* everything: the corn, the trees, the water, the cow, the human. Another type of animism is evident in the myths that feature everything in creation coming from the creator's bodily waste. Bumba, the Central African Boshongo supreme being, vomits creation. For the Wapangwa of Tanzania, the basis of creation by the all-present "Word" is excrement.

One of the most complex of African creation myths is that of the Dogon people of Mali and western Sudan. A world-parent story with a cosmic egg, it stresses harmony in the world from the perspective of an animistic religion.

What is the Dogon creation myth?

In the beginning, say the Dogon, there was a maternal world egg that was shaken by seven huge movements of the unformed universe, which caused the egg to break into two placentas, the egg having been fertilized by the creator, Amma. Each placenta contained a set of twins, in both cases one a male, one a female, although all four of the children contained both the male and female essence. The twins are called the Nummo. One of the male twins, named Yoruga, broke out of a placenta prematurely, and the piece of the sac from which he broke out became the earth. Yoruga tried to get back into his sac to reunite with his twin, but she had deserted their placenta for that of the other set of twins. So Yoruga descended to the earth and attempted to copulate with it, but no children resulted from that act. Amma sent the other occupants of the placentas down to earth to see what they could do about creating humans. It was the intercourse between these brothers, sisters, and cousins that led to the creation of humans. Because all humans are descended from these original twins, all humans are descendants of incestuous relations between a mother and her twin brother or a father and his twin sister. In the complexity of Dogon religion and mythology, then, brothers and sisters are considered "parents" of each other's children. All of this suggests a peculiar kinship system. In Dogon tradition, a man will, if possible, marry a first cousin fathered by his maternal uncle.

Are there other versions of the Dogon myth?

There are other versions of this myth. One version, perhaps "corrupted" by colonialism, says that Amma made the stars when he threw bits of earth into the sky. Acting as a *deus faber*, a craftsman god, he created the sun and the moon using the art of pottery. The sun is like a pot brought to a high heat and glazed with red copper. The moon, heated to a lower degree, was surrounded by white copper. Africans came from the sun, white people from the moon.

The myth goes on to tell how Amma flung some clay into space to make Earth, who lay flat on her back, her genitals being an anthill. When Amma attempted to have intercourse with Earth, her anthill genitals rose up to prevent his passage. Determined to have his way, Amma cut away the rising part of the anthill, thus instigating the practice of female circumcision. Because he had raped Earth, the first child of the union was the wicked jackal. In more intercourse, however, Amma filled Earth with water—the true seed of life—and the result was the spirit children known as the Nummo. Born of Amma's water, these twins contained the Supreme Being's essence. Dogons believe all of creation contains this essence. The Nummo are in the grasses, in their weaving, in their ritual drums.

Are there African flood myths?

There are many African flood myths. A Yoruba myth tells how, when the god Olorun ruled the sky and the goddess Olokun ruled the earth, the god Obatala gained permission to descend to earth to create dry land and creatures to live on it. After creating the land, he became bored and drank too much wine from the palm tree he had created. Then,

A ritual Dogon container from Mali includes carvings of the spirit children called the Nummo.

while drunk, he created new creatures in his general image, some of whom were understandably imperfect. The new humans built villages and a great city, and the gods were happy with Obatala's work—all the gods, that is, but Olokun, who resented what she saw as Obatala's intrusion into her territory. While Obatala was away on a visit to the sky, Olokun used her oceans to flood the land, killing many people and ruining their settlements. The people begged the trickster Eshu (Legba) to go up to heaven to tell the gods what was happening and to beg for help. Eshu agreed, but only if sacrifices were made to him and to Obatala. When this was done, Eshu carried the message to the sky and soon Olorun's son, Orunmila, came down and used spells to put an end to the deluge.

AFRICAN GODDESSES AND TRICKSTERS

Are there important African goddesses?

Goddesses play a major role in many African mythologies. Several are Supreme Being creators, such as Woyengi of the Ijaw, Mawu of Dahomey, and Njambi of the Bankongo people in the Congo. Earth mothers and fertility goddesses are ubiquitous. Examples are Mboze of the Woyo people of southwestern Congo, Oddudua or Olokun of the Yoruba, and Ala of the Ibo, who, as the personification of earth itself, carries the dead ancestors in her womb, which is the Underworld. Asase is the Ashanti goddess of earth. For the Krachi of Togo and Ghana, Asase Ya is the earth on which Wulbari, the sky, lay, leaving crowded space for their offspring until Wulbari decided to rise up above her. The Zulu goddess Nokhubulwane, the inventor of beer, permeates all aspects of nature. An unusual goddess is the Yoruba Oya. Perhaps more a concept that a personality, she can be a river, an animal, an aspect of human behavior. She represents justice, but, like the Indian Kali, is a goddess of violence and death.

What are the tricksters' characteristics and roles?

Typically, tricksters are creative, but they often challenge or undermine the creator's work. They have enormous appetites for food, for sex, and for power. Sometimes they are culture heroes, helping humanity in the face of the Supreme Being's power and arbitrariness. Tricksters can change shapes, often becoming animals, to achieve their questionable goals. Tricksters are essentially amoral, perhaps representing a state of consciousness that has not yet accepted the restraints of civilization. Tricksters play a major role in African mythology, perhaps because, in general, African mythology reveals a skeptical view of life and of deities, stressing the precariousness of existence, which precariousness is thus represented by the tricksters and their activities.

Who are the major tricksters in African mythology?

Many African tricksters stand out. Several are known primarily for their trickery in the course of theft or even murder. The Bantu Hlakanyana, who had once been a participant in creation, is such a trickster, as is another Bantu figure, Dikithi, who had one arm, one leg, and one eye. Easily the most famous African tricksters are the West African gods Eshu, also known as Elegbara or Legba, and Ananse (Anansi) the Spider.

Eshu is an *orisha,* one of the spirits of Yoruba and Fon mythology. His spirit apparently accompanied the slaves to the new world; he remains an important presence as Papa Legba in Voodoo in Haiti, Cuba, and elsewhere. Legba is the spirit of verbal and nonverbal communication, a god of fertility, and the guardian of crossroads. Like Hermes in Greece, he is a penetrator of the dark world. In Dahomey, his penetrating phallic symbol, like the phallic *herm* of Hermes, is often placed outside of dwellings as a protective talisman.

Ananse (Anansi) is ubiquitous among West African peoples. He is the Spider, the weaver of stories. The term *Anansesem* ("Spider Stories") refers to a whole collection of orally transmitted Ananse tales. Ananse tales travelled with slaves to America, where the trickster takes forms such as "Aunt Nancy" and Br'er Rabbit.

LEGBA AND ANANSE

What is the story of Legba?

Legba (Elegba, Eshu) came into being at the very beginning of creation when the creator still lived on earth.

One myth tells us that he was, in fact, the son of the creator and the facilitator of the creator's will among his human subjects, filling a kind of culture-hero role while the creator remained aloof. If the creator caused bad things to happen, Legba was blamed, and if good things happened, the creator was praised. The situation so irritated Legba that he confronted his father. "I have only done what you have asked me to do," he said, "and it only gets me into trouble, since I get blamed when you cause bad things to happen." The creator replied that kings should always be praised for good things and his servants should be blamed for bad ones: "That's just the way it is and always will be," he said. This conversation infuriated Legba further and he plotted a trick of revenge. Lying, he claimed to his father that he had heard rumors that thieves were planning to steal from his famous garden of fine yams. Furious, the creator proclaimed that anyone who stole his yams would be executed. That night Legba stole into his father's house and took the god's sandals. After putting them on, he made his way into the garden and took all the yams. The next morning he ran to the creator's house and announced that all the yams had been stolen, but pointed out that since the thief had left sandal prints it should be easy enough to find him. The creator called everyone together to see whose sandal prints had been left in the garden. But the prints were huge—much larger than any feet in the village. So Legba turned to his father and said, "Sir, do you think it's possible that you took the yams while sleep-walking?" "Of course not," cried the god, but when he put his feet into the prints there was a perfect match. Now the people began to grumble about the creator stealing from himself. The creator realized that his crafty son had tricked him, and in fury he left the world for the sky, leaving his son in charge on earth.

What is the story of Ananse?

Some say Ananse was the son of the sky god creator, who in some tales is Nyame, in some Wulbari, in some, other creators. His mother was the earth goddess. Some see Ananse as primarily a culture hero who brought humans gifts they needed in order to survive. Ananse, as a spider, was small, but he was especially cunning, and like other tricksters, he was not above stealing to accomplish his goals.

This wooden figure with coins, cowry shells, and cords is a symbol of Eshu (Legba).

The Ashanti people say that it was Ananse who, in fact, created the sun and other astral bodies, as well as the first people, although it was the sky god Nyame who gave them the breath of life. Like all tricksters, Ananse had an erotic appetite; he even seduced and stole away the sky god's daughter.

In a Krachi tale the sky god Wulbari heard Ananse bragging that he was cleverer than the high god himself. Wulbari decided to teach Ananse a lesson by sending him on a mission to earth to find something without telling him what the something was. "If you're so smart, you should know what I want," he said. Ananse went down to earth, took feathers from different birds, attached the feathers to himself, and flew back to heaven disguised as one of them (tricksters can take any shape they want). Wulbari was amazed to find the mysterious and beautiful bird perched on a tree. He asked the animals what it was. They suggested that Ananse might know. "I can't ask him, because I sent him to earth to find something," said Wulbari. The animals asked what that something was, and Ananse, who was actually the bird, overheard. "I didn't tell him," said Wulbari, "but I had in mind the sun, the moon, and darkness." The animals laughed and complimented the god for apparently outsmarting the trickster. But now, Ananse knew what Wulbari wanted, and, in fact, he collected the sun, the moon, and darkness, and placed them in a sack. He then returned to Wulbari. When he pulled darkness out of the sack no one could see anything. When he took out the moon, the animals could see a little bit. Finally he brought out the sun; those who looked at it went blind, but those who blinked did not. This is how blindness came into the world.

What is the myth of Ananse and storytelling?

Ananse was, above all, a storyteller. The mysterious power of language was crucial to him. An Ashanti myth tells how Ananse stole storytelling from Nyame. Ananse proposed to pay for the stories known only to Nyame, the high god. "Why should I sell them to you?" said the god. "In any case, the price is much too steep for you." Ananse asked what that price was. "It is the Python, the Leopard, the Hornets, and a Fairy," said Nyame. Ananse left and consulted with Aso, his wife, who told him what he must do. So, following his wife's advice, he took a stick with some vines to a place where he found the python. "My wife and I have been arguing about your length," said Ananse. "Well, measure with that stick," said the python. Ananse placed the stick next to the snake and then quickly used the vine to tie it to the stick. He delivered the captured python to Nyame. Then, also on the advice of Aso, he dug a hole in the leopard's hunting trail and set a trap over it with sticks. Naturally, the leopard came along and fell through the sticks into the hole. Ananse pretended to help the leopard out of the hole but managed to wound and capture him instead. He took his captive off to Nyame. Again following Aso's instructions, he poured water over a swarm of hornets and urged them to take cover from the "rain" in the gourd he was carrying. The hornets did as they were told, and Ananse closed the gourd and took it to Nyame. Finally, with Aso's help, the trickster carved a little doll, painted it with sticky sap, and placed some yam mash in its hands. He placed the doll in a place where the fairies enjoyed dancing and tied a string to its head. One of the fairies asked the doll for some of the mash, and Ananse, hidden behind a tree, used the string to make the doll's head nod. When the fairy thanked the doll and it did not respond, the fairy became angry and slapped it. But now she was stuck to the doll (an African version of the American "tar baby"). Ananse took the captured fairy off to Nyame, and the god had no choice but to hand the stories over to Ananse. This is why we have stories in the world, especially the Spider Tales.

AFRICAN HEROES

Who are the African mythic heroes?

The Bantu of Sesuto tell the story of Lituolone, a god-hero who was miraculously conceived and born of an old woman, without having been with a man. Lituolone was born fully adult and ready to take on a heroic quest. The world had been oppressed by an evil monster who had devoured all humanity but his mother. So it was that the young hero decided to be a monster slayer as were so many world heroes before him. Taking a knife, he challenged the monster and was immediately swallowed by it. Once inside its evil belly, Lituolone cut his way out, killing the monster and releasing captured humanity.

The mythic heroes of Africa, however, mostly tend to be culture heroes—especially tricksters—who represent the needs of ordinary people in the face of the general arbitrariness of the high gods, the supreme beings and creators who are either disgusted with people or withdrawn from them. Tricksters such as Ananse and Legba are heroes in that they successfully trick the Supreme Being. Thus, Legba reveals the creator god's unfairness and Ananse wrests the art of storytelling from him. Other culture heroes

Why are animals so prominent in African myths?

The centrality of animals in African mythology and in other animistic mythologies, such as those of the Native North American, reflects the sense that all things in nature are animated by the spirit world. In an earlier time, according to this perspective, animals and humans were much more involved in each other's lives than they are now and could communicate directly.

such as the Kikuyu Gikuyu teach the people how to survive. The trickster heroes reflect a general sense that the world is a dangerous place in which ordinary people must struggle to survive without much help from the privileged, including the creator. In this kind of a world, the trickster, however amoral, or even immoral, represents the aspirations and wish fulfillments of the downtrodden and becomes a hero.

Are there African heroines?

There are some African mythological heroines. An example is the Kikuyu maiden Wanjiru, who undergoes sacrifice for the good of her people. Her story involves not only the motif of sacrifice, but also of the descent into the Underworld and resurrection. According to the story, after three years of severe drought the people met in a field to dance for rain. A shaman told them that rain would not come without the sacrifice of the maiden Wanjiru, for whom each family would have to pay with a goat. When the goats were assembled at the dancing grounds, Wanjiru was produced by her family. Since she was the object being sold, Wanjiru was placed in the middle of the dance grounds. It was then that she began to sink into the ground. The people cried out in horror, but Wanjiru herself cried out, "Rain will come." As the girl continued to sink, people stepped forward to save her but were paid with goats to move aside. As she went under, Wanjiru called out, "My own people have done this to me." Then during the night, Wanjiru's fiancé decided to follow his beloved. Like Orpheus in the Greek myth, he sank into the Underworld intending to retrieve her, and, unlike Orpheus, he succeeded. When the couple appeared alive and well at the dance circle, the people were amazed. The couple married and the rains came.

The Wanjiru myth resembles one from the Ceram in Indonesia, in which a maiden named Hainuwele is sacrificed in a dance circle and becomes the source of the people's nourishment.

MESOAMERICAN AND SOUTH AMERICAN MYTHOLOGIES: MAYA, AZTEC, INCA

What do we mean by Mesoamerican and South American mythologies?

Mesoamerican mythologies are those of the indigenous peoples of Mexico and Central America. These mythologies include, most importantly, those of the Mayans and the Mexica (Aztec). The mythology of the Mexica developed directly from those of a series of earlier civilizations, including the Olmec and Toltec and the peoples of Monte Alban (Zapotec) and Teotihuacan.

South America is a continent of many peoples, but the dominant mythology that has come down to us is that of the Inca of Peru, with which much of the rest of South American mythology has much in common.

MESOAMERICA

What is the history of Mesoamerican cultures?

People practicing agriculture and living in villages existed in Mesoamerica at least as early as 7000 B.C.E., and by 2500 B.C.E. a culture had emerged along the Gulf coast of what is today Mexico (Veracruz, Tobasco) that can reasonably be called "pre-Olmec," that is, leading directly to the first of the great Mesoamerican civilizations, the Olmec. The Olmec flourished between about 1500 and 400 B.C.E. Meanwhile, further south in Mexico and well into Central America, Mayan civilization had emerged and remained strong from about 1500 B.C.E. until the Spanish conquest in the early sixth century. By 600 B.C.E. the Zapotec had developed a civilization centered in the city of Monte Alban in what today is Oaxaca. The great pyramid city of Teotihuacan, near today's Mexico City, was the center of another civilization. It lasted from about 200 B.C.E. until about 750 C.E. The next important Mesoamerican civilization was that of the Toltec of Tula, which flourished between 800 and 1000 C.E. and was the direct mythological ancestor of the Mexica, or Aztecs, who built the city of Tenochtitlan in what is today Mexico City and dominated Mesoamerica from about 1350 C.E. until the Spanish conquered them under Hernán Cortés in 1521.

Who were the Olmec?

The Olmec culture, in the area of what is now Veracruz and Tabasco, came into its own in about 1500 B.C.E. The Olmec became powerful and built what seem to have been the earliest of the Mesoamerican pyramids. Their stone sculptures, of which large heads may be seen today, are imposing. The Olmec had a writing system by 300 B.C.E. and a calendar and a great interest in astronomy. Their gods included the ubiquitous Feathered Serpent and other deities who are clearly the mythological ancestors of the deities we find in the later cultures of Monte Alban, Teotihucuan, the Toltec, and the Aztec. By 600 B.C.E., the Olmecs had lost much of their power, and by 300 B.C.E., the culture was essentially extinct.

An Olmec head is seen here displayed at the Museum of Anthropology in Xalapa, Mexico.

THE MAYA AND THE *POPOL VUH*

Who are the Maya?

The Maya established a series of city-states in Southern Mexico and Central America beginning in about 1500 B.C.E. Many would say that theirs was the most advanced of the pre-Columbian cultures of Mesoamerica. The civilization reached its zenith between 250 and 900 C.E. The Maya had a fully developed writing system, a sophisticated calendar, and a knowledge of astronomy. They also were advanced in their architecture, weaving, pottery, and stone carving. And, as did the other Mesoamericans, they built pyramids as part of their religious expression. Mayans continue to live in southern Mexico and Central America and to follow many of their ancient traditions. The Mayan myths are collected in the *Popol Vuh*.

What is the *Popol Vuh*?

What we know of the mythology of the Maya comes from a kind of hieroglyphic writing carved into stone monuments and codices (books written on bark paper) by the Maya themselves, and from books by the colonial Spanish. The most important of the Spanish sources is the mid-sixteenth-century *Popol Vuh* ("Book of the People"). The mythology it contains is specifically that of the Quiché Maya of Guatemala. The *Popol Vuh* was written in the Quiché Maya dialect, but in Latin script. It was transcribed and translated into Spanish in 1700 by a Spanish Dominican friar, Francisco Ximenez.

What was the Maya cosmology?

As with all myths of the Maya, there are different versions of the cosmology in different centers. Generally it was believed that the earth (Cab) was a flat surface with four corners representing the four directions and the four cardinal colors—red, white, black, yellow. The flat surface for some was actually the back of a giant crocodile. As for the sky, it too had four corners and was held up by four powerful gods, known as the Bacab, and/or by a world tree, the Yaxché (Ceiba Tree), which stood in the center of the whole cosmos. The sky equivalent of the earth crocodile in some traditions was the two-headed serpent. There were many layers of heaven (Caan), each controlled by a god. At the highest level was the Maize god, Hunab'Ku, the father of the sacred twins. The Underworld (Xibalba, or Metanal) also had many layers and was visited each night by the Sun.

THE MAYAN GODS AND HEROES

What was the Maya pantheon?

There are more than two hundred Mayan gods, and their names vary in different centers. The most famous of the gods was universally worshipped under different names in Mesoamerica. He was Gucumatz for the Quiché Maya, Kukulkan for the Maya of the Yucatán Mexico. He would be the even more famous Feathered Serpent or Quetzalcoatl among the Nahuatl-speaking cultures beginning with the Olmec and the Teotihuacan peoples. Gucumatz was a culture hero as well as a god. With Tepeu, he is the creator in the *Popol Vuh*. Many Maya believed he came to them from the sea and taught them the arts of civilization before returning to the sea and promising to return one day. He was a "once and future king" like King Arthur. Visitors to Chichen Itza in the Yucatán can watch the shadow of this god, as Kukulkan, the Feathered Serpent, slithering down the steps of the great pyramid there during the spring and fall equinoxes.

There are other important gods named in various Maya traditions. Itzamná is the

The maize god was at the highest level of the Mayan pantheon.

creator god and usually the sun god. He was once a culture hero who taught the people how to survive and is, therefore, sometimes confused with Kukulkan (Gucumatz) or with the Yucatán creator Kinich Ahau.

Chac, like the Aztec Tlaloc, was a rain and harvest god and a god of thunder. Yumil Kaxob, the Maize god, was dependent on him and was also affected by Ah Puch (Yum Cimil), the god of Death, who was marked with black spots and was associated with skulls and corpses, as was the Hindu goddess Kali. Ix-Chel was one of the great goddesses. Like the Hindu Devi, she is an aspect of a collective of goddesses (Akna). According to some sources, with Itzamná she produced the Bacabs, who hold up the world. Ek Chuah, who is black and who has a scorpion tail, is the god of war and of merchants, suggesting that war and the search for riches are related. Acan is a god of wine and intoxication, the Mayan Dionysos. A strange goddess is Ixtab, who represents suicide and is depicted with a rope around her neck. She takes the souls of suicide victims to paradise. The sacred twins Hunahpú and Xbalanque are of great importance to the Maya and bring to mind the many twins of Indo-European culture.

What was the Maya creation myth?

There are many versions of the Maya creation myth. The creation myth that dominates the *Popol Vuh* is an unusual story because what stands out is the mistakes of the creators. In the beginning, as in so many creation myths, there was chaos—undifferentiated nothingness in which the deities themselves were undifferentiated. Creation took place when the spiritual power, which was the potential for deities, in fact, became separated into the water-earth gods Tepeu and Gucumatz. These deities created the earth, the plants, and the animals. The gods wanted a being that could recognize them and worship them. They tried to create humans out of mud, but the beings turned back into mud. The first gods were joined by others, including the goddess Chirakan-Ixmucane. The new group tried to make humans out of wood; but these creatures were empty, with no sense of their creators.

Was there a Maya flood myth?

To put an end to the wooden humans, the gods sent a flood, and the god of death arrived with demons to kill off the unwanted people.

How were real humans created?

Finally the gods got it right. From plant life they produced four men and then four women to go with the four corners of the world.

Who were the Maya heroes?

The primary Maya heroes were the "hero twins," Hunahpú and Xbalanque (Hunter and Jaguar Deer). The heroes were miraculously conceived when the dead skull of a figure known as Hun Hunahpú spits into the hand of Xquic. Hun Hunahpú had been summoned to the Underworld for making too much noise while playing the Maya ball game and had been sacrificed there. Threatened in childhood by jealous older brothers, the twins turned these brothers into monkeys. The hero twins sought revenge for their father's sacrifice. As did he, they played the ball game noisily and were called to the Underworld, thus following the path taken there by so many heroes of myth. There they defeated the Underworld lords in the ball game and eventually killed them, decisively undermining the power of the lords of death. As did other heroes, they became monster slayers, defeating in particular the bird demon, Vucub-Caquix. And as did other heroes, they eventually achieved apotheosis as the sun and moon in the heavens.

A drawing of the Mayan hero twins Hunahpá and Xbalanqué based on the Izapa Stela.

MONTE ALBAN AND TEOTIHUACAN

Who are the Zapotec?

The ancestors of the people we know today as the Zapotecs built the first real city in Mesoamerica on the flat top of Monte Alban, the ruins of which are spectacularly accessible near present-day city of Oaxaca. The Monte Alban civilization gradually became the major southern Mexican power for some thousand years, beginning in about 600 B.C.E. As did the Olmec, the Teotihuacan people, and the Maya, the Zapotec built pyramids, had calendar and writing systems, and had an interest in astronomy. They worshipped a number of gods who seem to be related to those of the other early Mesoamerican cultures, including the Feathered Serpent, associated with the god/hero Quetzalcoatl.

Who were the Teotihuacan people?

The Teotihuacan culture, centered in the great pyramid city just northeast of present-day Mexico City, was established in about 250 B.C.E. By 500 C.E. Teotihuacan was one of the largest and best-appointed cities in the world. Not only did it have pyramids, large public squares, and wide central streets, it had a population of about 125,000. The pyramids celebrated the gods—including the familiar Feathered Serpent/Quetzalcoatl figure—and their astronomical cognates. Pyramids such as those in honor of the sun and

A reproduction of a drawing of the Great Goddess of Teotihuacan based on an ancient mural.

the moon and their related deities were decorated with mythological figures that resembled the deities depicted much later by the Toltec and Aztec. Like the Monte Alban culture, Teotihuacan collapsed in the mid-seventh century C.E.

THE TOLTEC AND AZTEC

Who were the Toltec?

The Toltec, who became dominant in Mesoamerica in the tenth century C.E., were a warlike and commercial people. They built their capital at Tollan, near present-day Tula, Mexico. They spoke Nahuatl and remained powerful until the late twelfth century C.E. when the Aztec became dominant and essentially adopted much of the Toltec mythological system, including the ever-present Quetzalcoatl figure. Human sacrifice was practiced by the Toltec, as it would be by the Aztec.

Who are the Mexica (Aztec)?

By the early 1500s, the Mexica, or Aztecs, the last of the great pre-Columbian Mesoamerican civilizations, dominated an empire of some six million people. In 1325 they had begun to build their capital, Tenochtitlan, on land that is today Mexico City. Their culture, and especially their mythology, developed from that of the Toltec. As did the Toltec, they spoke Nahuatl; and, like the Toltec, they were militaristic and commercial. The Toltec and Aztec shared a tradition based on sacrifice, solar dominance, and many of the same deities. Many of these traditions were inherited indirectly from the Olmec and Monte Alban peoples. Aztec civilization was still developing when the Spanish, led by Cortés, conquered it in 1521.

What was the Aztec pantheon?

The Aztec absorbed gods of the peoples they conquered as well as those, especially, of the Teotihuacan and Toltec civilizations, so their pantheon takes different form at different times. The consistently major Aztec gods are the following, beginning with the four creator gods of the four directions:

Quetzalcoatl, a version of the ubiquitous Mesoamerican Feathered Serpent, was Lord of the West, god of fertility and of wisdom. In some stories he plays the role of human culture hero.

Tezcatlipoca, Lord of the North, was the god of night, providence, and matter, and was sometimes a rival of Quetzalcoatl. Xipe-Totec was Lord of the East and the ambiguous god of war, agriculture, disease, and spring. Huitzilopochtli was Lord of the South, god of fire, the sun, and of war.

Tlaloc was the ancient rain, thunder, and earthquake god. He required child sacrifices.

Coatlicue, the mother of Huitzilopochtli, was the great goddess of fertility, life, and death.

What was the Aztec creation myth?

There are several Aztec creation myths—some from the Mexica themselves, some filtered down from earlier Mesoamerican cultures, especially the Toltec. According to one myth, a goddess, Omecihuatl, gave birth to a sacrificial knife, which fell to earth and became the Mexica and their gods. This story suggests the origins of the Aztec practice of human sacrifice. In another myth there was an original self-created dual-gendered deity, Ometeotl (made up of the male Ometecuhtli and the female Omecihuatl, or Tonacatecuhtli and Tonacacihuatl). The male and female sides of this deity mated and gave birth to the most important of the Aztec solar deities: Blue Huitzilopochtli, White Quetzalcoatl, Black Tezcatlipoca, and Red Xipe-Totec. These four deities can be seen as one and are sometimes called the "Four Tezcatlipocas." Huitzilopochtli was also the "Blue Tezcatlipoca," and Quetzalcoatl was the "White Tezcatlipoca." Some scholars have suggested that this concept represents a tendency towards monotheism.

The best known Aztec creation myth is that of the "Five Suns," a myth of creation in stages, which resembles the creation myth of some of the southwestern Native North Americans. The first "sun" world was said to have been ruled by Tezcatlipoca, god of the north and darkness. It was eaten by tigers. The second "sun" world was that of Quetzalcoatl, god of the west and magic. It was destroyed by Winds, and its human survivors became monkeys. The third "sun" world was that of Tlaloc, here the god of fire as well as of rain. It was lost to a rain of fire and its human survivors became birds. The fourth "sun" world belonged to Chalchihuitlicue, goddess of the east and water, Tlaloc's consort. It was destroyed by a great flood. The present "sun" world of the Aztecs, the fifth, is that of the fire god Xiuhtecuhtli. Earthquakes will be its end. Still another Aztec myth reports that Quetzalcoatl and his opposite, Tezcatlipoca ("Smoking Mirror"), created the fifth world, which was ruled by Huitzilopochtli.

The existence of the various "sun" worlds is based on a numerological system and a complex "Divine Calendar" (*tonalamatl*). The overall theme of the Aztec creation myths is the constant struggle of the sun against the forces of darkness, a struggle related to the practice of sacrifice. In one depiction of an early story, the sun god Tonatiuh sticks out his tongue, waiting for blood. In another depiction the sun is threatened by the dark Tezcatlipoca. Quetzalcoatl, an old man heading back to the west, is the setting sun. In still another rendition, the bright sun is Huitzilopochtli ("Hummingbird of the South"), depicted as the victorious warrior.

HUITZILOPOCHTLI
AND QUETZALCOATL

Who were the Aztec mythical heroes?

Although generally considered deities, two figures in Aztec mythology also play the role of hero, either as culture heroes who teach the people how to live or as archetypal heroes who represent specific qualities associated with what Joseph Campbell calls the universal hero, the "hero with a thousand faces." These figures are Quetzalcoatl, the Feathered Serpent, and Huitzilopochtli, the "Hummingbird of the South."

What is the myth of Huitzilopochtli?

Huitzilopochtli was the patron god of the Aztec. The great temple in the center of the Aztec capital, Tenochtitlan, where human sacrifice took place, was dedicated to him. Huitzilopochtli is said to have told the Aztec people to call themselves "Mexica." It was he who led them, as a culture hero, from Aztlán to Tenochtitlan. But it is a miraculous conception and birth myth that ties him archetypally to other heroes. Coatlicue, "She of the Serpent-woven Skirt," was lying on a mountaintop when a ball of feathers landed on her and she became pregnant. Her grown children were so outraged at what they saw as their mother's disgrace that they determined to kill her. But just before they arrived to act on their plan, Huitzilopochtli was born fully armed and adult, with blue limbs and his left leg covered in hummingbird feathers. With his blue shield and spear, he defeated his siblings and saved himself and his mother.

What is the myth of Quetzalcoatl?

Quetzalcoatl's myth is more complex. As a cultural hero to many Mesoamerican people, he taught the people the arts and the use of the calendar, and he gave them maize. In a golden age he was the king of the Toltec city of Tula (Tollan), the City of the Sun. He had light skin and a white beard. Quetzalcoatl's conception and birth mark him as a hero figure. His mother, Chimalman, was a virgin who became pregnant when a great god took the form of "morning" and breathed on her. Like the Buddha's mother, Maya, Chimalman died soon after giving birth to the hero, signifying his belonging to an entire culture rather than to a particular mother or family. At birth Quetzalcoatl was fully adult, endowed with all powers and wisdom, making him able to immediately help the people. Quetzalcoatl lived in a shining house—a veritable sun palace surrounded by beautiful gardens. But in time he was challenged by his dark opposite, Tezcatlipoca, who came down to Tula on spider webs, bringing cold death to the gardens. Quetzalcoatl knew that Tezcatlipoca had come to drive him out of Tula, so he burnt down his silver palace and went with his opposite to the ball court. As Quetzalcoatl was about to hurl the ball through the ring, Tezcatlipoca took the form of a jaguar and attacked him, chasing him through the streets of Tula and out into the countryside. As he fled, Quetzalcoatl became an old man. When he came to the sea, the great hero made a raft of snakes and sailed away. Some say that in Tlappallan (Middle Aztec heaven) he drank from a fountain of immortality and will return one day, as will Arthur, a "once and future king." Others say that he died and became a star in the heavens. There is a popular story that says when the light-skinned, white-bearded Cortés arrived in Tenochtitlan, the Aztec thought he was Quetzalcoatl returning.

Why did the Mesoamericans practice human sacrifice?

Mesoamericans, including the Aztec, believed that the gods demanded blood-letting as payment for balance in the world. Sacrifice could involve an individual's self-inflicted bleeding, the sacrifice of animals, or the sacrifice of people. Different gods required different types of sacrifice. Tlaloc, the ancient rain god, demanded children, whose tears might bring rain. Other gods were satisfied with war captives or slaves. For the Aztec, the Temple Mayor at Tenochtitlan was the favored place of sacrifice.

The Aztec mythic hero Quetzalcoatl, depicted here in the thirteenth-century Codex Borbonicus, gave his people the gifts of the calendar, maize, and the arts.

For a time the victim was treated respectfully as a representative of the god to whom the sacrifice would be made, but when the proper time came the victim's heart was removed by priests and the body thrown down the side of the pyramid to be beheaded.

It should be noted that many scholars question the popular ideas about Mesoamerican human sacrifice, suggesting that its existence has been greatly exaggerated, in some cases by the conquering Spanish, who hoped to justify the forced conversion of the native peoples to Christianity.

THE SOUTH AMERICANS

Who are the indigenous people of South America?

There are hundreds of indigenous groups in South America. Each has its own indigenous language and culture, as well as mythology. It is thought that most if not all of these peoples crossed into the Americas via the land mass that later became the Bering Strait. There is indication of South American agriculture by 6500 B.C.E. As permanent settlements developed over the next millennia, so did mythology. In the time just before the arrival of the Spanish conquistadors, led by Francisco Pizarro in 1526, South America, at least in the Andean region, was dominated by a people known as the Inca.

What are some South American creation myths?

Stories of creation are ubiquitous among South American peoples, as they are among peoples everywhere. In many cases, creation in South America was initiated by a supreme sun deity. In what is today Colombia, the Witoto creator himself emerged from the sound of words that articulated ancient myths and incantations. This concept is similar to the Indian Vedic concept of the sacred words of the *Vedas* themselves, or the sound of the sacred syllable, "Om." The Chibcha of Colombia say that originally an as-yet-unformed god contained the light of the world. When that god rose up, light was released and creation began, with birds spreading the light around the world. The Chamacoco of today's Paraguay say that the mother goddess Eschetewuarha was the wife of the supreme deity but was herself the creator. For the Shipibo of Peru, a solar goddess is the creator. Culture heroes play a major role in many South American creation myths as they do in Africa and in other parts of the world. Sometimes the creator is assisted by twins. Sometimes these twins represent different sides of creation, the good and the evil, the evil twin becoming, in effect, a mischievous trickster. The Carib

What mythological themes dominate in South American mythology?

Myths of creation, plant myths, and apocalyptic flood-type myths are common.

people of Guiana believe that Makunaima and his twin created the world, but also caused a great flood. Also in Guiana we find Tuminikar, a solar deity who helps humans, and his brother, Duid, the moon, who undermines everything the solar deity does. The Ona of Brazil have a supreme being who sent a culture hero named Kenos to the world. It was Kenos who created human sexual organs out of peat, which were then responsible for the creation of the Ona. After Kenos taught the people what they needed to know to live, he departed, turning things over to a set of twins who gave the people both new knowledge and death. As in Mayan culture, the creators were not always successful. In what is now Venezuela, the Taulipa culture hero attempted to create humans out of wax, which, of course, melted. Wisely, he chose clay at his next attempt.

What are some South American origin myths?

Plants are the basis of agricultural societies, and there are many South American plant origin myths. Some South American Indians say that vegetables grew first on a tree of life. Some tell agricultural myths involving sacrificial planting and rebirth of sacred beings, much as in the myths of the North American Corn Mother. Many of the Peruvian Indians, including the Inca, tell how the first people were starving until Pachacamac, a culture hero, impregnated a woman, then dismembered and "planted" her child, who "returned" in the spring as edible plants.

What are some South American apocalyptic and flood myths?

There is an apocalyptic theme in South American mythology. There are those who believe that the world will end in fire; others believe in a great deluge. Both ends are seen as punishment by the gods for the evils of humanity, especially the failure of the people to follow the instructions of the culture hero. The Yaghan of the Cape Horn area argue that the moon caused a great flood because humans had learned more than they should have about female "mysteries." A male and female pair always manages to escape the apocalypse so that the world can go on. The Canari of Ecuador tell of two boys who avoided the flood and were led by two parrots, which turned into girls. The boys and the girls got together to create a new race of people, the Canari.

THE INCA

Who were the Inca?

An Andean people, of uncertain origin, the Inca can be traced at least as far back as the twelfth century C.E. By the mid-fifteenth century they were the most powerful group in South America, with their capital at Cusco and with many highly developed settlements in the Inca Valley and elsewhere nearby, especially the spectacular one at Machu Pichu.

A leader known as Manco Cápac was the founder of the Kingdom of Cusco. It was he, followed by a leader, Pachacuti, known as "The Earth Shaker," who began the process by which the Inca became dominant, controlling what are today Peru, Bolivia, Ecuador, and parts of Chile. Inca kings were known as "the Inca." Among the most powerful of these was Túpac Inca Yupanqui and his son Huayna Cápac. By the time of the arrival of the Spanish, led by the conquistador Francisco Pizarro, there were troubles in the Inca Empire. A civil war had broken out between the sons of Huayna Cápac. It was the son named Atahualpa who prevailed, and it was he who negotiated with the small but well-armed Spanish army in 1532 C.E. Imprisoned as a hostage, Atahualpa was eventually executed by the Spanish, who installed Atahualpa's brother Manco Inca Yupanqui as a puppet ruler. Finally, after putting down several rebellions, the Spanish defeated the army of the last Inca emperor, Túpac Amaru, in 1572.

What is known of Inca religion and mythology?

Regrettably, since the Inca lacked a written language, not a great deal is known about their mythology. What is known was recorded by the Spanish colonists. We know that the Inca believed in an afterlife, in which the good went to one place, the bad to another less appealing one. We also know something of the Inca pantheon and the mythological stories of the creation and of Incan origins.

What was the Inca pantheon?

The Inca creator and high god, who had many characteristics of the ubiquitous storm god of world mythology, was Viracocha. His wife was Pachamama, the Great Mother and earth goddess, or, according to some, Mamacocha (Cochamama), a sea goddess. Their son was the sun god Inti, the patron of Cusco, the Inca capital, known also as the "Sun City." Inti's semi-historical son was the first Inca emperor, Manco Cápac, sent to the earth as a culture hero to lead the Inca and to teach them the ways of survival and civilization. Manco was married to his sister Mamaoello (Mama Kilya), a fertility and moon goddess. It was she and the culture heroine Mama Occlo who taught the people how to work with wool and to spin and weave. Other Inca deities included the rain god Apu Illapu, Kuychi the rainbow god, and Yakumama, a water goddess in the form of a snake.

What was the Inca creation myth?

Viracocha first created the earth and the sky. Then he decided to create a race of giants to live in his creation. When they became evil, he sent a flood to destroy them. It is said that he then plucked the sun and the moon from the depths of Lake Titicaca. Because the moon was as bright as the sun, the sun became jealous and threw ashes into the moon's face to darken it.

The real emphasis in the various versions of the Inca creation myth is on the creation of humans and the origins of the tribe. One account has it that Pachacamac made the first man and woman out of clay but that he forgot to give them food, and the man died. As in the case of the Mayan myth, imperfect creation is a theme here. Pachacamac then made the angry woman more angry by making her fertile and then cutting up her baby when it was born. He took the pieces of the dismembered body and planted them in the earth. Not surprisingly, given similar myths from around the world, the sacrifice of the baby resulted in plants that fed the people. This myth would seem to have as one purpose the justification of human—especially child—sacrifice practices. When Pachacamac tried to sacrifice the woman's second son, Wichama, the boy escaped and Pachacamac killed the mother. Now very angry himself, the boy chased the trickster-creator into the sea.

A story more sympathetic to Pachacamac considers him the sun god—in effect, Viracocha. It relates that he did, in fact, create a man and woman out of clay and that he then sent his own son and daughter, born of the goddess Pachamama, to act as culture heroes to the new humans. The son and daughter were the first Inca and his queen, Manco Cápac and Mama Oello.

An Incan drawing of the creation god Viracocha.

They represented the sun and moon, respectively. They lived at Lake Titicaca, but, as commanded by their father, they traveled around at will, leaving marks with a golden rod. It was at these marks that the people were to build the Inca cities. In the Valley of Huanacauri, the golden rod sank into the ground, and it was here that the Inca and his wife established the capital city of Cusco.

Like all Inca cities, Cusco was divided into northern and southern halves, one founded by the Inca, one by his wife.

Was there an Inca flood myth?

As noted above, Viracocha sent a flood to destroy the original race of giants who had become unruly. Another flood myth recorded in pictographs tells how a man and woman floating in a box survived the flood and were sent to Tiahuanaco to live and to create a new race.

Who were the Inca mythological heroes?

The heroes of Inca mythology were culture heroes such as the first Inca and his wife— the beings sent by the gods to teach the people the proper and fruitful ways to live. The Inca people, who for so long resisted the dominance of the conquistadors, are themselves seen as heroes by their descendants.

NATIVE NORTH AMERICAN MYTHOLOGIES

Who are the Native North Americans?

Although evidence—some of it controversial—of a human occupation of North America in the Paleolithic age exists, the people we refer to as "Native Americans," or "Indians," seem almost certainly to have begun their migration to North America from northeast Asia by way of the land bridge across the then-dry Bering Strait by about 10,000 B.C.E. These people gradually made their way over the centuries into various parts of the continent and continued into Meso and South America. By the time of Columbus and the conquistadors of the fifth and sixth centuries, North American Indians, like their southern neighbors, were peoples, numbering in the millions, of many "nations" and languages. The last arrivals in the part of North America that is now the United States were the Athabaskan people, known to us as the Navajo (Diné) and Apache, who did not make their way to the southwest until about 1400 C.E. Many Native Americans of the pre-Columbian period were hunter-gatherers with no written languages. Some—especially in Mesoamerica—gradually established cities. Others, like the pre-Pueblo and Pueblo peoples of what is now the southwestern United States, emerged into agricultural communities. As written language did not exist in Native North America, history was passed down orally and is sometimes difficult to differentiate from myth.

Is there a single Native North American mythology?

As there are many Native American peoples, there are just as many mythologies. Mythologies always reflect particular cultures. Yet, perhaps because of some common origins in Central Asia, the frequent contact of various tribes in the Americas, and because Native Americans, as do all of us, share a common humanity with common concerns, leading to common or archetypal motifs and patterns in their mythologies, it is possible to speak somewhat generally about Native American mythology. To at least some extent, Native American mythology is firmly based in nature, in the world around us rather than in the dominance of a sky god. Native American mythology, then, tends to be animistic. As in African mythology, the world around us is considered to be spiritually alive. It is true, however, that there is a nearly universal acceptance of a larger, if somewhat distant, spiritual unifying factor, a "Great Spirit" that non-Indians tend to equate with God. In many cases the Great Spirit is a creator, sometimes helped or undermined by a trickster. Many Indian cultures are matrilineal. That is, the family line descends from the mother. Among matrilineal Native Americans especially, principal female deities, such as Great Mother figure are important and central in creation myths. Creation myths are the most important myths in Native America, as in most cultures.

Is there a Native North American pantheon?

As indicated above, there are as many mythologies as there are tribes and, therefore, as many sets of deities. These sets do not tend to be family pantheons as they are, for instance, in Sumer, Egypt, Greece, and Rome. Yet there are specifically understood groups of gods or spirits who are in some sense related or who work together as a unit. Examples of these are the Hopi *kachina* and the Navajo *yeii*. Often there are groups that include a distant creator or Great Spirit, an Earth Mother, and sometimes a trickster. There are occasional examples of world-parent creator deities—a Sky Father and Earth Mother who, as in other cultures such as the Egyptian and the Greek, must be separated so that creation can take place.

NATIVE AMERICAN
SPIRITS AND CREATORS

Who are the *kachinas* and the *yeii*?

Indians of the American Southwest—particularly the Pueblo peoples and the Zuni and Hopi—have spirits known as *kachinas* (*katsinas*). The Hopi say that the kachinas come from their home in the San Francisco Peaks, above Flagstaff, Arizona, to visit the Hopi villages for important ceremonies, such as dances to bring rain. The kachinas are also spirits of the dead who can become clouds. Kachinas are highly individualized and are represented not only by masked Indian dancers in the ceremonies, but by doll figures used for purposes of religious instruction and/or tourist trade. Some Hopi believe that the fertility goddess Hahaiwutti is the "mother" of the kachinas, a idea that fits with the role of the spirits as clouds that produce rain. Some Hopi say that both Hopi ceremonies and the world itself will end when a kachina removes his mask in a dance.

The Athabaskan peoples we know as the Navajo (Dine) and Apache (Tinde) have somewhat similar figures to the kachinas. The Navajo call them *yeii*, the Apache *hactin*. Led by Talking God, the *yeii*, who are often depicted in sand paintings, participate in ceremonies as masked dancers. They are embodiments of natural powers and they figure importantly in creation myths.

Kachina dolls have become commonplace items in gift stores of the American West, but the kachinas are important spiritual icons, especially among the Pueblo, Zuni, and Hopi peoples.

What are some examples of the Great Spirit?

The Great Spirit is known by many names. In some cases he can be a personification of the sun, as he frequently is in Meso and South America, or of the sky. For some Hopi in the American southwest, the creator sun god is Tawa, who thinks creation into existence but who leaves the working out of the details to others, particularly to the more earth-oriented Spider Woman. This is in keeping with a matrilineal culture's leaving of religious matters to men while reserving earthly matters to women. A more common supreme being in Native American mythology is the Great Spirit whose name can also be translated as Great Power, Great Mystery, Great Manitou, or Kitchi Manitou. The Great Spirit is generally a noncorporeal being who, like the Hindu Brahman, is everywhere and nowhere and is the essential spirit reality in an animistic world. In the Great Plains, the Great Spirit is the ultimate *wakan* or "medicine man," representing the harmony sought by all. In some cases, as among the Cree, the Ojibwa, and many Algonquian peoples, spirits are in everything and are aspects of the Great Manitou, which is neither male nor female and which created the world *ex nihilo*—from nothing—by having a vision of it.

What are some examples of Native American world-parent deities?

The world-parent myth in animistic cultures usually involves the concept that the world literally *is* the parent deity. The Diegueñ of California tell how Tu-chai-pai made the   241 world by blowing ground tobacco between Mother Earth and Father Sky, who were so close together that he and his brother were too cramped to do anything about creating things. The Tobacco caused the sky to rise up.

The Zuni of New Mexico have a creation myth in which all life was conceived from the union of Earth Mother and Sky Father. But Earth Mother's womb became so full that she pushed Father Sky away from her and began to sink into the primal waters. The world parents were worried about the survival of their offspring, so Mother Earth kept their progeny in her womb. But eventually, Earth Mother spat into the water, causing foam, and breathed on the foam, allowing her children to emerge. When her offspring came out of her she announced that she would nurture them in her being. Father Sky would send the colder, but necessary, moisture from above.

THE NATIVE AMERICAN GREAT GODDESS

What are some examples of Native American Great Goddess deities?

The Great Goddess archetype is firmly established in Native American mythology—especially in matrilineal cultures. In some cases, the Great Mother *is* the world. The Okanagan goddess is the Mother of Everyone and at one time had been a human being who now lives as the Earth. Her flesh is the soil, her bones are the rocks, her hair the plants, her breath the wind.

A Cherokee Great Goddess is Grandmother Sun, a central source of nourishment and survival. Other Great Goddesses are crucial in the creation process, as is the case of Mother Earth in the world-parent myths. Particularly strong Native American Great Goddesses are Spider Woman (or Spider Grandmother), Changing Woman, Thinking Woman, White Buffalo Woman, and Sedna.

What is the story of the Cherokee Grandmother Sun?

The Cherokee sun is represented, somewhat unusually, by a goddess figure, Grandmother Sun, rather than by a male deity. As the Sun Goddess, she has a mythological sister in the Japanese Amaterasu. The Cherokee myth of Grandmother Sun includes a disappearing god theme—again, as in the story of Amaterasu. It also includes the flood theme. Each day, during her journey across the heavens, Grandmother Sun stopped in the center of the sky to visit her daughter's house. While there, she complained that her grandchildren, the people of the earth, never looked directly at her but rather squinted and looked away. Yet these same grandchildren always looked lovingly up at the moon god. One day, Grandmother Sun became so jealous and angry that she decided to remain for an extended period at her daughter's house in the middle of the sky. Naturally, her prolonged presence caused the world below to be parched with heat, causing the people to beg the spirits of the earth—the "Little Men"—for help.

The spirits suggested sending two men disguised as snakes up to the sky to kill the goddess. When the snake men failed, the spirits sent up a man disguised as a horned monster, but he failed, too. When a man disguised as a rattlesnake succeeded only in killing Grandmother's daughter, the goddess became so furious that she locked herself in the daughter's house, leaving the world cold and dark. Once again the people asked the advice of the Little Men, who suggested that the daughter could be brought back from the land of the dead in the west. Seven men were chosen to capture her and to bring her back in a box. Each man carried a magic wand. Arriving in the Dark Land they found the sun's daughter dancing with other ghosts.

As directed by the spirits, each man struck the girl with his wand, and after the seventh had done so and the daughter had fallen over, the men put her into the box and carried her away without the other dancers noticing. But on the way home the daughter cried out so miserably from inside the box that the men let her out. Immediately she took the form of a redbird and flew away. When the men arrived home with the empty box, Grandmother Sun gave up hope of ever seeing her daughter again and flooded the earth with her tears. It was only after the people danced for her and sang songs to her that Grandmother relented, stopped the flood, and once again bathed the earth in her light and warmth.

Who is Spider Woman?

Spider Woman, or Spider Grandmother, is a popular goddess. She, or figures like her, are particularly prevalent among the southwestern Pueblo cultures, especially the Hopi. The Navajo and Cherokee, too, have Spider Woman myths. Usually she is the primary agent in the creation process, weaving creation into existence, even if it is initiated by a more distant Great Spirit figure. Once the people are created, Spider Woman becomes their culture hero, teaching them how to live. A Hopi myth tells how the sun god Tawa began the creative process, but sent Spider Woman to lead the people through it. It was Spider Woman who led the people out of the *sipapu*, the spider hole by means of which they entered our world. Today the Hopi and other Pueblo Indians have sacred and social chambers—often underground—called *kivas*, in the center of the floors of which is always found a tiny *sipapu*, rep-

A sculpture by artist Lauren Raine depicts Spider Woman, a goddess and teacher popular among the Pueblo peoples.

243

resenting the place of emergence into this world and perhaps reminding them of the importance of Spider Woman. The Navajo of Canyon de Chelly in Arizona call a tall rock structure there "Spider Rock" in honor of Spider Woman.

Who is Changing Woman?

The Athabaskan peoples, the Navajo and the Apache, have a goddess known by several names. She can be called White Shell Woman or White Bead Woman, and especially for the Navajo, Changing Woman. Changing Woman plays an important role in the female puberty rite, which the Navajo call the *kinaalda*. Changing Woman provides women with the possibility of giving birth. It is said that one day First Man heard a baby crying and found the baby in a cradle of rainbows. He picked up the baby and took it to First Woman. After Talking God and House God told the first couple how important this baby was, the couple accepted the child as their own. After only two days the baby could sit up, and after four days she could talk. On the tenth day she appeared in a white shell and was named White Shell Woman and Changing Woman. Changing Woman became a virgin mother by the sun of the famous Navajo twin heroes, Monster Slayer and Born for Water. Their immaculate conception took place when a ray of the sun's light passed through a waterfall and landed on Changing Woman.

What is the *kinaalda* myth?

The young goddess who would become known as Changing Woman told her parents, First Man and First Woman, that she was experiencing her first menses. The delighted first couple decided on a celebratory ritual. First Woman would play the role of Ideal Woman. Ideal Woman dressed the maiden in special clothes and carefully brushed her hair. This all represented the girl's achievement of *hozho*, which is beauty, or harmony. Each day during the rite, the girl ran for a long distance toward the east, the place of the sun and of beauty. And each day Ideal Woman massaged her with the power of womanhood and fertility, which would lead eventually to the birth of the sacred hero twins. On the last day of the ceremony, Ideal Woman massaged her from head to toe, literally rubbing in the power of womanhood and the capacity later to produce the sacred twins. On the last day of the ceremony the girl became Changing Woman.

What is the *kinaalda*?

The religion of the Athabaskan peoples treats female puberty as one of the most important events in tribal life. The puberty rite involves the young girl's becoming a fertile woman and, in the process of the rite, taking on the curative powers of the fertility goddess, Changing Woman or White Shell Woman. The Navajo call the puberty rite the *kinaalda*. A myth is told that "explains" and provides the outline for the *kinaalda*.

Who is Thinking Woman?

Thinking Woman is a Great Goddess of several of the the Keres-speaking Pueblo Indians of New Mexico. Among the people of the Acoma Pueblo, an ancient village popularly known as "Sky City," as it sits on top of a butte, Thinking woman is a central figure in the creation myth. Her Indian name is Tsichtinako, and she is a corn goddess, who originally lived under the earth. She is, in fact, the personification of earth itself, the earth goddess who gives birth to two daughters: Iatiku ("Life Bringer") and Nautsiti ("Full Basket"). It is these two who direct the process by which the people and plants emerge from under the earth into our world.

Who is White Buffalo Woman?

White Buffalo Woman is a goddess of the Lakota Sioux. According to the myth of the White Buffalo Woman, a certain chief, Standing Hollow Horn, sent out a group of braves to hunt one morning during a period of great food shortage. The hunters saw a strange figure approaching them—really floating rather than walking toward them, making it clear to them that the figure was a spirit, a *wakan*. Soon they realized that the spirit had taken the form of a beautiful woman with strikingly shining eyes and two round red dots on her face. Her fine clothes were embellished with beautiful white buckskin. The woman's exquisite black hair was tied back with a strand of buffalo fur. In her hands she carried a mysterious bundle and some dried sage. This was Ptesan-Wi, White Buffalo Woman. Amazed, the braves stared at her, and one lunged toward her with desire, only to be consumed by a flash of lightning. White Buffalo Woman ordered a young man to go back to the chief and to instruct him to set up a sacred medicine tent with twenty-four poles. She would follow soon with great gifts.

When the spirit woman arrived where the Sioux had set up the medicine tent, she told the people to build an altar of red earth inside it. On the altar they were to place a buffalo skull. Now White Buffalo Woman circled the tent several times and then, in front of the chief, opened her bundle. From the bundle she took out the *chanunpa*, the sacred pipe that would from that day on be a central object in Sioux ritual. Acting as a culture hero, she instructed the people on how to use the pipe, how to grasp the stem with the left hand and to hold the bowl with the right, and how to pass it from person to person. In thanksgiving, the chief offered White Buffalo Woman the only nourishment they had, water and sweet grass. Sweet grass was dipped into a skin bag full of fresh water and was handed to her. This act, like the passing of the pipe, has always been an element of Sioux ritual. Next, White Buffalo Woman showed the people how to fill the pipe with red willow bark tobacco and how to walk around the medicine tent four times, representing the path of the sun. This was the Sacred Hoop, the Path of Life. White Buffalo Woman continued teaching the people how to use the pipe and how to pray, how to sing the pipe song, how to raise the pipe to Father Sky, how to lower it to Mother Earth, and how to point it to recognize the four directions. "The Sacred Pipe will collect all things together," she said, "the sky, the earth, the world, the people, and the pipe ritual will please Wakan Tanka, the Great Mystery." When she got up to leave, White Buffalo Woman promised to come back in every new cycle of time. The ages of creation were within her, she said, as she floated off into the red setting sun. As she went, she turned over four times, turning first into a black buffalo, then a brown one, then a red one, and finally into a pure white female buffalo calf. After this, the buffalo came to the Sioux and allowed themselves to be hunted and killed for food and clothing. And to this day the people wait for White Buffalo Woman to return.

Who is Sedna?

Sedna (Nuliajuk) is an Inuit sea spirit who plays a significant role in the creation of food. Sedna is one of many animistic goddesses, such as Corn Mother, for example, whose body becomes in some sense suste-

A modern drawing by Troy Hosea of the White Buffalo Woman, a goddess of the Lakota Sioux.

nance for her people. Some Inuit teach that Sedna, as a young girl, lived with her father, Anguta, until a giant sea bird, the fulmar, seduced her, convincing her to live with him in his nest across the sea. But the nest was foul and there was little food. Disgusted by the conditions, Sedna sent messages to her father, begging to be rescued. It took Anguta a year to arrive on the scene, but when he did get there he immediately killed the fulmar, and he and his daughter began their trip home in his boat. But, enraged by the murder of their leader, other fulmars used violent winds to chase Anguta's boat. Now, hoping to save himself from the storm by lessening the boat's weight, Anguta threw his daughter overboard. When she tried to hang on to the boat, he cut off her fingers, which instantly became the whales, seals, and other sea creatures on which the people still depend for food. After the storm Sedna swam up from the depths and climbed back into the boat. Her father was sleeping so she ordered his dogs to eat his hands and feet. When Anguta woke up, he was so furious that earth itself swallowed him.

NATIVE AMERICAN TRICKSTERS

What defines Native American tricksters?

There are many Native American tricksters, or many faces for the same archetypal figure. As we have seen, tricksters are all amoral, all possessed of great appetites for all kinds of pleasure. Carl Jung saw the trickster as the personification of our precivilized selves, the stage of our being which is full of imagination and desire but not yet controlled by the manners or restraints we associate with society. Thus, tricksters are shapeshifters and are often depicted in their animal rather than human form. All tricksters are creative, often assisting the creator but also bringing self-centered mischief to and, therefore, undermining creation. But tricksters can also be culture heroes, who teach the people survival techniques. The modern-day cognates of mythical Native American tricksters might be the shamans and medicine people who are said to have the power to descend to the spirit world, and the clowns and whipping boys in the Southwest pueblo dances, who are free to make taboo-defying jokes but who also punish members of the community who have strayed from the ceremonial path.

Who are some Native American tricksters?

Kumokums is a trickster of the Modoc Indians of California. Manabozho is an Algonquian trickster. Among tribes of the Midwest the trickster is sometimes the Great Hare. For many Plains Indians he is Iktome the Spider. In the Pacific Northwest he is Raven. And in many parts of the country we find the trickster Coyote. Coyote, Raven, and Iktome are particularly colorful figures.

Who is Coyote?

Coyotes exist in most parts of America, and, appropriately, so do Coyote trickster myths. Wherever he is, Coyote is both clever and foolish, creative and destructive, otherworldly and worldly, a supporter of community but also a loner. He will do anything for sex and for food, and he recognizes few social boundaries or taboos. Like cartoon figures such as Road Runner or Bugs Bunny, he is a braggart, and sometimes he becomes the butt of his own tricks. Like most tricksters, Coyote can also be a culture hero. A Papago myth tells how Coyote saved himself and Montezuma and Montezuma's people from the flood by warning the chief to build a huge canoe.

Two myths will serve to illustrate aspects of this figure's personality. The first is a creation myth of the Maidu of California. At the beginning of time, say the Maidu, when there was only darkness and the primordial waters, two beings suddenly emerged from the nothingness in a raft. These were Turtle and Earth-Initiate, who immediately began to create the world. Then one day, also out of nowhere, Coyote arrived with Rattlesnake, his pet. Coyote enjoyed watching Turtle and Earth-Initiate create the animals and First Man and First Woman out of clay. Then he thought, "If they can make things, so can I." But as hard as he worked, his creations failed and he laughed at them. When Earth-Initiate scolded him for laughing at the new creations, Coyote said he had not been laughing. This was the first lie told in the world. Meanwhile, Earth-Initiate continued, making a perfect world, even teaching the people how to remain forever young. But now Coyote became like the Serpent of Genesis—another trickster. When he visited the people of Earth-Initiate's world, the people told him how happy they were in their perfect world. This irritated Coyote, and he told the people he could show them how it would be better if sickness and death could become a part of life. Knowing nothing of sickness and death, the people wanted to know more. So Coyote, now a negative culture hero, taught them about competition by suggesting that they have a footrace. Meanwhile, Coyote

Coyote is an anthropomorphized trickster figure who often appears in myths of many of the Native American people. Both clever and foolish, creative and destructive, otherworldly and worldly, he is a supporter of community but also a loner.

had his pet, Rattlesnake, wait in a hole along the path of the race. But Coyote was to regret his own trick when it became evident that his own son would lead in the race and would be the victim of the waiting snake. When the boy fell dead, the people thought he did not get up because he was embarrassed by falling and thus losing the race. But Coyote knew better and wept the first tears in world. From then on people did not remain young. When they grew old, they died.

The second myth is a Rosebud Sioux tale told by Jenny Leading Cloud. One day Coyote and Iktome the Spider were walking along when they came to a rock named Iya. Coyote respected the rock, as he knew it had great powers. So he gave the rock his beautiful blanket as a gift. But later, when a storm came up, Coyote missed his blanket and wanted it back. Iktome warned him against it, but Coyote went back to Iya and demanded his blanket back. But the rock stopped him saying, "What is given is given." Coyote became enraged, tore the blanket off the rock and placed it on his own back. "There, that's that," cried Coyote. "Oh no, it isn't," the rock murmured. Now Coyote and Iktome went into a cave to wait out the storm. When the sun came out again, they sat down on the path to have a smoke and some fry bread. A strange rumbling noise caught their attention, however, and looking up they saw Iya the rock rolling toward them. "Run," Iktome shouted, and they did, but the rock was gaining on them. "Swim across the river," cried Iktome, and they did, but Iya rolled right along after them. When they tried to hide among trees, the rock simply knocked down the trees. Now Iktome had had enough: "Your problem!" he called as he descended into a spider hole, narrowly avoiding what happened to Coyote, who now lay flattened on the ground by the huge rock. Iya picked up the blanket and went away. Sometime later a man came along and thought Coyote was a rug. He took the rug home and placed it before his fireplace. But next morning the man's wife came to him and said,"I just saw that rug of yours running away across the field."

Who is Raven?

Raven, like Coyote, is often obscene, self-centered, and sometimes foolish. In a Northwest Indian myth that tells about the beginning of time, Raven is a creator—a self-created being living with his wife in a confined space. It is his bored wife who suggests to Raven that he create the earth. "But I don't know how," Raven said. "Well, then," answered his wife, "I'll create something," and she laid down to sleep with Raven watching her. During her sleep she lost her feathers, grew very fat, and, still sleeping, gave birth to twins. Like their mother, the twins had no feathers, and this upset Raven. The twins became aware of Raven, and when their mother finally woke up they pointed at him and asked, "What's that?"

"It's father," their mother answered.

The twins mocked their father's strange feathers and his harsh voice. Now Raven decided he had better create something, since his wife had succeeded in creating humans from herself. So he consulted some strange beings who said they were seeds and suggested that the new humans needed an earth where they could live; Raven should create one. Saying he would try, Raven flew off with one of the seed beings. In flight he urinated and defecated, and his excremental droppings became the element of earth—the trees, the rivers, the valleys. The seed being reminded Raven that the new people would have to eat, and so Raven made plants and animals for them. Eventually, Raven, acting as a culture hero, but also for his own pleasure, showed the people how to make new babies.

EARTH DIVERS AND EMERGERS

What types of creation myths exist in Native North America?

Several types of creation myths exist in Native North America. Creations from clay and other materials are represented here by the Coyote myth and Raven myth just discussed. World-parent creations usually involve the body of the first deities becoming elements of the world, as in the case of the Zuni world-parent myth, also treated earlier. Or, the parent is in some way sacrificed and his or her body parts become the world. By far the two most common types of creation myths among Native Americans are the earth-diver creation and the emergence creation.

What is the nature of the earth-diver creation?

In earth-diver creation myths, earth-making material must be brought up from the depths of the primordial waters—literally, the birth waters of earth. Usually an animal—but sometimes a god or a hero—is sent to retrieve the necessary substance. Earth-diver creations are prevalent especially among the eastern tribes of North America, such as the Iroquoian peoples. As Native Americans almost certainly originally crossed into America via the Bering Strait land bridge, it is not surprising that earth-diver creations are ubiquitous in Asia, particularly in Central Asia. Native Americans add an interesting element to the archetype, however. The earth-diver act itself is preceded in many American earth-diver myths by the motif of the woman who falls from the sky and becomes the sacrificial world parent. The Oneida of New York State are members of the Iroquois Federation, and as do the other Iroquois, they tell the story of Sky Woman.

What is the Oneida creation myth?

In the beginning, the Oneida say, earth did not exist; there was only the upper world and the primordial waters containing water animals below. The spirits lived in the upper world with the Great Spirit. One day the Great Spirit decided to uproot the great apple tree—a kind of world tree—that grew in the upper world. In its place was a gaping hole. The Great Spirit asked his daughter to go down through the hole to the waters below. In fact, he dropped his daughter—now we can call her Sky Woman—through the hole, and she slowly floated down toward the waters. From below, the animals saw her coming, shining like a star, and they realized she would need a dry landing place. So Beaver dove down into the waters hoping to find some soil, but he drowned. After several animals tried and failed, Muskrat succeeded in diving and bringing up the necessary earth. But he, too, died in the process. Turtle agreed to have the bit of earth placed on his back, and immediately it expanded into what is now North America. Sky Woman landed there and gave birth to twins—one good and one bad. The bad twin was so bad that Sky Woman died giving birth to him. But the good twin made good use of his mother's body, making her literally the world parent. He made her head the sun and other parts the moon and stars. The rest of her body he buried in the earth, making the soil fertile. From the soil he raised plants, but the bad twin put thorns on the plants. He made deer and bear, but the evil twin made poisonous snakes. When the good twin made humans out of the clay of his mother's earth, the bad twin made monkeys to mock them. After a long fight between the twins, the good twin prevailed and his brother was sent to a dark underground cave, from which he continued to send up problems for the world.

What is the nature of the emergence creation?

The emergence creation is found among many tribes of the American southwest. The Acoma people and other Pueblo tribes, and the Navajo, for example, all say that they emerged into this world from a world, or worlds, below the earth. In this emergence

This sipapu (the smaller hole next to the fire pit) found in an old Pueblo settlement in Mesa Verde National Park, represents the portal from which the ancestors of mankind emerged, according to myth.

process, the people move gradually from an insect or lower animal state to the human condition. As the people emerge from the womb of the earth, they are often led by a goddess. Spider Woman or Thinking Woman, for instance, assist the Acoma and Hopi people, in effect, acting as a birthing midwife.

What is the Navajo emergence myth?

The Navajo, the largest of the Native American nations, conceive of a series of domed worlds, one on top of another. The first world, deep underground, was an island of sorts in the primal waters of an endless ocean. The people there were the Insect people, who spent most of the time quarreling. They generally ignored their gods and acted inappropriately sexually. The gods sent a great flood to force them to leave the first world for the second. The second world was blue and was populated by the Swallow people. The Insect people got along with the Swallow people until one day an insect sexually assaulted a swallow. Having to flee, the Insect people, led by a locust, flew up to the third world—the Yellow World—where the Grasshopper people lived. But once again they acted inappropriately and were expelled up to the fourth world, which was populated by the Kisani, the Pueblo People. The Insect people got along with the Kisani and learned many things from them. Through ceremonies directed by the gods, they were cleansed and eventually First Man and First Woman came into being. But the people began quarreling and the men and women separated and then came back together. A figure known as Water Monster stole two young girls from the people, and after Coyote stole children belonging to Water Monster, the monster sent a terrible flood. The people—both the Insect People and the Kisani—were saved by hiding in a reed before escaping, again led by Locust, into our world, the fifth world.

What is the significance of the emergence creation in Native American mythology?

Clearly the Underworld, where the emergence myth begins, must remind us of the womb of Mother Earth—a dark wet place that contains the potential for life. The act of emergence from one world to the next is a kind of birthing and evolving process. Psychologically, this birthing process represents the human longing for greater consciousness and for fulfillment. Emergence believers typically have ceremonies—especially curing ceremonies—marking the possibility of a new beginning in the present time that mirrors the movement from a lower to a higher state in the creation story. The emergence myth is reflected in the feminine architecture of the earth-hugging Navajo structure, the hogan, and also by the circular kiva, with its symbolic birth entrance or *sipapu* in the center of the floor.

Are there flood myths in North America?

As is evident from the Navajo creation myth, floods, as in other cultures, serve a purpose of cleansing, leading to new birth. We have seen the flood motif in the Cherokee Grandmother Sun myth and in the Papago Coyote myth, in which the trickster saves himself and the people from a flood in a huge canoe. The Algonquian peoples have flood stories, including one in which the trickster Manabozho's rashness almost leads to his demise in a flood.

NATIVE AMERICAN HERO MYTHS

Are there Native American hero myths?

As in many cultures, tricksters and other beings may act as culture heroes who teach the people how to live. Coyote, Raven, and the Great Hare all fulfill such roles. There are nobler heroes as well, young men who successfully pursue vision quests for the good of their people. One of these heroes is an Ojibwa boy, Wunzh, who, during his quest, wrestles with and defeats a spirit who, after being buried, is reborn as corn.

Other examples of Indian heroes are Corn Mother (or Corn Grandmother) and a strange boy who was also a water jar. And there are also monster-slaying heroes.

Who is Corn Mother?

Corn Mother, whose stories are told by many Native American peoples, is an embodiment of the Indian belief in the animistic origin of corn. Certain Iroquoian speakers said that Corn Mother was really the Earth Mother and the mother of the creator himself and the source of plant food. When she died, corn grew from her breasts, and beans and squash from the rest of her body. The Arikara of the Plains have a myth of a murdered Corn Mother from whom corn grew. In the southwest many say that Corn Mother planted her heart in the earth and announced that instead of giving forth milk, the earth would produce corn. The Cherokee and the Penobscot of Maine have particularly haunting Corn Mother myths involving sacrifice and planting.

What is the Cherokee Corn Mother myth?

A hunter had a wife named Selu ("Corn") and a son. One day Selu was washing the meat brought to her by her husband when some of the blood from it spilled and became a little boy. His miraculous conception of course ties this little boy to heroes found in almost all mythologies around the world. One day the two boys decided to follow the hunter to see where he found so much meat. From behind some trees they watched as the hunter moved a slab away from a cave to release a deer, which he then shot before replacing the slab. After a few days the boys returned to the cave and pushed the slab aside, allowing a great number of animals to escape. From that day on, animals have hidden from hunters. Next the boys happened to see their mother produce corn and beans by rubbing her stomach and armpits. Revolted by what they had seen, they decided that Selu was a witch and had to be killed. Selu understood what the boys were thinking and volunteered to be killed. She told the boys they should bury her and then watch over her grave. The next day corn had sprung fully grown from the grave. When people heard of this miracle, they came to see for themselves. The boys gave them kernels to plant but warned them to watch over the seeds for seven nights. But the people fell asleep on the seventh night and as a result the corn grows more slowly now than it did for the two boys.

What is the Penobscot Corn Mother myth?

The Penobscot say that First Woman became sad when she realized that her people were hungry, so she told her husband, First Man, that he must sacrifice her in order to put a stop to her crying. When the horrified man asked the creator what to do, the creator said he must do what his wife wished him to do. The man, weeping bitterly, returned home, and his wife instructed him to wait until the sun was at the top of the sky. Then he was to kill her and have two of their sons drag her body back and forth by her silky yellow hair until all of her flesh was gone. Then the man and the boys were to leave the place for seven moons. After seven moons the man did return and there he found beautiful plants wearing his wife's beautiful hair. And on these plants were Corn Mother's final gift—the corn that keeps people alive and happy.

Who is Water Pot Boy?

The Tewa Indians living among the Hopi near the village of Walpi in northern Arizona have a hero story that contains many elements of the archetypal, or monomythic, world hero. These elements include the miraculous conception, the virgin birth, the search for the father, the descent into the Underworld, and rebirth.

A woman of the village had a beautiful daughter who refused to get married. She asked the daughter to help her make water pots, and one day the daughter was mixing clay by stomping on it to smooth it out. While she was doing so, some of it somehow entered her, and she became pregnant. Not believing the daughter when she claimed not to have had any contact with a man, the mother became angry, and her anger became horror when the young woman gave birth to boy who was not built like a boy but like a water pot. But the girl's father, strangely, was pleased with his water pot grandson. It took only about twenty days after his birth for Water Pot Boy to be able to play with the other children of the village, who loved playing with him. The boy's mother cried a lot over the fact that her strange little son had no legs or arms. He did have eyes and ears and a mouth for feeding at his top. One day when his grandfather was about to go off rabbit hunting, Water Pot Boy begged to go along. But the grandfather laughed and asked how a water pot boy could hunt without arms or legs. Still, the boy pleaded so hard that the grandfather gave in, and the boy rolled along beside him as they hunted below the mesa where they lived. When Water Pot Boy spied a rabbit, he rolled after it out of his grandfather's sight. Suddenly he banged against a rock and broke into many pieces. Out of the pieces sprang a fine boy dressed beautifully in lots of good leather, feathers, and turquoise. Now free to hunt properly, the boy quickly caught several rabbits and returned to his grandfather. The grandfather, of course, did not recognize his grandson in his new form. "Have you seen Water Pot Boy?" he asked. "And who are you?" "I am Water Pot Boy," said the boy, "your grandson." It was only after the boy explained what had happened in the collision with the rock that the grandfather believed him. Then the two went happily home. At first the boy's mother thought the handsome boy was a suitor and went off to hide. But she was happy when her father explained everything.

There came a day when Water Pot Boy asked his mother about his father. His mother explained that she had no idea who the father could be as she had never been with a man. Still, the boy was determined to go in search of his father and asked his mother to help him prepare for his journey. "I think I know where he is," said the boy, who now left his village and headed toward Horse Mesa Point. There he met a man standing near a spring. The man asked him where he was going, and the boy explained that he was looking for his father. "In fact," said the boy, "I think *you* are my father." The man tried to frighten the boy by glaring at him, but the boy kept looking directly at the man until the man relented, smiled, and embraced his son. The man took the boy over to the spring and they entered it together, diving down to where the man introduced him to all of his dead relatives. After a while the boy left the spring and returned to his village to explain things to his mother. Soon his mother became sick and died, and the boy went back to the spring, where he found his mother with the other shades of their relatives. His father greeted him and explained that in reality he was Red Water Snake and that he had made the boy's mother die so that they might live happily together in the spring with their relatives. The boy decided to join them, too, and they all live there together to this day.

What is an example of an Native American Monster Slayer myth?

Some Blackfoot tribe members tell the story of a young man named Kutoyis, who was miraculously conceived. It seems that an old man and his wife were at the mercy of a wicked son-in-law who had plenty to eat but gave the old people only scraps. One day he gave them an ugly clot of buffalo blood, which they placed in a pot to make soup. Suddenly they heard a child's cry, and when they took the top off the pot they found a baby boy there and immediately named it Kutoyis ("Blood-Clot"). Realizing that the wicked son-in-law would kill the boy as a future enemy if he found out about the child, , they disguised him as a girl. But it took only four days for Kutoyis to become a man, and immediately he killed the son-in-law. Now clearly marked by his birth and quick growth as a true hero, he did what heroes everywhere do: he went off on a quest to find and destroy the monsters that were oppressing the people. Finding the worst monster of all, Wind Sucker, who swallowed people at will, Kutoyis allowed himself to be swallowed and then killed the beast from within, thus freeing all the people who had been swallowed before.

MODERN MYTHS

Is there such a thing as a modern myth?

If by "myth" we mean a narrative which is itself not true and usually impossible, but which is important because it "explains" some otherwise unexplainable aspect of reality, there are narratives which may be called modern myths. It is important to note that in this sense modern myths differ from general literature in that literature usually deals with things that did not actually happen but which are generally believable or possible in themselves. According to the above definition of myth, there are modern creation myths and hero myths. There are also new deity myths, although people have generally tended to maintain at least formal adherence to traditional deities even as they have questioned the validity of the traditional hero narratives and, especially, the ancient creation myths.

MODERN ATTEMPTS TO EXPLAIN EXISTENCE

What is an example of a modern creation myth?

Many scholars and theologians have reminded us that, with the exception of religious fundamentalists, as the human race has evolved, so has its understanding of creation. If once we believed that Mother Earth was fertilized by Father Sun, or that a god created the world by thought or word, we have now been led by our clearer understanding of the nature of the universe to new creation stories which for our modern minds are as true as the Mother Earth or *ex nihilo* myths were for earlier generations. They are "true" to us because they are based in science, the thinking process to which the modern world ascribes. We "believe in" science as ancient peoples believed in other systems of thought.

So, for example, we explain creation by way of scientific hypotheses based on technologically based astral observation and experiments with particles. The current generally accepted theory of creation is the "Big Bang" theory, which depicts a universe that came into being out of the void in a matter of minutes as the result of one great explosion. According to the theory, our solar system developed from that explosion and the universe has been expanding ever since. When we add Charles Darwin's theory of evolution to the Big Bang theory, we have the story of a creation which is very much a continuing process.

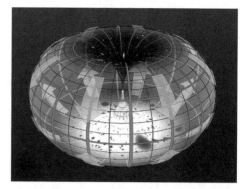

This illustration by Bryan Brandenburg depicts the Big Bagel Theory posited by physicist Howard Bloom about the dynamics of the origin of the universe.

In a book titled *The Universe Is a Green Dragon: A Cosmic Creation Story,* physicist Brian Swimme, echoing the thoughts of a "new age" philosopher/theologian, Thomas Berry, places the scientific theories in a more traditional mythic context that refers us back to the old cosmic egg creation and dragon myths. The universe, is "alive," he says, and has been since the "cosmic egg of the primeval fireball," which, like a dragon, poured forth creative fire.

What are examples of modern scientific myths that "explain" the world?

Many scientists use narratives in what they call "thought experiments" to explain difficult concepts of reality. Three of the most famous of these experiments are Schrödinger's Cat, the Twin Paradox, and the Gaia Hypothesis.

What is the story of Schrödinger's Cat?

Physicist Erwin Schrödinger (1887–1961) devised a thought experiment in which a live cat is placed in a box with a container of poison . The box also contains an atom of radioactive material that has a 50% chance of decaying in a set time. The decay will be recorded by a detector. The poison container will break and the cat will die if the radioactive material does not decay. So, it appears that there is a 50% chance that the cat will be dead after the previously set time for decay—or still alive. This seems to be logical, but Schrödinger tells us that according to the post-Newtonian world of quantum mechanics the cat is neither dead nor alive until we actually open the box and see what has happened. In other words, conscious observation is an integral part of any happening; conscious observation actually affects reality.

What is the Twin Paradox?

The Twin Paradox is the basis of a thought experiment narrative that "explains" Albert Einstein's Special Relativity theory. In the narrative, one twin goes into outer space by rocket and returns home to find that his twin brother has aged more than he has. The story attempts to demonstrate the reality of the concept of space-time continuum, which demonstrates that objects in motion experience time at a slower rate than objects not in motion.

What is the Gaia Hypothesis?

The Gaia Hypothesis is another theory—a thought model—developed in part by a British scientist named James Lovelock (1919–) It refers back to the old Greek myth of the origins of creation through the Great Earth Goddess Gaia and applies that myth to new "scientific" reality. It is a model that has as its scientific background the laws of thermodynamics: that energy can neither be created nor destroyed, the

Scientist and author James Lovelock proposed the Gaia Hypothesis in which the earth is seen as a living organism with all its components, including humans, analogous to cells in our bodies.

total amount of energy in the universe being constant, but in any exchange of energy in a closed system such as earth, there will always be less useable energy after the exchange. In other words, everything that is, everything being made up of energy, will be subject to decay, or entropy, as it is used. Energy used dissipates as heat. The Gaia Hypothesis expresses the possibility of ultimate tragedy. It emphasizes that the world is an ecological unity of which each part—including the human—can be considered something like a cell. Gaia—Earth—in this view, is a living organism that makes adjustments, analogous to conscious adjustments, to its needs for survival. The human race, which is perhaps the consciousness organ of Gaia, is not actually necessary for Gaia's survival, and if humans do more harm to Gaia in terms of energy dissipation, Gaia will dispense with humans. We naturally think here of realities such as the greenhouse effect and global warming. The Gaia Hypothesis, whether we believe it or not, does remind us that there is more to life than us and our "needs."

PSYCHOLOGY AND MYTH

How does psychology use myths?

Two of the founders of psychoanalysis, Sigmund Freud (1856–1939) and Carl Jung (1875–1961) were in their own ways involved with mythology. They both were concerned with the psychological meaning and the use of myths in their work, and both were responsible for certain psychological myths that remain to this day elements of our cultural vocabulary.

How did Freud use myths?

For Freud, myths—including those of God—were "primitive" expressions that reveal essential human neuroses. In *Totem and Taboo* (1913) he went so far as to suggest that the beginnings of myth and religion and society can be traced to the "Oedipus Complex."

The Oedipus Complex is a modern myth created by Freud. It concerns Freud's belief that the boy child has a natural subconscious sexual desire for his mother and a natural hostility toward his father, his rival for his mother's love. The theory takes its "plot" from the myth of Oedipus, the Greek hero who inadvertently murdered his father and married his mother, the story most famously told by Sophocles in his play *Oedipus the King*.

Neo-Freudians have used the term "Elektra Complex" to describe what they see as the girl child's love of the father and rivalry with the mother, a situation referring back to the *Oresteia*, the trilogy by the Greek playwright Aeschylus in which Agamemnon's daughter Elektra drives her brother Orestes to kill their mother, who had herself murdered their father.

Freud also created what might be called a psychological "myth," complete with characters. First, there is the "psyche," which we tend to speak of as if it were a tangible reality, much as we might discuss the "soul." In that psyche Freud saw three important characters, which have themselves become active beings in our common vocabulary. These are the ego, the superego, and the id. According to the Freudian model of the psyche, the *id* is our instinctive aspect; the *superego* our moralistic side, taught us by parents and society; and the *ego* is the mediating character between the conflicting impulses of the other two.

How did Jung use myths?

Jung's use of myths differs somewhat from Freud's. For Jung, myths were not symptoms of neuroses. Rather, they were cultural dreams providing insight into what he called the "collective unconscious," or collective memory, as opposed to the personal unconscious. The universal motifs of myths—the hero's quest, the flood, the trickster—are images of psychological tendencies, or archetypes, inherited by humans. Myths provide information about ourselves as cultures and as a species. In terms of psychoanalysis, Jung saw the archetypes of the collective unconscious as a symbolic language which could stimulate a level of information that could take the analyst and the analysand a step deeper than that provided by the personal unconscious stressed by Freud.

How did Joseph Campbell use myths?

Essentially, though influenced by Freud, Campbell worked from a Jungian perspective. In his most famous work, *The Hero with a Thousand Faces,* he concentrated on the hero archetype, tracing the universal or near-universal pattern of the collective hero's life journey in what he called the heroic "monomyth." The monomyth contains such elements as the miraculous conception and birth, the quest, the descent into the Underworld, and the return.

THE HEROIC MONOMYTH
AND MODERN GODS

What does the heroic monomyth have to do with us today?

Jung and Campbell, and others who take the psychological approach to myth, see the heroic monomyth as a universal mirror of the individual human's psychological journey through life from birth to individuation, or wholeness. The miraculous conception and birth of the hero speak to the awakening in our lives to the quest for Self and wholeness that lies ahead. The quest itself is the process by which the hero, representing the psychological voyager, is able to move beyond personal and historical limitations. The hero, sometimes after an initial refusal, accepts the call to adventure. This acceptance represents our own acceptance of the inner call to journey into the unknown in search of Self. As the mythical hero's quest requires overcoming several archetypal barriers—the *femme fatale*, the monster in the path—the psychological voyager, too, must overcome neuroses, obsessions, and other roadblocks. The mythical hero's descent into the Underworld becomes our "dark night of the soul," our descent into the dark world of the unconscious to find a way to wholeness. The mythical hero's return is our achievement of that wholeness.

What are some examples of modern deity myths?

Modern deity myths have, for the most part, been those expressing new understandings of the God of the monotheistic Abrahamic religions: Judaism, Christianity, Islam. For Christian theologian Paul Tillich (1886–1965), a personal god was an absurdity—a being rather than Being itself. For Jewish theologian Martin Buber (1878–1965), God was discovered only in contact between people. For Jesuit paleontologist Teilhard de Chardin (1881–1955), God was the culmination of an evolutionary process leading to something like the Hindu concept of Brahman, the essence of reality present everywhere but nondefinable. Philosopher-anthropologist Gregory Bateson (1904–1980) spoke of something he called "immanent mind," which is in the individual mind but also in the life all around us. Each individual mind is a subsystem of a larger universal mind "compara-

---

Why do modern humans continue to have gods?

The concept of divinity has been at the center of human consciousness for as long as there have been myths. We see the concept in prehistoric objects such as the Ice Age lion man and the Paleolithic cave dwellings discussed at the beginning of this book. We can assume that humans find comfort and explanation in gods and goddesses—explanations of the events of nature and comfort in a belief that we are part of a meaningful rather than random universe.

ble" to God. In the twenty-first century, theologians continue to reconsider the concept of god, seeing the deity as a guiding force "within," as neither male nor female, as present but somehow nor personal.

Are there examples of ancient myths being "rewritten" to fit modern ideologies?

A good example of this tendency is the Medusa myth, which has stimulated modern thinkers in the twentieth and twenty-first centuries to apply the myth to their own beliefs. This ancient Greek myth, with Roman additions by Ovid, tells the story of Medusa, a priestess of Athene, who was raped by the god Poseidon and then condemned by Athene for having polluted her temple as a result of that act. Medusa was turned into a Gorgon, a monster with snakes in her hair. Eye contact with her turned the gazer into stone. The hero Perseus, aided by Athene and other gods, decapitated Medusa. For the Greeks, Medusa was a monster—one of many in mythology—who, whatever the reasons for her state, needed to be killed by a monster-slaying hero. Sigmund Freud, however, saw Medusa's decapitation as a symbol of and, in a sense, a justification for his theory of castration fear. The French structuralist critic Roland Barthes (1915–1980) equates Medusa's "petrifying" (stonemaking) stare with conventional beliefs and opinions.

The brief years of the John F. Kennedy administration, including the Kennedys' private lives, have been idealized by Americans, who often think of it as a shining moment of history, something like the myth of Camelot and King Arthur (left to right: President Kennedy, John F. Kennedy Jr., Mrs. Kennedy, and Caroline Kennedy).

Hélène Cixous (1937–) and other feminists have turned the monstrous Medusa into a symbol of feminine resistance to the male-dominated phallocentric world.

How is myth used in politics?

Hitler used Germanic myths to justify actions of his Nazi party. A more benign example of the political use of myth is the general connection made by the press and politicians between the John F. Kennedy administration and King Arthur's Camelot. The young and handsome Kennedy with his beautiful family were Arthur and Guinevere. The young people and the hope that surrounded his presidency were reminiscent to the public of the Round Table and its aura.

How is myth used in popular culture?

There have been many attempts to create modern mythic heroes and situations that mirror ancient heroes and their deeds. Superman arrived on earth miraculously to save it from its own criminal darkness. His defenses, like those of all heroic monster-slayers, are supernatural and formidable. Although created to provide thrills, he might be said also to represent the continuing human quest for wholeness. Joseph Campbell (1904–1987), in his book *Myths to Live By*, suggests that the voyage to the moon expressed a similar "mythic" purpose. Space stories such as the Star Wars films can play a similar role. The argument made by Campbell and others is that modern humans continue to need myths to help them discover the paths to wholeness that were provided by the ancient myths for the people who came before us.

Why do humans have to create myths?

Religion scholar Bruce Lincoln (1948–) teaches that myths are useful because they explain reality and provide visions of what reality could be. He also points out that when myths are used to justify the superiority of the ideals and power of one group over another, they can be dangerous. Hitler's use of German mythology to justify the actions of Naziism is an example of the harmful power of myth.

If humans use myths to justify their actions and/or to explain reality, they also use them because they have to. Humans, as cultural historian Thomas Berry (1914–2009) suggests, might be said to be defined by the fact that they of all species make creation conscious of itself. Only humans are concerned constantly with what Aristotle defined as "plot," a narrative with a beginning, a middle, and an end. Like it or not, we are, by definition, travelers through plots—our own lives and our communal life as nations and as a species. Myths are cultural dreams, stories made up by cultures to explain the unknown, to keep the past alive, and to express hope for the future.

THE WORLD MYTH

Is there such a thing as a world myth?

A world myth does not exist if, by "world myth," we mean a myth that the world or most of the world accepts, even though there have been attempts in history by particular religions to convince the world to believe in their sacred narratives, their myths. A single world myth does not exist because myths need cultural clothes to become alive—to be real-ized. When myths from around the world are compared, however, a universal *shadow* myth—an archetypal world myth—does emerge.

PRINCIPAL COMPONENTS OF THE WORLD MYTH

What are the essential components of this archetypal world myth?

This world myth, first of all, establishes the existence of deities. Creation itself is the second element of the myth. All cultures have creation myths, and many cultures attach a flood myth to the creation story. The third component of the world myth is the lives of special beings we know as heroes.

Why are these three elements so universal?

They are universal because humans are universal. All individuals have different backgrounds; every culture is different from every other culture. Individuals look different from each other; each culture has its own traditions, differentiating itself from other cultures. But just as individuals are normally born with two eyes, two arms, two legs, and so forth, they are all born with a consciousness peculiar to humans in general. In the same way, all cultures, in order to survive, need to believe in their communal signifi-

265

How are the deities in the world myth both cultural
and archetypal—local and universal?

Creator gods are universal because we all have been created in some way; and they are local, because our communities, whether religions, nations, or whole cultures, require gods who represent our values. Mother/Earth goddesses are universal because we all came from mothers and because we all depend on the earth itself for nourishment; again, they are local, because different communities have various concepts of the feminine in the universe and of the nourishment their particular corners of the world produce. Gods who represent aspects of natural phenomena are universal for the obvious reason that we are all affected by these phenomena, and local because climate and the importance of particular natural events differ from place to place. Polynesian deities reflect the world of the Pacific Islands; the weather spirits of the North American woodlands reflect that natural world.

cance. Deity myths, creation myths, and hero myths speak to the universal human consciousness and to our universal desire to live in a meaningful rather than a random universe. Deities provide that meaningfulness even if the deities themselves, as in Greek mythology, for instance, tend to be arbitrary and even fickle. All cultures have creation myths because societies require some sense that their particular culture has significance. Cultures need to know their parentage and the details of their birth just as individuals do. Heroes exist because individuals and cultures need to envision human possibilities that transcend normal boundaries of existence.

Who are the primary deity archetypes in the world myth?

A Supreme Being who is also a creator is common. Supreme creator gods dominate most cultural pantheons. Earth or Mother goddesses are also common, however, as are animal-related gods and deities who represent various aspects of nature. Trickster gods are not universal, but they exist in sufficient number to suggest that the world myth needs them.

THE SUPREME BEING
AND GREAT GODDESS

Who are some of the major versions of the great Supreme Being in the world myth?

The Supreme Being takes form according to the cultural traditions from which or she springs.

The Hebrew Yahweh is a firm and even demanding father of a tribe. The Greek high gods Kronos and Zeus are arbitrary and dominating heads of families, reflecting the highly patriarchal culture of Greece. In cultures in which the emphasis is on warrior skills, the god is a warrior god such as the Norse Odin or the Vedic Indra. The Canaanite Baal, is more of a weather/storm god, like the Norse Thor or the Maori Tawhiri and the Aztec Tlaloc. In Egypt and South America the Supreme Beings—Ra and Viracocha, for example—are usually associated with the sun, as are the Inca Inti, the Hopi Tawa, and the Iranian Mithras. Amaterasu in Japan and Grandmother Sun among the Cherokee are sun *goddesses*. In India the Supreme Being takes many forms—Shiva, Vishnu, Devi—of the unknowable all-present Brahman, a conceptual reality that resembles Gregory Bateson's modern vision of something like God, as "Immanent Mind." In cultures such as the ancient Iranian and Zoroastrian, the Supreme Being, Ahura Mazda represents the positive aspect of a dualistic world. The Great Spirit of Native America is a metaphorical embodiment of an animistic essence in creation. In Africa, the often disappearing creator god reflects a cultural attitude toward those in authority.

What is the significance of the Supreme Being?

The Supreme Being is the centering force of the world myth, the reason for being.

Usually associated with the sky, with Heaven, the Supreme Being provides the world myth with a sense of the father above, someone who provides rules and order in the larger house which is the universe as well as in the house which is the local culture. Like a worldly father, he can be demanding and arbitrary. The Abrahamic god treats Job somewhat callously, and to many seems cruel when he demands that Abraham sacrifice his son Isaac. Zeus is cruel and a philanderer as well. The Supreme Being exists at a significant distance from us, in a sky that was long ago separated from Mother Earth. Sometimes, as in many African myths, he purposely and even disdainfully ignores us once he has finished his creating. The god above is a being with whom we try to have conversation through prayer or religious ritual, for instance, but who is difficult or impossible to reach. He is the father whose approval we long for but who remains out of our immediate range.

Who are some of the major versions of the Great Goddess in the world myth?

As does the Supreme Being, the Great Goddess takes the form appropriate to the given culture. In prehistoric cultures, such as the one in Çatal Hüyük, she is the large-bodied, full-breasted figure who exudes opulence and fertility. Similarly endowed Great Goddesses include the Sumerian Ninhursag, the Phrygian Cybele, the Greek Earth Mothers Gaia and Rhea, the Norse Freyja, the Aztec Coatlicue, the multi-breasted Artemis of Ephesus in Anatolia, and some Native American versions of Corn Mother.

The Great Mother can also be the *de facto* creator, as in the case of Gaia and, in some versions, the Egyptian Neith and the Native American Corn Mothers, the Acoma Thinking Woman, the Shinto Izanami, and the Iroquoian mothers who come down from the sky. **267**

What is the significance of the Great Goddess?

The Great Goddess has traditionally been associated with Earth itself and is, therefore, altogether accessible to us. If the Supreme Being has been an unknowable reality, Mother Earth speaks to us every day. Whether Devi or Gaia, or the Iroquois woman who falls from the sky, she produces food, takes back our dead, and provides us with a home. She is the mother we take for granted and often betray. The modern Gaia hypothesis speaks scientifically to that betrayal.

FERTILITY AND ANIMAL GODS

What are some examples of fertility deities?

Many goddesses and some gods are directly associated with aspects of fertility.

A 1738 plate illustration by Jan Wandelaar featuring Mother Earth on her throne. Mother Earth has become a popular incarnation of the Great Goddess to whom more people in the modern world seem to relate.

This group naturally includes the Great Mother Goddess and goddesses of love such as Aphrodite and Eros and the Sumerian Inanna. Dying and resurrecting gods such as Osiris and Baal are also clearly fertility deities and are celebrated as such.

What is the significance of fertility deities?

Fertility deities stand metaphorically for the processes of life that involve regeneration. Eros and his mother bring about the sexual desire that enables reproduction. Osiris, Baal, and Corn Mother are gods literally "planted" in the Great Mother so that they can be reborn as crops.

Are animal deities a significant part of the world myth?

As we have seen, deities with animal characteristics are common, especially in Egypt, where gods are commonly depicted with animal heads, and in animistic cultures, such as those in Africa and North America. Often humans associate particular animals with particular characteristics transferable to themselves. The lion is powerful, as is the Egyptian lion goddess Sekhmet. Bulls are symbols of power and fertility and are associated with figures such as Poseidon and Baal. Zeus takes animal forms to assert his sexual power over mortal women. In China, dragons are positive power symbols and, therefore, appear as the actual heads of powerful gods such as Fuxi and Nuwa. Athene is wise and is sometimes linked with the owl. Various animals as avatars are embodiments of the great Hindu god Vishnu. Quetzalcoatl, a central mythological figure of Mesoamerica, is the feathered serpent; serpents are symbols of mysterious power that comes from the earth. The Great Mother Goddess of Minoan Crete holds snakes in her raised hands as if to celebrate that power.

In animistic cultures such as those of Africa and Native North America, animals are animated by the same spirits that give soul to humans. The totem relationship with animals perhaps points back to a time when animals and humans were seen as living in full communication together.

Tricksters often take animal shapes. The African Ananse and the Native American Iktome are spiders. The Native American Coyote and the Great Hare take primary form from the animals for which they are named.

TRICKSTERS

Who are some examples of the trickster deity in the world myth?

Among the most important cultural versions of the trickster archetype are the Sumerian Enki, the Norse Loki, the African Legba and Ananse, and the Native Americans Iktome, Raven, and Coyote. Other gods or demigods generally associated with other aspects of life, sometimes display trickster characteristics. Hermes steals the cattle of Apollo, Krishna steals the clothes of the bathing Gopis. Several tricksters are best known for their negative role as underminers of creation. Satan plays a trickster role as a corrupter in the Garden of Eden; Susanowa is a trickster in his struggle against Amaterasu; the Iroquoian bad twin works against the creations of his good brother.

What is the significance of the trickster in the world myth?

The trickster is the divine representation of a state of being between early childhood

In the biblical story of the Garden of Eden the Serpent serves in the role of the trickster (1531 painting on beechwood by Lucas Cranach the Elder.)

269

and the attainment of the self-control necessary for civilized communal life. He is creative, but he has uncontrollable appetites and is amoral. In mythology, tricksters can take any shape, using these disguises to achieve their often reprehensible goals. In creation stories tricksters sometimes become devils, as in the case of the biblical Serpent. Tricksters can work against the creator, undermining his creation and representing the deep dualistic nature of the world, the eternal struggle between good and evil, day and night, life and death. Or they can be simply playful, as in the case of Hermes stealing Apollo's cattle. The Norse trickster, Loki, is a constant source of disturbance in creation and does a great deal to bring about the end of the world.

Are there other divine examples of the duality of the universe?

The Dying God figure can be an example of duality. Osiris is murdered, but his "planting" in the earth results in grain. Dionysos is "cooked" by the Titans, but he is reborn as a fertility god. Jesus is crucified, but is resurrected as what Christians call the "bread of life." Baldr is destroyed by Loki, but will return after Ragnarok to reestablish creation.

The sacred twins sometimes "explain" duality. The twin children of the Iroquoian Earth Mother represent the good and evil inherent in creation. Romulus and Remus perhaps represent the same conflict.

WAR IN HEAVEN AND THE CREATION

Is the war in heaven between deities a significant part of the world myth?

There are sufficient examples of this theme in world mythology to suggest that it is significant. The war in heaven can be a struggle between a creator and a trickster as in many African myths, or an all-out war such as the one in the Abrahamic tradition between God and his good angels on one hand and Satan and the bad angels on the other.

What are some other important examples of the war between the gods?

Perhaps the earliest documented war is that related in the *Enuma Elish* between the ancient goddess Tiamat and the Babylonian city god Marduk. The war in heaven between the Titans and the Olympians, as related by Hesiod, is a better-known example. The mythological texts of the Irish Celts describe the wars between the Tuatha de Danaan and the Fomorians and Firbolg. The Norse *Eddas* tell the stories of the Aesir versus the Vanir. In India it is the Devas against the Asuras. The war can be between individual deities. In China Zhuanxu fights Gonggong, much as in Japan Susanowa struggles against his sister Amaterasu, and in the Maasai tradition the black god fights the red god.

What is the significance of the war in heaven?

This war in some versions—the Babylonian and the Greek, for instance—can reflect a new religious system in opposition to an older one. Thus, the Marduk religion replaces the old Tiamat cult, and the Olympians replace the old Gaia-Kronos dynasty. The motif can also be another way of expressing a sense of the duality inherent in the universe.

What are the components—and general significance—of the creation story in the world myth?

The creation myth is universal because we all wonder where we came from. Humans have always wondered where they came from as individuals, and particularly as cultures. The world creation myth is expressed in several basic approaches. The most popular of these approaches is the *ex nihilo* creation—the creation from nothing. Another type of creation prominent in the world myth is the creation from the undifferentiated void—especially the cosmic egg or primordial maternal waters. Still another approach to creation is by

The theme of a war in heaven is shared by many cultures. In this illustration from John Milton's *Paradise Lost,* the angel Michael throws the rebellious angels out of heaven.

way of the procreative power of the world parents, gods who existed before the universe and who joined together to begin the creative process. Nearly always these parents—Geb and Nut in Egypt, Rangi and Papa in Polynesia, for example—have to be separated so that the particulars of creation can develop between them. In some cases a single world parent such as the Norse Ymir or the Babylonian Tiamat must be sacrificed so that his or her body can become the world. The first people emerge from all these processes that make up the archetypal world myth. It is, of course, most important that we humans know where we came from.

What are some examples of the *ex nihilo* creation?

One Egyptian creator, Atum, begins the world with his own bodily fluids. Other Egyptian creators produce the world from their own thoughts. The Indian creators—Prajapati, Brahma, Vishnu—all tend to create from inside their minds. The Native American Great Manitou has a vision of creation. The Acoma Thinking Woman thinks creation, and it is. Yahweh creates via the word; he says, "Let it be," and it is.

What is the significance of the *ex nihilo* creation?

The creation from nothing answers the universally tantalizing question about how we and the world came into being if there was once an infinite nothingness. Many religious systems have answered the question with the belief in, or creation of, a deity—a

Supreme Being of some sort—who always existed in some sense and always will exist. Perhaps this concept leads inevitably to monotheism or, at least, monism, the belief that all gods are expressions of one central essence of creation, such as the Hindu Brahman, of whom the great gods and goddesses may be said to be emanations.

What are some examples of the creation from chaos?

The concept of creation from chaos is close to that of the *ex nihilo* creation. But in this case it is a void—the undifferentiated chaos—that precedes the creation of the universe. The void can be the primordial waters. In Sumer and Babylon the waters are personified as Nammu or Tiamat. In India, Vishnu sleeps on the waters before the creation. In Native America, the primordial waters are the source of creation in earth-diver myths.

The undifferentiated earth itself can be the chaos. In Australian aboriginal culture, the ancestors created the world as they differentiated the void of Dreamtime.

The cosmic egg is another symbol of the primeval chaos. It is creation waiting to happen. In the Chinese story, Pangu emerges from the world egg, as do the Dogon Nummu twins.

Regarding the modern world of science, was the material out of which creation came in the Big Bang undifferentiated chaos or nothingness?

What is the significance of the creation from chaos?

At the center of the creation from chaos is an animistic sense that earth always possessed the potential (animus) for creation. If the *ex nihilo* creation is centered on an individual god, the chaos creation is centered more on Earth's potential, even on the maternal aspect of creation: the maternal waters, the egg which came before its contents.

What are some examples of the world-parent creation?

There are two types of the world-parent creation. One involves the union of sky and earth—Heaven and Earth as father and mother of the universe. In association with this archetype is almost always the story of the separation of the parents so that further creation may occur. The second type of world-parent creation is that of the dismemberment of a single primordial being so that he or she literally animates every aspect of creation.

Examples of Sky Father and Earth Mother are ubiquitous. In Sumer it was An and Ki uniting to form Anki. In India, Dyaus was Sky and his consort, Earth, was Prithvi. In Greece it was Gaia and Uranos; in China, Tian and Di, forming Tian Di, or Yin as Earth uniting with Yang as Sky.

What are some examples of the separation of the world parents?

In Sumer the Supreme Being Enlil pushed An and Ki apart to allow creation to continue between them. In the same way and for the same reason, Shu (Air) separated Geb and Nut in Egypt. Kronos separated Gaia and Uranos violently in Greece. The Diegueño in California say it was tobacco that caused Father Sky and Mother Earth to come apart. In Zuni, it is Mother Earth herself who tires of Father Sky's attentions and pushes him away.

What is the significance of the separation of the world parents?

The most obvious answer is that people have always been aware of the distance between sky and earth and their place in that space and have felt the need to explain the cosmic geography. There is also the very human feeling that children often have about the sexuality of their parents, the fear that sexual union leaves no room for them.

What are some examples of the animistic creation via the dismemberment of a world parent?

The Baylonian god Marduk defeats the ancient Mother Goddess Tiamat and dismembers her body, turning her body parts into an animistic world. The Norse gods, led by Odin, do the same thing with the androgynous giant Ymir. In the *Vedas,* the Purusha, the primal man, is sacrificed to become creation, his mouth becoming Brahman. A Chinese equivalent to Purusha was Pangu, the offspring of Yin and Yang, who emerged from the cosmic egg and whose body became the source of an animistic world. The Zulu Unkulunkulu's body, too, was the world, as was that of the Iroquoian Sky Woman.

A Babylonian artwork shows Marduk defeating the Mother Goddess Tiamat.

273

What other versions of the creation archetype exist?

In some cases the creator is a *deus faber,* a craftsman god. In Egypt, Ptah is depicted in one myth as creating the world on a potter's wheel. Several groups of far western Native Americans have myths in which the *deus faber* creates the world as a kind of tent, with poles representing the four directions. Two creation archetypes popular among other Native North Americans are the earth-diver creation and the emergence creation.

In the first, an animal usually dives into the primordial waters to bring up earth, which is placed on a turtle's back and which expands into the world. In the emergence creation, the people emerge into this world from a world below the earth.

What are some examples of the earth-diver creation?

In a Vedic myth in India, Vishnu sends agents to the depths on a creative mission. The Churning of the Ocean of Milk has earth-diver aspects. In Polynesia, Maui brings up islands from the depths, as do Izanami and Izanagi in Japan. In Native America, the Iroquois tribes in particular tell the tale of the animals who dive for earth in order that the woman who falls from the sky will have a place to land and eventually to create.

What is the significance of the earth-diver creation?

The earth-diver creation emphasizes the feminine, earth-based nature of creation from the primordial waters, which are stimulated by the divine world of spirits, such as the falling woman or Vishnu, the seeds of creation.

What are some examples of the emergence creation?

The emergence creation is centered primarily in what is now the southwestern United States. The Pueblo peoples and the Hopi all tell of their emergence from the earth, and the Navajo have an elaborate tale of the gradual emergence into a series of underground worlds before they achieved this world.

What is the significance of the emergence creation?

As does the earth-diver creation, the emergence archetype stresses the feminine side of creation. Earth literally gives birth to creation with the help of midwives such as Spider Woman and Thinking Woman's daughters.

What are some examples of creation by a goddess?

There are several examples of creation by goddesses beginning with the Sumero-Babylonian Nammu-Tiamat and the Egyptian Neith. Gaia in Greece and Izanami in Japan are female creators, as are several African goddesses, including Njambi, Mawu, and Woyengi, as well as the Aztec Omecihuatl.

Why is incest so prevalent in creation myths?

Incest is prevalent simply because the first beings are so often brother and sister that they have no choice but to unite for procreation. In Vedic creation myths, father-daughter incest is sometimes seen as a kind of original sin that corrupts creation.

It is corruption in creation that leads in many cultures to the flood myth.

THE FLOOD

What are some examples of the flood myth?

The flood myth is so much a part of the creation archetype that stories of the deluge exist in most cultures. The Sumerians and Babylonians told a flood myth that is similar to the one told in Genesis. The Sumerian Noah is Ziusudra (Utnapishtim in Babylon). The Roman flood heroes are Deucalion and Pyyrha; the Norse versions are Bergelmir and his wife. Gonggong's flood in China is overcome by the flood hero Yu. The Mayan flood takes place to correct a mistake of the creator. Almost always the flood is sent by the creator to punish imperfect or corrupt humans.

Why is the flood archetype so ubiquitous?

The flood myth is as ubiquitous as the human race's sense of its own imperfection and the need for a second chance. Apocalyptic myths such as the Norse Ragnarok can serve as the equivalent of the great deluge—the end of all things—as can the great war between the Pandavas and Kauravas in the Indian *Mahabharata*.

What is the significance of the flood myth?

The flood myth is the myth of punishment and a second chance. The flood hero is the new "first" human. Creation dies to the old

The biblical flood is a story not unique to the Judeo-Christian world but can be found in the mythology of many cultures (1866 illustration by Gustave Doré).

world and is born to the new out of the new primordial mother waters—the waters of the flood. Because of the flood, we have a new creation.

What role does the creation of humans play in the world myth?

Most myths, understandably, describe the creation of the first examples of the people who would create the myths. The Sumerians, the Chinese, the Hawaiians, the Maidu, and several Iroquoian tribes say that the first humans were made from clay. The Maya say that the gods made the first imperfect humans out of mud and wood. Body parts will do as well; God created Eve from Adam's rib (or from dust). Ymir produced the first Norse humans from his armpit. Most mythologies have characters known by various names but always meaning what the Navajo mean when they tell of First Man and First Woman.

THE HERO

What is a hero?

The hero is the third component of the world myth. The world hero is a special human being born to overcome barriers, to experience the extremes of human possibility. The hero overcomes the limitations of his or her own culture and so breaks new ground for the species. He becomes the world hero. In a comparison of heroes in myths from all corners of the world, the world hero emerges as an archetype, a shadow being behind the many heroes.

The hero life follows a pattern, which has been called a "monomyth." The life begins with a miraculous conception and unusual birth. Sometimes the hero is born with adult abilities. The hero is threatened in some way as a child and is often hidden away or abandoned. Later he or she must demonstrate the hero status by some important act. Eventually there is a quest of some sort, one that involves tests and trials—a search for a parent, the diverting relationship with a *femme fatale*, the fight with a monster, a descent into the Underworld. The hero achieves his goal or sometimes he dies, but in some sense returns.

What are some examples of the hero's miraculous conception and/or birth?

A clear indication of the world hero is a miraculous conception and unusual birth. The ancient Akkadian king, Sargon, was said to have been born of a virgin. Jesus, too, was the product of a virgin birth; his mother herself is said to have been the result of an "Immaculate Conception." Abraham's son Isaac was born to a barren mother. In Phrygia, Attis was conceived by a pomegranate seed in his mother, the Great Goddess, in her form as Nana. Horus was conceived when his mother, Isis, succeeded in arousing the dead Osiris. Many versions of the world hero are fathered by gods: Herakles and Perseus are fathered by Zeus, Theseus by Poseidon. Rama's wife Sita was born of the Earth. The

Who are some world heroes?

The world hero, as Joseph Campbell suggests, wears many cultural masks, has many faces. He emerges early in Mesopotamia in Gilgamesh and later in the Middle East in Horus, Jesus, Mithras, and others. Greek mythology has many representatives: Herakles, Theseus, Perseus, for example. King Arthur is a later world hero, as is the Norse Volsung and Sigurd. In India Draupadi, the wife of the Pandavas in the *Mahabharata* has characteristics of the world hero, as does the Buddha, the Ceramese maiden Hainuwele, and the African maiden Wanjiru. The Mesoamerican Quetzalcoatl, in his human form, is a world hero, and so are Native Americans such as Kutoyis and Water Pot Boy.

Buddha's mother, Maya, conceived him in a dream via a white elephant. It was a grain of wheat that was responsible for Taliesin's conception. The Aztec goddess Coatlicue conceived Huitzilopochtli via a ball of feathers. A piece of clay led to the birth of Water Pot Boy, a blood clot to the birth of Kutoyis. Quetzalcoatl was conceived when his mother was entered by divine breath. The Navajo sacred twins were the result of a sun ray, which lingered on the body of the goddess Changing Woman.

What is the significance of the miraculous conception and birth?

Birth is always miraculous. It is a miracle that speaks to the universal longing for a new beginning. We long for the hero who can represent not only the given culture, but all of us. The hero is conceived outside the "normal" process because the hero belongs not to any one family but to the whole culture. Like all the first humans in myth, the hero is conceived and born mysteriously because, as did Adam in the Bible or the Navajo First Man and First Woman, he or she springs from the eternal essence. The world hero represents our second chance. It is significant that even if the hero is fathered by a god, he can only be meaningful to us as a fellow human if he enters the world via the biological doorway, which is the human mother.

What are some examples of the hero being born with adult characteristics?

The Greek Herakles, the Irish Cuchulainn, the Norse Volsung, the Indian Krishna, the Buddha, the Aztec Huitzilopochtli, and the Native American Kutoyis all share, with many versions of the world hero, the fact that they are born with adult powers—in fact, essentially skipping childhood.

Why is the hero sometimes born with adult powers?

The immediate adulthood of the hero is another sign—along with his immaculate conception—that he belongs to no particular parents, but to a whole culture and the world. He comes to us via the mother, but normal parenting for him is seen here as superfluous.

What are some examples of the hero being threatened and abandoned or hidden during childhood?

The world hero is a threat to the status quo and is immediately threatened in childhood. Sometimes he is actually abandoned, sometimes he is successfully hidden away for his protection. In the Jesus story, King Herod feels so threatened when the magi tell him they have come to worship a new king, that he orders the killing of all newborn boys in his land. Kamsa does the same thing in the Krishna story. Jesus is taken to Egypt, and Krishna is sent away to a foster family. In Iran, other magi announce the birth of Zoroaster to King Duransarum, and he attempts to stab the child. In Egypt, Isis hides the young Horus in the Delta to save him from his violent uncle, Seth. Sigurd, Moses, and Sargon are all hidden away from threatening forces. King Acrisius tries to rid himself of Perseus by abandoning him in the river. Jocasta and Laius give up the baby Oedipus to the wilderness.

The heroine Draupadi (right) used a miraculous sari to protect her from those who meant her harm.

The world hero is often protected by animals or people of the lower classes—"ordinary" people. Romulus and Remus are abandoned and raised by a wolf. Sigurd grows up with a smith, Krishna with cowherders.

What is the significance of the threat and abandonment in childhood?

The hero is a threat to the status quo because the hero always represents advancement to a different reality. Not surprisingly, then, the newborn hero is almost immediately threatened by the kings, jealous fathers, or demons who cannot accept a force for new understanding.

What are some examples of the world hero's early revelatory acts?

Signs of the divine essence of the world hero are demonstrated in childhood. Krishna kills a demon while still in the cradle. As a boy, Arthur removes the sword from the rock, and Theseus succeeds in retrieving his father's shoes and sword. Cuchulainn, as a child, kills the giant watchdog of Culann. Jesus impresses the elders at the temple in Jerusalem. Draupadi, as the young wife of the Pandava brothers in the *Mahabharata*, reveals her inner divinity when, with Krishna's help, she overcomes the attempt of the evil Kauravas to strip her of her miraculous sari.

What is the significance of these revelatory acts?

They are clear indications, like the miraculous conception, of the hero status. The young hero is able to break through natural barriers, to do what ordinary mortals are unable to do.

What is the hero's "call"?

Once an adult, the hero receives an internal or external call to action. In some cases he refuses the call at first. Moses, for instance, expresses his reluctance to lead his people out of Egypt as instructed by the voice in the Burning Bush. Odysseus is reluctant to leave his wife and child to fight in the Trojan War. Tolkien's Bilbo and Frodo in *The Hobbit* and in *The Lord of the Rings*, respectively, would have preferred to remain in the comforts of their homes rather than to follow the adventurous paths outlined by Gandalf. But the point is that the hero must leave home precisely because he must be a groundbreaker; so the world hero finally accepts the call and begins the necessary quest.

In other words, as does the Buddha or Sophocles's Antigone the hero accepts the call of a "higher law."

What are some examples of the hero's quest?

The quest is the central act in the world hero's life; it is the unfolding of the very purpose of the hero's existence, the reason for his being. The world hero, in all of his or her masks, undertakes the quest. The quest can take many forms, depending on the "landscape" of the particular culture. The oldest recorded quest is that of the Sumero-Babylonian hero Gilgamesh for eternal life. In the Bible, Moses seeks the Promised Land. In Greece, Theseus seeks the Minotaur in the Labyrinth and his father on a journey from his birthplace to Athens. The Native American Water Pot Boy also searches for his father—the source of his identity. Jason seeks the Golden Fleece. Aeneas looks for the new Troy, Rome. Muhammad on his Night Journey seeks God and higher knowledge. King Arthur and his knights search for the Holy Grail.

What events characterize the quest?

The quest always involves specific trials or tests. Herakles must complete his twelve labors. Perseus must find a way to kill Medusa without being turned to stone. There are always temptations that threaten to throw the hero off course. One such temptation for male heroes is the *femme fatale*—the temptress who embodies sexuality. Gilgamesh refuses the temptation of the great love goddess Inanna, as Cuchulainn will refuse Morrigan later. Odysseus must eventually leave Calypso and Circe. Aeneas must resist the temptation to stay with Dido rather than continuing on his quest. King Arthur and some of his knights are tempted by Morgan Le Fay. The Buddha is tempted by lust under the Bodhi Tree. Lleu is killed by Blodeuwedd, Maui is killed by his *femme fatale*.

279

Perhaps the single most important trial facing the world hero is the monster he hopes to slay.

What are some examples of the hero as monster slaying?

The killing of the monster is a major heroic goal. Gilgamesh and his friend Enkidu kill the monster Humbaba. Marduk slays Tiamat. Theseus kills the Minotaur, King George and Sigurd kill the Dragon. Perseus kills Medusa. Herakles kills the Nemean Lion and other monsters. The Mayan twins kill the bird demon. The Blackfoot Kutoyis kills the monster who eats humans.

What is the significance of monster slaying?

The monster is the demon which must be slain if the hero is to survive. In terms of our own lives, the monster represents our own inner demons, whatever they may be. The monster is what eats away at our reason for being.

What are some examples of the hero in the Underworld?

The descent to the Underworld, sometimes in death, is the ultimate trial facing the world hero on his quest. Full knowledge requires the facing of the ultimate challenge. Heroes descend to the Underworld to understand ultimate things or to bring back a lost person.

Inanna descends to her negative self, her sister Ereshkigal. In this way she learns what she needs to know of supreme negativity. Baal descends because he is the seed which must be planted before plants can return in the spring. Jesus descends to defy Satan, to "harrow" Hell. Osiris descends in death to become king of the Underworld. Odysseus and Aeneas make their journeys to the Land of the Dead to seek guidance from those who have already completed their quests. Orpheus goes, hoping to retrieve a lost love. Wanjiru and Hainuwele go as objects of sacrifice to bring prosperity to their people.

What is the significance of the Underworld descent ?

The descent into the Underworld is a metaphor for what has been called the "night journey of the soul." It speaks to the need of individuals to descend into the self to face the

A hellish vision of the Underworld by seventeenth-century artist Jan Brueghel the Elder.

demons and other dangers that lie there. The world hero on the descent is the germinating seed in the great mother. Having spent the allotted time in the depths, the hero can return as the one who has broken through the barriers that stand in the way of growth and self-knowledge.

The returning hero, like Jesus, the revived Osiris, or Arthur as the "once and future king," is our symbol of hope.

What is the overall significance of the heroic quest?

The heroic quest is finally significant insofar as it reflects our lives. If it has nothing to do with us, it is mere fantasy. In many cases the hero searches for something lost or for something his culture associates with its identity. The Holy Grail sought by Arthur's knights is at the religious center of the culture Arthur represents. For us it is a symbol of whatever we need to find to know ourselves and to achieve wholeness, freedom from our demons. The difficult trials that face the hero—and us, metaphorically—represent the powerful guardians at each threshold that stand between us and progress—the giants, the femmes fatales, the evil kings. But the hero returns with something learned. Inanna returns from the Underworld with a fuller knowledge of the whole world she rules rather than just the positive side of it. Wanjiru, Hainuwele, Jesus, and Osiris return as sources for material or spiritual food for their people. Osiris returns as grain, Hainuwele as vegetables, Corn Mother as corn. These are all versions of the boon or great gift that the world hero brings on the quest.

What else does the hero have to do with us?

In myths as in dreams, all the characters and actions are the direct products of those who dreamed them. In this sense, the hero of the world myth is analogous to the Ego or Persona of dream. All cultures dredge up trials and demons peculiar to their traditions. But it is to the universal world hero who emerges from a comparison of his or her many emanations that we must look for insight into our collective consciousness, our human psyche. We can relate to the world hero to the extent that we understand the need to succeed, to persevere against seemingly impossible odds. And we can relate to the nationalistic, familial, or ethnic loyalty that versions of this hero, in particular cultural clothes, represent. These, after all, are values we all preach in our schools, homes, legislatures, and places of worship.

It is also true that the archetypal world hero can evolve. It is to our current versions of the hero that we must look to discover how that change is taking place. To study the hero is to gaze into a mirror.

THE WORLD MYTH

What then is the world myth?

The world myth tells us that in some sense there are deities in the universe. These deities, like humans, fought in the distant past to achieve some sort of order in "heaven." There are Father gods, Mother goddesses, tricksters, and spirits in all aspects of nature. It was a deity who created the world, and that creation has been explained to us in sacred texts in a variety of ways. Along with deities and ordinary humans like us, there have always been a special class of people, or demigods, known as heroes. When we compare these heroes, we see that in actuality they are masks for a single world hero who stands for our own path through life, our own striving for wholeness, and the realization of our potential as individuals, as cultures, and as a species.

APPENDIX 1: PARALLEL MYTHOLOGY: CHART OF UNIVERSAL MYTHOLOGICAL TYPES AND THEMES

All myths are cultural. That is, they are realized by particular cultures and wear the "clothes" of those cultures. Yet, if we compare the myths of the world, certain universal themes or motifs—archetypal constructs—emerge. Several of these motifs and corresponding cultural examples of them are listed here. Certain examples are expressions of more than one motif. Chapters in which the myths appear are noted in parentheses.

Animal or Part-Animal Deities

Ice Age—(XVI)

Egyptian—Sphinx (III)

Egyptian—Amun, Anubis, Horus, Hathor, et al., with animal heads (III)

Minoan—White Bull of Poseidon (IV)

Greek—Zeus as Swan, Bull, etc. (V)

Indian—many of Vishnu's avatars (IX)

Indian—Hanuman Monkey King—*Ramayana* (IX)

Chinese—Fuxi, Nuwa, et al., have dragon heads (X)

African—Bulu—Zambe's animals (XIII)

Mesoamerican—the Feathered Serpent (XIV)

Native North American tricksters—Coyote, Great Hare, Spider , et al. (XV)

Native North American earth-divers—Turtle, Muskrat, et al. (XV)

Sioux—White Buffalo Woman (XV)

Navajo—Insect People (XV)

Animist Spirits

Tibetan—Bon—nature spirits (IX)

Japanese—Shinto *kami* (X)

Central Asian—Tengri (XI)

African—spirits in all things—Orishas (XIII)
Native North American—spirits and "Great Spirit" in all things (XV)
Hopi—kachina (XV)
Navajo—Yeii (XV)
Cherokee—Little Men (XV)
Inuit—Sedna (XV)

Apocalypse—End of the World

Norse—Ragnarök (VIII)
Indian—destruction of the world at end of each age (IX)
Indian—*Bhagavadgita,* the final war (IX)
South American—many end-of-the-world myths (XIV)

Creation Begun by a Goddess

Sumerian-Babylonian—Nammu/Tiamat (II)
Egyptian—Neith (III)
Greek—Gaia (IV)
Japanese—Izanami (X)
Australian—Eingana, Yhi (XII)
Nigerian Ijaw—Woyengi (XIII)
Dahomey—Mawu (XIII)
Congo Bankongo—Njambi (XIII)
Aztec—Omecihuatl (XIV)
Shipibo—solar goddess creator (XIV)
Acoma—Thinking Woman (XV)
Iroquoian—Sky Woman falls to earth (XV)

Creation from Nothing (*Ex Nihilo*) or from Chaos

Egyptian—Amun or Atum via masturbation (III)
Egyptian—Ptah via thought and word (III)
Egyptian—Atum—produced Shu and Tefnut via thought (III)
Indian—Prajapati via his mind (IX)
Indian—Brahma—via his mind (IX)
Indian—Vishnu—via his mind in sleep (IX)

Indian—Vedic golden cosmic egg (IX)

Chinese—Pangu in cosmic egg (X)

Japanese—spontaneous creation of gods—Izanami and Izanagi (X)

Central Asian—all creations (XI)

Australian—Dreamtime creation (XII)

Hawaiian—Kane (XII)

Maori—Io (XII)

Dogon—world egg (XIII)

Mayan—Tepeu and Gucumatz (XIV)

Aztec—Ometeotl—contains both genders (XIV)

Witoto—creator from words (XIV)

Chibcha—creation from light (XIV)

Native North American—Great Manitou creates via a vision (XV)

Modern—the Big Bang (XVI)

Creation of an Animistic World via Dismemberment or Waste

Babylonian—Marduk dismembers Tiamat (II)

Canaanite—Baal (II)

Norse—Odin, Vili, and Vé dismember Ymir (VIII)

Indian—sacrifice of Purusha (IX)

Chinese—Pangu becomes universe (X)

Zulu—Unkulunkulu's body is the world (XIII)

Boshongo—Bumba vomits creation (XIII)

Okanagan—Great Mother's body is the world (XV)

Northwest Native North Americans—Raven creates with excrement (XV)

Iroquoian—Sky Woman's body becomes the world (XV)

Native North American—Corn Mother (Grandmother) sacrificed and planted (XV)

Creation via Earth-Divers

Indian—Vishnu sends agent to depths (IX)

Indian—Vishnu—Churning Ocean of Milk (IX)

Japanese—Izanagi and Izanami and primal waters (X)

Central Asian—all creations (XI)

Polynesian—Maui brings up island from depths (XII)

Iroquoian—Sky Woman and animal-divers (XV)

Creation via Emergence

Japanese—from the earth (X)

Navajo—Journey of the Insect People (XV)

Hopi—Spider Woman guides the people from below (XV)

Pueblo Indians—emergence from below via the sipapu (XV)

Creation via Father Sky and Mother Earth/World Parents

Sumerian—An + Ki (II)

Babylonian—Apsu and Tiamat (II)

Greek—Gaia and Uranos (IV)

Indian—Dyaus and Prithvi (IX)

Chinese—Tian Di: tian = sky, di = earth (X)

Chinese—Yin=earth, Yang=sky (X)

Maori—Rangi (Sky) and Papa (Earth) (XII)

Hawaii—Ao and Po (XII)

Zuni—Father Sky and Mother Earth (XV)

Creation via Separation of the World Parents

Sumerian—Enlil separates An and Ki (II)

Babylonian—Marduk destroys Apsu-Tiamat (II)

Egyptian—Shu separates Geb and Nut (III)

Greek—Kronos separates Gaia and Uranos (IV)

Hittite—Heaven and Earth separated (IV)

Chinese—Zhong and Li separate the two worlds (X)

Japanese—separation of Izanami and Izanagi (X)

Maori—separation of Rangi and Papa (XII)

Krachi—separation of Wulbari (Sky) and Asase Ya (Earth) (XIII)

Diegeueño—California—Mother Earth-Father Sky separated by tobacco (XV)

Zuni—Earth Mother pushes Father Sky away from her (XV)

Culture Heroes

Egyptian—Osiris and Isis (III)

Greek—Prometheus—gift of fire (IV)

Chinese—Nuwa (X)

Chinese—Fuxi (X)

Chinese—Qi—helped with flood (X)

Chinese—Yi (X)

Chinese—Gun—stole soil to stop the flood (X)

Polynesian—Maui (XII)

Kikuyu—Gikuyu (XIII)

Ashanti—Ananse steals storytelling from creator (XIII)

Mayan—Gucumatz (Kukulkcan), Feathered Serpent (XIV)

Aztec—Quetzalcoatl and Huitzilopochtli (XIV)

Inca—Pachacamac—plants a child for food (XIV)

Inca—first Inca king and queen—Manco Cápac and Mama Occlo (XIV)

Navajo—Talking God (XV)

Acoma—girl twins of Thinking Woman (XV)

Sioux—White Buffalo Woman (XV)

Papago—Coyote saves people (XV)

Northwest Native Americans—Raven (XV)

Iroquoian—good twin (XV)

A Devil or Trickster Undermines Creation

Hebrew—Satan in Garden of Eden (II)

Zoroastrian—Angra Mainyu (II)

Egyptian—Apophis (III)

Japanese—Susanowo (X)

Central Asian—Erlik and others interfere with creator (XI)

Ashanti—Ananse undermines creator (XIII)

Yoruba—Legba undermines creator (XIII)

Carib—bad twin undermines creator (XIV)

Maidu—Coyote and Rattlesnake bring death (XV)

Iroquoian—bad twin brings trouble (XV)

Dying Gods

Sumerian—Inanna and Dumuzi/Tammuz (II)

Canaanite—Baal (II)

Phrygian—Attis (II)

287

Christian—Jesus (II)

Egyptian—Osiris (III)

Greek—Dionysos (V)

Greek/Phoenecian—Adonis (V)

Norse—Odin (VIII)

Norse—Baldr (VIII)

Japanese—Izanami (X)

Polynesian—Maui dies in Hine (XII)

Fertility and Love Deities

Sumerian—Inanna (II)

Arabic—Al-Uzza (II)

Canaanite—Dagan (II)

Canaanite—Baal (II)

Canaanite—Asherah (II)

Arabic—al-Uzza (II)

Phrygian—Cybele and Attis (II)

Egyptian—Isis (III)

Greek/Anatolian—Artemis (V)

Greek—Aphrodite (V)

Greek—Hera (V)

Greek—Demeter (V)

Greek—Dionysos (V)

Roman—Ceres (VI)

Roman—Cupid (VI)

Welsh—Branwen (VII)

Norse—Freyr (VIII)

Norse—Freyja (VIII)

Japanese—Inari, goddess of—rice (X)

Australian—Anjea (XII)

Australian—Julunggul (XII)

Australian—Djanggawuls (XII)

Polynesian—Hina (XII)

Polynesian—Maui (XII)

Iroquoian—Sky Woman (XV)

Native American—Corn Mother (XV)

First Humans

Sumerian—Enki creates humans out of clay (II)

Hebrew—Adam and Eve and Garden of Eden (II)

Norse—from Ymir's armpit or from the ash tree (VIII)

Chinese—Nuwa makes them from clay (X)

Central Asian—God creates humans from clay (XI)

Australian—Yhi's creations (XII

Australian—Djanggawuls' creations (XII)

Hawaiian—humans from clay (XII)

Bulu—Zambe's first humans (XIII)

Mayan—imperfect—out of mud and wood (XIV)

Taulipa—imperfect—out of wax (XIV)

Aztec—imperfect—out of clay (XIV)

Maidu—Turtle and Earth-Initiate make them from clay (XV)

Iroquoian—good twin makes them from clay (XV)

Navajo—First Man and First Woman (XV)

Penobscot—First Man and First Woman (XV)

The Flood Myth and Flood Hero

Sumerian and Babylonian—Ziusudra/Utnapishtim and Anu and Ea's Flood (II)

Hebrew—Noah and Yahweh's Flood (II)

Egyptian—Ra sends beer to calm Sekhmet (III)

Roman—Deucalion and Pyyrha (VI)

Irish—Fintan (VII)

Norse—Bergelmir and his wife (VIII)

Indian—Manu and the Fish (IX)

Chinese—Gonggong's flood—flood hero Yu (X)

Australian—Lizard's Flood (XII)

Polynesian—many flood myths (XII)

Yoruba—Olokun's flood (XIII)

Mayan—flood sent to end imperfect creation (XIV)

Aztec—Fourth world destroyed by Tlaloc's flood (XIV)

Yaghan—world flooded as punishment (XIV)

Canari—two boys and parrots as flood heroes (XIV)

Inca—flood to destroy early race of giants (XIV)

Papago—Coyote saves people from flood (XV)

Navajo—Water Monster's Flood (XV)

Algonquian—Manabozho and the flood (XV)

The Great Earth Mother Goddess

Anatolia—Çatal Hüyük Goddess (II)

Sumerian—Ninhursag (II)

Phrygian—Cybele (II)

Arabia—Allat (II)

Egyptian—Hathor (III)

Egyptian—Isis (III)

Egyptian—Nut III)

Minoan—Snake Goddess (IV)

Greek—Gaia (IV)

Greek—Rhae (IV)

Greek—Demeter and Persephone (V)

Greek/Anatolian—Artemis (V)

Etruscan—Uni (VI)

Greek—Artemis of many breasts in Asia Minor (V)

Roman—Juno (VI)

Celtic—continental—Sulis (Belisama) (VII)

Irish—Danu (Ana) (VII)

Welsh—Don (VII)

Norse—Frigg (VIII)

Norse—Freyja (VIII)

Indian—Indus Valley—pre-Devi goddess (IX)

Indian—Vedic—Prithvi (IX)

Indian—Parvati—wife of Shiva (IX)

Indian—Sarasvati—wife of Brahma (IX)

Indian—Sri-Lakshmi—wife of Vishnu (IX)

Indian—Devi (IX)

Chinese—Nuwa (X)

Central Asian—Great Mother at world tree (XI)

Australian—Eingana (XII)

Australian—Waramurungundi (XII)

Yoruba—Olokun (Oddudua) (XIII)

Ibo—Ala (XIII)

Ashanti—Asase (XIII)

Zulu—Nokhubulwane (XIII)

Mayan—Ix-Chel (XIV)

Aztec—Coatlicue (XIV)

Inca—Pachamama (XIV)

Zuni—Mother Earth (XV)

Okanagan—Mother of All (XV)

Cherokee—Grandmother Sun (XV)

Hopi, Navajo, Cherokee—Spider Woman or Spider Grandmother (XV)

Acoma—Tsichtinako ("Thinking Woman") (XV)

Iroquoian—Sky Woman comes to earth (XV)

Native American—Corn Mother (XV)

Modern—Gaia Hypothesis (XVI)

Other Goddesses with Dominant Power

Sumerian/Babylonian—Inanna/Ishtar (II)

Egyptian—Hathor (III)

Egyptian—Isis (III)

Greek—Athene (V)

Greek—Artemis (V)

Roman—Venus (VI)

Irish—Morrigan (VII)

Indian—Devi (IX)

Indian—Kali (IX)

Indian—Durga (IX)

Chinese—Guanyin (X)

Japanese—Kannon (male or female) (X)

Hawaiian—Pele—(XII)

Yoruba—Oya—(XIII)

Navajo—Changing Woman (XV)

Sioux—White Buffalo Woman (XV)

Inuit—Sedna (XV)

Monomythic Heroes

Sumerian and Babylonian—Gilgamesh (II)

Akkadian—Sargon (II)

Persian—Zoroaster (II)

Persian—Mithra (II)

Hebrew—Moses (II)

Islamic—Muhammad (II)

Christian—Jesus (II)

Egypt—Horus and Osiris (III)

Greek—Theseus (IV, V)

Greek—Odysseus (IV)

Greek—Achilles (IV)

Greek—Perseus (V)

Greek—Herakles (V)

Greek—Jason (V)

Etruscan—Tages (VI)

Roman—Aeneas (VI)

Irish—Cuchulainn (VII)

Irish—Fionn (VII)

Welsh—King Arthur (VII)

Norse—Volsung (VIII)

Norse—Sigmund—sword from the rock (VIII)

Norse—Sigurd (VIII)

Germanic—Siegfried (VIII)

Indian—Krishna (IX)

Indian—the Pandava Brothers (IX)

Indian—Draupadi—wife of the Pandavas (IX)

Indian—Rama (IX)

Indian—Sita (IX)

Central Asian—Genghis Khan (XI)

Central Asian—Alp Kara Aslan (XI)

Central Asian—Buqu Khan (XI)

Polynesian—Maui in some stories XII)

Kikuyu—Wanjiru—sacrificial maiden (XIII)

Ceramese—in Indonesia—sacrificial Hainuwele (XIII)

Bantu—Lituolone (XIII)

Mayan—Hero Twins—Hunahpu and Xbalanque (XIV)

Toltec and Aztec—Quetzalcoatll (XIV)

Tewa—Water Pot Boy (XV)

Blackfoot—Kutoyis (XV)

Modern—Hero with a Thousand Faces (Campbell) (XVI)

Modern—political heroes (XVI)

The Hero is Miraculously Conceived or Miraculously Born

Akkadian—Sargon (II)

Hebrew—Isaac by Abraham and Sarah (II)

Christian—Jesus by Virgin Mary (II)

Iranian—Mithraism—Mithras from a rock (II)

Iranian—Zoroastrian—Saoshyant (II)

Phrygian—Attis via Nana and Pomegranate (II)

Egyptian—Horus from dead Osiris (III)

Greek—Perseus (V)

Greek—Herakles (V)

Greek—Theseus (V)

Etruscan—Tages (VI)

Roman—Aeneas (VI)

Roman—Romulus and Remus (VI)

Irish—Cuchulainn (VII)

Welsh—Taliesen (VII)

Welsh—King Arthur via Merlin's magic (VII)

Norse—Volsung (VIII)

Indian—Krishna IX)

Indian—Karna (IX)

Indian—Vyasa (IX)

Indian—Sita (IX)

Indian—Satyavati (IX)

Indian—Buddha (IX)

Tibetan—Tara (IX)

Chinese—Yu (X)

Chinese—Qi (X)

Chinese—Huang Di (X)

Chinese—Fuxi (X)

Central Asian—Genghis Khan (XI)

Central Asian—Buqu Khan (XI)

Central Asia—Alp Kara Aslan (XI)

Polynesian—Maui (XII)

Bantu—Lituolone (XIII)

Mayan—Hero twins from spit of Hun Hunaphu (XIV)

Aztec—Coatlicue conceives Huitzilopochtli via ball of feathers (XIV)

Aztec—Chimalman conceives Quetzalcoatl via divine breath (XIV)

Navajo—Twins conceived via sun ray on Changing Woman (XV)

Tewa—Water Pot Boy conceived by clay (XV)

Blackfoot—Kutoyis conceived by clot of blood (XV)

The Hero is Born with Adult Powers

Greek—Herakles (V)

Etruscan—Tages (VI)

Irish—Cuchulainn (VII)

Norse—Volsung (VIII)

Indian—Krishna (IX)

Indian—the Buddha (IX)

Chinese—Huang Di (X)

Chinese—Qi (X)

Chinese—Yu (X)

Bantu—Lituolone (XIII)

Aztec—Huitzilopochtli (XIV)

Aztec—Quetzalcoatl (XIV)

Tewa—Water Pot Boy grows up fast (XV)

Blackfoot—Kutoyis (XV)

The Hero is Threatened in Childhood

Hebrew—Moses vs. Pharaoh (II)

Christian—Jesus vs. Herod (II)

Iranian—Zoroaster (II)

Egyptian—Horus vs. Seth (III)

Greek—Herakles vs. Hera (V)

Greek—Perseus vs. Acrisius (V)

Greek—Jason vs. Pelias (V)

Irish—Cuchulainn vs. 150 attackers (VII)

Welsh—Taliesen (VII)

Indian—Krishna vs. Kamsa (IX)

The Hero Is Abandoned, Cast Away, or Hidden in Childhood

Akkadian—Sargon (II)

Hebrew—Moses (II)

Christian—Jesus—flight into Egypt (II)

Egyptian—Horus (III)

Greek—Perseus (V)

Greek—Oedipus (V)

Roman—Romulus and Remus and the wolf (VI)

Welsh—Taliesen (VII)

Norse—Sigurd, lives with smith (VIII)

Indian—Krishna—grows up with cow herders (IX)

Maori—Maui as baby thrown into sea (XII)

Blackfoot—Kutoyis disguised as girl (XV)

The Hero Refuses or Accepts the Call

Hebrew—Moses asks "Why me?" (II)

Christian—Jesus in Garden of Gethsamane (II)

Greek—Achilles pretends to be a girl (IV)

Greek—Odysseus pretends to be insane (IV)

Greek—Antigone answers "higher law" (V)

Roman—Aeneas responds to Venus (VI)

Welsh—King Arthur pulls the sword from the rock (VII)

Indian—Buddha—call of enlightenment (IX)

Tewa—Water Pot Boy (XV)

The Hero Quest

Sumerian and Babylonian—Gilgamesh and Enkidu for Eternal Life (II)

Hebrew and Christian and Islamic—Abram/Abraham/Ibrahim for a Promised Land (II)

Hebrew—Moses and the Promised Land (II)

Islamic—Muhammad's Night Journey (II)

Christian—Kingdom of God (II)

Iranian—Zoroaster (II)

Iranian—Mithras (II)

Greek—Daedalus and Icarus (IV)

Greek—Theseus in the Labyrinth (IV)

Greek—Odysseus tries to get home (IV)

Greek—Perseus' search for Medusa (V)

Greek—Herakles and the twelve Labors (V)

Greek—Jason and the Golden Fleece (V)

Roman—Aeneas and the founding of Rome (VI)

Welsh—King Arthur's Round Table and the Holy Grail (VII)

Indian—Rama—quest for Sita (IX)

Chinese—Yu—quest to end the flood (X)

Ojibwa—Wunzh's vision quest (XV)

Tewa—Water Pot Boy searches for his father (XV)

Blackfoot—Kutoyis seeks monsters to kill (XV)

Modern—Jung—quest for wholeness (XVI)

The Hero Faces a *Femme Fatale*

Sumerian and Babylonian—Gilgamesh refuses Inanna/Ishtar (II)

Babylonian—Gilgamesh and Siduri (II)

Greek—all the Greek/Trojan heroes and Helen of Troy (IV)

Greek—Odysseus and Circe and Calypso (IV)

Greek—Agamemnon and Clytemnestra (V)

Greek—Theseus and Medea (V)

Greek—Hippolytus and Phaedre (V)

Greek—Jason and Medea (V)

Roman—Aeneas and Dido (VI)

Irish—Cuchulainn and Morrigan and Queen Medb (VII)

Welsh—Lleu killed by Blodeuwedd (VII)

Welsh—King Arthur, Percival, Gawain, Galahad, et al., and Morgan Le Fay (VII)

Indian—Rama and the forest demon (IX)

Indian—Buddha faces temptation of lust (IX)

Polynesian—Maui and Hina (XII)

The Hero as Monster Slayer

Sumerian and Babylonian—Gilgamesh and Enkidu slay Humbaba (II)

Babylonian—Marduk slays Tiamat (II)

Greek—Theseus kills the Minotaur (IV)

Greek—Odysseus and Cyclops (IV)

Greek—Perseus and Medusa (V)

Greek—Herakles and Nemean Lion, Lernean Hydra, et al. (V)

Greek—Theseus (V)

Norse—Sigurd and Fafnir the dragon (VIII)

Indian—Krishna (IX)

Chinese—Yi (X)

Polynesian—Maui fails, defeated by Hine (XII)

Bantu—Lituolone (XIII)

Mayan—Hero Twins defeat Bird Demon (XIV)

Navajo—twin named Monster Slayer (XV)

Blackfoot—Kutoyis (XV)

The Hero Searches for the Father

Christian—Jesus (II)

Greek—Telamachos searches for Odysseus (IV)

Greek—Theseus (V)

Roman—Aeneas searches Underworld (VI)

Tewa—Water Pot Boy searches for his father (XV)

Modern—Freud—Oedipus Complex (XVI)

The Hero or Deity Descends to the Underworld

Sumerian—Inanna to Ereshkigal (II)

Sumero-Babylonian—Inanna/Ishtar (II)

Canaanite—Baal (II)

Christian—Jesus (II)

Egypt—Osiris (III)

Greek—Odysseus to Shades (IV)

Greek—Theseus (V)

Greek—Herakles (V)

Greek—Orpheus and Eurydice (V)

Roman—Aeneas (VI)

Irish—Cuchulainn (VII)

Irish—Oisin (VII)

Japanese—Izanagi and Izanami (X)

Samoan—Maui—descends to get fire (XII)

Kikuyu—Wanjiru (XIII)

Mayan—Hero Twins descend (XIV)

Tewa—Water Pot Boy goes to depths of the water (XV)

Blackfoot—Kutoyis descends into monster's belly (XV)

The Hero Is Resurrected or Reborn

Christian—Jesus (II)

Egyptian—Osiris—revival by Isis (III)

Greek—Hyacinth as flower (V)

Greek—Herakles (V)

Welsh—Lleu (VII)

Welsh—King Arthur—the "once and future king" (VII)

Indian—Krishna ascends to Vishnu (IX)

Kikuyu—Wanjiru (XIII)

Ceramese—Indonesia—Hainuwele (XIII)

High God/Supreme Being

Sumerian—Enlil (II)

298   Babylonian—Anu (II)

Babylonian—Marduk (II)

Hebrew—Elohim/Yahweh (II)

Canaanite—El and Dagan and Baal (II)

Christian—God (II)

Arabic—Allah (II)

Zoroastrian—Ahura Mazda (II)

Egypt—Ra, Amun Ra (III)

Minoan—Diwe (IV)

Hittite—Kumarbi (IV)

Hurrian—Alahu (V)

Greece—Zeus (IV, V)

Roman—Jupiter (VI)

Etruscan—Tinia (VI)

Irish—the Dagda (VII)

Norse—Odin (VIII)

Germanic/Anglo-Saxon—Wotan/Woden (VIII)

Indian—Vedic Indra (IX)

Indian—Brahman concept (IX)

Indian—Shiva or Vishnu or Devi (IX)

Chinese—Shang Di or Tian Di or Yu Di or Di Ku or T'ai or Huang Di (X)

Japanese—Amaterasu—goddess (X)

Central Asian—Ulgen, et al. (XI)

Polynesian—Rangi, Ta'aroa, Ao, Io, Kane (XII)

Nigerian—Yoruba—Oluron (XIII)

Ashanti—Nyame (XIII)

Boshongo—Bumba (XIII)

Inca—Viracocha (XIV)

Native North American—Great Spirit, Great Mystery, Great Manitou (XV)

Modern—Teilhard's God (XVI)

Modern—Bateson's "Immanent Mind" (XVI)

Homosexuality

Sumerian and Babylonian—Gilgamesh and Enkidu (II)

Phrygian—Agdistis and Attis (II)

Egyptian—Horus and Seth III)

Greek—Herakles and Hylas on the *Argo* (V)

Greek—Apollo and Hyacinth (V)

Greek—Zeus and Ganymede (V)

Incest

Egyptian—all the original gods—brother/sister (III)

Greco-Roman—Cinyras and Myrrha (VI)

Welsh—Lleu born from Aranrhod and Gwydion (VII)

Indian—some creation myths (IX)

Indian—Brahma and daughter Sarasvati (IX)

Australian—Djanggawuls (XII)

Dogon—twin incest (XIII)

Mythical Mythmakers

Greek—Homer (IV)

Irish—Amairgen (VII)

Welsh—Taliesen (VII)

Indian—Vyasa—the *Mahabharata* and the *Vedas* (IX)

Indian—Valmiki—the *Ramayana* (IX)

Chinese—flood hero Yu—the *Shanhaijing* (X)

Pantheons

Sumerian—the Anunnaki (II)

Egyptian—the Ennead (III)

Egyptian—the Ogdoad (III)

Minoan—Linear B pantheon (IV)

Greek—the Olympians (IV, V)

Roman—triad of Jupiter, Mars, and Quirinus (VI)

Celtic—continental—triad of Teutates, Esus, Taranis (VII)

Irish—Tuatha de Danann (VII)

Welsh—Family of Don (VII)

Norse—the Aesir and the Vanir (VIII)

Indian—Vedic triads: Varuna, Mitra, and Aryaman; Indra, Agni, and Surya (IX)

Indian—Hindu triads of Shiva, Vishnu, and Brahma (or Devi) (IX)

Chinese—Five August Emperors (X)

Japanese—Amaterasu, Susanowo, Tsukiyomi, et al. (X)

Maori—Family of Rangi and Papa (XII)

Aztec—Quetzalcoatl, Tezcatlipoca, Xipe-Totec, Huitzilopochtli, Tloloc, Coatlicue, et al. (XIV)

Inca—Family of Viracocha (or Pachacamac) (XIV)

Primordial Waters

Sumerian—Nammu (II)

Babylonian—Tiamat (II)

Indian—Vishnu-based creation myths (IX)

Japanese—Japanese islands formed from it (X)

Central Asian—all creation myths (XI)

Zuni—Earth Mother breathes on it (XV)

Native North American—all earth-diver creations (XV)

Maidu—Turtle and Earth-Initiate (XV)

Inuit—Sedna and the Sea (XV)

Storm/Weather God

Canaanite—El and Baal (II)

Norse—Thor (VIII)

Germanic/Anglo-Saxon—Thunr, Thunor (VIII)

Chinese—Huang Di (X)

Maori—Tawhiri (XII)

Mayan—Chac (XIV)

Aztec—Tloloc (XIV)

Solar Deities

Sumerian Babylonian—Utu/Shamash (II)

Iranian—Mithraism—Mithra (II)

Egyptian—Ra (III)

Egyptian—Akhenaten's Aten (III)

Greek/Roman—Apollo (V, VI)

Irish—Lugh (VII)

Indian—Vedic Surya (IX)

Japanese—Amaterasu—goddess (X)

Australian—Wala, Bila—goddesses (XII)

Mayan—Itzamná (XIV)

Aztec—Tonatiuh (XIV)

Inca—Inti (XIV)

Cherokee—Grandmother Sun (XV)

Hopi—Tawa (XV)

Sacred Texts

Sumerian and Babylonian—Gilgamesh Epic (II)

Babylonian—*Enuma Elish* (II)

Hebrew—Bible (Torah and "Old Testament" additions) and *Talmud* (II)

Christian—Bible (*New Testament)* (II)

Islam—Qur'an and *Hadith* (II)

Egyptian—*Pyramid* and *Coffin Texts*, *Book of the Dead* (III)

Greek—Homer's *Iliad, Odyssey* (IV, V)

Greek—*Homeric Hymns* (IV, V)

Irish—*The Book of Invasions,* the *Tain, The Book of Leinster,* The Yellow Book of Lecan, *The Book of the Dun Cow* (VII)

Welsh—the *Mabinogion* (VII)

Norse—*Volsung Saga, Poetic Edda, Prose Edda* (VIII)

Indian—*Vedas, Brahmanas, Upanishads, Puranas* (IX)

Indian—the epics: *Mahabharata* (with *Bhagavadgita*), *Ramayana* (IX)

Chinese—*Shanhaijing, Chuci, Huainanzi* (X)

Japanese—*Kojiki, Nihongi* (X)

Mayan—*Popol Vuh* (XIV)

Trickster

Sumerian—Enki (II)

Greek—Hermes steals Apollo's cows (V)

Norse—Loki (VIII)

Norse—Odin as shapeshifter (VIII)

Indian—Krishna steals Gopi clothes (IX)

Central Asian—all creation myths—Erlik et al. (XI)

Australian—Bamapana (XII)

Australian—Crow (XII)

Polynesian—Maui (XII)

Yoruba and others—Legba (Eshu) (XIII)

Bantu—C (XIII)

Bantu—Dikithi (XIII)

West African—Ananse (Spider) (XIII)

Carib—one sacred twin a trickster (XIV)

Modoc—California—Kumokums (XV)

Plains Native Americans—Iktome (XV)

Midwest Native Americans—Great Hare (XV)

Northwest Native Americans—Raven (XV)

Native North American—Coyote (XV)

Algonquian—Manabozho (XV)

Twins

Greek—Dioscuri (V)

Roman—Castor and Pollux (VI)

Roman—Romulus and Remus (VI)

Indian—the Asvins (IX)

Central Asian—bad and good sons (XI)

Dogon—the Nummo (XIII)

Mayan—Hunahpu and Xbalanque (XIV)

Carib—one bad one good (XIV)

Navajo—Monster Slayer and Born for Water (XV)

Acoma—girl twins—Iatiku ("Life Bringer") and Nautsiti ("Full Basket") (XV)

Iroquoian—twins born to Sky Woman: one bad, one good (XV)

Underworld Deity

Sumerian—Ereshkigal (II)

Egyptian—Osiris (III)

Greek—Hades (V)

Celtic—continental—Taranis (VII)

Welsh—Beli (VII)

Norse—Hel (VIII)

War among the Gods

Babylonian—Marduk vs. the old gods (II)

Canaanite—Yamm and El vs. Baal (II)

Hurrian—Alahu vs. Anu (IV)

Hittite—Kumarbi vs. son Tesub (IV)

Greek—Olympians vs. Titans (IV)

Irish—Tuatha vs. Firbolg and Fomarians (VII)

Norse—Aesir vs. Vanir (VIII)

Norse—Ragnarök (VIII)

Indian—Indra vs. Vritra, Devas vs. Asuras (IX)

Chinese—Chiyou vs. Huang Di (X)

Chinese—Zhuanxu vs. Gonggong (X)

Japanese—Amaterasu vs. Susanowo (X)

Maori—Tawhiri, et al. vs. Tu, et al. (XII)

Hottentot—Goab vs. Gaunab (XIII)

Maasai—black vs. red god (XIII)

The World Center—Tree/Mountain

Sumerian—Huluppu Tree (II)

Hebrew—Forbidden Tree (II)

Arabic—Dhat Anwat Tree (II)

Islam—the Kabah (II)

Christianity—the Cross (II)

Norse—Yggdrasil (VIII)

Indian—Mount Meru (IX)

Japanese—the Heavenly August Pillar (X)

Central Asian—creator's tree (XI)

Mayan—Yaxché (XIV)

APPENDIX 2: SELECTED MYTHOLOGICAL TEXTS

The myths included here are intended to give the reader at least a glimpse, albeit in translation, of the stories as they would originally have been told. In most cases, somewhat archaic texts have been chosen because they are in the public domain and because they convey to the modern reader something of the timelessness and antiquity of the myths in contrast to the contemporary paraphrasing and retelling of myths in the regular chapters of this book. Particularly in the cases of the Inanna (Ishtar) descent myth, the Gilgamesh flood myth, the Egyptian *Book of the Dead* spells, and the Odin hanging myth, the reader would do well to read the mysterious texts simply in order to enter into the mood of the various pieces without worrying a great deal about their precise meaning.

The texts have been chosen to represent a wide range of the world's mythological traditions, from ancient Mesopotamia to Native North America and Africa.

THE DESCENT OF INANNA (ISHTAR) INTO THE LOWER WORLD

(From *The Civilization of Babylonia and Assyria: Its Remains, Language, History, Religion, Commerce*, trans. M. Jastrow, 1915. www.sacred-texts.com)

This myth is one of the world's oldest. It describes the terrifying journey of the great Sumero-Babylonian goddess Inanna (Ishtar) to her sister Ereshkigal's realm in the Underworld.

To the land of no return, the land of darkness,
Ishtar, the daughter of Sin [the moon-god] directed her thought,
Directed her thought, Ishtar, the daughter of Sin,
To the house of shadows, the dwelling, of Irkalla,
To the house without exit for him who enters therein,
To the road, whence there is no turning,
To the house without light for him who enters therein,
The place where dust is their nourishment, clay their food.

They have no light, in darkness they dwell.
Clothed like birds, with wings as garments,
Over door and bolt, dust has gathered.
Ishtar on arriving at the gate of the land of no return,
To the gatekeeper thus addressed herself:

"Gatekeeper, ho, open thy gate!
Open thy gate that I may enter!
If thou openest not the gate to let me enter,
I will break the door, I will wrench the lock,
I will smash the door-posts, I will force the doors.
I will bring up the dead to eat the living.
And the dead will outnumber the living."
The gatekeeper opened his mouth and spoke,
Spoke to the lady Ishtar:
"Desist, O lady, do not destroy it.
I will go and announce thy name to my queen Ereshkigal."
The gatekeeper entered and spoke to Ereshkigal:
"Ho! here is thy sister, Ishtar …
Hostility of the great powers …."
When Ereshkigal heard this,
As when one hews down a tamarisk she trembled,
As when one cuts a reed, she shook:
"What has moved her heart [seat of the intellect] what has stirred her liver [seat of the
    emotions]?
Ho there, does this one wish to dwell with me?
To eat clay as food, to drink dust as wine?
I weep for the men who have left their wives.
I weep for the wives torn from the embrace of their husbands;
For the little ones cut off before their time.
Go, gatekeeper, open thy gate for her,
Deal with her according to the ancient decree."
The gatekeeper went and opened his gate to her:
"Enter, O lady, let Cuthah greet thee.
Let the palace of the land of no return rejoice at thy presence!"

He bade her enter the first gate, which he opened wide, and took the large crown off her
    head:
"Why, O gatekeeper, dost thou remove the large crown off my head?"
306   "Enter, O lady, such are the decrees of Ereshkigal."

The second gate he bade her enter, opening it wide, and removed her earrings:

"Why, O gatekeeper, dost thou remove my earrings?"

"Enter, O lady, for such are the decrees of Ereshkigal."

The third gate he bade her enter, opened it wide, and removed her necklace:

"Why, O gatekeeper, dost thou remove my necklace?"

"Enter, O lady, for such are the decrees of Ereshkigal."

The fourth gate he bade her enter, opened it wide, and removed the ornaments of her breast:

"Why, O gatekeeper, dost thou remove the ornaments of my breast?"

"Enter, O lady, for such are the decrees of Ereshkigal."

The fifth gate he bade her enter, opened it wide, and removed the girdle of her body studded with birth-stones.

"Why, O gatekeeper, dost thou remove the girdle of my body, studded with birth-stones?"

"Enter, O lady, for such are the decrees of Ereshkigal."

The sixth gate he bade her enter, opened it wide, and removed the spangles off her hands and feet.

"Why, O gatekeeper, dost thou remove the spangles off my hands and feet?"

"Enter, O lady, for thus are the decrees of Ereshkigal."

The seventh gate he bade her enter, opened it wide, and removed her loin-cloth.

"Why, O gatekeeper, dost thou remove my loin-cloth?"

"Enter, O lady, for such are the decrees of Ereshkigal."

Now when Ishtar had gone down into the land of no return,

Ereshkigal saw her and was angered at her presence.

Ishtar, without reflection, threw herself at her [in a rage].

Ereshkigal opened her mouth and spoke,

To Namtar, her messenger, she addressed herself:

"Go Namtar, imprison her in my palace.

Send against her sixty diseases, to punish Ishtar.

Eye-disease against her eyes,

Disease of the side against her side,

Foot-disease against her foot,

Heart-disease against her heart,

Head-disease against her head,

Against her whole being, against her entire body."

After the lady Ishtar had gone down into the land of no return,

The bull did not mount the cow, the ass approached not the she-ass,

To the maid in the street, no man drew near.

The man slept in his apartment,

The maid slept by herself.

[The second half of the poem, the reverse of the tablet, continues as follows:]

The countenance of Papsukal, the messenger of the great gods, fell, his face was troubled.

In mourning garb he was clothed, in soiled garments clad.

Shamash [the sun-god] went to Sin [the moon-god], his father, weeping,

In the presence of Ea, the King, he went with flowing tears.

"Ishtar has descended into the earth and has not come up. The bull does not mount the cow, the ass does not approach the she-ass.

The man does not approach the maid in the street,

The man sleeps in his apartment,

The maid sleeps by herself."

Ea in the wisdom of his heart, formed a being,

He formed Asu-shu-namir the eunuch.

Go, Asu-shu-namir, to the land of no return direct thy face!

The seven gates of the land without return be opened before thee,

May Ereshkigal at sight of thee rejoice!

After her heart has been assuaged, her liver quieted,

Invoke against her the name of the great gods,

Raise thy head, direct thy attention to the khalziku skin.

"Come, lady, let them give me the khalziku skin, that I may drink water out of it."

When Ereshkigal heard this, she struck her side, bit her finger,

Thou hast expressed a wish that can not be granted.

Go, Asu-sbu-iaamir, I curse thee with a great curse,

The sweepings of the gutters of the city be thy food,

The drains of the city be thy drink,

The shadow of the wall be thy abode,

The thresholds be thy dwelling-place;

Drunkard and sot strike thy cheek!"

Ereshkigal opened her mouth and spoke,

To Namtar, her messenger, she addressed herself.

"Go, Namtar, knock at the strong palace,

Strike the threshold of precious stones,

Bring out the Anunnaki, seat them on golden thrones.

Sprinkle Ishtar with the waters of life and take her out of my presence.

Namtar went, knocked at the strong palace,

Tapped on the threshold of precious stones.

308   He brought out the Anunnaki and placed them on golden thrones,

He sprinkled Ishtar with the waters of life and took hold of her.

Through the first gate he led her out and returned to her her loin-cloth.

Through the second gate he led her out and returned to her the spangles of her hands and feet.

Through the third gate he led her out and returned to her the girdle of her body, studded with birth-stones.

Through the fourth gate he led her out and returned to her the ornaments of her breast.

Through the fifth gate he led her out and returned to her her necklace.

Through the sixth gate he led her out and returned her earrings.

Through the seventh gate he led her out and returned to her the large crown for her head.

[The following lines are in the form of an address—apparently to some one who has sought release for a dear one from the portals of the lower world.]

"If she (Ishtar) will not grant thee her release,

To Tammuz, the lover of her youth,

Pour out pure waters, pour out fine oil;

With a festival garment deck him that he may play on the flute of lapis lazuli,

That the votaries may cheer his liver [his spirit].

Belili [sister of Tammuz] had gathered the treasure,

With precious stones filled her bosom.

When Belili heard the lament of her brother, she dropped her treasure,

She scattered the precious stones before her,

"Oh, my only brother, do not let me perish!

On the day when Tammuz plays for me on the flute of lapis lazuli, playing it for me with the porphyry ring.

Together with him, play ye for me, ye weepers and lamenting women!

That the dead may rise up and inhale the incense."

THE EPIC OF GILGAMESH
TABLET XI
THE STORY OF THE FLOOD

(Maureen Gallery Kovacs, translation. Stanford University Press, 1998)

This ancient myth of the flood is found in the various versions of the epic tale of the Sumerian hero Gilgamesh, one of the world's oldest stories. The version here is a translation of the Akkadian-Babylonian text. The Gilgamesh flood resembles Noah's flood in the Bible.

Gilgamesh spoke to Utanapishtim, the Faraway:
> "I have been looking at you,
> but your appearance is not strange—you are like me!
> You yourself are not different—you are like me!
> My mind was resolved to fight with you,
> (but instead?) my arm lies useless over you.
> Tell me, how is it that you stand in the Assembly of the Gods, and have found life!"

Utanapishtim spoke to Gilgamesh, saying:
> "I will reveal to you, Gilgamesh, a thing that is hidden,
> a secret of the gods I will tell you!
> Shuruppak, a city that you surely know,
> situated on the banks of the Euphrates,
> that city was very old, and there were gods inside it.
> The hearts of the Great Gods moved them to inflict the Flood.
> Their Father Anu uttered the oath (of secrecy),
> Valiant Enlil was their Adviser,
> Ninurta was their Chamberlain,
> Ennugi was their Minister of Canals."

Ea, the Clever Prince, was under oath with them
so he repeated their talk to the reed house:

> "Reed house, reed house! Wall, wall!"
> O man of Shuruppak, son of Ubartutu:
> Tear down the house and build a boat!
> Abandon wealth and seek living beings!
> Spurn possessions and keep alive living beings!
> Make all living beings go up into the boat.
> The boat which you are to build,
> its dimensions must measure equal to each other:
> its length must correspond to its width.
> Roof it over like the Apsu.

I understood and spoke to my lord, Ea:

> "My lord, thus is the command which you have uttered
> I will heed and will do it.
> But what shall I answer the city, the populace, and the Elders!"

Ea spoke, commanding me, his servant:

> "You, well then, this is what you must say to them:
> 'It appears that Enlil is rejecting me
> so I cannot reside in your city,
> nor set foot on Enlil's earth.
> I will go down to the Apsu to live with my lord, Ea,

310

and upon you he will rain down abundance,
a profusion of fowl, myriad fishes.
He will bring to you a harvest of wealth,
in the morning he will let loaves of bread shower down,
and in the evening a rain of wheat!'"

Just as dawn began to glow
the land assembled around me,
the carpenter carried his hatchet,
the reed worker carried his (flattening) stone....
The child carried the pitch,
the weak brought whatever else was needed.
On the fifth day I laid out her exterior.
It was a field in area,
its walls were each 10 times 12 cubits in height,
the sides of its top were of equal length, 10 times 12 cubits each.
I laid out its (interior) structure and drew a picture of it.
I provided it with six decks,
thus dividing it into seven (levels).
The inside of it I divided into nine (compartments).
I drove plugs (to keep out) water in its middle part.
I saw to the punting poles and laid in what was necessary.
Three times 3,600 (units) of raw bitumen I poured into the bitumen kiln,
three times 3,600 (units of) pitch ...into it,
there were three times 3,600 porters of casks who carried (vegetable) oil,
apart from the 3,600 (units of) oil which they consumed
and two times 3,600 (units of) oil which the boatman stored away.
I butchered oxen for the meat,
and day upon day I slaughtered sheep.
I gave the workmen ale, beer, oil, and wine, as if it were river water,
so they could make a party like the New Year's Festival.
... and I set my hand to the oiling.
The boat was finished by sunset.
The launching was very difficult.
They had to keep carrying a runway of poles front to back,
until two-thirds of it had gone into the water.
Whatever I had I loaded on it:
whatever silver I had I loaded on it,
whatever gold I had I loaded on it.
All the living beings that I had I loaded on it,

I had all my kith and kin go up into the boat,
all the beasts and animals of the field and the craftsmen I had go up.
Shamash had set a stated time:
> "In the morning I will let loaves of bread shower down,
> and in the evening a rain of wheat!
> Go inside the boat, seal the entry!"

That stated time had arrived.
In the morning he let loaves of bread shower down,
and in the evening a rain of wheat.
I watched the appearance of the weather—
the weather was frightful to behold!
I went into the boat and sealed the entry.
For the caulking of the boat, to Puzuramurri, the boatman,
I gave the palace together with its contents.
Just as dawn began to glow
there arose from the horizon a black cloud.
Adad rumbled inside of it,
before him went Shullat and Hanish,
heralds going over mountain and land.
Erragal pulled out the mooring poles,
forth went Ninurta and made the dikes overflow.
The Anunnaki lifted up the torches,
setting the land ablaze with their flare.
Stunned shock over Adad's deeds overtook the heavens,
and turned to blackness all that had been light.
The … land shattered like a … pot.
All day long the South Wind blew …,
blowing fast, submerging the mountain in water,
overwhelming the people like an attack.
No one could see his fellow,
they could not recognize each other in the torrent.
The gods were frightened by the Flood,
and retreated, ascending to the heaven of Anu.
The gods were cowering like dogs, crouching by the outer wall.
Ishtar shrieked like a woman in childbirth,
the sweet-voiced Mistress of the Gods wailed:
> "The olden days have alas turned to clay,
> because I said evil things in the Assembly of the Gods!
> How could I say evil things in the Assembly of the Gods,
> ordering a catastrophe to destroy my people!!
> No sooner have I given birth to my dear people
> than they fill the sea like so many fish!"

The gods—those of the Anunnaki—were weeping with her,
the gods humbly sat weeping, sobbing with grief,
their lips burning, parched with thirst.
Six days and seven nights
came the wind and flood, the storm flattening the land.
When the seventh day arrived, the storm was pounding,
the flood was a war—struggling with itself like a woman writhing (in labor).
The sea calmed, fell still, the whirlwind (and) flood stopped up.
I looked around all day long—quiet had set in
and all the human beings had turned to clay!
The terrain was as flat as a roof.
I opened a vent and fresh air (daylight!) fell upon the side of my nose.
I fell to my knees and sat weeping,
tears streaming down the side of my nose.
I looked around for coastlines in the expanse of the sea,
and at twelve leagues there emerged a region (of land).
On Mt. Nimush the boat lodged firm,
Mt. Nimush held the boat, allowing no sway.
One day and a second Mt. Nimush held the boat, allowing no sway.
A third day, a fourth, Mt. Nimush held the boat, allowing no sway.
A fifth day, a sixth, Mt. Nimush held the boat, allowing no sway.
When a seventh day arrived
I sent forth a dove and released it.
The dove went off, but came back to me;
no perch was visible so it circled back to me.
I sent forth a swallow and released it.
The swallow went off, but came back to me;
no perch was visible so it circled back to me.
I sent forth a raven and released it.
The raven went off, and saw the waters slither back.
It eats, it scratches, it bobs, but does not circle back to me.

Then I sent out everything in all directions and sacrificed (a sheep).
I offered incense in front of the mountain-ziggurat.
Seven and seven cult vessels I put in place,
and (into the fire) underneath (or: into their bowls) I poured reeds, cedar, and
myrtle.
The gods smelled the savor,
the gods smelled the sweet savor,
and collected like flies over a (sheep) sacrifice.
Just then Beletili arrived.
She lifted up the large flies (beads) which Anu had made for his enjoyment:
    "You gods, as surely as I shall not forget this lapis lazuli around my neck,

may I be mindful of these days, and never forget them!
The gods may come to the incense offering,
but Enlil may not come to the incense offering,
because without considering he brought about the Flood
and consigned my people to annihilation."
Just then Enlil arrived.
He saw the boat and became furious,
he was filled with rage at the Igigi gods:
"Where did a living being escape?
No man was to survive the annihilation!"
Ninurta spoke to Valiant Enlil, saying:
"Who else but Ea could devise such a thing?
It is Ea who knows every machination!"
La spoke to Valiant Enlil, saying:
"It is yours, O Valiant One, who is the Sage of the Gods.
How, how could you bring about a Flood without consideration
Charge the violation to the violator,
charge the offense to the offender,
but be compassionate lest (mankind) be cut off,
be patient lest they be killed.
Instead of your bringing on the Flood,
would that a lion had appeared to diminish the people!
Instead of your bringing on the Flood,
would that a wolf had appeared to diminish the people!
Instead of your bringing on the Flood,
would that famine had occurred to slay the land!
Instead of your bringing on the Flood,
would that (Pestilent) Erra had appeared to ravage the land!
It was not I who revealed the secret of the Great Gods,
I (only) made a dream appear to Atrahasis, and (thus) he heard the secret of the gods.
Now then! The deliberation should be about him!"
Enlil went up inside the boat
and, grasping my hand, made me go up.
He had my wife go up and kneel by my side.
He touched our forehead and, standing between us, he blessed us:
"Previously Utanapishtim was a human being.
But now let Utanapishtim and his wife become like us, the gods!
Let Utanapishtim reside far away, at the Mouth of the Rivers."

They took us far away and settled us at the Mouth of the Rivers.

"Now then, who will convene the gods on your behalf,
that you may find the life that you are seeking!

Wait! You must not lie down for six days and seven nights."
Soon as he sat down (with his head) between his legs
sleep, like a fog, blew upon him.
Utanapishtim said to his wife:

> "Look there! The man, the youth who wanted (eternal) life!
> Sleep, like a fog, blew over him."

His wife said to Utanapishtim the Faraway:

> "Touch him, let the man awaken.
> Let him return safely by the way he came.
> Let him return to his land by the gate through which he left."

Utanapishtim said to his wife:

> "Mankind is deceptive, and will deceive you.
> Come, bake loaves for him and keep setting them by his head
> and draw on the wall each day that he lay down."

She baked his loaves and placed them by his head
and marked on the wall the day that he lay down.
The first loaf was dessicated,
the second stale, the third moist, the fourth turned white…,
the fifth sprouted gray (mold), the sixth is still fresh.
the seventh—suddenly he touched him and the man awoke.
Gilgamesh said to Utanapishtim:

> "The very moment sleep was pouring over me
> you touched me and alerted me!"

Utanapishtim spoke to Gilgamesh, saying:

"Look over here, Gilgamesh, count your loaves!
You should be aware of what is marked on the wall!
Your first loaf is dessicated,
the second stale, the third moist, your fourth turned white,
the fifth sprouted gray (mold), the sixth is still fresh.
The seventh—at that instant you awoke!"

Gilgamesh said to Utanapishtim the Faraway:

"O woe! What shall I do, Utanapishtim, where shall I go!
The Snatcher has taken hold of my flesh,
in my bedroom Death dwells,
and wherever I set foot there too is Death!"

HOME EMPTY-HANDED

Utanapishtim said to Urshanabi, the ferryman:

> "May the harbor reject you, may the ferry landing reject you!
> May you who used to walk its shores be denied its shores!
> The man in front of whom you walk, matted hair chains his body,
> animal skins have ruined his beautiful skin.
> Take him away, Urshanabi, bring him to the washing place.
> Let him wash his matted hair in water like ellu.
> Let him cast away his animal skin and have the sea carry it off,
> let his body be moistened with fine oil,
> let the wrap around his head be made new,
> let him wear royal robes worthy of him!
> Until he goes off to his city,
> until he sets off on his way,
> let his royal robe not become spotted, let it be perfectly new!"

Urshanabi took him away and brought him to the washing place.
He washed his matted hair with water like ellu.
He cast off his animal skin and the sea carried it off.
He moistened his body with fine oil,
and made a new wrap for his head.
He put on a royal robe worthy of him.
Until he went away to his city,
until he set off on his way,
his royal robe remained unspotted, it was perfectly clean.
Gilgamesh and Urshanabi boarded the boat,
they cast off the magillu-boat, and sailed away.

The wife of Utanapishtim the Faraway said to him:

> "Gilgamesh came here exhausted and worn out.
> What can you give him so that he can return to his land (with honor)!"

Then Gilgamesh raised a punting pole
and drew the boat to shore.
Utanapishtim spoke to Gilgamesh, saying:
> "Gilgamesh, you came here exhausted and worn out.
> What can I give you so you can return to your land?
> I will disclose to you a thing that is hidden, Gilgamesh.
> … I will tell you.
> There is a plant… like a boxthorn,
> whose thorns will prick your hand like a rose.
> If your hands reach that plant you will become a young man again."

316

Hearing this, Gilgamesh opened a conduit (to the Apsu)
and attached heavy stones to his feet.
They dragged him down, to the Apsu they pulled him.
He took the plant, though it pricked his hand,
and cut the heavy stones from his feet,
letting the waves throw him onto its shores.
Gilgamesh spoke to Urshanabi, the ferryman, saying:

> "Urshanabi, this plant is a plant against decay
> by which a man can attain his survival.
> I will bring it to Uruk-Haven,
> and have an old man eat the plant to test it.
> The plant's name is 'The Old Man Becomes a Young Man.'
> Then I will eat it and return to the condition of my youth."

At twenty leagues they broke for some food,
at thirty leagues they stopped for the night.
Seeing a spring and how cool its waters were,
Gilgamesh went down and was bathing in the water.
A snake smelled the fragrance of the plant,
silently came up and carried off the plant.
While going back it sloughed off its casing.
At that point Gilgamesh sat down, weeping,
his tears streaming over the side of his nose.

> "Counsel me, O ferryman Urshanabi!
> For whom have my arms labored, Urshanabi!
> For whom has my heart's blood roiled!
> I have not secured any good deed for myself,
> but done a good deed for the 'lion of the ground'!"
> Now the high waters are coursing twenty leagues distant,
> as I was opening the conduit I turned my equipment over into it.
> What can I find (to serve) as a marker for me!
> I will turn back (from the journey by sea) and leave the boat by the shore!"

At twenty leagues they broke for some food,
at thirty leagues they stopped for the night.
They arrived in Uruk-Haven.
Gilgamesh said to Urshanabi, the ferryman:

> "Go up, Urshanabi, onto the wall of Uruk and walk around.
> Examine its foundation inspect its brickwork thoroughly—
> is not (even the core of) the brick structure of kiln-fired brick,
> and did not the Seven Sages themselves lay out its plan!

One league city, one league palm gardens, one league lowlands, the open area of the Ishtar Temple, three leagues and the open area of Uruk it encloses."

NOAH'S FLOOD

This is the biblical story of Noah and the flood in the King James translation of Genesis 7 and 8.

CHAPTER 7

1 And the LORD said unto Noah, Come thou and all thy house into the ark; for thee have I seen righteous before me in this generation.

2 Of every clean beast thou shalt take to thee by sevens, the male and his female: and of beasts that *are* not clean by two, the male and his female.

3 Of fowls also of the air by sevens, the male and the female; to keep seed alive upon the face of all the earth.

4 For yet seven days, and I will cause it to rain upon the earth forty days and forty nights; and every living substance that I have made will I destroy from off the face of the earth.

5 And Noah did according unto all that the LORD commanded him.

6 And Noah *was* six hundred years old when the flood of waters was upon the earth.

7 And Noah went in, and his sons, and his wife, and his sons' wives with him into the ark, because of the waters of the flood.

8 Of clean beasts, and of beasts that *are* not clean, and of fowls, and of every thing that creepeth upon the earth,

9 There went in two and two unto Noah into the ark, the male and the female, as God had commanded Noah.

10 And it came to pass after seven days, that the waters of the flood were upon the earth.

11 In the six hundredth year of Noah's life in the second month, the seventeenth day of the month, the same day were all the fountains of the great deep broken up, and the windows of heaven were opened.

12 And the rain was upon the earth forty days and forty nights.

13 In the selfsame day entered Noah, and Shem, and Ham, and Japheth, the sons of Noah, and Noah's wife, and the three wives of his sons with them into the ark;

14 They, and every beast after his kind, and all the cattle after their kind, and every creeping thing that creepeth upon the earth after his kind, and every fowl after his kind, every bird of every sort.

15 And they went in unto Noah into the ark, two and two of all flesh, wherein *is* the breath of life.

16 And they that went in, went in male and female of all flesh, as God had commanded him: and the LORD shut him in.

17 And the flood was forty days upon the earth; and the waters increased, and bare up the ark, and it was lift up above the earth.

18 And the waters prevailed, and were increased greatly upon the earth; and the ark went upon the face of the waters.

19 And the waters prevailed exceedingly upon the earth; and all the high hills, that *were* under the whole heaven, were covered.

20 Fifteen cubits upward did the waters prevail; and the mountains were covered.

21 And all flesh died that moved upon the earth, both of fowl, and of cattle, and of beast, and of every creeping thing that creepeth upon the earth, and every man:

22 All in whose nostrils *was* the breath of life, of all that *was* in the dry *land*, died.

23 And every living substance was destroyed which was upon the face of the ground, both man, and cattle, and the creeping things, and the fowl of the heaven; and they were destroyed from the earth: and Noah only remained *alive*, and they that *were* with him in the ark.

24 And the waters prevailed upon the earth an hundred and fifty days.

Chapter 8

1 And God remembered Noah, and every living thing, and all the cattle that *was* with him in the ark: and God made a wind to pass over the earth, and the waters asswaged;

2 The fountains also of the deep and the windows of heaven were stopped, and the rain from heaven was restrained;

3 And the waters returned from off the earth continually: and after the end of the hundred and fifty days the waters were abated.

4 And the ark rested in the seventh month, on the seventeenth day of the month, upon the mountains of Ararat.

5 And the waters decreased continually until the tenth month: in the tenth *month*, on the first *day* of the month, were the tops of the mountains seen.

6 And it came to pass at the end of forty days, that Noah opened the window of the ark which he had made:

7 And he sent forth a raven, which went forth to and fro, until the waters were dried up from off the earth.

8 Also he sent forth a dove from him, to see if the waters were abated from off the face of the ground;

9 But the dove found no rest for the sole of her foot, and she returned unto him into the ark, for the waters *were* on the face of the whole earth: then he put forth his hand, and took her, and pulled her in unto him into the ark.

10 And he stayed yet other seven days; and again he sent forth the dove out of the ark;

11 And the dove came in to him in the evening; and, lo in her mouth *was* an olive leaf pluckt off: so Noah knew that the waters were abated from off the earth.

12 And he stayed yet other seven days; and sent forth the dove; which returned not again unto him any more.

13 And it came to pass in the six hundredth and first year in the first *month*, the first *day* of the month, the waters were dried up from off the earth: and Noah removed the covering of the ark, and looked, and, behold, the face of the ground was dry.

14 And in the second month, on the seven and twentieth day of the month, was the earth dried.

15 And God spake unto Noah, saying,

16 Go forth of the ark, thou, and thy wife, and thy sons, and thy sons' wives with thee.

17 Bring forth with thee every living thing that *is* with thee, of all flesh, *both* of fowl, and of cattle, and of every creeping thing that creepeth upon the earth; that they may breed abundantly in the earth, and be fruitful, and multiply upon the earth.

18 And Noah went forth, and his sons, and his wife, and his sons' wives with him:

19 Every beast, every creeping thing, and every fowl, *and* whatsoever creepeth upon the earth, after their kinds, went forth out of the ark.

20 And Noah builded an altar unto the LORD; and took of every clean beast, and of every clean fowl, and offered burnt offerings on the altar.

21 And the LORD smelled a sweet savour; and the LORD said in his heart, I will not again curse the ground any more for man's sake; for the imagination of man's heart *is* evil from his youth; neither will I again smite any more every thing living, as I have done.

22 While the earth remaineth, seedtime and harvest, and cold and heat, and summer and winter, and day and night shall not cease.

THE EGYPTIAN BOOK OF THE DEAD
THE PAPYRUS OF ANI

(From *The Egyptian Book of the Dead*, trans. E.A. Wallis Budge, 1895.)

The Book of the Dead describes ritual spells related to the treatment of the dead as mummies in ancient Egypt. Certain deities play central roles here—especially Osiris, the god of the Underworld.

THE CHAPTER OF THE PRAISE OF HATHOR, LADY OF AMENTET

Hathor, Lady of Amentet, the Dweller in the Great Land, the Lady of Ta-Tchesert, the Eye of Ra, the Dweller in his breast, the Beautiful Face in the Boat of Millions of Years, the Seat of Peace of the doer of truth, Dweller in the Boat of the favoured ones....

THE CHAPTER OF THE FOUR LIGHTED LAMPS WHICH ARE MADE FOR THE SPIRIT-SOUL

Behold, thou shalt make four rectangular troughs of clay wherein thou shalt scatter incense, and thou shalt fill them with the milk of a white cow, and by means of these thou shalt extinguish the lamps. The Osiris Nu, the steward of the overseer of the seal, whose word is truth, saith: The fire cometh to thy KA, O Osiris Khenti-Amenti! The fire cometh to thy KA, O Osiris Nu, whose word is truth. The ordering of the night cometh after the day. [The fire cometh to thy KA, O Osiris, Governor of those who are in Amenti], and the two sisters of Ra come likewise. Behold it (the fire) riseth in Abtu, and it cometh; I cause it to come, the Eye of Horus. It is set in order upon thy brow, O Osiris Khenti-Amenti; it is set in thy shrine and riseth on thy brow; it is set on thy brow, O Osiris Nu, it is set on thy brow. The Eye of Horus protecteth thee, O Osiris Khenti-Amenti, and it keepeth thee in safety; it casteth down headlong all thine enemies for thee, and all thine enemies have fallen down headlong before thee. O Osiris Nu, the Eye of Horus protecteth thee, it keepeth thee in safety, and it casteth down headlong all thine enemies. Thine enemies have fallen down headlong before thy KA, O Osiris Khenti-Amenti. The Eye of Ra protecteth thee, it keepeth thee in safety, and it hath cast down headlong all thine enemies. Thine enemies have fallen down headlong before thy KA, O Osiris Nu, whose word is truth. The Eye of Horus protecteth thee, it keepeth thee in safety, it hath cast down headlong for thee all thine enemies, and thine enemies have fallen down headlong before thee. The Eye of Horus cometh. It is sound and well, it sendeth forth light even as doth Ra in the horizon. It covereth the powers of Suti with darkness, it mastereth him, and it bringeth its flame against him by its own command. The Eye of Horus is sound and well, thou eatest the flesh thereof, thy body possesseth it. Thou acclaimest it. The Four Fires enter into thy KA, O Osiris Khenti-Amenti, the Four Fires enter into thy KA, O Osiris Nu, the steward of the overseer of the seal, whose word is truth.

Hail, ye sons of Horus, Kesta, Hapi, Tuamutef, and Qebhsenuf, ye have given your protection to your divine Father Osiris Khenti-Amenti, give ye your protection to the Osiris Nu, whose word is truth. Now therefore inasmuch as ye have destroyed the Opponent of Osiris Khenti-Amenti, who liveth with the gods, having smitten Suti with his right hand and arm when dawn came upon the earth, and Horus hath become master [of Suti], and hath avenged his divine Father himself; and inasmuch as your divine Father hath been made to flourish through the union of the KA of Osiris Khenti-Amenti, which ye effected, and the Eye of Horus hath avenged him, and hath protected him, and hath cast down headlong for him all his enemies, and all his enemies have fallen down before him, even so do ye destroy the Opponent of the Osiris Nu, the steward of the overseer of the seal, whose word is truth. Let him live with the gods, let him smite his enemy, let him destroy him, when light dawneth on the earth. Let Horus be master and avenge the Osiris Nu, and let the Osiris Nu flourish through his union with his KA which ye have effected. O Osiris Nu, the Eye of Horus hath avenged thee. It hath cast down headlong all thine enemies for thee, and all thine enemies have been cast down headlong before thee.

Hail, Osiris Khenti-Amenti, grant thou light and fire to the perfect Heart-soul which is in Hensu. And [O ye Sons of Horus], grant ye power unto the living heart-soul of the Osiris Nu by means of his fire. Let him not be repulsed, and let him not be driven back at the doors of Amentet! Let his offerings of bread and of linen garments be brought unto him among the lords of funeral oblations. O offer ye praises, as unto a god to the Osiris Nu, the destroyer of his Opponent in his form of Truth, and in his attributes of a god of truth.

RUBRIC: [This Chapter] shall be recited over four torches of atma cloth, which hath been anointed with the finest Thehennu unguent, and the torches shall be placed in the hands of four men who shall have the names of the pillars of Horus written upon their shoulders, and they shall burn the torches in the beautiful light of Ra, and this shall confer power and might upon the Spirit-soul of the deceased among the stars which never set. If this Chapter be recited for him he shall never, never perish, and he shall become a living soul for ever. These torches shall make the Spirit-soul to flourish like Osiris Khenti-Amenti, regularly and continually for ever. It is a struggle. Thou shalt not perform this ceremony before any human being except thine own self, or thy father, or thy son, because it is an exceedingly great mystery of the Amentet, and it is a type of the hidden things of the Tuat. When this ceremony hath been performed for the deceased, the gods, and the Spirit-souls, and the dead shall see him in the form of Khenti-Amenti, and he shall have power and dominion like this god.

If thou shalt undertake to perform for the deceased that which is ordered in this "Chapter of the four blazing torches," each day, thou shalt cause the form of the deceased to come forth from every hall [in the Tuat], and from the Seven Halls of Osiris. And he shall live in the form of the God. He shall have power and dominion corresponding to those of the gods and the Spirit-souls for ever and ever. He shall enter in through the secret pylons and shall not be turned back in the presence of Osiris. And it shall come to pass, provided that the following things be done for him, that he shall enter in and come forth. He shall not be turned back. No boundary shall be set to his goings, and the sentence of the doom shall not be passed upon him on the Day of the Weighing of Words before Osiris—never, never.

And thou shalt perform whatsoever [is written in] this book on behalf of the deceased, who shall thereby become perfect and pure. And thou shalt "open his mouth" with the instrument of iron. And thou shalt write down these things in accordance with the instructions which are found in the books of Prince Herutataf, who discovered them in a secret coffer (now they were in the handwriting of the god [Thoth] himself and had been deposited in the Temple of the goddess Unnut, the Lady of Unu) during a journey which he was making in order to inspect the temples, and the temple-estates, and the sanctuaries of the gods. And thou shalt perform these ceremonies secretly in the Tuat-chamber of the tomb, for they are mysteries of the Tuat, and they are symbolic of the

things which are done in Khert-Neter.

And thou shalt say: I have come, I have advanced hastily. I cast light upon his (the deceased's) footsteps. I am hidden, but I cast light upon his hidden place. I stand up close to the Tet. I stand up close to the Tet of Ra, I turn back the slaughter. I am protecting thee, O Osiris.

RUBRIC: This Chapter shall be recited over a Tet of crystal, which shall be set upon a brick made of crude mud, whereupon this Chapter hath been inscribed. Thou shalt make a cavity in the west wall [of the tomb], and having turned the front of the Tet towards the east, thou shalt wall up the cavity with mud which hath been mixed with extract of cedar. This Tet shall drive away the enemies of Osiris who would set themselves at the east wall [of the tomb].

And thou shalt say: I have driven back thy foes. I keep watch over thee. He that is upon his mountain (Anpu) keepeth watch over thee ready for the moment when thy foes shall attack thee, and he shall repulse them for thee. I will drive back the Crocodile at the moment when it attacketh thee, and I will protect thee, O Osiris Nu.

RUBRIC: This Chapter shall be recited over a figure of Anpu made of crude mud mixed with incense. And the figure shall be set upon a brick made of crude mud, whereupon this Chapter hath been inscribed. Thou shalt make a cavity in the east wall, and having turned the face of the figure of Anpu towards the west wall [therein] thou shalt wall up the cavity. This figure shall repulse the enemies of Osiris, who would set themselves at the south wall.

And thou shalt say; I am the belt of sand round about the hidden coffer. I turn back the force of the blazing fire of the funerary mountain. I traverse the roads, and I protect the Osiris Nu, the steward of the overseer of the seal, whose word is truth.

RUBRIC: This Chapter shall be recited over a brick made of crude mud whereon a copy of this Chapter hath been inscribed. And thou shalt place a reed in the middle thereof, and thou shalt smear it with pitch, and set light thereto. Then thou shalt make a cavity in the south wall, and, having turned the front of the brick towards the north, thou shalt wall the brick up inside it. [It shall repulse the enemies of the Osiris Nu] who would assemble at the north wall.

And thou shalt say: O thou who comest to set fire [to the tomb or mummy], I will not let thee do it. O thou who comest to cast fire [herein], I will not let thee do it. I will burn thee, and I will cast fire upon thee. I protect the Osiris Nu, the steward of the overseer of the seal, whose word is truth.

RUBRIC: This Chapter shall be recited over a brick of crude mud, whereon a copy of this Chapter hath been inscribed. [And thou shalt set upon it] a figure of the deceased made of palm wood, seven fingers in height. And thou shalt perform on it the ceremony of "Opening the Mouth." Then thou shalt make a cavity in the north wall, and having [placed the brick and the figure inside it], and turned the face of the figure towards the south, thou shalt wall up the cavity. [It shall repulse the enemies of the Osiris Nu], who would assemble at the south wall.

And behold, these things shall be done by a man who is washed clean, and is ceremonially pure, and who hath eaten neither meat nor fish, and who hath not [recently] had intercourse with women. And behold, thou shalt make offerings of cakes and ale to these gods, and shalt burn incense on their fires. Every Spirit-soul for whom these things shall be done shall become like a holy god in Khert-Neter, and he shall not be turned back at any gate in Amentet, and he shall be in the following of Osiris, whithersoever he goeth, regularly and continually.

THE ODYSSEY

(From *The Odyssey*, Book VI, by Homer, trans. Samuel Butler, 1900.)

In this classic translation of Homer's *Odyssey*, Samuel Butler tends to use the Latin spellings of the Greek heroes. Thus, Odysseus is Ulysses, Poseidon is Neptune, Zeus is Jove (Jupiter), and Athene is Minerva. This is the tender story of the hero's friendship with the young woman Nausikaa (Nausicaa).

So here Ulysses (Odysseus) slept, overcome by sleep and toil; but Minerva (Athene) went off to the country and city of the Phaeacians—a people who used to live in the fair town of Hypereia, near the lawless Cyclopes. Now the Cyclopes were stronger than they and plundered them, so their king Nausithous moved them thence and settled them in Scheria, far from all other people. He surrounded the city with a wall, built houses and temples, and divided the lands among his people; but he was dead and gone to the house of Hades, and King Alcinous, whose counsels were inspired of heaven, was now reigning. To his house, then, did Minerva hie in furtherance of the return of Ulysses.

She went straight to the beautifully decorated bedroom in which there slept a girl who was as lovely as a goddess, Nausicaa, daughter to King Alcinous. Two maid servants were sleeping near her, both very pretty, one on either side of the doorway, which was closed with well-made folding doors. Minerva took the form of the famous sea captain Dymas's daughter, who was a bosom friend of Nausicaa and just her own age; then, coming up to the girl's bedside like a breath of wind, she hovered over her head and said:

"Nausicaa, what can your mother have been about, to have such a lazy daughter? Here are your clothes all lying in disorder, yet you are going to be married almost immediately, and should not only be well dressed yourself, but should find good clothes for those who attend you. This is the way to get yourself a good name, and to make your father and mother proud of you. Suppose, then, that we make tomorrow a washing day, and start at daybreak. I will come and help you so that you may have everything ready as soon as possible, for all the best young men among your own people are courting you, and you are not going to remain a maid much longer. Ask your father, therefore, to have a waggon and mules ready for us at daybreak, to take the rugs, robes, and girdles; and you can ride, too, which will be much pleasanter for you than walking, for the washing-cisterns are some way from the town."

When she had said this Minerva went away to Olympus, which they say is the everlasting home of the gods. Here no wind beats roughly, and neither rain nor snow can fall; but it abides in everlasting sunshine and in a great peacefulness of light, wherein the blessed gods are illumined for ever and ever. This was the place to which the goddess went when she had given instructions to the girl.

By and by morning came and woke Nausicaa, who began wondering about her dream; she therefore went to the other end of the house to tell her father and mother all about it, and found them in their own room. Her mother was sitting by the fireside spinning her purple yarn with her maids around her, and she happened to catch her father just as he was going out to attend a meeting of the town council, which the Phaeacian aldermen had convened. She stopped him and said:

"Papa dear, could you manage to let me have a good big waggon? I want to take all our dirty clothes to the river and wash them. You are the chief man here, so it is only right that you should have a clean shirt when you attend meetings of the council. Moreover, you have five sons at home, two of them married, while the other three are goodlooking bachelors; you know they always like to have clean linen when they go to a dance, and I have been thinking about all this."

She did not say a word about her own wedding, for she did not like to, but her father knew and said, "You shall have the mules, my love, and whatever else you have a mind for. Be off with you, and the men shall get you a good strong waggon with a body to it that will hold all your clothes."

On this he gave his orders to the servants, who got the waggon out, harnessed the mules, and put them to, while the girl brought the clothes down from the linen room and placed them on the waggon. Her mother prepared her a basket of provisions with all sorts of good things, and a goat skin full of wine; the girl now got into the waggon, and her mother gave her also a golden cruse of oil, that she and her women might anoint themselves. Then she took the whip and reins and lashed the mules on, whereon they set off, and their hoofs clattered on the road. They pulled without flagging, and carried not only Nausicaa and her wash of clothes, but the maids also who were with her.

When they reached the water side they went to the washing-cisterns, through which there ran at all times enough pure water to wash any quantity of linen, no matter how dirty. Here they unharnessed the mules and turned them out to feed on the sweet juicy herbage that grew by the water side. They took the clothes out of the waggon, put them in the water, and vied with one another in treading them in the pits to get the dirt out. After they had washed them and got them quite clean, they laid them out by the sea side, where the waves had raised a high beach of shingle, and set about washing themselves and anointing themselves with olive oil. Then they got their dinner by the side of the stream, and waited for the sun to finish drying the clothes. When they had done dinner they threw off the veils that covered their heads and began to play at ball, while

Nausicaa sang for them. As the huntress Diana [Artemis] goes forth upon the mountains of Taygetus or Erymanthus to hunt wild boars or deer, and the wood-nymphs, daughters of Aegis-bearing Jove [Zeus], take their sport along with her (then is Leto proud at seeing her daughter stand a full head taller than the others, and eclipse the loveliest amid a whole bevy of beauties), even so did the girl outshine her handmaids.

When it was time for them to start home, and they were folding the clothes and putting them into the waggon, Minerva began to consider how Ulysses should wake up and see the handsome girl who was to conduct him to the city of the Phaeacians. The girl, therefore, threw a ball at one of the maids, which missed her and fell into deep water. On this they all shouted, and the noise they made woke Ulysses, who sat up in his bed of leaves and began to wonder what it might all be.

"Alas," said he to himself, "what kind of people have I come amongst? Are they cruel, savage, and uncivilized, or hospitable and humane? I seem to hear the voices of young women, and they sound like those of the nymphs that haunt mountain tops, or springs of rivers and meadows of green grass. At any rate I am among a race of men and women. Let me try if I cannot manage to get a look at them."

As he said this he crept from under his bush, and broke off a bough covered with thick leaves to hide his nakedness. He looked like some lion of the wilderness that stalks about exulting in his strength and defying both wind and rain; his eyes glare as he prowls in quest of oxen, sheep, or deer, for he is famished, and will dare break even into a well-fenced homestead, trying to get at the sheep—even such did Ulysses seem to the young women, as he drew near to them all naked as he was, for he was in great want. On seeing one so unkempt and so begrimed with salt water, the others scampered off along the spits that jutted out into the sea, but the daughter of Alcinous stood firm, for Minerva put courage into her heart and took away all fear from her. She stood right in front of Ulysses, and he doubted whether he should go up to her, throw himself at her feet, and embrace her knees as a suppliant, or stay where he was and entreat her to give him some clothes and show him the way to the town. In the end he deemed it best to entreat her from a distance in case the girl should take offence at his coming near enough to clasp her knees, so he addressed her in honeyed and persuasive language.

"O queen," he said, "I implore your aid—but tell me, are you a goddess or are you a mortal woman? If you are a goddess and dwell in heaven, I can only conjecture that you are Jove's daughter Diana, for your face and figure resemble none but hers; if on the other hand you are a mortal and live on earth, thrice happy are your father and mother—thrice happy, too, are your brothers and sisters; how proud and delighted they must feel when they see so fair a scion as yourself going out to a dance; most happy, however, of all will he be whose wedding gifts have been the richest, and who takes you to his own home. I never yet saw any one so beautiful, neither man nor woman, and am lost in admiration as I behold you. I can only compare you to a young palm tree which I saw when I was at Delos growing near the altar of Apollo—for I was there, too, with much people after me, when I was on that journey which has been the source of all my troubles. Never yet did such a young plant shoot out of the ground as that was, and I admired and wondered at it exactly as I now admire and wonder at yourself. I dare not clasp your knees, but I am in great distress; yesterday made the twentieth day that I had been tossing about upon the sea. The winds and waves have taken me all the way from the Ogygian island, and now fate has flung me upon this coast that I may endure still further suffering; for I do not think that I have yet come to the end of it, but rather that heaven has still much evil in store for me.

"And now, O queen, have pity upon me, for you are the first person I have met, and I know no one else in this country. Show me the way to your town, and let me have anything that you may have brought hither to wrap your clothes in. May heaven grant you in all things your heart's desire—husband, house, and a happy, peaceful home; for there is nothing better in this world than that man and wife should be of one mind in a house. It discomfits their enemies, makes the hearts of their friends glad, and they themselves know more about it than any one."

To this Nausicaa answered, "Stranger, you appear to be a sensible, well-disposed person. There is no accounting for luck; Jove gives prosperity to rich and poor just as he chooses, so you must take what he has seen fit to send you, and make the best of it. Now, however, that you have come to this our country, you shall not want for clothes nor for anything else that a foreigner in distress may reasonably look for. I will show you the way to the town, and will tell you the name of our people; we are called Phaeacians, and I am daughter to Alcinous in whom the whole power of the state is vested."

Then she called her maids and said, "Stay where you are, you girls. Can you not see a man without running away from him? Do you take him for a robber or a murderer? Neither he nor any one else can come here to do us Phaeacians any harm, for we are dear to the gods, and live apart on a land's end that juts into the sounding sea, and have nothing to do with any other people. This is only some poor man who has lost his way, and we must be kind to him, for strangers and foreigners in distress are under Jove's protection, and will take what they can get and be thankful; so, girls, give the poor fellow something to eat and drink, and wash him in the stream at some place that is sheltered from the wind."

On this the maids left off running away and began calling one another back. They made Ulysses sit down in the shelter as Nausicaa had told them, and brought him a shirt and cloak. They also brought him the little golden cruse of oil, and told him to go wash in the stream. But Ulysses said, "Young women, please to stand a little on one side that I may wash the brine from my shoulders and anoint myself with oil, for it is long enough since my skin has had a drop of oil upon it. I cannot wash as long as you all keep standing there. I am ashamed to strip before a number of good-looking young women."

Then they stood on one side and went to tell the girl, while Ulysses washed himself in the stream and scrubbed the brine from his back and from his broad shoulders. When he had thoroughly washed himself, and had got the brine out of his hair, he anointed himself with oil, and put on the clothes which the girl had given him; Minerva then made him look taller and stronger than before, she also made the hair grow thick on the top of his head, and flow down in curls like hyacinth blossoms; she glorified him about the head and shoulders as a skilful workman who has studied art of all kinds under Vulcan and Minerva enriches a piece of silver plate by gilding it—and his work is full of beauty. Then he went and sat down a little way off upon the beach, looking quite young and handsome, and the girl gazed on him with admiration; then she said to her maids:

"Hush, my dears, for I want to say something. I believe the gods who live in heaven have sent this man to the Phaeacians. When I first saw him I thought him plain, but now his appearance is like that of the gods who dwell in heaven. I should like my future husband to be just such another as he is, if he would only stay here and not want to go away. However, give him something to eat and drink."

They did as they were told, and set food before Ulysses, who ate and drank ravenously, for it was long since he had had food of any kind. Meanwhile, Nausicaa bethought her of another matter. She got the linen folded and placed in the waggon, she then yoked the mules, and, as she took her seat, she called Ulysses:

"Stranger," said she, "rise and let us be going back to the town; I will introduce you at the house of my excellent father, where I can tell you that you will meet all the best people among the Phaeacians. But be sure and do as I bid you, for you seem to be a sensible person. As long as we are going past the fields—and farm lands, follow briskly behind the waggon along with the maids and I will lead the way myself. Presently, however, we shall come to the town, where you will find a high wall running all round it, and a good harbour on either side with a narrow entrance into the city, and the ships will be drawn up by the road side, for every one has a place where his own ship can lie. You will see the market place with a temple of Neptune [Poseidon] in the middle of it, and paved with large stones bedded in the earth. Here people deal in ship's gear of all kinds, such as cables and sails, and here, too, are the places where oars are made, for the Phaeacians are not a nation of archers; they know nothing about bows and arrows, but are a sea-faring folk, and pride themselves on their masts, oars, and ships, with which they travel far over the sea.

"I am afraid of the gossip and scandal that may be set on foot against me later on; for the people here are very ill-natured, and some low fellow, if he met us, might say, 'Who is this fine-looking stranger that is going about with Nausicaa? Where did she find him? I suppose she is going to marry him. Perhaps he is a vagabond sailor whom she has taken from some foreign vessel, for we have no neighbours; or some god has at last come down from heaven in answer to her prayers, and she is going to live with him all the rest of her life. It would be a good thing if she would take herself off and find a husband somewhere else, for she will not look at one of the many excellent young Phaeacians who are in with her.' This is the kind of disparaging remark that would be made about me, and I could not complain, for I should myself be scandalized at seeing any other girl do the like, and go about with men in spite of everybody, while her father and mother were still alive, and without having been married in the face of all the world.

"If, therefore, you want my father to give you an escort and to help you home, do as I bid you; you will see a beautiful grove of poplars by the road side dedicated to Minerva;

it has a well in it and a meadow all round it. Here my father has a field of rich garden ground, about as far from the town as a man's voice will carry. Sit down there and wait for a while till the rest of us can get into the town and reach my father's house. Then, when you think we must have done this, come into the town and ask the way to the house of my father Alcinous. You will have no difficulty in finding it; any child will point it out to you, for no one else in the whole town has anything like such a fine house as he has. When you have got past the gates and through the outer court, go right across the inner court till you come to my mother. You will find her sitting by the fire and spinning her purple wool by firelight. It is a fine sight to see her as she leans back against one of the bearing-posts with her maids all ranged behind her. Close to her seat stands that of my father, on which he sits and topes like an immortal god. Never mind him, but go up to my mother, and lay your hands upon her knees if you would get home quickly. If you can gain her over, you may hope to see your own country again, no matter how distant it may be."

So saying she lashed the mules with her whip and they left the river. The mules drew well and their hoofs went up and down upon the road. She was careful not to go too fast for Ulysses and the maids who were following on foot along with the waggon, so she plied her whip with judgement. As the sun was going down they came to the sacred grove of Minerva, and there Ulysses sat down and prayed to the mighty daughter of Jove.

"Hear me," he cried, "daughter of Aegis-bearing Jove, unweariable, hear me now, for you gave no heed to my prayers when Neptune was wrecking me. Now, therefore, have pity upon me and grant that I may find friends and be hospitably received by the Phaeacians."

Thus did he pray, and Minerva heard his prayer, but she would not show herself to him openly, for she was afraid of her uncle Neptune, who was still furious in his endeavors to prevent Ulysses from getting home.

METAMORPHOSES

(From Matamorphoses, by Ovid, trans. Sir Samuel Garth, John Dryden, et al., 1717.)

This is a classic translation of one of the most popular of Ovid's tales, the tragic story of Orpheus and Eurydice. Again, Roman versions are used for the names of the mythological characters.

BOOK THE TENTH
The Story of Orpheus and Eurydice

Thence in his saffron robe, for distant Thrace,
Hymen departs, thro' air's unmeasur'd space;
By Orpheus call'd, the nuptial Pow'r attends,

But with ill-omen'd augury descends;
Nor chearful look'd the God, nor prosp'rous spoke,
Nor blaz'd his torch, but wept in hissing smoke.
In vain they whirl it round in vain they shake,
No rapid motion can its flames awake.
With dread these inauspicious signs were view'd,
And soon a more disastrous end ensu'd;
For as the bride, amid the Naiad train,
Ran joyful, sporting o'er the flow'ry plain,
A venom'd viper bit her as she pass'd;
Instant she fell, and sudden breath'd her last.

When long his loss the Thracian had deplor'd,
Not by superior Pow'rs to be restor'd;
Inflam'd by love, and urg'd by deep despair,
He leaves the realms of light, and upper air;
Daring to tread the dark Tenarian road,
And tempt the shades in their obscure abode;
Thro' gliding spectres of th' interr'd to go,
And phantom people of the world below:
Persephone he seeks, and him who reigns
O'er ghosts, and Hell's uncomfortable plains.
Arriv'd, he, tuning to his voice his strings,
Thus to the king and queen of shadows sings.

Ye Pow'rs, who under Earth your realms extend,
To whom all mortals must one day descend;
If here 'tis granted sacred truth to tell:
I come not curious to explore your Hell;
Nor come to boast (by vain ambition fir'd)
How Cerberus at my approach retir'd.
My wife alone I seek; for her lov'd sake
These terrors I support, this journey take.
She, luckless wandring, or by fate mis-led,
Chanc'd on a lurking viper's crest to tread;
The vengeful beast, enflam'd with fury, starts,
And thro' her heel his deathful venom darts.
Thus was she snatch'd untimely to her tomb;
Her growing years cut short, and springing bloom.
Long I my loss endeavour'd to sustain,
And strongly strove, but strove, alas in vain:
At length I yielded, won by mighty love;
Well known is that omnipotence above!

But here, I doubt, his unfelt influence fails;
And yet a hope within my heart prevails.
That here, ev'n here, he has been known of old;
At least if truth be by tradition told;
If fame of former rapes belief may find,
You both by love, and love alone, were join'd.
Now, by the horrors which these realms surround;
By the vast chaos of these depths profound;
By the sad silence which eternal reigns
O'er all the waste of these wide-stretching plains;
Let me again Eurydice receive,
Let Fate her quick-spun thread of life re-weave.
All our possessions are but loans from you,
And soon, or late, you must be paid your due;
Hither we haste to human-kind's last seat,
Your endless empire, and our sure retreat.
She too, when ripen'd years she shall attain,
Must, of avoidless right, be yours again:
I but the transient use of that require,
Which soon, too soon, I must resign entire.
But if the destinies refuse my vow,
And no remission of her doom allow;
Know, I'm determin'd to return no more;
So both retain, or both to life restore.

Thus, while the bard melodiously complains,
And to his lyre accords his vocal strains,
The very bloodless shades attention keep,
And silent, seem compassionate to weep;
Ev'n Tantalus his flood unthirsty views,
Nor flies the stream, nor he the stream pursues;
Ixion's wond'ring wheel its whirl suspends,
And the voracious vulture, charm'd, attends;
No more the Belides their toil bemoan,
And Sisiphus reclin'd, sits list'ning on his stone.

Then first ('tis said) by sacred verse subdu'd,
The Furies felt their cheeks with tears bedew'd:
Nor could the rigid king, or queen of Hell,
Th' impulse of pity in their hearts repell.

Now, from a troop of shades that last arriv'd,
Eurydice was call'd, and stood reviv'd:
Slow she advanc'd, and halting seem to feel

The fatal wound, yet painful in her heel.
Thus he obtains the suit so much desir'd,
On strict observance of the terms requir'd:
For if, before he reach the realms of air,
He backward cast his eyes to view the fair,
The forfeit grant, that instant, void is made,
And she for ever left a lifeless shade.

Now thro' the noiseless throng their way they bend,
And both with pain the rugged road ascend;
Dark was the path, and difficult, and steep,
And thick with vapours from the smoaky deep.
They well-nigh now had pass'd the bounds of night,
And just approach'd the margin of the light,
When he, mistrusting lest her steps might stray,
And gladsome of the glympse of dawning day,
His longing eyes, impatient, backward cast
To catch a lover's look, but look'd his last;
For instant dying, she again descends,
While he to empty air his arms extends.
Again she dy'd, nor yet her lord reprov'd;
What could she say, but that too well he lov'd?
One last farewell she spoke, which scarce he heard;
So soon she drop'd, so sudden disappear'd.

All stunn'd he stood, when thus his wife he view'd
By second Fate, and double death subdu'd:
Not more amazement by that wretch was shown,
Whom Cerberus beholding, turn'd to stone;
Nor Olenus cou'd more astonish'd look,
When on himself Lethaea's fault he took,
His beauteous wife, who too secure had dar'd
Her face to vye with Goddesses compar'd:
Once join'd by love, they stand united still,
Turn'd to contiguous rocks on Ida's hill.

Now to repass the Styx in vain he tries,
Charon averse, his pressing suit denies.
Sev'n days entire, along th' infernal shores,
Disconsolate, the bard Eurydice deplores;
Defil'd with filth his robe, with tears his cheeks,
No sustenance but grief, and cares, he seeks:
Of rigid Fate incessant he complains,
And Hell's inexorable Gods arraigns.

This ended, to high Rhodope he hastes,
And Haemus' mountain, bleak with northern blasts.

And now his yearly race the circling sun
Had thrice compleat thro' wat'ry Pisces run,
Since Orpheus fled the face of womankind,
And all soft union with the sex declin'd.
Whether his ill success this change had bred,
Or binding vows made to his former bed;
Whate'er the cause in vain the nymphs contest,
With rival eyes to warm his frozen breast:
For ev'ry nymph with love his lays inspir'd,
But ev'ry nymph repuls'd, with grief retir'd.

A hill there was, and on that hill a mead,
With verdure thick, but destitute of shade.
Where, now, the Muse's son no sooner sings,
No sooner strikes his sweet resounding strings.
But distant groves the flying sounds receive,
And list'ning trees their rooted stations leave;
Themselves transplanting, all around they grow,
And various shades their various kinds bestow.
Here, tall Chaonian oaks their branches spread,
While weeping poplars there erect their head.
The foodful Esculus here shoots his leaves,
That turf soft lime-tree, this, fat beach receives;
Here, brittle hazels, lawrels here advance,
And there tough ash to form the heroe's lance;
Here silver firs with knotless trunks ascend,
There, scarlet oaks beneath their acorns bend.
That spot admits the hospitable plane,
On this, the maple grows with clouded grain;
Here, watry willows are with Lotus seen;
There, tamarisk, and box for ever green.
With double hue here mirtles grace the ground,
And laurestines, with purple berries crown'd.
With pliant feet, now, ivies this way wind,
Vines yonder rise, and elms with vines entwin'd.
Wild Ornus now, the pitch-tree next takes root,
And Arbutus adorn'd with blushing fruit.
Then easy-bending palms, the victor's prize,
And pines erect with bristly tops arise.
For Rhea grateful still the pine remains,

For Atys still some favour she retains;
He once in human shape her breast had warm'd,
And now is cherish'd, to a tree transform'd.

THE WORDS OF ODIN THE HIGH ONE

(From The Hávamál: *The Words of Odin the High One from the Elder or Poetic Edda* [*Saemund's Edda*], ed. D.L. Ashliman, trans. Olive Bray, 1908. http://www.pitt.edu/~ dash/havamal.html#runes.)

This is the strange story of the Norse god Odin, who hung on the world tree for nine days in search of the meaning of the ancient occult writings, or runes. As Inanna descended to the Underworld to understand its mysteries, Odin dies in a sense, to understand Earth's deepest meanings.

ODIN'S QUEST AFTER THE RUNES

137.

I trow I hung on that windy Tree
nine whole days and nights,
stabbed with a spear, offered to Odin,
myself to mine own self given,
high on that Tree of which none hath heard
from what roots it rises to heaven.

138.

None refreshed me ever with food or drink,
I peered right down in the deep;
crying aloud I lifted the Runes
then back I fell from thence.

139.

Nine mighty songs I learned from the great
son of Bale-thorn, Bestla's sire;
I drank a measure of the wondrous Mead,
with the Soulstirrer's drops I was showered.

140.

Ere long I bare fruit, and throve full well,
I grew and waxed in wisdom;
word following word, I found me words,
deed following deed, I wrought deeds.

141.

Hidden Runes shalt thou seek and interpreted signs,
many symbols of might and power,
by the great Singer painted, by the high Powers fashioned,
graved by the Utterer of gods.

142.

For gods graved Odin, for elves graved Daïn,
Dvalin the Dallier for dwarfs,
All-wise for Jötuns, and I, of myself,
graved some for the sons of men.

143.

Dost know how to write, dost know how to read,
dost know how to paint, dost know how to prove,
dost know how to ask, dost know how to offer,
dost know how to send, dost know how to spend?

144.

Better ask for too little than offer too much,
like the gift should be the boon;
better not to send than to overspend.

……

Thus Odin graved ere the world began;
Then he rose from the deep, and came again.

HAINUWELE

The story of Hainuwele from Ceram in Indonesia is one of many in the world myth in which the hero becomes a scapegoat—a sacrificial victim—for the good of all. (Source: Leeming, *Oxford Companion to World Mythology,* 167–168.)

Among the first nine families of the West Ceram people, who originally emerged from bananas in the Molucca Islands in what is now Indonesia, there was a hunter called Ameta, whose dog one night was attracted by the scent of a wild pig. The pig escaped into a pond but drowned. Ameta dragged it out of the pond and was surprised to find a coconut impaled on its tusk. Ameta was sure this coconut must be a great treasure because there were as yet no coconut palms on earth. He wrapped the coconut like a baby in a cloth, decorated it with a snake figure, and took it home. He planted it according to instructions received in a dream, and in three days a coconut palm tree had grown to full height. In three more days it blossomed, and Ameta climbed it to retrieve some of the fruit. He cut his finger while collecting the fruit, and a baby girl emerged from the mixture of blood and sap. The dream messenger instructed Ameta to wrap the girl in the snake-decorated cloth and to bring her home. This he did, and he was amazed when in a very few days, the girl, whom he named Hainuwele ("Coconut Branch"), was fully grown and defecating valuable things like bells and dishes.

Soon it was time for the first nine families to perform what is called the Maro dance at a place called the Nine Dance Grounds. As always, the women sat in the center of the grounds handing out betel nut to the men, who danced around them in a spiral. Hainuwele sat in the very center. On the first night she, too, handed out betel, but on the second night she gave the dancers coral, on the third fine pottery, and on each successive night something still more valuable.

The people became jealous of Hainuwele's wealth and decided to kill her. Before the ninth night's dance, they prepared a deep hole at the center of the ceremonial grounds, and during the dance they edged Hainuwele into the hole and covered her with earth.

Ameta soon missed his "daughter," and discovered through his magical skills that she had been murdered during the Maro dance. He immediately took nine pieces of palm leaf to the dance grounds and stuck them into the earth, the ninth one at the very center of the grounds. When he pulled out that piece of palm he found bits of Hainuwele's flesh and hair attached to it. He dug up the body, dismembered it, and buried the pieces, all but the arms in various places in the dance grounds. Within minutes there grew the plants that are to this day the staples of the Ceramese diet.

Then the goddess Mulua Satene, angry at the murder of Hainuwele, an aspect of herself, struck several of the first people with an arm of the dead maiden, and these people become the first animals.

ANANSE STEALS STORY-TELLING

This is the tale of how the African trickster Ananse (Anansi) steals the art of story-telling from the High God. (Source: E2BN online—Ananse Texts.)

Anansi stretched his eight legs as he sat in the middle of his web, watching the people around their fires in the evening. They were restless and the children were bored. "How can I help them?" Anansi said to himself—he rather liked people, being one himself sometimes. "I know, stories! They need stories to tell and to listen to... mmm" he thought.

He knew that all the stories were kept in a beautiful wooden box by Nyame, the Sky God. He also knew that Nyame kept the box close to him at all times. For this, he would not be able to use trickery and sneak it away from the Sky God.

As the great sun rose in the morning sky, Anansi spun a beautiful silken thread, long enough to reach all the way to the clouds and he scampered up to heaven to talk to Nyame.

He knew he must be polite and on his best behaviour. He bowed low. "Oh Nyame, great and wise god of the Sky, I wish to have your box of stories to take back to the people. What is your price?"

Nyame's laughter thundered out, shaking the clouds around. "Ho, ho, ho, little Anansi. My price is much too high for someone like you. Great princes and rich villages have tried to buy my box, but none has been able to pay the price."

"I will pay," said Anansi stoutly, "I will give you your price. Name it."

"Very well little one. My price is Onini, the python who can swallow a goat; Osebo, the leopard with teeth as sharp as spears; Mmoboro, the hornet whose sting is like red hot needles and Mmoatia, the bad-tempered fairy that no-one can see. Bring to me all of these and my box with all the stories shall be yours."

"I … I … w … will bring them," stuttered Anansi as he backed away to the sound, once again, of Nyame's thunderous laughter.

Swinging down his silken thread, Anansi knew he could be in trouble—any one of these dangerous creatures could end his life, like the lives of those who had tried before. He shared the problem with his wife Aso, and together they devised a plan to tackle first Onini, the python who can swallow a goat.

The next morning, Anansi marched into the forest waving a big palm stick and muttering, "She's wrong, I know she is. He is much bigger and longer than this stick. Why does she not give him the respect he deserves? I know I am right and she is wrong. But will she listen? No."

As he approached the water hole, the sleek head of Onini, the python, appeared over a branch in front of him. "What are you muttering about in this way, Anansi? You have disturbed my rest." he hissed, irritably.

"Oh great Onini, it is my wife. She declares that you are shorter than this palm stick … I say that you are certainly longer, but will she listen? I don't know how to prove that I am right."

"It is easy, you foolish spider," jeered the python as he slithered off the branch. "Lay your stick on the ground and I will lie beside it. We shall soon see who is right."

And so it happened, but the python had difficulty keeping his coils stretched out straight and did not seem to measure the full length.

"Let me use my silk to keep you fastened to the stick, as I am sure that we can then prove how very wrong my wife is, and how great in length and strength you are, oh Onini," suggested Anansi.

And so it happened, and when Onini was fully bound,

"You foolish python," jeered the spider, "now you shall come with me to Nyame."

So saying, he hauled him up his silken thread to the clouds and presented him to the Sky God who merely said. "I see what I see. There remains what remains."

Anansi swung down his silken thread and once more consulted with his wife, and together they thought hard and devised a plan to ensnare Osebo, the leopard with teeth as sharp as spears.

Anansi searched in the forest until he came across the route that the leopard took every night to the water hole. He then looked around for a suitable place and dug a deep hole, too deep even for a leopard to escape from. It was exhausting work but little Anansi was very determined.

When he was satisfied, he carefully laid sticks across the hole and covered them with leaves and covered them with dusty earth.

By the time evening came, the hole was invisible and a tired Anansi went home to his supper and his bed, where he slept like a log.

As the great sun rose in the morning sky, Anansi went for a walk in the forest and heard screeching and scrabbling. Hurrying forward, he came to the pit and there saw an angry Osebo, desperately trying to claw his way up out of the hole.

He looked in and said, "Good morning Osebo, why are you in this hole?"

"You foolish spider" snarled Osebo, "cannot you see I have fallen into a trap? You must help me to get out."

"Oh dear no, I cannot do that," and Anansi started to back away adding, "You would eat me and my wife and children if I helped you out."

"Come back, come back," purred Osebo, " I promise little one, I will do no such thing if only you will help me."

"For that promise, I will indeed help you to get out," said Anansi and went to the nearby willowy tree he had spotted yesterday. He pulled its top to reach down over the hole, tied it in place with his silk, and then spun another long, strong and sticky thread to reach down into the pit.

"Wind this thread well around your tail," he called down to Osebo. When it was fastened, Anansi cut the silk holding the tree top down. It whooshed up into the air, taking the leopard with it by his tail.

As Osebo spun round and round the top of the tree, the rest of Anansi's strong, sticky thread wound round and round his body. When he was completely trussed, Anansi went up and snipped the thread from the tree and Osebo landed with a bump on the ground.

"You foolish leopard," chuckled the spider, "now you shall come with me to Nyame."

So saying, he hauled him up his silken thread to the clouds and presented him to the Sky God who merely said. "I see what I see. There remains what remains."

Anansi swung down his silken thread and once more consulted with his wife, and together they thought and discussed and devised a plan to trap Mmoboro, the hornet whose sting is like red hot needles.

They hollowed out a large calabash and filled it with water. Anansi cut down a large plantain leaf and took it and the filled gourd to a tree in which there was a hornets' nest.

He poured half the water over his head so that he was dripping and then threw the rest of the water over the hornets' nest, so that it too was dripping. Anansi then held the plantain leaf over his head as though sheltering from rain as the angry Mmboro started to swarm out towards him.

"Oh dear, oh dear," wailed Anansi, "the rains have come early. You poor creatures you have no shelter. Come, take cover in my calabash until the storm is over."

"Thank you, thank you, Anansi," buzzed the Mmboro as they flew into the gourd. When the last one had entered, Anansi clapped the plantain leaf over the hole and wound his silk around it to hold it in place.

"You foolish Mmboro," crowed the spider, "now you shall come with me to Nyame."

So saying, he hauled the calabash up his silken thread to the clouds and presented it, filled with the angry buzzing hornets, to the Sky God who merely said. "I see what I see. There remains what remains."

Anansi swung down his silken thread and once more consulted with his wife, and together they thought and discussed and argued, until at last they devised a plan to capture Mmoatia, the bad tempered fairy whom no one can see.

Anansi carved a doll from the wood of the gum tree. He then plastered it with sticky gum.

Meanwhile, his wife Aso, pounded yams into a paste with eggs and oil to make ano, which fairies love.

They knew the places the fairies like to play and dance, although they could not see them; so in the middle of the hot day when all creatures are at rest, Anansi crept very quietly to the lovely clearing and sat the doll on the grass with the dish of yams beside it.

He spun a fine thread from the doll's head to his hiding place in the trees. Then he waited.

As evening drew on, he heard a little voice saying, "Hello, little gum baby, may I have some of your ano?"

Anansi pulled the silken thread and the doll's head nodded. "Oooh lovely," squeaked the voice and Anansi watched as the dish appeared to float up into the air and the yam started to disappear. Soon it was all gone, the dish dropped to the ground and the voice said, "Thank you."

Anansi remained still and then the voice spoke again more loudly, "Thank you". And then again angrily "I said THANK YOU. Answer me or I shall have to slap you on your crying place."

Almost immediately, the doll's head wobbled and the voice squeaked, "Let me go, or I shall slap you on the other side." Soon the doll's head wobbled again and then rocked from side to side.

"Aaaah, let me go or I shall kick you," screamed the fairy voice.

Thump, thump came the sound of feet landing on the sticky gum doll and it began to roll and bounce and toss around the clearing as the fairy's voice shrieked ever more loudly.

Anansi leapt from his hiding place and in no time had his sticky thread wound round and round the doll and its captive fairy.

"You foolish Mmoatia," whooped the spider, "now you shall come with me to Nyame."

So saying, he hauled the gum doll up the silken thread, with the invisible angry fairy still screaming threats, to the Sky God who stood and said. " You have paid my price. Great princes and rich villages tried and failed, but you, Anansi, have succeeded."

He called out loudly, "Listen to me, all you who can hear. Praise Kwaku Anansi for he has paid the price for the Sky God stories and they shall be given to him. Henceforth they shall be known as "spider stories".

So saying, he bent down and lifted the beautiful wooden box and gave it to Anansi who had paid the price so that the people would have stories to tell for ever.

CHARACTERS IN MYTHOLOGY

Abraham (Abram, Ibrahim)—the biblical patriarch, sacred to Jews, Christians, and Muslims, whose sons Ishmael (Ismail) and Isaac were instrumental in the origins of monotheistic religions. God sent Abraham to Canaan, the "Promised Land."

Achilles—the most feared Greek hero in Homer's *Iliad* whose argument with King Agamemnon caused problems for the Greeks in the Trojan War.

Acrisius—the King of Argos in Greece, the father of Danaë, and the grandfather of Perseus.

Actaeon—the unfortunate young man who happened upon the goddess Artemis (Diana) bathing and was punished when the goddess turned him into a stag and had his own hounds tear him to pieces.

Adam and Eve—the biblical first humans, created by Yahweh in the Garden of Eden. Urged on by Satan disguised as a serpent, they committed the first sin by eating the fruit of the Forbidden Tree.

Adonis—the product of the incestuous relationship between Myrrha and her father, Cinyras. According to Ovid in his *Metamorphoses,* his mother was turned into a tree, from which he was born. Adonis became the lover of Venus, but was killed by a wild boar and became the center of a dying-and-rising god cult in Phoenecia.

Aeëtes—the king of Colchis, where Jason travelled to obtain the Golden Fleece.

Aegeus—the father or surrogate father of the Greek hero Theseus.

Aeneas—the hero of Virgil's Roman epic, *The Aeneid*. Born a Trojan, he left Troy after its fall and began the process by which the "New Troy," Rome, would be founded.

Aeolus—a Greek wind god. In Homer's *Odyssey*, he gave Odysseus a bag of winds meant to help the hero sail home.

Aesir—the pantheon of Norse mythology, headed by Odin. Originally the Aesir fought against an older pantheon, the Vanir, but eventually the two pantheons joined to become an enlarged Aesir.

Aeson—the father of Jason, the hero of the *Argonauts*, the epic about the search for the Golden Fleece.

Aethra—the mother of the Greek hero Theseus either by the god Poseidon or the human Aegus.

Agamemnon—the King of Mycenae, the leader of the Greeks against the Trojans in the Trojan War. He was murdered by his wife upon his return home from the war.

Agave—the mother of King Pentheus in Euripides' play, the *Bacchae*. It was she who, under the influence of a Bacchanal frenzy, tore her own son to pieces as a sacrifice to the god Dionysos.

Agdistis—the would-be lover and ultimate enemy of the Phrygian man-god Attis.

Agni—the Vedic god of fire in India.

Ahura Mazda—the supreme being of the ancient Persian (Iranian) religion, Mazdaism, and of its successor, Zoroastrianism.

Ahuras—the gods of ancient pre-Islamic Persia (Iran).

Aighistos—the relative of Agamemnon whom Agamemnon left in charge of Mycenae when he was away fighting the Trojan War. Aighistos became the lover of the king's wife, Clytemnestra, and assisted her in the returning king's murder.

Ajax—one of the major Greek heroes in the Trojan War.

Alcestis—In Euripides' play, the *Alcestis,* Alcestis was the brave young wife who offered to go to the Underworld to save her husband from that fate.

Alcinous—the father of Nausikaa and the king of Phaiakia. He helped Odysseus return home to Ithaka.

Alkmene—the mother of the Greek hero Herakles by Zeus.

Allah—the Arabic/Islamic name for God.

Allat—a pre-Islamic Arabic goddess.

Amairgen—the poet-prophet who played a significant role in the founding of Ireland.

Amaterasu—the great sun goddess and primary deity of Japan, the ancestor of the ruling family.

Amida Buddha—the great Buddha of the Pure Land form of Buddhism in Japan.

Amma—the creator god of the Dogon people in Africa.

Amphitryon—the husband of Alkmene, the mother of Herakles by Zeus. Zeus had disguised himself as Amphitryon in order to sleep with Alkmene.

Amun—the chief god and creator in the Egyptian center of Karnak. He was sometimes associated with the sun god as Amun Ra.

An and Ki—the Sky Father and Earth Mother of ancient Sumer who formed the universe, Anki.

Ananse (Anansi)—the trickster, the Spider, of the mythology of West Africa.

Anat—the sister and/or consort of the god Baal in Canaanite mythology.

Anchises—the father of Aeneas, the hero of Virgil's Roman epic, *The Aeneid*.

Andromache—the wife of Hector, the Trojan hero of Homer's *Iliad*.

Andromeda—became the wife of the Greek hero Perseus after he killed Medusa. She had been tied to a rock as a sacrifice to a sea monster.

Angra Mainyu—the negative power in opposition to the positive Ahura Mazda in Mazdaism and Zoroastrianism in ancient Persia (Iran).

Anki—see An and Ki

Antigone—a daughter of King Oedipus of Thebes and the heroine of Sophocles' play, *Antigone,* who got into trouble with King Creon when she disobeyed his orders not to bury her condemned brother.

Antiope—an Amazon whom the Greek hero Theseus married. She produced Hippolytus.

Anu—the Babylonian version of the old Sumerian sky god, An.

Anubis—the jackal-headed primary funerary god of ancient Egypt. He assisted in judging the dead in the Underworld.

Anunnaki—the name for the pantheon of ancient Sumer.

Ao and Po—the Sky Father and Earth Mother of Polynesian Hawaii.

Aonghus—the Irish trickster-like god and son of the "All Father," the Dagda of the Tuatha de Danann.

Aphrodite—the Greek goddess of love, married to Hephaistos. She was born of the foam in the sea resulting from the castration of the first Sky God, Uranos.

Apollo (Pajawone)—one of the greatest of the Greek Olympian and Roman gods, associated with prophecy, light, reason, and the sun.

Apophis—the serpent god representative of chaos in ancient Egypt, who struggles against the divine order represented by the Supreme Being.

Apsu—the Babylonian version of the Sumerian Abzu. He represented the fresh waters which mated with Tiamat, the salt waters, to form the first deities.

Aranrhod—the dawn goddess of Welsh mythology, the mother of Dylan and Lleu, by an incestuous relationship with her brother, Gwydion.

Ares (Are, Enuwarijo)—the Greek god of War.

Argonauts—the crew of the Argo, the ship used by the Greek hero Jason on his quest for the Golden Fleece, the quest described in the epic *The Argonauts*.

Ariadne—the daughter of King Minos of Crete. She helped Theseus defeat the Minotaur and left the island with him only to be abandoned on the island of Naxos. The god Dionysos took pity on her there and married her.

Arjuna—one of the Pandava brothers who fought against the Kauravas in the Indian epic, the *Mahabharata*. It is he who has the central discussion with Krishna in the *Bhagavadgita*. His father was the god Indra.

Artemis (Atemito)—the Greek goddess associated with the hunt, virginity, and sometimes the moon. Her brother was Apollo, her mother, Leto, her father, Zeus. In Anatolia she was a fertility goddess with many breasts.

Arthur, King—the legendary Celtic king whose court was at Camelot and who presided over a group of questing, chivalrous followers known as the Knights of the Round Table.

Asase Ya and Wulbari—Mother Earth and Sky God for the Krachi people of Africa.

Ascanius (Iulius)—the son of Aeneas in Virgil's Roman epic, *The Aeneid*

Ashtart (Astarte)—a Canaanite fertility goddess, perhaps a mythological predecessor of Aphrodite.

Asvin Twins—twins among the gods of Vedic India.

Ask and Embla—the first humans, made by the Norse gods out of an ash tree and an elm tree.

Astyanax—the son of the Trojans Hector and Andromache.

Asuras—the demons in Indian Vedic mythology. They were opposed by the gods known as the *devas*.

Aten—the solar deity proclaimed by the Egyptian pharaoh Akhenaten to be the major, if not the only, deity.

Athene (Atana Potinija)—one of the greatest Greek deities. Often called Pallas Athene, she was the patron deity of Athens and the goddess of wisdom. She was born of Zeus's head, and the Parthenon in Athens was built in her honor.

Athirat (Asherah)—one of several Canannite fertility goddesses.

Atlas—the Titan condemned by Zeus to hold up the world.

Atreus—the king who gave his name to the House of Atreus, the family dynasty of Mycenae in Greece. The House of Atreus was a family cursed by horrific crimes of the past, which would be repeated in the present and future. Agamemnon, the son of Atreus, murdered by his wife, was a king of the House of Atreus during the time of Homer's *Iliad*.

Attis—a Phrygian man-god associated with death and rebirth. His rites were popular in Rome along with those of the Great Goddess Cybele.

Atum—a version of the Egyptian creator god. He created by way of his own bodily fluids and was sometimes associated with the sun god Ra as Atum-Ra.

Audumla—the great cow of Norse mythology from whom flowed the four rivers of milk drunk by the giant Ymir at creation.

Aunt Nancy—a form the African trickster Ananse took among the African slaves in America.

Avalokitesvara—the greatest of the Bodhisattvas, who becomes in effect, a god in Tibetan Buddhism. Tibetans say he was their progenitor and that he is reincarnated in the Dalai Lama.

Baal—the most important of the Canaanite gods: a storm god, a god of fertility, and a dying and resurrected god.

Bacabs—the Mayan gods who hold up the world.

Bacchus—a Roman version of the Greek Dionysos. He was associated with drink and eroticism.

Balar—the one-eyed Fomorian giant—the Fomorian Goliath—who fought against the Irish Tuatha de Danann and was killed by the slingshot of Lugh—the Tuatha David.

Baldr—the dying god of the Norse Aesir. He would return to rule after the end of the world events of Ragnarök.

Banba—one of the triune queens of Ireland met by the Milesians on their way to a truce meeting at Tara.

Belenus—a solar god of the Continental Celts.

Belisama—a Continental Celtic Great Goddess figure, associated by the Romans with Minerva.

Bergelmir and wife—the "Noah and wife" of the Norse flood myth.

Bhima—one of the Pandava brothers who fought against the Kauravas in the Indian epic, the *Mahabharata*. He is the son of the wind god, Vayu.

Blodeuwedd—a *femme fatale* in Welsh mythology. She plots to kill her husband, Lleu.

Brahma—one of the ancient Indian triad that also included Shiva and Vishnu. Brahma is the creator.

Brahman (Atman)—the ultimate deity of Vedantic Hinduism of which all other deities are only an aspect. Brahman is neither male nor female. Brahman is everywhere and nowhere, the essence of existence. Discovered internally by the individual, Brahman is Atman.

Bran—the King of Britain in Welsh mythology—a giant and the brother of Branwen. Although decapitated, his head continued to talk.

Branwen—the sister of Bran in Welsh mythology. She was a goddess of love and was mistreated when she married the King of Ireland.

Brigid—the daughter of the Dagda in Irish mythology. Later she would be assimilated into Christianity as a virgin and a saint.

Brynhild—a shield maiden in the Norse story of Sigurd.

Buddha (Siddhartha Gautama, Shakyamuni)—the great Buddha who found enlightenment under the Bodhi Tree.

Bull of Heaven—the natural companion in many Middle Eastern mythologies of the fertility goddess. A symbol of male power, he was sometimes opposed by heroes such as Gilgamesh.

Bumba—the Supreme Being of the central African Boshongo.

Buraq—the winged horse on which Muhammad took his Night Journey from Mecca to Jerusalem.

Buri, Bor, and Bestla—emerged from the ice licked by the cow Audumla at the beginning of creation in Norse mythology. Buri's son Bor and his mate, the frost giantess Bestla, gave birth to the gods Odin, Vili, and Vé.

Cadmus—the son of the Greek god Ares and the founder of the city of Thebes.

Calypso—the nymph/witch in Homer's *Odyssey*, who kept Odysseus on her island for a time as a lover, even as he longed to return home to his wife.

Cassandra—a prophetess, a daughter of King Priam and Queen Hecuba of Troy. She was also the captive and mistress of King Agamemnon and suffered death with him when he returned to Mycenae after the Trojan War.

Cassiopeia—the mother of the Greek hero Perseus's wife, Andromeda.

Castor and Polydeuces (Pollux)—the Greek and Roman versions of the Indo-European twins motif. Known in Greece as the Dioscuri (sons of God), because they were fathered by Zeus (visiting Leda as a swan), they accompanied the Greek hero Jason on his quest for the Golden Fleece.

Cepheus—the father of Andromeda, the wife of the Greek hero Perseus.

Cerberus—the three-headed dog that guarded the entrance to the Greek Underworld, Hades.

Ceres—the Roman Earth Goddess, roughly equivalent to the Greek Demeter.

Ceridwen—the magician who in Welsh mythology, was said to have magically conceived the poet prophet Taliesen.

Cesair—said in some versions of Irish mythology to be the granddaughter of Noah and, with her father, to have "discovered" Ireland.

Chagan-Shukuty—a Central Asian version of the Buddha (Shakyamuni), said to have assisted the creator god in his work.

Chalchihuitlicue—the Aztec goddess of the east and water to whom the fourth sun world of creation belonged.

Changing Woman—an important Navajo goddess, associated particularly with the female puberty ceremony, the kinaalda.

Chimalman—the virgin mother of the great Mesoamerican hero and god, Quetzalcoatl.

Chirakan-Ixmucane—a Mayan goddess who was a member of a group of gods who tried to make humans out of wood.

Chiron—a centaur renowned for his wisdom and learning in Greek mythology. He "home-schooled" the hero Jason.

Chiyou—the son of the Chinese god of war. He led a rebellion in Heaven.

Chrysaor—the warrior who sprang from Medusa's decapitated head after she was killed by the Greek hero Perseus. Chrysaor's father was in all likelihood Poseidon, who had raped Medusa.

Chryseis—the war-prize mistress of King Agamemnon. He was forced to return her to her father.

Chrysippos—the beautiful son of King Pelops in Greek mythology. He was raped by Laius, his tutor and future king of Thebes.

Cinyras—the beautiful son of Pygmalion and his humanized statue. He eventually had a daughter, Myrrha, who tricked him into an incestuous relationship and was later, according to Ovid's *Metamorphoses,* turned into a tree to evade her father's horrified wrath. She gave birth, as a tree, to Adonis.

Circe—the nymph-witch who in Homer's *Odyssey,* turned men into pigs. Odysseus, however, tamed her with the help of the gods, and he became her lover for a while.

Clytemnestra—the wife of and murderer of King Agamemnon of Mycenae. She was a daughter of Zeus by way of his liaison as a swan with Leda.

Coatlicue—the Aztec Great Goddess of fertility, life, and death and the mother of the god Huitzilopochtli.

Conchobar—the King of Ulster in Irish mythology.

Conla—the son of the Irish hero Cuchulainn. His father kills him without realizing who he is.

Cormac Mac Art—the Irish high king saved by Fionn.

Corn Mother (Corn Grandmother)—a goddess of fertility who takes many forms, usually as a scapegoat to be killed and "planted," in Native North American mythology.

Coyote—a ubiquitous trickster in Native North American mythology.

Creon (Theban)—succeeded Oedipus as king of the Greek city of Thebes after Oedipus's disgrace. He entered into a struggle with Oedipus's daughter Antigone, described in *Antigone,* by Sophocles.

Creusa—the wife of the Trojan Aeneas. She died before the couple could escape the burning Troy at the end of the Trojan War.

Cuchulainn—the primary hero of Irish mythology. He is especially important as a brave warrior in the epic, *The Tain.*

Cupid—a Roman boy-god, usually seen as Venus's son and always associated with the pangs of love caused by wounds from his arrows. He is roughly equivalent to the Greek Eros.

Cybele—the Great Mother goddess of ancient Phrygia. Her myth is associated with that of the man-god Attis.

Cyclops Polyphemos—the monstrous one-eyed son of Poseidon, tricked and blinded by Odysseus in Homer's *Odyssey.*

Daedalus—the master craftsman who in Crete created the Labyrinth for the Minotaur. He also designed the wings by which he and his son Icarus could escape from the island.

Daevas—demons working against Ahura Mazda in the religion of pre-Islamic Iran.

Dagan—a name for the Canaanite high god.

Dagda (the Dagda)—the supreme druid, the "All Father" and "good god" of the Tuatha de Danann in Irish mythology.

Danaans—people of the ancient Greek city of Argos, originally founded by Danaus. Homer sometimes uses the word to refer to the Greeks in general.

Danaë—the daughter of King Acrisius of Argos and the mother of the Greek hero Perseus, by Zeus in a shower of gold.

Danaus—the founder of Argos. The Danaans take their name from him.

Danu (Ana)—the ancient Mother Earth Goddess of Ireland. Thus, the Tuatha de Danann.

Dechtire—the mother of the Irish hero Cuchulainn by the god Lugh in his form as a fly.

Delilah—the *femme fatale* who brought about the downfall of the Hebrew hero Samson.

Demeter (Da-mater)—the Earth Goddess—literally "the Mother"—of ancient Greece, the sister of Zeus, the mother of Persephone.

Demodokos—the blind minstrel storyteller who perhaps serves as a self-portrait of Homer in the episode of *The Odyssey* that takes place in Phaiakia.

Deucalion and Pyyrha—the couple that survived the great flood described in Ovid's *Metamorphoses.* Deucalion was a son of Prometheus.

Devaki—the mother of Krishna, the Indian hero and avatar of Vishnu.

Devas—the good forces, the gods who prevailed over the less-good Asuras in the Vedic heaven of Indian mythology.

Devi—a collective name for the Great Goddess of India. In effect, she has replaced Brahma as the third member of the Hindu triad, along with Shiva and Vishnu.

Di Jun—one of the supreme deities of ancient China.

Di Ku (Gaoxin)—one of the supreme deities of ancient China.

Dian Cecht—the Tuatha de Danann healer in Irish mythology.

Diana—Roman goddess of the hunt, who is roughly equivalent to the Greek Artemis.

Dictys—the fisherman who took in Danaë and her son Perseus when they arrived in their chest on the island of Seriphos.

Dido—the queen of Carthage, who fell in love with the Trojan hero Aeneas when he spent time in Carthage on his way to find Rome, the "New Troy."

Dionysos (Dionysus)—one of the Greek gods. He was associated with wine and with religious ecstasy and drama.

Dioscuri—means "sons of God." Another name for Castor and Polydeuces because they were the children of Leda and Zeus.

Dis Pater—the Underworld god of the Continental Celts.

Djanggawuls—figures involved in the creation during the Dreamtime of the Australian aboriginal people.

Don—the Great Mother of Welsh mythology, the equivalent of the Irish Danu (Anu). Thus, the Welsh pantheon is the "Family of Don."

Donn—a name for the god of death in Irish mythology.

Donn Cuailnge—the famous stolen bull at the center of the war described in the Irish epic, *The Tain.*

Draupadi—the wife of all five Pandava brothers in the Indian epic, the *Mahabharata.* She can be seen as an incarnation, or avatar, of the goddess Lakshmi, the wife of Vishnu.

Dumuzi (Tammuz)—the shepherd husband of the great Sumerian/Babylonian goddess Inanna (Ishtar).

Durga—a violent aspect of the Indian goddess Devi. It was she who defeated the demon Mahisha, who threatened the universe itself.

Duryodhana—the leader of the Pandava enemies, the Kauravas in the great struggle described in the Indian epic *The Mahabharata.*

Dyaus (Dyaus Pitar)—the "father god" of the Sky, who mated with Prithvi (Earth) to begin creation in the Indian Vedas. "Dyaus" is the root for Zeus and "deus" (God).

Dylan—the sea god in ancient Wales, the child of Aranrhod.

Ea—the Babylonian god of wisdom and the waters, the equivalent of the Sumerian Enki.

Earth-Initiate—the creator, along with Turtle, of the Maida Indians of California.

Echo—the nymph who longed for Narcissus in the myth retold by Ovid in the *Metamorphoses.*

Ector, Sir—the guardian of King Arthur during his childhood.

Efnisien—a bringer of strife in Welsh mythology—especially in connection with Bran and Branwen.

Einstein's Twins—the characters in Einstein's thought experiment about space time.

El (Elib)—the head god and creator of the Canaanite pantheon as listed in Ugarit.

Elektra—the sister of Orestes, and the driving force behind the revenge killing of her mother, Clytemnestra, who had murdered her father, King Agamemnon.

Ellil—the Baylonian storm god, the equivalent of the Sumerian Enlil.

Elohim—or Yahweh, a name for the Hebrew God.

Emer—the wife of Cuchulainn in Irish mythology.

Enki—a god of wisdom and the waters in Sumerian mythology. He was also sometimes a trickster.

Enkidu—the close friend of Gilgamesh in the Sumerian/Babylonian epic of Gilgamesh. Together the two heroes killed the demon Hawawa (Humbaba).

Enlil—the Sumerian national god, a storm deity.

Enmerkar—a semi-divine Sumerian legendary king who was said to have invented writing.

Ennead—the name for the nine great gods of the Egyptian city of Heliopolis, including: Atum (Atum-Re), Shu and Tefnut, Geb and Nut, Osiris and Isis, and Seth and Nephtys.

Epimetheus ("Afterthought")—the brother of the Titan Prometheus ("Forethought") in Greek mythology. Prometheus warned his hasty brother not to accept gifts from the Olympians, but Epimetheus accepted the first woman, Pandora, from them. She arrived to be his wife with a box, which she opened, releasing all the evils of the world.

Epona—a Celtic horse goddess.

Ereshkigal—the sister of Inanna (Ishtar) in Sumer and Babylonian mythology. She was goddess of the Underworld, where Inanna paid her a notable visit.

Eriu—one of the triune eponymous goddesses of Ireland, as her name indicates clearly.

Erleg Khan—one of many Central Asian trickster-devils, or evil brothers, who undermined the creator's work.

Erlik—essentially the same as Erleg in Central Asia.

Eros—the Greek god of love, usually thought of as the son of Aphrodite.

Eschetewuarha—a South American creator goddess in what is today Paraguay.

Eseg Malan—a good god for the Buryats of Central Asia. He lives in the west.

Eteocles—a son of Oedipus who waged war against his brother Polynices.

Etna—a Mesopotamian hero, the King of Kish.

Eumaeos—Odysseus's loyal swineherd in Homer's *Odyssey*. He helped Odysseus defeat the suitors who wanted Penelope.

Europa—the young woman who became the mother of King Minos when the Greek god Zeus took the form of a bull and abducted her.

Eurycleia—Odysseus's loyal nurse in Homer's *Odyssey*.

Eurydice—the musician Orpheus's unfortunate wife, who was almost, but not quite, released from the Greek hell, Hades.

Eurynome—the mother of the Three Graces in Greek mythology.

Eurytheus—the king of Tiryns for whom Herakles performed his twelve labors.

Evander—the Etruscan hero who came to Aeneas's aid in his war with Turnus near the end of Virgil's Roman epic, *The Aeneid.*

Family of Don—the Welsh pantheon.

Fafnir—the human form of the dragon killed by Sigurd in Norse mythology.

Fates—the Greek Moirai, the three spinning crones who spun out and cut life.

Fenrir—the giant wolf, the son of Loki in Norse mythology; he would swallow Odin at the end of time.

Fergus mac Roich—the great Ulster warrior, foster father of Cuchulainn, and lover of Queen Medb in the Irish *Tain*.

Fintan—the husband of Cesair in Irish mythology; he turned himself into a salmon to avoid death from the flood.

Fionn mac Cumhail (Demna)—the hero of the medieval Fenian cycle of Irish mythology.

Firbolg—the fourth wave of "invaders" in the myth of early Ireland. Eventually they were overcome by the Tuatha de Danann.

First Man and First Woman—the first people in Navajo mythology. They, of course, exist in the mythologies of many cultures.

Five August Emperors—the legendary first five emperors of China: Huang Di, Zhuanxu, Di Ku, Yao, Shun.

Fomorians—the one-legged, one-armed violent race that opposed the Tuatha de Danann in Irish mythology.

Fotla—one of the three eponymous queens of Ireland.

Freyja (Freya)—the main goddess of the early Norse fertility deities, the Vanir.

Freyr—the main fertility god of the Norse Vanir, the brother or husband of Freyja. Freyja and Freyr form a triad with their father, Njord.

Frigg—the wife of the high god Odin in Norse mythology—the highest ranking goddess. Associated with childbirth, she is the mother of the dying god Baldr.

Furies (Erinyes, Eumenides)—as the Erinyes, the much-feared avengers who demanded allegiance to the old blood-based revenge law. Eventually tamed by Athene, they became the Eumenides, the "Venerable Ones."

Fuxi—one of the "three August Ones" of Chinese mythology, often depicted as a snake. He was the emperor brother of Nuwa.

Gaia—the world-originating Earth and Mother Goddess in the Greek creation myth told by Hesiod.

Galahad, Sir—one of the most loved and gentle of King Arthur's knights of the Round Table. In some stories he is said to have found the Holy Grail in the Chapel Perilous.

Ganesha (Ganapati)—the much-worshipped elephant-headed god, son of Shiva and Parvati in Indian mythology.

Ganga—the personification of the Ganges, the river of purification for Hindus. She rides on a great water beast and descends from heaven to earth.

Ganymede—a young boy, prince of Troy, with whom Zeus fell in love and carried off to Olympus to become the immortal cupbearer of the gods in Greek mythology.

Geb and Nut—the brother and sister offspring of Shu and Tefnut in Egyptian mythology. Geb was the earth. His sister-wife Nut was separated from him to become the sky.

Gikuyu—the Kikuyu culture hero in Africa.

Gilfaethwy—a son of the Mother Goddess Don in Welsh mythology.

Gilgamesh—the Sumerian and later Babylonian hero who sought eternal life in the epic named for him.

Glauce—the princess of Corinth, who was to replace Medea as Jason's wife in Greek mythology.

God—name many use for the Supreme Being in Judaism, Christianity, and Islam.

Goibhniu—the smith god—the Hephaistos—of Irish mythology.

Goliath—the Philistine giant defeated by David in Hebrew mythology.

Gonggong—a Chinese demon god with a serpent's body. He caused havoc in his war with the supreme deity.

Gopis—the cow-herding girls who served as playmates of—and a source of tricks for—the young Krishna in Indian mythology.

Gordias—the Phrygian king who gave his name to the Gordion Knot tied by his son, King Midas.

Gorgons—the monstrous three sisters, one of whom was Medusa, killed by Perseus in Greek mythology.

Graiae—three sisters of the Gorgons in Greek mythology. They had only one tooth and one eye to share between them.

Grandmother Sun—the sun goddess of the Cherokee Indians.

Great Hare—a popular Native North American trickster and culture hero.

Great Spirit—(Great Manitou, Great Mystery, Kitchi Manitou)—a common term used to designate the Supreme Being of Native North American mythology.

Guanyin (Kannon)—a popular Chinese goddess of mercy. She is the feminine *yin* that balances the male *yang*. She also exists in Japan as Kannon and is sometimes depicted as a male.

Gucumatz (Kukulkan, Feathered Serpent)—the Mayan version of the popular Mesoamerican "Feathered Serpent"—the culture hero and god who would emerge later as Quetzalcoatl.

Gun—the Chinese descendant of the Yellow Emperor and the father of Yu. Gun and Yu fought against the great flood.

Gwydion—the son of the Welsh Mother Goddess, Don, and the greatest of storytellers.

Hachiman—the Japanese Shinto god of War.

Hades—the Greek name for the Underworld and for the god—a brother of Zeus—who was its overlord, ruling with his wife, Persephone.

Haemon—the son of King Creon in Thebes. He died with his beloved Antigone.

Hagar—the slave mistree of Abram (Abraham) in the Bible. She was the mother of Ishmael (Ismail).

Hainuwele—The Ceramese (Indonesian) maiden who becomes a sacrificial victim. Her death provides food for her people.

Hanuman—the monkey king who, with his army, worked with Rama to free Sita in the Indian epic, the *Ramayana*.

Hathor—the ancient Egyptian cow goddess, the Eye of Heaven.

Hawawa (Humbaba)—the monster killed by the Sumerian/Babylonian hero Gilgamesh.

Hebe—a daughter of Zeus and Hera who waited on her parents until she married the deified Herakles and bore him two heavenly sons.

Hector—the son of the Trojan king, Priam, and the greatest of the Trojan warriors in Homer's *Iliad*.

Hecuba—the wife of King Priam of Troy and the mother of Hector in Homer's *Iliad*.

Heimdall—the Norse god who guarded the rainbow bridge that connected Asgard, the home of the gods, with Midgard, the home of humans.

Hel—the offspring of Loki who rules the land of the dead (Hel) in Norse mythology.

Helen—the offspring of Leda and Zeus in his form as a swan, she married King Menelaus of Sparta and was the cause of the Trojan War, described in Homer's *Iliad*, when she ran off with the Trojan prince, Paris, and became known as "Helen of Troy."

Helios—a Greek sun deity.

Hephaistos (Apaitioji)—the lame Greek smith god who married Aphrodite.

Herakles (Hercules)—the greatest Greek hero, a son of Zeus and Perseus's grand-daughter Alkmene, known for his Twelve Labors.

Hermaphroditus—The son of the Greek gods Hermes and Aphrodite. As told by Ovid, he became androgynous when the gods answered the prayers of a water nymph who accosted him while he was bathing and joined their bodies.

Hermes (Emma)—the messenger god of the Greeks, the son of Zeus and Atlas's daughter Maia.

Hesperides—seven daughters of Atlas in Greek mythology. They guarded the apples taken by Herakles in one of his Twelve Labors.

Hestia—one of the original Olympians, a sister of Zeus and guardian of the hearth and home.

Hina—a consort of the Polynesian trickster hero Maui and the source of his struggle with Te Tuna, the eel.

Hippolytus—the son of the Greek hero Theseus and the Amazon Antiope, sister of the queen, Hippolyta.

Hod—the blind Norse god tricked by Loki into killing Baldr.

Homer—the legendary author of the Greek epics, *The Iliad* and *The Odyssey*.

Horus—the falcon-headed son of the Egyptians Osiris and Isis. He struggles with Seth for dominance.

Huang Di—the famous Yellow Emperor, one of the Five August Emperors of China. He was also seen as a Thunder God.

Huitzilopochtli—one of the most important of the Aztec deities. He is the sun god and the war god, miraculously conceived by his mother Coatlicue and a feather.

Hunab'Kù—the Mayan maize god, the father of the sacred twins.

Hunahpu and Xbalanque—the sacred twins of the Mayan in Mesoamerica. After descending the the Underworld, they arise as the sun and moon.

Hyacinth—the boy beloved of the Greek god Apollo. He was killed by the jealous god of the North Wind, but was resurrected as a beautiful flower.

Hylas—the boy loved by the Greek hero Herakles. He disappeared during the voyage of the Argonauts.

Icarus—the unfortunate son of the Greek craftsman Daedalus. Icarus died when he ignored his father's warnings and flew too close to the sun.

Igraine—the mother of King Arthur.

Iktome—one of several tricksters in Native North American mythology.

Inanna (Ishtar)—the greatest of the Sumerian/Babylonian goddesses, she was above all associated with the fertility of the land.

Inari—the Japanese Shinto god of rice.

Indra—a Vedic king of the gods in India.

Inti—the sun god of the Inca in South America, the son of the creator, Viracocha, and the father of the Inca founder, Manco Capac.

Io—an unfortunate woman seduced by the Greek king god Zeus while she was a priestess of Zeus's wife, Hera. Hera had no mercy on her.

Iphigenia—the daugther of King Agamemnon and Queen Clytemnestra of Mycenae in Greek mythology. It was Agamemnon's decision to sacrifice her that led to his wife's anger against him.

Isaac—the son of Abraham by his wife, Sarah in the Bible.

Ishmael (Ismail)—the son of Abraham and his slave Hagar in the Bible.

Isis—the sister-wife of the man-god Osiris in Egypt. It is she who revives Osiris and protects their offspring, Horus.

Ismene—the sister of the Greek heroine of Sophocles' *Antigone* who refuses to help her sister in her attempt to bury their brother.

Itzamná—the high god of the Mesoamerican Maya, he is also a culture hero who invented writing.

Ix-Chel—the Mayan goddess of fertility and the wife of Itzamná.

Izanagi and Izanami—the first parents of the Japanese Shinto creation following the separation of Heaven and Earth. They are the ancestors of the sun goddess Amaterasu.

Jacob (Israel)—the son of Isaac, renamed Israel by Yahweh in the Bible.

Jason—the Greek hero who went in search of the Golden Fleece with companions known as the Argonauts. His wife was Medea.

Jesus—the hero of the story told in the Christian section of the Bible known as the New Testament.

Jiandi—a name for the Chinese supreme deity.

Jibril—the Arabic name for the angel Gabriel, who gave Muhammad the words to the holy book, the Qur'an.

Jocasta—the unfortunate mother-wife of the Greek hero and king of Thebes, Oedipus.

Jormundgand—the serpent offspring of Loki. He surrounds the human world, Midgard, biting his own tail.

Juno—the Roman goddess, wife of Jupiter, roughly equivalent to the Greek Hera.

Jupiter (Iuppiter, Jove)—the high god of Rome—roughly equivalent to the Greek Zeus.

Kachina—spirit figures in the Native North American Hopi religion.

Kali—a violent form of the Indian goddess Devi, she is sometimes seen as a wife of Shiva.

Kaliya—a serpent demon-king killed by Krishna in Indian mythology.

Kami—the Shinto god/spirit figures of Japan.

Kamsa—the evil king in Hindu mythology who is related to Krishna's mother and attempts to kill the newborn Krishna by massacring the innocents, as did King Herod in the Bible.

Karna—a miraculously conceived hero allied with the Kauravas in the Indian epic *The Mahabharata*.

Kauravas—the cousins of the Pandavas who became the enemy in the war described in the Indian epic, the *Mahabharata*.

Kay, Sir—the son of Sir Ector in the Arthurian tales. While Arthur was a boy, he acted as Kay's squire.

Khnum—the ram-headed creator god of Esna in ancient Egypt.

Khonsu—the moon god of ancient Egypt.

Kingu—the son of Apsu in the Babylonian creation epic, the *Enumma Elish*, he led the war for Tiamat and Apsu against the forces of Marduk.

Krishna—the greatest of the avatars of the god Vishnu in Hindu mythology. Sometimes Krishna acts as a god, sometimes as a human.

Kronos—the son of Gaia and Uranos in the old Greek religion; he castrates his father and becomes—until his son Zeus defeats him—the king of the gods.

Kumbari—the Kronos of Hurrian mythology who defeated his deity father and then was defeated by his own son.

Kumokums—a trickster among Native North American tribes in California.

Kunti—the mother of the hero Karna by the sun god in the Indian epic, the *Mahabharata*.

Kutoyis (Blood Clot)—the monster-killing hero of the Native North American Blackfoot tribe.

Laius—the Greek King of Thebes, married to Jocasta, who had been unwittingly killed by his successor and son, Oedipus, in Sophocles' *Oedipus the King*.

Lakshmana—the loyal brother of Rama in the Indian epic the *Ramayana*.

Lakshmi (Sri)—a form of the Hindu goddess Devi, signifying prosperity; she is married to the great god Vishnu.

Lancelot, Sir—one of the knights of King Arthur's Round Table, who betrays the king by having an affair with Queen Guinevere.

Lavinia—the daughter of King Latinus in the Roman epic *The Aeneid*. After a war between a former suitor and Aeneas, she marries Aeneas.

Leda—the Greek queen of Sparta who is seduced or raped by Zeus in his form as a swan and who then lays eggs, producing—depending on the story source—Clytemnestra, Helen of Troy, and the twins, Castor and Polydeuces (Pollyx).

Legba (Eshu, Elegbara)—the famous west African trickster.

Leto—the mother of the Greek gods Apollo and Artemis by Zeus; she is much persecuted by Zeus's jealous wife, Hera.

Life Bringer and Full Basket twins—the creator twin daughters of Thinking Woman. They are culture heroes to the Acoma people in Native North America.

Lituolone—a Bantu African miraculously conceived, he is a monster-killing god-man.

Lleu—a god-hero of Welsh mythology who was betrayed by his wife, Blodeuwedd.

Llyr—the father of Bran and Branwen in Welsh mythology, who possibly is the source for King Lear.

Lohiau—the human lover of Pele in Hawaiian mythology.

Loki—the usually evil trickster god in Norse mythology; responsible for the death of Baldr and in a sense, for the end of the world.

Lugh—the Irish god-hero whose Welsh cognate is Lleu. He led the Tuatha de Danann in the final battle with the Fomorians and, David-like, killed the giant Balor with his slingshot.

Lughaid of Munster—the decapitator of the Irish hero Cuchulainn.

Maat—the eponymous personification of the cosmic order known as *maat* in Egytian mythology. She is a goddess married to Thoth and is the daughter of the high god, Atum.

Macha—one of several Irish goddesses of war.

Mama Occlo—an Inca culture heroine.

Mamacocha (Cochamama)—an Inca Sea goddess. Some say she was the mother of Inti by Viracocha.

Mamaoello (Mama Kilya)—the wife of the Inca founder Manco Cápac.

Manabozho—an Algonquian Indian trickster of Native North America.

Manco Cápac—the legendary founder of the Inca in South America.

Manu—the demiurge who is the progenitor of the human race at the beginning of each age.

Marduk—the city god of ancient Babylon who, as the hero of the creation epic the *Enumma Elish*, defeated the ancient goddess Tiamat and became the chief Babylonian god.

Mars—the Roman god of war, who, as also a fertility and agricultural deity, was more important in Rome than his roughly equivalent Ares was in Greece.

Mary (Maryam)—the mother of Jesus, said to have conceived him by an aspect of God without losing her virginity.

Math—a Welsh god known for magical powers; he was the brother of the mother goddess Don.

Matholwych—the King of Ireland who married the Welsh Branwen and then treated her badly, leading to a devastating war between the Welsh and the Irish.

Mathonwy—the father of the goddess Don in Welsh mythology.

Maui—the popular Polynesian trickster deity who is also a culture hero.

Maya—the mother of the Buddha.

Medb (Maeve)—the sometimes wicked queen of Connaught in the great war described in the Irish epic, *The Tain*.

Medea—the sorcerous daughter of the King of Colchis who helped the Greek hero Jason obtain the Golden Fleece. She was later betrayed by Jason and took violent revenge, according to Euripides in his play *Medea*.

Medusa—the monstrous Gorgon with snake-filled hair who was killed by the Greek hero Perseus.

Megara—the first wife of the Greek hero Herakles, who killed her in a fit of rage caused by the always-jealous Hera.

Membe—the Bulu African creator god.

Menelaus—the Greek king of Sparta, husband of Helen of Troy, brother of Agamemnon.

Mentor—in *The Odyssey*, Athene takes the form of Odysseus's old friend Mentor to guide Odysseus's son, Telamachos, in his search for his father.

Mercury—the Roman god who has a cognate in the Greek Hermes.

Merlin—the wizard who leads the process by which Arthur becomes King of Britain.

Metis—the first wife of Zeus, she helped him overpower his father, Kronos.

Midas—the King of the Phrygians after his father Gordias. He asked that everything he touched be turned to gold and suffered the obvious results.

Mil of Spain—the founder of the Milesians, the Celts who were the final "invaders" of Ireland in the creation process.

Mimir—the wise god of Norse mythology decapitated by the Vanir. Odin preserved his head and put it in Mimir's Well at the base of the world tree, Yggdrasill.

Minerva—the Roman cognate of Athene; less important in Rome than Athene was in Greece.

Minos—the King of Minoan Crete—perhaps a son of Zeus.

Minotaur—the monstrous bull man resulting from the union of Queen Pasiphae of Crete and the great white bull of Poseidon. The Minotaur was confined to the Labyrinth built by Daedalus.

Mithra—an ancient Iranian solar god corresponding to the Indian Vedic Mitra. He was much admired in Rome.

Mitra—the brother of Varuna in Vedic India, he represents perfection and proper laws.

Mnemosyne—the Greek personification of Memory, she is the daughter of Gaia and Uranos. Some say Zeus was her father and that she gave birth to the Muses.

Monster Slayer and Born for Water twins—the sacred twins of the Navajo creation myth.

Mordred—the product of an incestuous relationship involving King Arthur; Mordred and Arthur are eventually killed in a war fought between their two armies.

Morgan Le Fay—said to be King Arthur's half sister. She has magical powers and is sometimes Arthur's enemy, though some say she led the mortally wounded king to the mysterious land of Avalon.

Morrigan—one of a triune of Irish goddesses of war. She is also associated with fertility and is Cuchulainn's enemy.

Moses (Musa)—the leader of the Hebrews traveling toward the Promised Land and the receiver of Yahweh's laws.

Mot—the Canaanite god of death, the brother and enemy of Baal.

Muhammad—the prophet of Islam who received the word of Allah via the angel Jibril (Gabriel).

Muses—the nine daughters of Mnemosyne associated with the arts.

Mut—the wife of the Egyptian high god, Amun, in Thebes.

359

Myrrha—daughter of Cinyras, who tricked her father into an incestuous relationship. According to Ovid's *Metamorphoses*, she was turned into a tree to evade her father's horrified wrath. She gave birth, as a tree, to Adonis.

Nakula and Sahadeva—the twin brothers in the Pandava family in the Indian epic, the *Mahabharata*. They were fathered by the twin gods, the Asvins.

Nammu—a Sumerian fertility goddess who personifies the primordial ocean—the maternal waters (like Tiamat in Babylon). Some say she was the original goddess, the mother of An and Ki.

Narcissus—the boy who fell in love with his own reflection and wasted away, told of by the Roman poet Ovid in his *Metamorphoses*.

Nausikaa—the modest young princess who greeted and helped Odysseus when in Homer's *Odyssey* he landed naked and nearly drowned in Phaiakia.

Neith—one of the early great mother goddesses of Egypt; she came from the primordial waters (Nun) and was said to have created humans and deities.

Nephtys—the sister-wife of the wicked Seth and the sister of Osiris and Isis in Egyptian mythology. She helped Isis revive Osiris.

Neptune—the Roman cognate of the more important Greek god Poseidon.

Nerthus—the early Germanic earth goddess, literally "Mother Earth."

Nestor—one of the Greek heroes of Homer's *Iliad,* he is king of Pylos. In *The Odyssey,* Telemachos visits him, seeking information about the missing Odysseus.

Nibelungs—the name applied to the people, the land, and the treasure of the hero Siegfried (the Norse Sigurd) in the Germanic epic the *Nibelungenlied*.

Ninhursag—representing fertility and birth, she is one of the four major gods of ancient Sumerian mythology.

Ninigi-no-Mikoto—the grandson of the Japanese sun goddess Amaterasu. He was sent by Amaterasu to earth to rule, and is seen as the immediate ancestor of the Japanese royal family.

Ninlil—the wife of the Sumerian god Enlil, she was known as "Lady Air."

Njord—one of the old Vanir race of Norse fertility gods; the father of Freyja and Freyr.

Noah (Nuh)—the flood hero of the great flood in the Bible; warned by God, he and his family built an ark and survived the deluge.

Nuada—a king of the Tuatha de Danaan who lost his hand in a battle in Ireland with the Firbolg.

NummoTwins—in Africa, the Dogon version of the sacred twins; the intermediaries between the creator and humanity, they emerged from the cosmic egg.

Nuwa—a great mother goddess of Chinese mythology.

Nyambe (Nyame)—the moon goddess in Ghana in Africa and the mother goddess of the Ashanti. Also the creator god in parts of Africa.

Obatala—an African Yoruba culture hero and imperfect creator.

Odin—the great high god of Norse mythology.

Odysseus (Ulysses)—the wily hero of *The Odyssey*, the Greek epic by Homer.

Oedipus—the unfortunate hero of the Greek play by Sophocles, *Oedipus the King*. He unwittingly killed his father and married his mother by whom he had four children.

Ogdoad—the pantheon of eight deities in the ancient Egyptian religious center, Hermopolis. The gods were Amun and Amunet (the invisible forces); Heh and Hehet (infinity); Kek and Keket (darkness); and Nun and Naunet (primal waters).

Ogma—the Irish god of eloquence who led the dead to the Underworld.

Oisin—an Irish warrior, the son of Fionn, leader of the Fenians.

Olokun (Oddudua)—the African Yoruba earth goddess and ruler.

Olorun—the African Yoruba sky god ruler.

Olympians—the divine family of Zeus who lived on the Greek Mount Olympus.

Orestes—the son of Agamemnon and Clytemnestra who, as described in the *Oresteia* by the Greek playright Aeschylus, took revenge against his mother for her murder of his father.

Orishas—the spirits which inhabit the earth in various African mythologies, especially the Yoruban.

Orpheus—the Greek musician who attempts to retrieve his dead wife from the Underworld and fails tragically.

Osiris—the god-man in Egyptian mythology who is killed by his brother Seth, revived by his sister-wife Isis, and becomes King of the Underworld.

Otsirvani—a Central Asian creator god.

Pachacamac—the Inca creator of humans.

Pachamama—the earth goddess wife of the Inca high god Viracocha; usually said to be the mother of Inti.

Pandavas—the family of five brothers, all married to Draupadi, who fight against the Kauravas in the Indian epic *The Mahabharata*. They are Yudhishthira, Arjuna, Bhima, and the twins Nakula and Sahadeva, all fathered by gods.

Pandora—in Greek mythology, the first human woman created by the gods, given to Epimetheus as his wife. Out of curiosity, she opened a box from the gods, releasing all evils into the world.

361

Pangu—in Chinese mythology, the first living creature to emerge from the cosmic egg; his body became the animistic source of the world. He separated heaven and earth.

Paris—the Trojan prince who caused the Trojan War described in Homer's epic *The Iliad* by running off with the Greek King Menelaus's wife, Helen.

Partholon—the leader of one of the early "invasions" leading to the creation of Ireland.

Parvati—the Hindu "Daughter of the Mountain," the nurturing version of the great goddess Devi; the wife of Shiva.

Pasiphae—the wife of King Minos of Crete, who in a Greek myth, falls in love with the great white bull of Poseidon, and by the bull becomes the mother of the terrible bull-man, the Minotaur.

Patroklos—the best friend of the Greek hero Achilles. He is killed in Homer's *Iliad*.

Pegasus—the winged horse in Greek mythology, born of the severed head of the monstrous Medusa.

Pele—the volcano goddess of Hawaii.

Pelias—the uncle and enemy of the Greek hero Jason who usurps the throne of Iolcus.

Pelops—the father of Atreus of the House of Atreus.

Penelope—the faithful wife of Odysseus in the Greek epic, *The Odyssey*.

Pentheus—the king of Thebes who doubts the power of the Greek god Dionysos in Euripides' play, *The Bacchae,* and pays for his disbelief with a terrifying death.

Percival (Parsifal)—one of the most famous of King Arthur's Knights of the Round Table who search for the Holy Grail.

Peredur—a Welsh version of Percival.

Persephone—the young daughter of the Greek earth goddess Demeter, who is abducted by Hades to become his wife and Queen of the Underworld.

Perseus—the Greek hero who killed Medusa.

Phaedre—a daughter of King Minos of Crete, the sister of Ariadne. She became the wife of Theseus.

Philomela—a princess of the Greek state of Attica, she was raped by Tereus, a king in Thrace, who was married to Procne, her sister. Tereus cuts out her tongue to prevent her from revealing his crime.

Pluto—the Roman god of the Underworld, roughly equivalent to the Greek Hades.

Polynices—one of the sons of the Greek King Oedipus of Thebes.

Poseidon (Posedaone)—the Greek god of the Sea and most powerful brother of the high god, Zeus.

Prajapati—the primary creator god of the *Brahmanas* in India.

Priam—the king of Troy in Homer's Greek epic *The Iliad*.

Priapus—a son of Aphrodite and, possibly, Dionysos in Greek mythology. He is usually an ithyphallic fertility figure.

Prithvi—Mother Earth in the Vedic tradition of India.

Procne—the wife of Tereus, who rapes her sister Philomela.

Proetus—a Greek sea god sometimes called the "Old Man of the Sea."

Prometheus—the Titan who in Greek mythology was punished by Zeus for stealing fire for humans.

Pryderi—a Welsh hero, the son of the goddess Rhiannon and Pwyll.

Ptah—the primary creator god of the Memphite tradition in ancient Egyptian religion.

Purusha—the "first man" of the Indian *Rigveda*; he became the original "sacrifice" out of which the world was made.

Pwyll—a Welsh hero, husband of Rhiannon, father of Pryderi.

Pygmalion—the Cypriot king who fell in love with the statue he made of a woman who, in answer to his prayers, came to life and became his wife.

Python—the great serpent slain by the Greek god Apollo at the sanctuary at Delphi.

Qi—the Chinese hero and founder of the Shang Dynasty.

Quetzalcoatl—the great Mesoamerican god-hero and sometimes creator or culture hero associated with the more ancient figure, the Feathered Serpent.

Quirinus—originally a Sabine god, he formed an archaic Roman triad of important gods with Jupiter and Mars; he represented community.

Ra (Re)—the Egyptian Supreme Being and personification of the sun.

Radha—one of the cow-herding Gopis in Indian mythology; the particular favorite of Krishna.

Rama—the hero of the Indian epic, the *Ramayana;* one of the two greatest avatars of the Indian god Vishnu.

Rangi and Papa—a Polynesian embodiment of Father Sky and Mother Earth.

Ravana—the multi-headed, multi-armed demon of Lanka who held Sita captive in the Indian epic, the *Ramayana*.

Raven—a ubiquitous trickster figure among Northwest Native North Americans.

Regin—the smith who brought up the hero Sigurd in Norse mythology.

Rerir—in Norse mythology, a grandson of Odin who was the husband of Volsung's mother.

Rhae—a personification of Earth and the mother of the first generation of Olympians in Greek mythology.

Rhiannon—a Welsh goddess queen, wife of Pwyll, daughter of the King of the Underworld.

Romulus and Remus—the founding twins of Rome. Sons of Mars and the mortal Rhae Silvia, they were suckled by a wolf and cared for later by a shepherd.

Rudra—an early Vedic form of what became the great Indian god Shiva.

Sarai (Sarah)—the wife of the patriarch Abraham and mother of Isaac in the Bible.

Sarasvati—the wife of the Indian god Brahma; she is goddess of the arts and learning.

Sargon I—the legendary heroic king of Akkad in Mesopotamia.

Satan—a name for the devil in the biblical tradition; the corrupter of Adam and Eve.

Satyavati—in Indian mythology, the fisherwoman daughter of a fish and the mother of the legendary poet Vyasa.

Satyrs—the ithyphallic followers of the Greek god Dionysos; thus, symbols of fertility.

Sedna—the Inuit sea spirit and creator goddess.

Sekhmet—the lion-headed wife of the creator Ptah in the Memphite religion of ancient Egypt. She was sent by Ra to punish humanity.

Sentata—the name first given to the Irish hero Cuchulainn.

Seth (Set, Typhon)—the brother of and murderer of Osiris and the eternal enemy of Osiris and Isis' son, Horus.

Seveki—a Central Asian spirit.

Shamash—See Utu

Shang Di—one of many names for the Chinese Supreme Being.

Shem—a son of the biblical flood hero, Noah, and the founder of the Semites.

Shesha (Ananta, Vasuki)—the world serpent in Indian mythology; Vishnu sleeps on him before creation.

Shiktur—a name for the mischievous trickster-devil who undermines creation in Central Asian mythology.

Shiva—the great Indian Destroyer god and Yogi god of Hindu mythology.

Shlomo—a name for the trickster-devil figure who undermines creation in Central Asian—in this case, Buryat—mythology.

Shu and Tefnut—the parents of Geb and Nut; they represent Air and Moisture; they emerged from Atum in the Egyptian theology of Heliopolis.

Sidh—fairies—the name given to the Irish Tuatha de Danann after their final defeat when they retreated to underground places.

Siduri—the beautiful nymphlike woman with whom Gilgamesh has a relationship during his journey.

Sigmund—a descendant of the Norse god Odin and the father of the Norse hero Sigurd. In Germany he is Siegmund.

Sigurd—the greatest of the Norse heroes, the remover of the sword from the sacred oak, the dragon-slaying son of Sigmund. In Germany he is Siegfried.

Sita—the wife of the Vishnu avatar Rama in the Indian epic the *Ramayana*. She is an avatar of the goddess Lakshmi.

Sky Woman—the woman who falls from the sky in the earth-diver myths of the Eastern Native North Americans.

Sky Woman's Twins—the children of Sky Woman, who continue the creation process, one doing good, one doing harm.

Sombov—a name for a Central Asian creator god.

Spider Woman—one of the most important of Southwestern Native North American goddesses. She taught the Navajo how to weave and led some of the people up through the sipapu (hole in the earth) during the Emergence Creation.

Stygian Nymphs—these were the nymphs in Greek mythology who had possession of certain objects required by Perseus in his killing of Medusa.

Surya (Savitar)—the Indian Vedic god of the sun.

Susanowo—the brother and rival of the great Japanese sun goddess Amaterasu.

Ta'aroa—the Tahitian name for the Polynesian Supreme Being.

Tages—the Etruscan prophet miraculously born.

Taliesen—the Welsh poet/prophet; the equivalent of the Irish Amairgen.

Talking God—an important Native American Navajo god in the creation story; the protector of the Changing Woman.

Tammuz—the Baylonian name for the Sumerian husband of the goddess Ishtar (Inanna).

Tane (Kane)—the Polynesian tree and forest deity.

Tangaroa (Tangaloa, Kanaloa)—the Maori version of the Polynesian god of the sea.

Tantalus—a king in Asia Minor who served up his son Pelops in a stew for the gods and was punished by being made to suffer "tantalizing" hunger and thirst forever in the presence of food and drink in the Underworld.

Tara—the female counterpart, or aspect, of the bodhisattva Avalokitesvara in Tibetan Buddhist mythology.

Tata and Nena—the survivors of the Aztec flood myth.

Tawa—a name for a Hopi Indian sun-creator god.

Tawhiri—a Polynesian storm god.

Te Tuna—the eel, or the penis; the Polynesian rival to the hero-trickster Maui.

Telemachos—the son of the Greek hero Odysseus, who goes in search of his father in Homer's *Odyssey*.

Tengri—a Turko-Mongol creator in Central Asia.

Tepeu—with Cucumatz, the Mayan creator in the *Popol Vuh*.

Tereus—the evil king in Thrace who married Procne and raped and de-tongued her sister Philomela.

Tessup (Tesub)—a Hittite god and rival of his father for control of the gods.

Tezcatlipoca—in Mesoamerican mythology, a sometimes rival of Quetzalcoatl but also a creator and culture hero, Lord of the North, a god of fertility and wisdom.

Theseus—the Greek hero who defeated the Minotaur and was perhaps a son of Poseidon.

Thinking Woman—a Native North American goddess of the Pueblo Southwest, the primary creator of the Emergence Creation story in Acoma.

Thor (Thunor, Thunr)—the Norse/Germanic thunder-weather-storm god.

Thoth—a moon and wisdom god in ancient Egypt.

Tiamat—the Mesopotamian primal goddess of salt waters, defeated by the Babylonian hero Marduk in the *Enuma Elish*.

Tiandi—a Chinese name for the supreme deity—the union of Sky (*tian*) and Earth (*di*).

Tiresias—the blind prophet of Greek mythology, who also experienced life both as a man and as a woman.

Titans—the children of the original Greek gods who were defeated by the Olympians, led by Zeus.

Tlaloc—the Mesoamerican rain god.

Tristan and Iseult—star-crossed lovers of Welsh and Cornish mythology.

Tsukuyomi—the Japanese moon god born of Izanagi's right eye.

Tu (Tumatauenga)—the Maori war god.

Tuatha de Danann—the divine family who defeated the Fomorians and Firbolg in Ireland and were eventually overcome by the Milesians.

Tu-chai-pai—the creator for the Diegueño Indians of California.

Turnus—the rival to Aeneas at the end of the Roman Virgil's epic *The Aeneid*.

Tyr—the war god among the Norse Aesir.

Ulgen (Num)—one of the creator gods or assistants to the creator in Central Asian mythology.

Umai—a Central Asian fertility goddess.

Uranos—the embodiment of Sky in relation to Gaia (Earth) at the beginning of creation in Greek mythology.

Urshanabi—the ferryman who took the Mesopotamian hero Gilgamesh across the river to visit the flood hero Utnapishtim (Ziusudra).

Uther Pendragon—the father of King Arthur by Igraine.

Utnapishtim—the Babylonian name for the Sumerian flood hero, Ziusudra.

Utu (Shamash)—a name for the Mesopotamian sun god.

Valkyries—Odin's maids in Valhalla in Asgard in Norse mythology; they served the dead warriors mead and pork.

Valmiki—the legendary author of the Indian epic, the *Ramayana*.

Vanir—the old fertility gods of Norse mythology; they fought for a time against the Odin-led Aesir.

Varuna—an Indian high sky god in the Vedas.

Vasudeva—the earthly father of the Hindu Vishnu avatar Krishna.

Vayu—the Vedic god of the wind in India.

Vé—a brother of the Norse god Odin.

Venus—the Roman goddess of love, more important in Rome than the roughly equivalent Aphrodite in Greece; the mother of Aeneas, the founder of Rome.

Vesta—the Roman goddess of sacred fire, patroness of the Vestal Virgins, roughly equivalent to the Greek Hestia.

Vidar—a son of the Norse god Odin who will destroy the wolf Fenrir at the end of the world.

Vili—a brother of the Norse god Odin.

Viracocha—the Incan creator high god.

Vishnu (Narayana)—one of the three great gods of Hindu India; the preserver with many avatars including Krishna and Rama.

Vishvakarman—the divine architect who holds the universe together in the Indian *Rigveda*.

Volsung—the founder of the Volsungs in Norse mythology; the family of Sigmund and Sigurd.

Vrita—the negative demon killed by the Indian Vedic king god Indra.

Vulcan—the Roman equivalent of the Greek smith god Hephaistos.

Vyasa—the legendary creator of the *Mahabharata* and other important Indian texts.

Wakan Tanka—the Great Mystery or Great Spirit of Plains Indians in North America.

Wanjiru—a central African heroine who undergoes a sacrificial death and resurrection.

Water Pot Boy—a Tewa hero in southwestern Native America who has a miraculous conception and searches for his father.

White Buffalo Woman (Ptesan-Wi)—an important goddess and culture heroine of the Plains Indians—especially the Sioux—of North America.

Wind Sucker—a North American Blackfoot Indian monster killed by the hero Kutoyis ("Blood Clot").

Woden (Wotan)—the German/Anglo Saxon name for the Norse god Odin.

Wulbari—in Africa, the Krachi Sky god.

Xihe—the Chinese goddess who gave birth to the ten suns.

Xipe-Totec—the Aztec Lord of the East, a creator god and sometimes rival of Quetzal-coatl.

Xiuhtecuhtli—the Aztec fire god, the god of the last Aztec creation, the fifth sun.

Yahweh—a name for the Hebrew God of the Torah.

Yakumama—an Inca water goddess in the form of a snake.

Yama—the brother of Manu and the basis of material used to make the world in some Vedic texts in India.

Yamm—an old Canaanite water god who wants to be head god.

Yao—one of the Five August Emperors of China.

Yeii—Navajo spirit figures in North America.

Yhi—a creator goddess in the Dreamtime of the Karraur Aborigine of Australia.

Yi—the Chinese culture hero who shot down nine of the unnecessary suns born from Xihe.

Yinglong—the Chinese dragon whose tail formed channels to the sea against the great flood.

Ymir—the Norse giant from whose body the gods made the world.

Ynakhsyt—a Central Asian earth mother responsible for cattle.

Yoruga—one of the Dogon Nummo Twins; he broke out of his cosmic egg sac prematurely.

Yu—the Chinese flood hero who finally put an end to the deluge.

Yudhishthira—the leader of the Pandava clan in the Indian epic *The Mahabharata*.

Yumil Kaxob—the Mayan maize god.

Yurlunger—a snake deity in Australian Aborigine Dreamtime; he swallows two Dreamtime creator sisters, but regurgitates them.

Zagreus—a Thracian form of the Greek god Dionysos.

Zambe—the son of the African Bulu creator, sent to earth to act as a culture hero.

Zeus (Diwe)—the king of the Olympian gods of Greece.

Zhurong (Zhuanxu, Gaoyang)—the Supreme Being and founder of the Chu people in China.

Ziusudra—the Sumerian name for the flood hero in the epic of Gilgamesh.

Zoroaster (Zarathustra)—the hero and central figure of the Persian (Iranian) religion, Zoroastrianism.

Zuni Earth Mother and Sky Father—the creators of the Zuni world.

Glossary

Abrahamic—A term referring to the biblical story of Abraham. Because Jews, Christians, and Muslims all trace their origins to Abram/Abraham/Ibrahim, these religions are often called the Abrahamic religions.

Animistic myths—Myths that reflect understandings of the world based on the concept that everything contains spirit (*animus*). African and Native North American myths tend to be animistic. Myths of the dismemberment and/or "planting" of World Parents leading to creation are animistic because everything in creation contains the spirit of and is "animated" by the World Parent, as in the case, for instance, of the Babylonian Tiamat or the Norse Ymir.

Apocalypse—An apocalypse is the end of the world. Apocalypse myths are myths of that end. The Norse Ragnarök is an example.

Archetype—A universal symbol or pattern. The term is used primarily in psychology by Carl Jung and his followers in religious studies by Mircea Eliade and his followers, and in literary criticism by scholars such as Northrop Frye. The heroic monomyth, for instance, outlined especially by mythologist Joseph Campbell, is concerned with the hero archetype.

Aryans—A term sometimes used for the Indo-Iranians who are said to have descended from the north into India and Iran in ancient times, bringing with them Indo-European linguistic, cultural, and religious traditions.

Avatar—An incarnation of a god. In Hinduism the avatars of the god Vishnu—notably Krishna and Rama—are particularly important. Vishnu's wife Lakshmi also has avatars in Sita and Draupadi.

Chaos—An undifferentiated, un-ordered reality or void before creation takes place—the nothingness before the Big Bang, for instance.

Chaos creation—Creation from chaos is a type of creation in which the world comes from elements already in existence but not yet ordered or differentiated—the void or a cosmic egg, for instance.

Cosmogony—The study of the creation of the cosmos (Greek *kosmos*, meaning "order" + *genesis*, meaning "birth"). A creation myth is sometimes a cosmogony and so is the modern Big Bang theory.

Creation Myths—All cultures have myths that explain the creation of their cultures and/or of the world in general. Creation myths provide some significance in the universe to those who create them.

Creatrix—A term sometimes used to distinguish a female creator from a male one.

Cuneiform—Usually thought to be the first form of writing, a system of pictographs carved into clay tablets. The ancient Sumerians probably invented it.

Deities—Humans have seemingly forever felt it necessary to believe in particular deities—gods and goddesses—both to explain the nature of things and also to assure themselves that the world and the universe are meaningful rather than merely random.

Deus Otiosus or Deus Absconditus—The god who withdraws or disappears. This theme is particularly prevalent in African myths. The creator god frequently becomes disgusted by his human creations and retires from the world.

Dualism—The sense that the world is marked by a struggle between two opposites, usually good and evil. Dualism exists in many religious systems, such as Christianity and Zoroastrianism, and in Native American myths about twins: one bad, one good.

Earth-Diver Creation—An archetype of creation especially popular in parts of Native North America, it usually involves an animal's diving into the primordial waters to find the material with which to create the world.

Emergence Creation—A creation archetype popular among southwestern Native Americans, it involves the emergence of the first people by stages from within the earth.

Epics—Epics are long poems depicting the actions of a culture and its heroes. Epics can be oral, that is, passed on by word of mouth, as apparently Homer's *Iliad* and *Odyssey* were, or they can be literary, as in the case of Virgil's *Aeneid*.

Eschatological myths—Myths that deal with the end of things. The Norse Ragnarök story is eschatological, as is any story of a "Last Judgment."

Etiological myths—Etiology is the study of origins. Etiological myths explain the origins of traditions and natural phenomena. Creation myths have strong etiological aspects.

Ex nihilo Creation—The most common type of creation myth, the *ex nihilo* (from nothing) myths tell, for example, of the creation of the world by the creator's words or thoughts when there was nothing but a void. The *ex nihilo* creation is closely related to the Creation from Chaos type and is sometimes indistinguishable from it.

Fertility Deity—Fertility deities are those particularly associated with sexuality and the fruition of humans and elements of their world. In Greece, Aphrodite is a fertility goddess who is sexually magnetic. Dionysos is a fertility god who is associated with the harvesting of the grape.

Hero—In mythology a hero is a human male or female who has special powers, usually derived from having a divine parent or miraculous origin. He or she embodies the aspirations of a people. Hero myths tell the stories of heroes.

Hieroglyphics—The ancient Egyptian form of writing, hieroglyphic symbols were both ideograms (signifying ideas) and phonograms (signifying phonetics). The Greeks believed that writing was invented by the Egyptian god they called Thoth, and the word *hieroglyphic* means "God's Words" (*hieros*, meaning "sacred" + *glypho*, meaning "inscription").

Indo-European—The Indo-Europeans were people who perhaps once spoke a common language and who migrated into India, Iran, Anatolia, and Europe, probably during the middle of the third millennium B.C.E. Eventually, various languages—such as English and the Romance languages—evolved from a supposed proto-Indo-European language.

Matriarchal—Matriarchal societies are those in which matriarchs (women leaders) are dominant.

Matrilineal—Matrilineal societies are those in which a person's name, and sometimes property rights, come from the female rather than the male line.

Mesolithic—In archeology and mythology, scholars refer to the Mesolithic period of the Stone Age, the time between the Paleolithic and the Neolithic eras (c. 10,000–8000 B.C.E.).

Metaphor—Myths and their components can often be seen as metaphorical, that is, as representations or symbols of a culture's ideas and beliefs rather than as factual reality.

Minoans—The people of ancient Crete are called Minoans after the name of their mythical king, Minos.

Miraculous Conception and Birth—In the heroic monomyth, the hero is recognized as a hero from the beginning because of a miraculous conception or birth. In some cases the hero's mother has not experienced sexual intercourse and thus remains a virgin, as in the story of Jesus' nativity. Sometimes the hero is fathered by a god by way of a natural element such as the wind or a sun ray.

Monomyth—A term coined by James Joyce and used primarily by mythologist Joseph Campbell to refer to the universal or archetypal pattern of hero myths around the world. The heroic monomyth contains archetypal patterns such as the miraculous conception, the quest, and the descent to the Underworld. Monomythic heroes are heroes whose lives contain several of these patterns.

Monotheism—The belief in a single god, such as the Hebrew/Jewish Yahweh, the Christian God, and the Muslim Allah. Some see the Egyptian pharaoh Akhenaten as a monotheist. Some might consider the Vedantic Hindu concept of Brahman as at least pointing to monotheism.

Myth—A narrative, usually religious in nature, which explains reality, expresses a sense of a culture's place in reality, but which to some within and outside the culture is more metaphorical and symbolic than literal.

Mythology—The study of myths and also a collection of myths, sometimes called **mythography**. We can study the concept of myths and we can read Greek mythology or Egyptian mythology, or world mythology.

Mythos—The Greek term from which our word *myth* is derived.

Neolithic—The New (*neo*) Stone (*lith*) Age (c. 8000–3000 B.C.E.), just before the Copper or Bronze Age.

Ontological myths—The study of being. Ontological myths explain the nature of being or existence.

Pagan—A term commonly applied to nonmonotheistic beliefs, especially pantheism.

Paleolithic—The old Stone Age. The prehistoric period (c. 75,000–10,000 B.C.E.)

Pantheism—The belief in many deities. The ancient Greek and Egyptian religions and mythologies are pantheistic rather than monotheistic.

Pantheon—A pantheon (*pan*, meaning "all" + *theos*, meaning "gods") is a collection of deities belonging to a particular cult or religion. Highly organized pantheons such as those in Greece and Egypt are divine families usually headed by a Father God, thus reflecting the realities of a patriarchal culture.

Patriarchal—Cultures and traditions dominated by male rather than female leaders are patriarchal, as opposed to matriarchal.

Patrilineal—A culture is patrilineal rather than matrilineal if family lines and names are passed down through the paternal (male) line.

Primordial—Used synonymously with "primal" and "primeval" in myths to denote original forms out of which creation emerged. The primordial waters in many myths are analogous to the birth waters of real life.

Quest—In heroic myths the quest is the central act—the process by which the hero proves himself or herself. In the Arthurian myth, the Round Table heroes go on a quest for the Holy Grail.

Resurrection and Rebirth—The act of returning to life after a period of death. Osiris in Egypt and Jesus both experience resurrection. In some religions and mythologies, people are reborn in different forms after death.

Ritual or Rite—A set form of actions that celebrate or reenact a mythological event or belief.

Scapegoat—An archetypal aspect of the lives of heroes such as the Indian Sita, the African Wanjiru, or Jesus in which the hero is sacrificed to save the lives of others or of a whole society.

Scripture—Generally the word "scripture" refers to a given society's sacred texts—in some cases the "word of God.". For Jews and Christians the Bible is scripture, for Hindus the Vedas and other ancient texts are scripture. For Muslims the Qur'an is the holy book, or scripture.

Semites—Semitic peoples are those of the Middle East who speak Semitic languages. The ancient Babylonians, Canaanites, and Hebrews were Semites, as are modern Arabs and Jews.

Shaman—A holy person—called a "Medicine Man" or "Medicine Woman" by some Native Americans—who communicates with the spirit world and has the power to cure.

Symbol—Myths are full of symbols. A church steeple is a symbol of the idea of reaching up to God. Thor's hammer and Zeus's thunderbolt are symbols of power.

Teleological myth—Myths that express the connection between natural processes and a final purpose or design.

Theism—The belief in gods or a god, for the most part personal ones as opposed to concepts. Monotheists are, by definition, theists whereas Gregory Bateson (the concept of "Immanent Mind") is not.

Triad—The concept of three dominant gods as in Hinduism's Shiva, Vishnu, and Brahma. This differs from the Christian dogma of the Trinity in which God has three aspects, Creator, Redeemer, and Spirit.

Void, the—In the *ex nihilo* creation myths, the creator exists in a state of nothingness, or void, before he or she creates the universe. Such is the case of Yahweh in the biblical book of Genesis.

World-Parent Creation—Creation in which a primal being is in some way turned into the elements of reality, as in the Norse creation.

Bibliography

Abrahams, Roger D. *African Folktales*. New York: Pantheon, 1983.

Adams, Richard E. W. *Prehistoric Mesoamerica*, rev. ed. Norman: University of Oklahoma Press, 1991.

Allouche, Adel. "Arabian Religions." In Mircea Eliade, ed. *The Encyclopedia of Religion*, vol. 1, pp. 363–367. New York and London: Macmillan, 1987.

Andersen, Johannes C. *Myths and Legends of the Polynesians*. New York: Dover, 2011.

Apollodorus. *The Library*. James G. Frazer, trans. London: Heinemann, 1921.

Apollonius of Rhodes. *The Voyage of the Argo*. E. V. Rieu, trans. Baltimore: Penguin, 1959.

Armstrong, Karen. *Muhammad: A Biography of the Prophet*. San Francisco: Harper, 1992.

———. *A History of God: The 4,000-Year Quest of Judaism, Christianity, and Islam.* Ballantine, 1994.

———. *A Short History of Myth*. Edinburg: Canongate, 2006.

Artigas, Mariano. *The Mind of the Universe: Understanding Science and Religion*. Philadelphia: Templeton, 2000.

Ashton, W. G., trans. *Nihongi*. Tokyo: Charles Tuttle, 1972.

Barbour, Ian G. *Myths, Models, and Paradigms: A Comparative Study in Science and Religion*. New York: Harper and Row, 1970.

Baring, Anne, and Jules Cashford. *The Myth of the Goddess: Evolution of an Image*. New York: Viking, 1991.

Bateson, Gregory. *Steps to an Ecology of the Mind*. New York: Ballantine Books, 1972.

Beier, Ulli. *The Origin of Life and Death: African Creation Myths*. London: Heinemann, 1966.

Best, Robert. *Noah's Ark and the Ziusudran Epic: Sumerian Origins of the Flood Myth*. Winona Lake, IN: Eisenbanus, 1999.

Bierhorst, John. *The Mythology of South America*. New York: Oxford University Press, 2002.

———. *The Mythology of North America*. New York: William Morrow, 1985.

Bierlein, J. F. *Parallel Myths*. New York: Ballantine Books, 1994.

Birrell, Anne. *Chinese Mythology: An Introduction*. Baltimore: Johns Hopkins University Press, 1993.

Bloch, Raymond. "Etruscan Religion." Carol Dean-Nassau and Marilyn Gaddis Rose, trans. In Mircea Eliade, ed. *The Encyclopedia of Religion*, vol. 5, pp. 182–185. New York and London: Macmillan, 1987.

Boer, Charles, trans. *The Homeric Hymns*. Chicago: Swallow Press, 1970.

Bonnefoy, Yves. *Roman and European Mythologies*. Chicago: University of Chicago Press, 1991.

———. *Greek and Egyptian Mythologies*. Chicago: University of Chicago Press, 1992.

Bonnefoy, Yves, with Wendy Doniger, trans., ed. *Asian Mythologies*. Chicago: University of Chicago Press, 1993.

Buck, William, trans. *The Ramayana*. Berkeley: University of California Press, 1976.

Budge, E. A. W. *Egyptian Religion*. New York: Bell, 1959.

———. *The Gods of the Egyptians, or Studies in Egyptian Mythology*. New York: Dover, 1969.

Buxton, Richard. *The Complete World of Greek Mythology*. New York: Thames and Hudson, 2004.

Campbell, Joseph. *The Hero with a Thousand Faces*. Princeton, NJ: Princeton University Press, 1968.

———. *The Masks of God*. 4 vols. New York, 1970.

———. *Myths to Live By*. New York: Viking, 1972.

Chadwick, Nora K., ed. *The Celts*, new ed. New York: Penguin Books, 1997.

Cixous, Hélène. "The Laugh of the Medusa," trans. Kieth Cohen and Paula Cohen in *Signs*, Vol. 1, no. 4, Summer 1976: 875-893.

Clarke, Lindsay. *Essential Celtic Mythology*. San Francisco: HarperCollins, 1997.

Coogan, Michael D. *The Oxford History of the Biblical World*. Oxford and New York: Oxford University Press, 1998.

Crossley-Holland, Kevin. *The Norse Myths*. New York: Pantheon, 1980.

Cunliffe, Barry. *The Ancient Celts*. New York: Oxford University Press, 1997.

Dalley, Stephanie. *Myths from Mesopotamia* (World's Classics series), rev. ed. Oxford and New York: Oxford University Press, 2000.

Davies, Paul, and John Gribbin. *The Matter Myth: Dramatic Discoveries That Challenge Our Understanding of Physical Reality*. New York: Simon & Schuster, 2007.

Doty, William G. *Myth: A Handbook*. Westport, CT: Greenwood Press, 2004.

———. *Mythography: The Study of Myths and Rituals*. 2nd ed. Tuscaloosa, AL: University of Alabama Press, 2000.

Douglas, Mary. *Natural Symbols: Explorations in Cosmology*. New York: Pantheon, 1970.

Dundes, Alan, ed. *The Flood Myth*. Berkely: University of California Press, 1988.

Durkheim, Emile. *The Elementary Forms of Religious Life.* J.W. Swain, trans. London: Allen & Unwin, 1915.

Eliade, Mircea. *Cosmos and History: The Myth of the Eternal Return.* New York: Harper Torchbooks, 1954.

———, ed. *The Encyclopedia of Religion.* 16 vols. New York: Macmillan, 1987.

———. *Gods, Goddesses, and Myths of Creation.* New York: Harper & Row, 1974.

———. *Myth and Reality.* New York: Harper & Row, 1963.

———. *Patterns in Comparative Religion.* New York: Sheed & Ward, 1958.

———. *The Sacred and the Profane.* New York: Harcourt, Brace, 1959.

Ellis, Peter Berresford. *Dictionary of Celtic Mythology.* New York: Oxford University Press, 1992.

Erdoes, R., and A. Ortiz, eds. *American Indian Myths and Legends.* New York: Pantheon, 1988.

Faulkner, R. O. *The Ancient Egyptian Book of the Dead.* C. Andrews, ed. London: British Museum, 1985.

Fee, Christopher, with David Leeming. *Gods, Heroes, and Kings: The Battle for Mythic Britain.* New York: Oxford University Press, 2001.

Frankel, Valerie Estelle. *From Girl to Goddess: The Heroine's Journey through Myth and Legend.* Jefferson, NC: McFarland, 2010.

Frazer, Sir James. *The Golden Bough.* 12 vols. London: Macmillan & Co., 1907–15—especially volume 4, "The Dying and Reviving Gods").

Freud, Sigmund. "Medusa's Head" and "The Infantile Genital Organization" in *The Standard Edition of the Complete Psychological Works of Sigmund Freud,* ed. and trans. James Strachey. New York: Vintage, 1999.

———. *Totem and Taboo.* New York: Moffat, Yard, 1918.

Frye, Northrop. *Anatomy of Criticism.* Princeton: Princeton University Press, 1957.

——— *The Great Code: The Bible and Literature.* New York: Harcourt Brace Jovanovich, 1982.

Gardner, John, and John Maier, eds. *Gilgamesh.* New York: Knopf, 1984.

Gimbutas, Marija. *The Language of the Goddess.* London: Thames & Hudson, 2001.

Gnoli, Gherardo. "Zoroastrianism." In Mircea Eliade, ed. *The Encyclopedia of Religion,* vol. 15, pp. 579–591. New York and London: Macmillan, 1987.

Graves, Robert. *The Greek Myths,* 2 vols. Baltimore, MD: Penguin, 1955.

———. *The White Goddess.* New York: Farrar, Straus & Giroux,

Green, Miranda. *Celtic Myths* (Legendary Past series). London: British Museum Press, 1993.

Greene, Brian. *The Elegant Universe.* New York: W.W. Norton, 1999.

Gribbon, John. *In Search of Schrödinger's Cat.* New York: Bantam, 1984.

Hamilton, Edith. *Mythology.* New York, 1953.

Hammonds, Carolyn, trans. *The Seven Commentaries on the Gallic War* (by Julius Caesar). New York: Oxford University Press, 1998.

Hansen, William. *Classical Mythology*. New York: Oxford University Press, 2004.

Harrison, Jane. *Epilegomena to the Study of Greek Religion and Themis: A Study of the Social Origins of Greek Religion*. Hyde Park, NY: University Books, 1962.

———. *Mythology*. New York: Harcourt, 1963.

Heidel, Alexander. *The Gilgamesh Epic and Old Testament Parallels*. Chicago: University of Chicago Press, 1949.

Hesiod. *Theogony*. Norman O. Brown, trans. Indianapolis, IN: Bobbs-Merrill, 1953.

Hillman, James. *The Myth of Analysis: Essays on Psychological Creativity*. New York: Harper and Row, 1978.

Hinnels, J. R. *Persian Mythology*. London: Hamlyn, 1975.

Hollander, Lee M., trans. *The Poetic Edda* (by Snorri Sturluson). Austin: University of Texas Press, 1962.

Homer. *Iliad*. Richard Lattimore, trans. Chicago: Phoenix Books, 1961.

———. *The Odyssey of Homer*. Robert Fitzgerald, trans. Garden City, NY: Doubleday, 1963.

Hyde, Lewis. *Trickster Makes the World: Mischief, Myth, and Art*. New York: Farrar, Strauss & Giroux, 2010.

Hynes, William J., and William G. Doty. *Mythical Trickster Figures: Contours, Contexts, and Criticisms*. Tuscaloosa: University of Alabama Press, 1997.

Jones, Gwyn, and Thomas Jones, trans. *The Mabinogion*, rev. ed. Rutland, VT: Charles E. Tuttle, 1993.

Jung, Carl Gustav. *The Archetypes and the Collective Unconscious*. New York: Pantheon Books, 1959.

———. *Four Archetypes: Mother/Rebirth/ Spirit/Trickster*. R. F. C. Hull, trans. Princeton: Princeton University Press, 1969.

———. *Symbols of Transformation*. New York: Harper, 1962.

Jung, Carl Gustav, and C. Kerenyi. *Essays on a Science of Mythology: The Myth of the Divine Child and the Mysteries of Eleusis*. R. F. C. Hull, trans. Princeton: Princeton University Press, 1963.

Kinsella, Thomas, trans. *The Tain*. Oxford: Oxford University Press, 1970.

Kitagawa, Joseph M. "Japanese Religion: An Overview." In Mircea Eliade, ed. *The Encyclopedia of Religion*, vol. 7, pp. 520–538. New York and London: Macmillan, 1987.

Kramer, Samuel Noah. *Sumerian Mythology*. 1944. Rev. ed., Philadelphia: University of Pennsylvania Press, 1998.

Kramer, Samuel Noah, and John Maier. *Myths of Enki: The Crafty God*. New York: Oxford University Press, 1989.

Knappert, Jan. *Islamic Legends*. 2 vols. Leiden: Brill, 1985.

———. *The Encyclopedia of Middle Eastern Mythology and Religion.* Shaftesbury, Rockport, Brisbane: Element, 1993.

Larrington, Carolyne, ed. *The Feminist Companion to Mythology.* London: Pandora, 1992.

Leeming, David A. *A Dictionary of Asian Mythology.* New York: Oxford University Press, 2001.

———. *Creation Myths of the World: An Encyclopedia.* 2 vols. Santa Barbara: ABC-CLIO, 2010).

———, ed. *Encyclopedia of Psychology and Religion.* 3 vols. New York: Springer, 2013.

———. *From Olympus to Camelot: The World of European Mythology.* New York: Oxford University Press, 2003.

———. *Jealous Gods and Chosen People: The Mythology of the Middle East.* New York: Oxford University Press, 2004.

———. *Medusa: In the Mirror of Time.* London: Reaktion Books, 2013.

———. *Myth: A Biography of Belief.* New York: Oxford University Press, 2002.

———. *Mythology: The Voyage of the Hero.* 3rd edition. New York: Oxford University Press, 1998.

———. *The Oxford Companion to World Mythology.* New York: Oxford University Press, 2005.

———. *The World of Myth.* 2nd ed. New York: Oxford University Press, 2013.

Leeming, David, and Jake Page. *Goddess: Myths of the Female Divine.* New York: Oxford University Press, 1994.

———. *God: Myths of the Male Divine.* New York: Oxford University Press, 1996.

———. *The Mythology of Native North America.* Norman, OK: University of Oklahoma Press, 1998.

———. *Myths, Legends, & Folktales of America.* New York: Oxford University Press, 1999.

Leeming, David A., and Margaret Leeming. *A Dictionary of Creation Myths.* New York: Oxford University Press, 1994.

Leick, Gwendolen. *A Dictionary of Ancient Near Eastern Mythology.* London and New York: Routledge, 1991.

Lévi-Strauss, Claude. *Myth and Meaning.* New York: Schocken Books, 1979.

———. *The Raw and the Cooked.* John and Doreen Weightman, trans. New York: Harper & Row, 1969.

———. *Structural Anthropology.* New York: Basic Books, 1963.

Lewis, Mark Edward. *The Flood Myths of Early China.* Albany, NY: State University of New York Press, 2006.

Lincoln, Bruce. "Indo-European Religions." In Mircea Eliade, ed. *The Encyclopedia of Religion,* vol. 7, pp. 198–204. New York and London: Macmillan, 1987.

———. *Myth, Cosmos, and Society: Indo-European Themes of Creation and Destruction.* Cambridge, MA: Harvard University Press, 1986.

———. *Theorizing Myths: Narratives, Ideology, and Scholarship.* Chicago: University of Chicago Press, 1999.

Lindow, John. *Norse Mythology: A Guide to the Gods, Heroes, Rituals, and Beliefs.* New York: Oxford University Press, 2001.

Livingstone, David *The Dying God: The Hidden History of Western Civilization.* London: Thames & Hudson, 2001.

Long, Charles H. *Alpha: The Myths of Creation* New York: Scholars Press, 1963.

Lord, Albert B. *The Singer of Tales.* New York: Atheneum, 1960.

Lovelock, James E. *Gaia: A New Look at Life on Earth.* New York: Oxford University Press, 1979.

Luke, Helen M. *Woman Earth and Spirit: The Feminine in Symbol and Myth.* New York: Crossroad Publishing, 1984.

MacAlister, R. A. S. *Lebor Gabala Erenn* [Book of Invasions]. 5 vols. Dublin: Irish Text Society, 1956.

Mallory, J. P. *In Search of the Indo-Europeans: Language, Archaeology and Myth.* London: Thames & Hudson, 1989.

Markale, Jean. *The Great Goddess: Reverence of the Divine Feminine from the Paleolithic to the Present.* Rochester, VT: Inner Traditions, 1999.

McLean, Adam. *The Triple Goddess: An Exploration of the Archetypal Feminine.* Grand Rapids, MI: Phanes Press, 1989.

Momigliano, Arnaldo. "Roman Religion: The Imperial Period." In Mircea Eliade, ed. *The Encyclopedia of Religion,* vol. 12, pp. 462–471. New York and London: Macmillan, 1987.

Moreman, Christopher. *Beyond the Threshold: Afterlife Beliefs and Experience in World Religion.* Lanham, MD: Rowman & Littlefied, 2010.

Morford, Mark, and Robert Lenardon. *Classical Mythology.* New York, Oxford University Press, 2011.

Moseley, Michael E. *The Incas and Their Ancestors.* London: Thames & Hudson, 1992.

Mudrooroo [Colin Thomas Johnson]. *Aboriginal Mythology.* Scranton, PA: Thorsons, 1995.

Murdock, Maureen. *The Heroine's Journey.* Boston: Shambala, 1990.

Narr, Karl J. "Paleolithic Religion." Matthew J. O'Connell, trans. In Mircea Eliade, ed. *The Encyclopedia of Religion,* vol. 11, pp. 149–159. New York and London: Macmillan, 1987.

Neumann, Eric *The Great Mother: An Analysis of the Archetype.* New York: Bollingen Foundation, 1963.

Nilsson, Martin. *The Mycenaean Origin of Greek Mythology.* New York: W.W. Norton, 1963.

O'Flaherty, Wendy Doniger. *Hindu Myths: A Sourcebook Translated from the Sanskrit.* Harmondsworth, UK: Penguin, 1975.

Okpewho, Isadore. *Myth in Africa.* London: Cambridge University Press, 1983.

382

Ovid. *Ovid's Metamorphoses*. Charles Boer, trans. Dallas, TX: Spring Publications, 1989.

Panikkar, Raimundo. "Deity." In Mircea Eliade, ed. *The Encyclopedia of Religion*, vol. 4, pp. 264–276. New York and London: Macmillan, 1987.

Parrinder, Geoffrey. *African Mythology*. London: Hamlyn, 1982.

Pearson, Carol. *The Hero Within: Six Archetypes We Live By*. San Francisco, HarperOne, 1998.

Pinch, Geraldine. *Egyptian Mythology: A Guide to the Gods, Goddesses, and Traditions of Ancient Egypt*. New York: Oxford University Press, 2002.

Puhvel, Jaan. *Comparative Mythology*. Baltimore: Johns Hopkins University Press, 1987.

Radin, Paul. *The Trickster: A Study in American Indian Mythology*. New York: Philosophical Library, 1956.

Read, Kay Almere, and Jason J. Gonzalez. *MesoAmerican Mythology*. New York: Oxford University Press, 2000.

Rundle Clark, R. T. *Myth and Symbol in Ancient Egypt*. London: Thames & Hudson, 1959.

Sandars, N. K., trans. *The Epic of Gilgamesh*. Harmondsworth, UK: Penguin, 1973.

Schilling, Robert. "Roman Religion: The Early Period." Paul C. Duggan, trans. In Mircea Eliade, ed. *The Encyclopedia of Religion*, vol. 12, pp. 445–461. New York and London: Macmillan, 1987.

Schwartz, Howard. *Tree of Souls: The Mythology of Judaism*. New York: Oxford University Press, 2004.

Segal, Robert. *Myth: A Very Short Introduction*. New York and Oxford: Oxford University Press, 2004.

Soyinka, Wole. *Myth, Literature & the African World*. Cambridge, UK: Cambridge University Press, 1976.

Sproul, Barbara C. *Primal Myths: Creation Myths around the World*. San Francisco: HarperCollins, 1991.

Srejovich, Dragoslav. "Neolithic Religion." Veselin Kostic, trans. In Mircea Eliade, ed. *The Encyclopedia of Religion*, vol. 10, pp. 352–360. New York and London: Macmillan, 1987.

Swimme, Brian. *The Universe Is a Green Dragon: A Cosmic Creation Story*. Santa Fe, NM: Bear & Co., 1984.

Sullivan, Lawrence E. "Supreme Beings." In Mircea Eliade, ed. *The Encyclopedia of Religion*, vol. 14, pp. 166–181. New York and London: Macmillan, 1987.

Takeshi, Matsumae. "Japanese Religion: Mythic Themes." In Mircea Eliade, ed. *The Encyclopedia of Religion*, vol. 7, pp. 545–552. New York and London: Macmillan, 1987.

Tedlock, Dennis, ed. and trans. *Popol Vuh*. New York: Touchstone, 1996.

Ulanov, Ann, and Barry Ulanov. *Religion and the Unconscious*. Philadelphia: Westminster Press, 1975.

Van Buitenan, J. A. B., trans. *The Mahabharata*. Chicago: University of Chicago Press, 1973–1978.

Vasquez, Juan Adolfo. "South American Religions: Mythic Themes." In Mircea Eliade, ed. *The Encyclopedia of Religion*, vol. 13, pp. 499–506. New York and London: Macmillan, 1987.

Vergil (Virgil). *Aeneid*. Robert Fitzgerald, trans. New York: Vintage, 1990.

Walker, Barbara. *The Woman's Encyclopedia of Myths and Secrets*. New York: HarperOne, 1983.

Wasilewska, Ewa. *Creation Stories of the Middle East*. London and Philadelphia: Jessica Kingsley, 2000.

Weigle, Marta. *Creation and Procreation: Feminist Reflections on Mythologies of Cosmogony and Parturition*. Philadelphia: University of Pennsylvania Press, 1989.

Weston, Jessie. *From Ritual to Romance: An Account of the Holy Grail from Ancient Ritual to Christian Symbolism*. New York: Doubleday, 1957.

Williams, George M. *Handbook of Hindu Mythology*. New York: Oxford University Press, 2003.

Wolkstein, Diane, and Samuel Noah Kramer. *Inanna: Queen of Heaven and Earth*. New York: Harper & Row, 1983.

Yang, Lihui, and An Deming. *Handbook of Chinese Mythology*. New York: Oxford University Press, 2008.

Young, Jean I., trans. *The Prose Edda of Snorri Sturluson: Tales from Norse Mythology*. Berkeley: University of California Press, 1954.

Zerries, Otto. "South American Religions: An Overview." In Mircea Eliade, ed. *The Encyclopedia of Religion*, vol. 13, pp. 486–499. New York and London: Macmillan, 1987.

Zimmer, Heinrich. *Myths and Symbols in Indian Art and Civilization*. Princeton, NJ: Princeton University Press, 1972.

Zolbrod, Paul G. *Dine Bahane: The Navajo Creation Story*. Albuquerque: University of New Mexico Press, 1984.

Zuesse, Evan M. "African Religions: Mythic Themes." In Mircea Eliade, ed. *The Encyclopedia of Religion*, vol. 1, pp. 70–82. New York and London: Macmillan, 1987.

Index

Note: (ill.) indicates photos and illustrations.

A

abandonment, 278, 295
Abildgaard, Nicolai Abraham, 148 (ill.)
Abraham, 25, 27–28, 29, 30, 32, 276
Abram, 27
Abzu, 19
Acallamh na Senorach ("The Colloquy of the Ancients"), 133
Acan, 228
Achaeans, 57
Achilles, 55 (ill.)
    Achilles' heel, 170
    Aeneas, 118
    Aeneid, 115, 116
    Iliad, 57, 58
    miraculously conceived, 90
    Odyssey, 59, 61, 62, 63
    Peleus, 88
    Trojan War, 89
Acoma, 250, 251
Acoma Pueblo, 245
Acrisius, 85, 87, 278
Actaeon, 75
Adad, 312
Adam, 27, 29, 32, 276, 277
Adam of Bremen, 144
Adonis, 34, 74, 79, 119, 121, 150
Aeëtes, King, 88
Aegeus, 52, 83–84, 101
Aegisthus, 94, 94 (ill.), 95
Aeneas
    Aeneid, 22, 115–18, 121–22
    hero's quest, 279
    Iliad, 114
    Underworld, 280
    Venus, 113
    warrior hero, 109
Aeneid (Virgil), 4, 24, 115–18, 121–22
Aeschylus
    Dionysos festival, 69, 71, 80, 90
    Freud, Sigmund, 260
    Oresteia, 93–96, 97
    Ovid, 119

Aesir, 146–47, 148–49, 270
Aeson, 87
Aethra, 72, 83–84
African mythologies
    Ananse, 221–22
    animals, 223
    animism, 216
    colonialism, 215–16
    definition, 215
    Dogon creation myth, 217–18
    flood myths, 218–19
    goddesses, 219
    heroes and heroines, 222–23
    Legba, 220–21, 221 (ill.)
    Supreme Beings, 216–17
    tricksters, 219–20
Agamemnon, 94 (ill.)
    Agamemnon, 93–95
    Elektra, 101, 260
    Homer, 57
    hubris, 116
    Iliad, 58, 62
    individual heroism, 115
    Mycenae, 56
    Odyssey, 63
    Trojan War, 89
    Zeus, 72
Agamemnon (Aeschylus), 93–95
Agdistis, 34
Agni, 160, 160 (ill.), 165, 167
Ah Puch, 228
Aha, 35
Ahura Mazda, 33, 267
Ailill, 131
Ajax, 96
Ajyst, 198
Akhenaten, 8, 47–48
Akkadians, 18
Ala, 219
Alalu, 78
al-Buraq, 30
Alcestis (Euripides), 101
Alcinous, 60, 324, 326, 327, 329
Alexander the Great, 34, 69–70
Algonquian, 252

Alinga, 206
Alkmene, 67, 81
Allah, 29, 30–31, 198
Allat, 28
Alp Kara Aslan, 203
al-Uzzá, 28
Amairgen, 4, 127, 130–31, 133, 135
Amaterasu
    brothers, 194
    Grand Shrine, 195
    Grandmother Sun, 242
    Japanese war in heaven, 192–93
    Supreme Being, 267
    Susanowa, 269, 270
Amenhotep IV, 47
Amentet, 320, 322
American Indian mythologies. *See* Native North American mythologies
Ameta, 335–36
Amida Buddha, 194
Amma, 217, 218
Amphitryon, 81
Amulius, King, 111
Amun, 39, 40, 42
Amunet, 40
Amun-Ra, 39, 41, 47–48
Amycus, 88
An, 13, 14, 17, 19, 43, 64, 272
Ana, 129
Ananse, 7, 213, 220, 221–22, 269, 336–40
Anansi, 220
Ananta Shesha, 163
Anat, 27
Anatolia, 53
Anchises, 116, 118
ancient Egyptians, 35
Andromache, 57
Andromeda, 87
Angerona, 111
Anghir, 201
Angra Mainyu, 33
Angrboda, 151
Anguta, 246

Ani, 320
animal deities, 268–69, 283
animal heads, 41–42
animism, 216, 285
animist spirits, 283–84
animistic creation, 273
Anjea, 207
Anki, 272
Anpu, 323
Antigone, 96, 99 (ill.), 279
Antigone, 96, 99–100
Antiope, 84
Anu, 19, 20, 22, 310, 312
Anubis, 38, 46
Anunnaki, 13, 308, 312
Ao, 210, 211
Aonghus, 129, 149
Apache, 244
Apaitioji, 53
Aphrodite
    Aeneas, 114
    Argonautica, 89
    desire, 113
    fertility deity, 268
    Hesiod's creation myth, 64, 67
    Homeric Hymns, 56
    Iliad, 57
    incarnation of Isis, 48
    love, 74
    origins, 78
    Roman Republic, 112
    sexuality, 76, 214
    trickster myth, 9
Aplu, 110
apocalypse, 152
apocalyptic, 235
Apollo
    cattle, 269, 270
    Classical Greek pantheon, 74–75
    disease curer, 126
    Etruscan god, 110
    Eumenides, 96
    Greco-Roman mythology, 119
    Homeric Hymns, 56
    homosexuality, 77
    Iliad, 57, 58
    Minoan pantheon, 53
    Oedipus the King, 98
    oracle, 97, 98
    Python, 155
    Zeus, 66, 67, 76
Apollodorus, 51, 71, 119
Apollonius of Rhodes, 71, 81, 88
Apophis, 38, 44
Apples of the Hesperides, 83
Apsu, 19, 20
Apu Illapu, 236
Arabs, 28, 29
Aranrhod, 136, 137, 138
Arawn, King, 138
archaic Greek mythology, 63–67

archetype, 7–8
Are, 53
Ares
    Aphrodite, 9, 74, 76, 214
    Hera, 67
    Jason and the Golden Fleece, 88
    Mars, 113
    Minoan pantheon, 53
Arete, Queen, 62
Argives, 57
Argonautica, 88–89
Argonauts, 88
Ariadne, 51, 52, 53, 84
Arikara, 253
Aristophanes, 71, 90, 92
Aristotle, 2, 70, 92, 96, 98–99
Arjuna, 109, 169, 170, 171, 175, 175 (ill.)
Artemis
    Etrusan god, 110
    Greek pantheon, 75
    Homeric Hymns, 56
    masculinized, 76
    Minoan pantheon, 53
    Odyssey, 326
    origins, 78–79
    Roman Republic, 113
    world myth, 267
    Zeus, 66–67
Arthur, King, 140–42, 142 (ill.)
    Celts of Wales, 135
    Fionn, 133, 134
    Herakles, 81
    hero myth, 7
    hero's quest, 279
    Kennedy Camelot, 262 (ill.), 263
    sacred beast, 82
    Sigmund, 154
    symbol of hope, 281
    Welsh hero, 138
    world hero, 277, 278
Artumes, 110
Aruru, 22
Aryaman, 160
Aryans, 158
Asase, 219
Asase Ya, 219
Ascanius, 115, 116, 118, 122
Asgard, 144
Asherah, 26, 28, 54
Ashliman, D. L., 334
Ashtart, 26
Ashur, 19–20, 21
Ashvin twins, 109, 165, 171
Asian mythology. *See* Central Asian
    mythology; Chinese mythology;
    Japanese mythology
Aso, 222, 339
Assyrians, 18
Astarte, 26, 54, 78, 109–10
Astvat-Ereta, 33

Astyanax, 57
Asuras, 270
Asu-sbu-iaamir, 308
Asu-shu-namir, 308
Atana Potinija, 53
Atemito, 53
Aten, 47
Athabaskan peoples, 240, 244
Athene
    Clashing Rocks, 88
    Eumenides, 96
    Greek pantheon, 74
    Herakles, 82, 83
    Homeric Hymns, 56, 57
    Iliad, 58
    masculinized, 76
    Medusa, 86, 87, 262
    Minoan pantheon, 53
    Odysseus, 61
    Odyssey, 58, 59, 62, 324
    owl, 269
    Parthenon, 69, 75 (ill.)
    Poseidon, 72
    Zeus, 67
Athens, 69–70
Athirat, 26
Atlas, 66, 67
Atrahasis, 314
Attis, 34, 79, 122–23, 150, 276
Atugan, 198
Atum, 38, 40, 42, 44, 271
Atum Khepri, 42
Atum-Ra, 38, 40, 42, 43, 44, 46
Atys, 334
Audumla, 147, 155
Augean Stables, 82
Augeas, 82
Augustus, Emperor, 4, 114, 115, 118, 122
Augustus Caesar, 108
Australian Aborigine mythology
    basis for, 205
    creation myths, 207–8
    Dreaming/Dreamtime, 205–6, 206 (ill.)
    flood myths, 208
    indigenous people of Australia, 205
    mythic heroes, 209
    pantheon, 206–7
Avalokites´vara, 177, 188, 194
avatar, 164, 168
Aztec, 230–32

B

Baal, 26, 150, 267, 268, 280
Baal Cycle, 26–27
Babylonians, 19–24
Bacab, 227

Bacchae, 102–3
Bacchylides, 70, 84
Badarian culture, 35
Balabhadra-Rama, 168
Balar, 130
Baldr, 145, 147, 149–50, 153, 270
Bale-thorn, 334
Banba, 131
Barnabas, 123
Barraiya, 207
Barthes, Roland, 262
Bateson, Gregory, 261, 267
Battle Gray, 132, 133
Battles of Mag Tuired, 130
Beaver, 250
Being, 261
Belenus, 126
Beletili, 313
Belides, 331
Belisama, 126
Beltene, 133
Bendigeidfran, 136 (ill.)
Bergelmir, 148, 275
Berry, Thomas, 258, 263
Bestla, 147, 334
Bhagavadgita, 170
Bhima, 171
Biame, 207
Bible, 27
Big Bang theory, 258, 258 (ill.)
Bila, 206
Bilbo, 279
birth, 277
black god, 270
Black Surt, 147
Black Tezcatlipoca, 231
Blackfoot, 255
Blodeuwedd, 137, 137 (ill.), 138, 279
Blue Huitzilopochtli, 231
Blue Wolf, 203
Bodhisattva Kannon, 194
bodhisattvas, 176, 177
The Book of Invasions, 128, 129, 130–31
Book of the Dead, 38–39, 320–24
Bor, 147
Bormo, 126
Born for Water, 244
Bosphorus, 72
Boyi, 180
Brahma, 167, 167 (ill.)
    ex nihilo creation, 271
    Hindu creation myth, 163, 164 (ill.)
    Hindu pantheon, 165, 166
    Mahisha-asura, 175
    Puranas, 161
    Shakti, 174
    Shiva, 173
    tripartization, 109
    Vishnu, 168

Brahman
    animistic creation via dismemberment of world parent, 273
    Bhagavadgita, 170
    ex nihilo creation, 272
    Hindu pantheon, 165
    modern deity myth, 261
    Parade of Ants, 166
    Shiva, 173
    Supreme Being, 267
    Upanishads, 161
Brahmanas, 159, 160, 160 (ill.)
Bran, 136–37
Branwen, 136–37
Bray, Olive, 334
Brigid, 129
Briseis, 57
Brodowski, Antoni, 99 (ill.)
Brynhild, 155
Buber, Martin, 261
Buddha
    Buddhism, 175, 176 (ill.), 176–77
    Japanese Buddhist pantheon, 194
    Maˉyaˉ, Queen, 9
    Muhammad, 31
    Tages, 109
    Vishnu, 168
    world hero, 277, 279
Buddhism, 175–77, 188, 194
Budge, E. A. Wallis, 320
Buga, 198
Bugs Bunny, 247
Bull God, 11
bulls, 53
Bumba, 217
Buninka, 201
Bunjil, 209
Bunyan, Paul, 9, 9 (ill.)
Buqu Khan, 203
Buri, 147, 155
Burkhan, 202
Burning Bush, 279
Buryat creation myth, 201–2
Buryats, 200
Butler, Samuel, 324

C

Caan, 227
Cadmus, 97, 103
Caesar Augustus, 113
Calypso, 22, 59, 117, 279
Cambridge Ritualists, 5
Camelot, 263
Campbell, Joseph
    archetypal hero, 81
    Cuchulainn, 132
    dreams, 8

hero myths, 7, 10
    monomyth, 260, 261
    myths in popular culture, 263
    Neanderthals, 3
    universal hero, 232
    universalist approach to mythology, 5, 6
    world heroes, 277
Canaanites, 25
Canari, 235
Cangjie, 179, 184
Carib, 234–35
Carpet Snake, 208
Cassandra, 93, 94
Cassiopeia, Queen, 87
Castor, 88, 109
Cattle of Geryon, 83
Celtic mythology, 125, 126–27. *See also* Irish mythology; Welsh mythology
Celts, 125
Celts of Wales, 134–35
Central Asian mythology
    Buryat creation myth, 201–2
    cosmology, 198
    creation myths, 200–203
    definition, 197–98
    deities, 198–99
    geography of Central Asia, 197
    heroes, 203
    Master Spirits, 199–200
    Mongolian creation myth, 202
    people of Central Asia, 197
    shamans, 199 (ill.), 200
    Siberian creation myths, 202–3
    themes, 198
    tricksters, 200
    Tungus creation myth, 201
    Turkic creation myth, 200–201
Cepheus, King, 87
Cerberus, 83, 330, 332
Cercyon, 84
Ceres, 110
Ceridwen, 135
Ceryneian Hind, 82
Cesair, 127, 128
Chadwick, John, 50
Chagan-Shukuty, 202–3
Chalchihuitlicue, 232
Chamacoco, 234
Changing Woman, 242, 244, 277
Chaos, 6, 38, 64, 163
chaos, 46, 184, 188, 191, 228, 272
Charybdis, 61, 116, 117 (ill.)
Cherokee, 242, 243, 252
Cherokee Corn Mother, 253
Chibcha, 234
Chimalman, 233
Chimera, 87
Chimpanzee, 215

Chinese mythology
  age of, 180
  Buddhism, 188
  Chinese people, 179
  Chinese writing, 179
  Chuci, 180
  Confucius, 187
  creation myth, 182–83
  creation of humans, 183
  dragons, 186 (ill.), 186–87
  Five August Emperors, 181–82
  flood myth, 183
  Fuxi, 184
  Guanyin, 188, 188 (ill.)
  Gun, 185
  heroes, 184, 186
  historicizing, 187
  Huainanzi, 180
  Nuwa, 182
  pantheon, 180–82
  Qi, 185
  separation of Heaven and Earth, 183
  shamanism, 189
  Shanhaijing, 180
  sources of, 179–80
  Soushenji, 180
  T'ai, 184
  Taoism, 187–88
  unified ethnic-based, 179
  war in heaven, 182
  Yi, 185
  yin and yang, 184
  Yu, 185
Chirakan-Ixmucane, 228
Chiron, 87
Chiyou, 182, 183
Christianity, 31–32
Chrysaor, 87
Chryseis, 57
Chrysippos, 97
Chuci, 180
Cigfa, 139
Circe, 22, 60–61, 89, 117, 279
City Dionysia, 90–92
Cixous, Hélène, 263
Classical Greek mythology
  Aeschylus, 93–96
  Antigone, 99–100
  Aphrodite, 74, 78
  Apollo, 74–75
  Ares, 74
  Argonautica, 88–89
  Aristotle, 92
  Artemis, 75, 78–79
  Athene, 74
  Bacchae, 102–3
  cave myth, 104–5, 105 (ill.)
  Classical Greek history, 69–70
  Demeter, 73, 79
  Dionysian mysteries, 79–80

Dionysos, 75–76, 79 (ill.), 79–80
  dramas, 90–103
  Elusinian mysteries, 80
  Euripides, 100–103
  everyday life, 90
  Ganymede, 77, 77 (ill.)
  gods as reflection of actual human life, 76
  Greek god origins, 78–79
  Greek gods and human life, 76–78
  Hades, 72–73
  Hephaistos, 74
  Hera, 72
  Herakles, 81 (ill.), 81–83
  Hermes, 75
  hero sagas, 79–81
  Hestia, 73
  homosexuality, 77, 77 (ill.)
  Jason and the Golden Fleece, 87–89, 88 (ill.)
  meaning of hero myths, 89–90
  Medea, 101–2
  Medusa, 86–87
  mystery cults, 79–81
  Oedipus Cycle, 96–100
  Oedipus the King, 97
  Olympians, 71–76
  Orpheus, 104
  Orphism, 103–4
  pantheon, 71–76
  Persephone, 73
  Perseus, 85–87
  philosophical myths, 104, 105
  Poseidon, 72
  prominent contributors to, 71
  psychological meaning of, 90
  punishment of the guilty, 100
  role of, 70
  Sophocles, 96–100
  Theseus, 83–85
  Twelve Labors, 82–83
  Zeus, 71–72, 72 (ill.), 77, 77 (ill.)
Cleopatra, 35
Clytemnestra, 58, 72, 88, 93–95, 94 (ill.), 96, 101
Coatlicue, 231, 232, 267, 277
Cochamama, 236
Codex Regius, 144
Coffin Texts, 38, 42, 44
colonialism, 215–16
Conchobar, 131, 132
Confucius, 187
Constantine, 123
Consus, 110
Continental Celts, 125–26, 126–27
Cormac Mac Art, 134
Corn Grandmother, 252
Corn Mother, 253
  archetype, 8
  fertility deity, 268
  hero myth, 7

heroic quest, 281
  origin myths, 235, 246
  world myth, 267
Cortés, Hernán, 226, 231, 233
Coyote, 7, 9, 213, 247–48, 248 (ill.), 249, 252, 269
Cranach, Lucas, 269 (ill.)
creation begun by a goddess, 284
creation from nothing, 284–85
creation myths, 284–86
  African, 217–18
  Australian Aborigine, 207–8
  Aztec, 231–32
  Central Asian, 200–203
  Chinese, 182–83
  Egyptian, 42–44
  Hindu, 163
  Inca, 236–37
  Irish, 127
  Japanese, 191
  Mayan, 228
  modern myths, 257–58
  Native North American, 249–52
  nature of, 6–7
  Norse, 147
  Polynesian, 211–12
  South American, 234–35
  Sumerian, 14
  world myth, 271–75, 276
creation of animistic world via dis-memberment or waste, 285
creation via earth-divers, 285
creation via emergence, 286
creation via Father Sky and Mother Earth/world parents, 286
creation via separation of world parents, 286
Creon (Corinthian king), 101–2
Creon (of Thebes), 97, 98, 99–100
Cretan Bull of Minos, 82
Crete, 78
Creusa, 116
Crow, 207
crucifixion, 32
Cuchulainn, 109, 131–33, 132 (ill.), 172, 277, 278, 279
Culann, 132, 278
cult of Isis, 48
culture heroes, 286–87
cuneiform script, 12, 17 (ill.)
Cupid, 113, 116
Cuthah, 306
Cybele, 8, 34, 78, 79, 122–23, 267
Cycladic mythology, 49–50
Cyclops, 63, 64, 116
The Cyclops (Euripides), 91

D

Daedalus, 50, 51, 51 (ill.), 119
Dagan, 25

Dagda, 129
Dagon, 25
Daïn, 335
Dalai Lama, 177
Damgalnuna, 20
Damkina, 20
Damona, 126
Danaans, 57
Danaë, 72, 85
Danu, 129, 136
Dark Elves, 145
Darwin, Charles, 258
David, 21, 25
Davidian culture, 158
Dechtire, 132
deity descending to the Underworld, 298
deity myths
    Babylonian, 19
    modern, 257, 261
    nature of, 7
    primary, 6
    Sumerian, 15–16
    world myth, 266
Delian League, 69, 70
Demeter
    Eleusinian mysteries, 80
    Homeric Hymns, 56
    Isis, 48
    Minoan pantheon, 54
    origins, 79
    Persephone, 73
    Rhea, 65
    Zeus, 66, 67, 104
Deming An, 187
Demna, 134
Demodokos of Phaiakia, 55, 58, 60
Demophon, 80
Dendera, 39
Deucalion, 119–20, 275
deus faber, 274
Devaki, 168
Devas, 270
Devi, 158, 161, 166, 174, 267
devil undermines creation, 287
Dharma, 171
Di, 272
Di Jun, 180, 185
Di Ku, 181–82, 185
Dian Cecht, 130
Diana, 110, 113, 326
Diana Aricana, 109
Dictys, 85
Dido, 22, 279
Dido, Queen, 116, 117, 118
Dikithi, 220
Dionysian mysteries, 79–80
Dionysos, 75–76, 79 (ill.)
    Aphrodite, 74
    Bacchae, 102–3
    Dionysian mysteries, 79–80

duality of the universe, 270
    festival, 69, 70, 90
    Greek drama, 92
    heroes of tragedy, 99–93
    Homeric Hymns, 56
    Midas, 34
    Minoan religion, 53, 54
    origins, 79
    Orphism, 104
    resurrection, 46
    satyrs, 91
    Zeus, 67
Dioscuri, 88
Dis Pater, 129
dismemberment, 274, 285
dithyramb, 91
Diwe, 53
Diwonusojo, 53–54
Djanggawul Sisters, 207
Dogon creation myth, 217–18
Don, 136
Donn, 129
Donn Cuailnge, 131, 132
Doré, Gustave, 275 (ill.)
Doty, William G., 2
Dragon, 280
Dragon King, 188
dragons, 186 (ill.), 186–87
Draupadi, 164, 171, 175, 277, 278 (ill.), 278–79
Dreaming/Dreamtime, 205–6, 206 (ill.), 208
dreams, 8
Dryden, John, 329
duality of the universe, 270
Duid, 235
Duke of Cornwall, 141
Dumuzi, 14, 15, 16, 19, 21, 213
Duransarum, King, 278
Durga, 166, 174–75, 207
Durkheim, Émile, 5, 5 (ill.)
Duryodhana, 171
Dvalin the Dallier, 335
dwarfs, 145
Dyaus, 163, 165, 272
Dyaus Pitar, 160
Dying God, 270
dying gods, 287–88
Dylan, 137
Dymas, 324
Dynastic periods, 37

E

Ea, 19, 20, 22, 23, 308, 310
Eagle, 207
Earth, 183, 186
Earth Mother, 242, 253, 272
earth-diver creation, 249–50, 274, 285

Earth-Initiate, 247
East Asian mythology. *See* Chinese mythology; Japanese mythology
Echo, 119, 120–21
Ector, Sir, 141
Edain Echraide, 138
Efnisien, 136
Efrawg, 141
ego, 260
Egyptian mythology
    ancient Egyptians, 35
    animal heads, 41–42
    Book of the Dead, 38–39
    challenges to old sun god creator, 47–48
    Coffin Texts, 38
    creation myths, 42–44
    cult of Isis, 48
    deities, 41
    Dynastic periods, 37
    flood myth, 47
    forced separation of world parents, 43
    Geb, 40–41
    Great Goddess, 41
    Greco-Roman world of late antiquity, 48
    Hamito-Semitic language, 35–36
    Heliopolis, 40
    hieroglyphs, 36
    Horus, 44–47, 45 (ill.)
    humanity, 44
    incest, 41
    Isis, 44–47, 45 (ill.)
    main religious centers, 39–40
    Nut, 40–41
    Osiris, 44–47, 45 (ill.)
    pantheons, 40–42
    Pyramid Texts, 38
    pyramids, 37
    Rosetta Stone, 36, 36 (ill.)
    Solar Barque myth, 43–44
    Sphinx, 37
    war between Horus and Seth, 46–47
Eingana, 207
Einstein, Albert, 258
Eitaku, Kobayashi, 192 (ill.)
Ek Chuah, 228
El, 25, 26
Elegbara, 220
Elektra, 95, 96, 260
Elektra, 101
Elektra Complex, 260
The Elementary Forms of the Religious Life (Durkheim), 5
Elephant, 215
Elffin, 135
Eliade, Mircea, 5–6
Elib, 25

Eliot, T. S., 121
Ellil, 19
Elusinian mysteries, 80
Emaa, 53
emergence creation, 250–53, 251 (ill.), 274, 286
emperor-god cult, 122–23
end of the world, 284
Eneferu, 37
Enkai, 217
Enki, 15 (ill.)
    Babylonian deity, 19
    flood, 17
    Gilgamesh, 18
    Inanna, 15, 16
    Sumerian pantheon, 14
    trickster, 149, 269
Enkidu, 17–18, 22, 24, 280
Enlil, 13–14, 16, 18, 19, 272, 310, 314
Enmerkar, King, 12
Ennead, 41
Ennugi, 310
Enuma Elish, 19–20, 21
Enuwarijo, 53
Epic of Gilgamesh, 12, 17, 17 (ill.), 19, 21–24, 309–18
Epimetheus, 67
Era, 53
Ereshkigal
    Inanna, 15, 16, 280, 305, 306, 307
    Sumerian pantheon, 14
    Tammuz, 19
Erinyes, 64
Eriu, 131
Er-Kishi, 201
Erleg Khan, 202
Erlik, 200, 201, 202
Eros, 64, 67, 74, 113, 268
Erra, 314
Erragal, 312
Erymanthian Boar, 82
Es, 198
Eschetewuarha, 234
Esculus, 333
Eseg Malan, 200
Eshu, 219, 220
Esus, 126–27
Etana, 20–21
Eteocles, 99
Etruscan gods, 109–10
Etruscans, 107, 109
Eumaeos, 61
The Eumenides (Aeschylus), 95–96
Euripides, 69, 71, 80, 90, 91, 100–103, 119
Europa, 51, 72, 77, 119
Eurycleia, 61
Eurydice, 119, 329–34
Eurytheus, King, 82

Eurytion, 83
Evander, 118
Evans, Arthur, 49
Eve, 27, 29, 32, 276
ex nihilo creation, 271–72
Exodus, 27

F

Fafnir, 154, 155
Father Sky, 242, 245, 273, 286
Father Sun, 257
Feathered Serpent, 227, 229, 231
femme fatale, 296–97
femme fatale trial, 280
Fenian Cycle, 130, 133–34
Fenrir, 147, 149, 151, 152
Ferdiad, 132, 132 (ill.)
Fergus mac Roich, 131
Fertile Crescent, 11
fertility deities, 268, 288–89
Festivity, 66
Fides, 110
Fidi Mkulla, 217
filid, 127
Finegas, 134
Finn Mac Cool, 133–34
Finnbhenach, 131, 132
Fintan, 128
Fionn mac Cumhail, 131
Firbolg, 128, 130, 155, 270
first humans, 289
First Man, 244, 247, 252, 253, 276, 277
First Woman, 244, 247, 252, 253, 276, 277
Fisher King, 141
Five August Emperors, 181–82
Five Suns, 231–32
Fjorgyn, 146
flood heroes, 289–90
flood myths, 289–90
    African, 218–19
    Australian Aborigine, 208
    Babylonian, 23, 24
    Chinese, 183
    creation myths, 7
    Egyptian, 47
    Epic of Gilgamesh, 309–18
    factually based, 8
    Hindu, 164
    Inca, 237
    Indian, 164
    Mayan, 228
    Native North American, 252
    Noah's flood, 318–20
    Norse, 148
    Polynesian, 212
    Roman, 119–20
    South American, 235

Sumerian, 17
    world myth, 275 (ill.), 275–76
Fomorians, 128, 130, 270
forced separation of world parents, 43
Fotla, 131
Four Tezcatlipocas, 231
Frazer, Sir James, 5, 122
Freud, Sigmund, 5, 65, 259, 260, 262
Freyja, 146, 148, 267
Freyr, 146, 149, 152
Frigg, 147, 149
Frodo, 279
Fujin, 193
Fupao, 181
Furies, 64, 95, 96, 331
Fuxi, 184, 186, 269

G

Gabriel, 29, 30
Gaels, 130
Gaia, 66 (ill.)
    Classical Greek pantheon, 71
    creation, 275
    Enumu Elish, 20
    Gaia Hypothesis, 259
    Great Goddess, 267, 268
    Great Mother, 7
    Herakles, 83
    Hesiod, 64–65, 66
    Medusa, 86
    world-parent separation, 183, 272
Gaia Hypothesis, 259
Gaia-Kronos dynasty, 271
Gaius Cassius Longinus, 108
Galahad, 141
Gan Bao, 180
Ganapati, 166
Ganesha, 4, 161, 162, 166, 170, 171 (ill.), 171–72, 174
Ganga, 173–74
Ganges, 173–74
Gangleri, 144
Ganymede, 76, 77, 77 (ill.), 119
Garden of Eden, 269, 269 (ill.)
Garm the Hound, 152
Garth, Samuel, 329
[click]-Gaunab, 217
Gawain, 141
Geb
    air and water, 44
    birth, 42
    creation myth, 271
    ground, 40–41
    joining with Nut, 64
    Pyramid Texts, 38

separation of Heaven and Earth, 183
separation of world parents, 272
Shu, 43
Gecko Man, 206
Gemmei, Empress, 190
Genesis, 27
Genghis Khan, 203, 203 (ill.)
Geoffrey of Monmouth, 135, 140
George, King, 280
Germanic mythology, 145–46
Geryon, 83, 87
Giants, 64
Gikuyu, 217
Gilfaethwy, 136, 137
Gilgamesh, 23 (ill.)
    ancient Sumer, 8
    Babylonia human hero, 20–21
    epic, 4
    Epic of Gilgamesh, 21–24, 309–18
    flood, 7
    hero figure, 17–18
    hero's quest, 279, 280
    Humbaba, 280
    Inanna, 15, 131, 172
    world hero, 277
Gilgamesh Epic, 12, 17, 17 (ill.), 19, 21–24, 309–18
Gimbutas, Marija, 3
Ginnungagap, 147
Girdle of Hippolyte, 83
Glauce, 101, 102
Gnowee, 206
God, 261–62, 267, 270, 276, 279
    goddesses with dominant power, 291–92
Gofannon, 136
Goibhniu, 129
Gokula, 168
The Golden Bough (Frazer), 5
Golden Fleece, 87–89, 88 (ill.)
Gonggong, 182, 183, 270, 275
Gopalas, 169
Gopis, 169, 169 (ill.), 269
Gordias, King, 34
Gorgons, 65, 72, 86–87, 262
Gorilla, 215
Gornias, 133
Graces, 66
Graiae, 86
Gram, 154, 155
Grand Shrine to Amaterasu, 195
Grandmother Sun, 242–43, 252, 267
Grannus, 126
Grasshopper, 251
Graves, Robert, 62
Great Earth Mother goddesses, 290–91

Great Goddess, 41, 267–68, 268 (ill.), 276
Great Hare, 247, 252, 269
Great Manitou, 271
Great Mother, 7, 8, 268
Great Mother Goddess of Minoan Crete, 269
Great Spirit, 241, 250, 267
Great Tortoise, 163
Great Ziggurat, 13 (ill.)
Greco-Roman mythology, 119
Greco-Roman world of late antiquity, 48
Greek mythology, 113. See also archaic Greek mythology; classical Greek mythology; Cycladic mythology; Minoan mythology
Grimnismal, 144
Gronw Pebyr, 137, 137 (ill.)
Guanyin, 181, 188, 188 (ill.)
Gucumatz, 227, 228
Guérin, Pierre-Narcisse, 94 (ill.)
Guinevere, 142, 263
Gullinkambi, 152
Gullveig, 148–49
Gun, 184, 185
Gungnir, 146, 152
Gwawl, 138
Gwern, 136 (ill.)
Gwion Bach, 135
Gwri, 139
Gwydion, 136, 137–38
Gylfaginning, 144
Gylfi, 144

H
Hachiman, 193
Hades
    Classical Greek pantheon, 72–73
    Elusinian mysteries, 80
    Herakles, 83, 85
    Odyssey, 324
    Orphism, 104
    Perseus and Medusa, 86, 87
    Rhea, 65
    Zeus, 66
Haemon, 99
Haemus, 333
Hagar, 28, 29
Hahaiwutti, 240
Hainuwele, 223, 277, 280, 281, 335–36
Haiwa, 29
Ham, 25, 318
Hamito-Semitic language, 35–36
Hammurabi, 19
Han, 179
Hanish, 312
Hanuman, 173

Hapi, 321
Harappan culture, 158
Harrison, Jane Ellen, 5, 5 (ill.)
Hathor
    Book of the Dead, 320
    Coffin Texts, 44
    cow goddess, 39, 40, 42, 46
    Earth Mother, 79
    Great Goddess, 41
    moon goddess, 53
Hati, 152
Hawawa, 22
Heaven, 183, 186
heaven, war in, myths. See war in heaven myths
Hebrews, 25
Hecataeus of Miletus, 125
Hector
    Aeneid, 116, 118
    Euripides, 101
    fact-based myth, 8
    Iliad, 57, 58, 62, 63, 114
Hecuba (Euripides), 101
Heh, 40
Hehet, 40
Heid, 149
Heimdall, 152
Heimdallr, 146
Hel, 145, 149, 151
Helen of Troy
    Aeneid, 116
    Dioscuri, 88
    Euripides, 101
    Mycenaean-Archaic Greek mythology, 57
    Odyssey, 58, 59, 60, 61, 62, 63
    Zeus, 72
Heliopolis, 40
Helios, 82
Hephaestus, 74
Hephaistos, 53, 58, 67, 74, 76, 214
Hera
    Classical Greek pantheon, 72
    Etruscan god, 109–10
    Hephaistos, 74
    Hestia, 73
    Jason, 89
    Minoan pantheon, 53
    Rhea, 65
    Zagreus-Dionysos, 104
    Zeus, 57, 66–67, 71, 76, 81–82, 83, 103, 113
Herakleopolis, 40
Herakles, 81 (ill.)
    Aeneid, 116
    Argonautica, 88
    Athene, 74
    born with adult characteristics, 277
    Classical Greek hero, 80–81
    Geryon, 87

Gilgamesh, 17
  as Greek hero, 89, 90
  Herakleopolis, 40
  hero's miraculous conception,
    276
  Hesiod, 64, 67
  homosexuality, 78
  Jason, 88
  Jesus, 31
  monster-slayer, 280
  Ovid, 119
  Theseus, 52, 85
  Twelve Labors, 81–83, 279
  Underworld, 32
  world hero, 277
Hercules, 123, 129. *See also* Herakles
Hermaphroditus, 74
Hermes
  African tricksters, 220
  Aphrodite, 74
  Bacchae, 103
  cattle theft, 76, 269, 270
  Eumenides, 96
  Greek pantheon, 75
  Hades, 73
  Herakles, 83
  Hermopolis, 40
  herms, 70
  Minoan pantheon, 53
  Odyssey, 59, 60
  Perseus, 86
  Phrixus, 87
  Zeus, 67
Hermod, 149–50
Hermopolis, 40
hero myths
  Australian Aborigine, 209
  boon, 10
  Greek, 89–90
  Irish, 130
  modern, 257
  Native North American, 252–55
  nature of, 7
  religious, 8–9
  Sumerian, 17–18
  world myth, 266, 276–82
hero quest, 279–80, 296
The Hero with a Thousand Faces
  (Campbell), 6, 7
Herod, 21, 170, 278
Herodotus, 69, 70, 125
heroes abandoned, cast away, or
  hidden in childhood, 295
heroes as monster slayers, 297
heroes born with adult powers,
  294–95
heroes descending to the Underworld, 298
heroes facing a *femme fatale,*
  296–97

heroes miraculously conceived or
  born, 293–94
heroes resurrected or reborn, 298
heroes searching for the Father, 297
heroes threatened in childhood, 295
heroes who refuse and/or accept the
  call, 295–96
Heroic Black Lion, 203
heroic monomyth, 261
hero's call, 295
Herutataf, Prince, 322
Heryshef, 40
Hesiod, 63–67, 64 (ill.)
  Archaic Age, 54, 70
  creation myth, 64–65
  gods of nature, 71
  Greek creation myth, 4
  history of, 63–64
  human life myths, 67
  Medusa, 86
  Ovid, 119
  war in heaven, 65–66, 78, 270
  Works and Days, 114
  Zeus, 66–67
Hesperides, 83
Hestia, 65, 67, 73, 113
hieroglyphs, 36–40
high gods, 298–99
Hi'iaka', 210–11
Hina, 213–14
Hinayana, 176
Hindu cosmology, 162
Hindu mythology
  Agni, 167
  Aryans, 158
  avatar, 164
  avatars, 168
  Bhagavadgita, 170
  Brahma, 167, 167 (ill.)
  Brahman, 161
  Brahmanas, 160, 160 (ill.)
  Devi, 174
  Durga, 174–75
  Ganesha, 171 (ill.), 171–72
  Hindu cosmology, 162
  Hindu creation myths, 163
  Hinduism, 157–58
  Indian cultural history, 157
  Indian flood myth, 164
  Indo-Europeans, 158
  Indra, 166
  Kali, 174–75
  Krishna, 168–70, 169 (ill.)
  Mahabharata, 170–71
  Mount Meru, 162, 162 (ill.)
  mythic heroes, 175
  myth-makers, 161–62
  pantheon, 165–66
  Parade of Ants, 166
  Parvatī, 174
  post-Vedic Hinduism, 161–62

pre-Indo-European period, 158
Puranas, 161
Rama, 172–73
Shakti, 174
Shiva, 173–74
Sita, 172–73
Sri-Lakshmi, 168
stages of development, 159
Surya, 167
Upanishads, 160–61
Vedas, 159–60
Vedic culture, 159–61
Vishnu, 167–68
wars in heaven, 166
Hinduism, 157–58
Hine-nui-te-po, 213
Hippocrates, 69
Hippolytus, 84, 101
Historia Brittonum (Nennius), 135
Historia Regum Britanniae (Geoffrey of Monmouth), 135
Historical Cycle, 130
Hitler, Adolf, 263
Hjordia, 154
Hlakanyana, 219–20
Hljod, 153
Hnes, 40
Hod, 147
Hodr, 149
Holy Grail, 141–42, 279, 281
Homer, 2 (ill.). *See also Iliad*
  (Homer); *Odyssey* (Homer)
  Aeneas, 114
  Aeneid, 115
  Daedalus, 51
  Gilgamesh, 24
  Hera, 76
  Hesiod, 63
  Homer-like authors, 4, 170, 172
  Medusa, 86
  Mycenaean Greeks, 50, 54–57
  mythos, 2
  Odyssey vs. *Iliad,* 62
  Oedipus, 97
  Ovid, 119
Homeric epics, 70, 71
Homeric Hymns, 56
homosexuality, 77, 77 (ill.), 299–300
Honir, 149
Hope, 67
Hopi, 243, 251, 254
Horus
  Book of the Dead, 321, 322
  Coffin Texts, 39
  Eleusinian mysteries, 80
  Isis, 48, 278
  miraculous conception, 276
  Osiris/Isis/Horus cult, 44–47, 45
    (ill.)
  sacred kingship, 36–37, 41

Seth, 38, 46–47
world hero, 277
House God, 244
House of Atreus, 96, 97
House of Thebes, 97
Hu, 187–88
Hu Yingling, 180
Huainanzi, 180
Huang Di, 181, 181 (ill.), 182, 185, 186, 187
Huayna Cápac, 236
hubris, 115–16
Huitzilopochtli, 231, 232, 277
Human, 215
human sacrifice, 233–34
humanity, 44
Humbaba, 22, 280
Hun Hunaphú, 228–29
Hunab'Ku, 227
Hunahpú, 228
Hundun, 187–88
Hvergelmir, 147
Hyacinth, 77–78, 119
Hyksos, 35
Hylas, 78, 88
Hymen, 329
Hypsipyle, 88

I

Iatiku, 245
Iblis, 29
Ibrahim, 27, 29, 30
Icarus, 50, 51, 119
id, 260
Igraine, 141
Iktome the Spider, 247, 248, 269
Iliad (Homer), 57–58, 62–63, 114, 118, 131, 170
Ilib, 25
Inanna
    Aphrodite, 78
    Babylonian deity, 19
    descent myth, 16–17, 152, 280, 305–9
    Dionysos, 79
    Dumuzi, 213
    fertility deity, 268
    Gilgamesh, 17, 22, 131, 172, 279
    Minoan pantheon, 54
    sexuality, 214
    Sumerian deity myth, 15
    Sumerian hymns, 38
    Sumerian pantheon, 14
Inari, 193
Inca, 235–37
incest, 41, 275, 300
Indian mythology. *See* Buddhism; Hindu mythology

Indian (Native) mythologies. *See* Native North American mythologies
Indo-Europeans, 108–9, 158
Indra, 160, 160 (ill.), 163, 165, 166, 167, 171, 267
Indus Valley, 158
Insect people, 251–52
Insular Celts, 127–29
Inti, 267
Inuit, 246
Invasions, 128
Io, 72, 77, 212
Iou, 110
Iphigenia, 93, 101
Iphikles, 82
Irish mythology. *See also* Celtic mythology
    Amairgen, 127
    Battles of Mag Tuired, 130
    The Book of Invasions, 128, 130–31
    creation myth, 127
    Fenian Cycle, 133–34
    Fionn mac Cumhail, 133–34
    Firbolg, 128
    hero stories, 130
    Insular Celts, 127–29
    Invasions, 128–29
    Patrick, Saint, 133, 134 (ill.)
    sources, 127
    Tain Bo Cuailnge, 131–32
    Tuatha de Danann, 129–31
Irkalla, 305
Iroquoian Earth Mother, 253, 270
Iroquoian mothers, 267
Iroquoian twins, 269, 270
Isa, 29, 30
Isaac, 27, 28, 29, 32, 267, 276
Iseult, 139 (ill.), 140
Ishmael, 28, 29
Ishtar
    Aphrodite, 54, 78
    Babylonian deity, 19
    descent myth, 305, 306, 309
    Etana, 21
    Gilgamesh, 22
Isis
    cult, 48
    Eleusinian mysteries, 80
    Geb and Nut, 40
    Horus, 43, 276, 278
    Imperial Rome, 122–23
    Osiris, 43
    Osiris/Isis/Horus cult, 44–47, 45 (ill.)
    Pyramid Texts, 38
Islamic mythology, 29
Ismail, 29
Ismene, 99
Israelites, 25
Itchita, 198

Itzamná, 227–28
Iulus, 115, 116
Iunu, 40
Iuppiter, 109, 110, 111, 112
I'wai, 209
Iweriadd, 136–37
Ix-Chel, 228
Iya, 248
Izanagi, 191–92, 192 (ill.), 193, 274
Izanami, 191–92, 192 (ill.), 193, 267, 274, 275

J

Jacob, 25, 27, 28
Jan Brueghel the Elder, 281 (ill.)
Janaka, King, 172
Japanese mythology
    Amaterasu, 192–93
    Buddhist pantheon, 194
    creation myth, 191
    heroes, 194–95
    influence of Chinese culture, 189
    Izanagi and Izanami, 191–92, 192 (ill.)
    Japanese people, 189
    Kojiki, 190
    modern, 195
    Nihon shoki, 190
    pantheons, 193–94
    Shinto, 190 (ill.), 190–91
    Shinto pantheon, 193–94
    sources of, 189–91
Japheth, 318
Jason, 7, 71, 74, 90, 101–2, 102 (ill.), 119, 279
Jason and the Golden Fleece, 87–89, 88 (ill.)
Jesus
    Arthurian legend, 142
    ascension, 170
    Attis, 34
    Christian myths, 31–32
    Christianity, 123
    circumcision, 28
    descent myth, 16
    duality of the universe, 270
    hero myth, 90
    Herod, 21, 278
    Holy Grail, 141
    Islamic mythology, 29
    Mary nursing, 48
    miraculous conception, 276
    Muhammad, 30–31
    Passion, 32
    resurrection, 9, 32
    Underworld, 280, 281
    Virgil, 114
    world hero, 277, 280

Jiandi, 185
Jibril, 29, 30
Jimmu, 194 (ill.), 195
Job, 267
Jocasta, 97, 98–99, 278
John, 31, 32
Jormungand, 145, 146, 149, 151, 152, 155
Joseph of Arimathea, 141, 142
Jotunheim, 145
Jötuns, 335
Jove, 120–21, 324, 326, 327, 329
Joy, 66
Judaism, 27
Julius Caesar, 108, 115, 119, 122, 125, 126–27
Julunggul, 207
Julus, 115
Jung, Carl, 5, 5 (ill.), 6, 7–8, 246, 259, 260, 261
Juno, 110, 113, 116, 118, 120–21
Jupiter
    Aeneid, 116, 118
    Barnabas, 123
    Dyaus, 165
    Etruscan mythology, 110
    Indo-European mythology, 109
    Julius Caesar, 126, 127
    Odyssey, 324
    Ovid, 119–21
    Roman Republic mythology, 113
Jupiter Dolichenus, 112
Jupiter Latiaris, 109, 110

K

kachinas, 240, 240 (ill.), 274
Kali, 166, 174–75, 207, 210, 219, 228
Kaliya, 155
Kalki, 168
kami, 274
Kami-no-Kaze, 193
Kamsa, 168
Kanaloa, 210, 212
Kane, 210, 212
Kangaroo, 208
Kannon Bosatsu, 194
Karna, 171
Karora, 207
Kaurava cousins, 171
Kay, Sir, 141
Kek, 40
Keket, 40
Kennedy, Caroline, 262 (ill.)
Kennedy, Jacqueline, 262 (ill.)
Kennedy, John F., 262 (ill.), 263
Kennedy, John F., Jr., 262 (ill.)
Kenos, 235
Kesta, 321

Keto, 65, 86
Khafra, 37
Khenti-Amenti, 321
Khmun, 40
Khnum, 42
Khonsu, 39
Khonvum, 217
Ki, 13, 14, 17, 43, 64, 272
Kikuyu Gikuyu, 223
kinaalda, 244
Kingu, 20
Kinich Ahau, 228
Kisani, 251–52
Kojiki, 190, 191
Kore, 80
Kramer, Samuel Noah, 18
Krishna, 168–70, 169 (ill.)
    Arjuna, 175 (ill.)
    avatar, 164, 175
    Bhagavadgita, 170
    born with adult characteristics, 277
    Brahma Vaivarta Purana, 161
    Kaliya, 155
    Mahabharata, 170–71
    Radha, 174
    revelatory acts, 278–79
    threatened and abandoned in childhood, 278
    trickster, 269
Kronos, 20, 25, 64, 65–66, 74, 266, 272
Kudnu, 206
Kui, 187
Kukulkan, 227
Kumarbi, 26, 78
Kumokums, 247
Kurma, 168
Kutoyis, 255, 277, 280
Kuychi, 236
Kwaku Anansi, 340

L

Labyrinth, 49, 50, 51, 52, 53
Ladon, 83
Laeg, 131
Laertes, 61
Laestrygonians, 60
Laius, 97, 98–99, 278
Lakota Sioux, 245
Lakshmana, 172
Lakshmi, 163, 164, 165–66, 172
Lancelot, Sir, 142
Latinus, King, 118
Leabhar Buide Leacain (The Yellow Book of Lecan), 130
Leabhar Gabhá (The Book of Invasions), 128
Leaning Cloud, Jenny, 248

Lear, King, 136
Lebor Laignech (The Book of Leinster), 130
Lebor na hUidre (Book of the Dun Cow), 130
Leda, 72, 77, 88
Legba, 219, 220–21, 221 (ill.), 222, 269
Leig, 133
Leighton, Frederic, 85 (ill.)
Lenus, 112
Lernean Hydra, 82
Lethaea, 332
Leto, 66, 326
Levant, 11
Lévi-Strauss, Claude, 5, 5 (ill.), 6
Li, 183
The Libation Bearers (Aeschylus), 95
Lif, 153
Lifthrasir, 153
Lihui Yang, 187
Lilith, 15
Lincoln, Bruce, 263
Ling Lun, 184
Little Men, 242–43
Lituolone, 222
Liu An, 180
Lizard Man, 206
Lleu, 137, 138, 279
Lleu Llawgyffes, 138
Lludd, 136
Llwyd, 140
Llyr, 136, 139
Locust, 252
Lohiau, 210–11
Loki, 147, 149–50, 151, 151 (ill.), 152, 269, 270
Lono, 211
Lord, Alfred, 56
love deities, 288–89
Lovelock, James, 259, 259 (ill.)
Lucan, 126
Lucretia, 109
Lugh, 129, 129 (ill.), 130, 131, 132
Lughaid of Munster, 133
Luke, 31, 32
Luxor, 47

M

Maasai, 217
Mabinogion, 135
Macha, 130, 131, 138
Mahabharata, 4, 170–71
Mahadevi, 174
Mahayana, 177
Mahayana Buddhism, 176
Mahisha-asura, 175
Maia, 67

Maidu, 247
Makunaima, 235
Malory, Sir Thomas, 140
Mama Kilya, 236
Mama Occlo, 236
Mama Oello, 237
Mamacocha, 236
Mamaoello, 236
Manabozho, 247, 252
Manat, 28
Manawydan, 139, 140
Manco Cápac, 235, 236, 237
Manco Inca Yupanqui, 236
Mandara, 163
Manookian, Arman, 213 (ill.)
Mantis, 216
Manu, 112, 164
Mara the Fiend, 177
Marc Antony, 35, 114
Marcus Antonius, 108
Marcus Junius Brutus, 108
Marduk, 20 (ill.)
    Enuma Elish, 19–20, 21
    Tiamat, 1, 26, 147, 270, 273, 273
        (ill.), 280
Mares of Diomedes, 82
Mark (Bible), 31, 32
Mark of Cornwall, King, 140
Mars
    Constantine, 123
    Greco-Roman myth, 9
    Indo-European mythology, 109
    Julius Caesar, 126
    Jupiter-Mars-Quirinus triad, 127
    Roman Republic and Greek
        mythology, 113
    Romulus and Remus, 111, 112
Mars Lenus, 112
Mary, 29
Maryam, 29
The Masks of God (Campbell), 6
Master Spirits, 199–200
Mater Matuta, 111
Math, 136, 137–38
Matholwych, 136, 137
Mathonwy, 136, 137
Matsya, 164, 168
Matthew, 31, 32
Maui, 210, 212–14, 213 (ill.), 274,
    279
Maui Ti'itit'i, 213
Mawu, 219, 275
Maya, 226, 277
Ma⁻ya⁻, Queen, 9, 176
Mayan mythology
    cosmology, 227
    creation myth, 228
    creation of humans, 228
    flood myth, 228
    heroes, 228–29, 229 (ill.)
    Maya, 226

pantheon, 227–28
Popol Vuh, 226–27
Mayan twins, 280
Mazdaism, 33
Mboze, 219
Medb, Queen, 131
Medea, 84, 89, 101–2, 102 (ill.), 119
Medus, 84
Medusa, 65, 72, 86–87, 90, 119,
    262–63, 280
Megard, 82
Membe, 215
Memphis, 39
Menelaus, King, 57, 58, 59, 61
Mentor, 59
Mercury, 110, 116, 123, 126, 129
Merimde, 35
Merlin, 141
Merneptah, 25
Meru, 163
Mesoamerican mythologies. See
    also Mayan mythology; South
    American mythologies
    Aztec, 230–32
    Aztec creation myth, 231–32
    Aztec mythical heroes, 232
    Aztec pantheon, 231
    definition, 225
    Huitzilopochtli, 232
    human sacrifice, 233–34
    Mesoamerican cultures, 225–26
    Mexica, 230–31
    Olmec, 226, 226 (ill.)
    Quetzalcoatl, 233, 233 (ill.)
    Teotihuacan people, 229–30,
        230 (ill.)
    Toltec, 230
    Zapotec, 229
Metamorphoses (Ovid), 4, 118–22,
    329–34
Metanal, 227
Metis, 66
Miach, 130
Michael (angel), 271 (ill.)
Midas, 34, 119
Middle East, definition, 11
Middle Eastern mythologies. See
    also Sumerian mythology
    Abraham, 27–28
    Akkadians, 18
    Arabs, 28, 29
    Assyrians, 18
    Attis, 34
    Baal Cycle, 26–27
    Babylonian deities, 19
    Babylonian flood, 23, 24
    Babylonian human heroes,
        20–21
    Babylonians, 19–24
    Bible, 27
    Canaanites, 25–26

Christianity, 31–32
Enuma Elish, 19–20, 21
Gilgamesh Epic, 21–24, 23 (ill.)
Hebrews, 25
Islamic mythology, 29
Israelites, 25
Judaism, 27
Middle East, definition, 11
Mithraism, 32–33
Muhammad, 29–31
Night Journey to Jerusalem, 30
    (ill.), 30–31
origins of, 12
Passion of Jesus, 32
Phoenicians, 25
Phrygians, 33–34
prehistoric, 11–12
Qur'an, 30
Semites, 18
Zoroastrianism, 32–33
Middle Stone Age, 3
Midgard, 145, 147
Milesians, 130–31
Milton, John, 271 (ill.)
Mimir, 149, 152, 154
Minerva
    Brigid, 129
    Etruscan-Roman period, 113
    Julius Caesar, 126
    Odyssey, 324, 325, 326, 327–28,
        329
Minoan mythology
    Daedalus, 51, 51 (ill.)
    Greeks, 50
    Labyrinth, 52
    Mesopotamians and Egyptians,
        50
    Minoan history, 49–50
    Minotaur, 51–52, 52 (ill.)
    pantheon, 53–54
    religion, 53
    Theseus, 52, 52 (ill.)
Minos, 49, 51–52, 53, 72, 84, 119
Minotaur, 52 (ill.)
    birth of, 51–52
    Cretan Bull of Minos, 82
    Greek mythology, 50
    Labyrinth, 51
    Minos, 49
    Theseus, 52, 84, 90, 119, 279,
        280
miraculous birth, 293–94
miraculous conception, 277, 293–94
Mithra, 32, 33
Mithraism, 32–33
Mithras, 122–23, 123 (ill.), 267, 277
Mitra, 32, 33, 160, 165
Mmoatia, 337, 339–40
Mmoboro, 337, 338–39
Mnemosyne, 64, 66

modern myths
  ancient myths re-written,
    262–63
  Campbell, Joseph, 260
  creation myths, 257–58
  definition, 257
  deity myths, 261–62
  Freud, Sigmund, 260
  Gaia Hypothesis, 259
  heroic monomyth, 261
  human need to create myths, 263
  Jung, Carl, 260
  politics, 263
  popular culture, 263
  psychology, 259–60
  Schrödinger's Cat, 258
  scientific, 258–59
  Twin Paradox, 258–59
Mongolian creation myth, 202
monomyth, 260, 261
monomythic heroes, 292–93
Monster Slayer, 244, 255
monster slayers, 280, 297
Montezuma, 247
Mordred, 142
Morgan Le Fay, 142, 279
Morrigan, 131, 132–33, 172, 279
Moses, 27, 29, 30, 31, 135, 278, 279
Mot, 26, 27
Mother Earth, 242, 245, 250, 252,
  257, 273, 286
Mother Goddess, 11
mountain, 304
Mt. Nimush, 313
Muda, 206
Muhammad, 28, 29–31, 279
Mulua Satene, 336
Musa, 29, 30, 31
Muses, 66, 333
Muskrat, 250
Muspell, 147
Mut, 39, 41
Mycenae, 78
Mycenaean mythology
  Homer, 54–57
  Homeric Hymns, 56
  Iliad, 57–58, 62–63
  Mycenaean history, 54
  Odyssey, 58–63
  Trojan War, 57–58
Myrrha, 119, 121
myth
  definition, 1–2
  derivation of, 2
  origin of, 2–3
myth-makers, 3–4, 300
mythographers, 4–6
Mythological Cycle, 130
mythology
  definition, 2
  prehistoric, 2–3

mythos, 2
myths
  archetype, 7–8
  burden or boon, 10
  creation myths, 6–7
  deity myths, 7
  dreams, 8
  factually based, 8
  hero myths, 7, 8–9, 10
  philosophy and psychology of,
    7–10
  reasons for telling, 10
  religious, 8–9
  trickster, 9
  types of, 6–7

N

Nakula, 171
Nammu, 13, 14, 17, 19, 272
Nammu-Tiamat, 275
Namtar, 307, 308
Nana, 276
Nanna, 13 (ill.), 14, 16, 19
Naqada culture, 35
Narashimba, 168
Narayana, 163
Narcissus, 119, 120–21
Narmer, King, 35
narrative, 1
Nataraja, 173
Native American mythologies. *See*
  Native North American mythologies
Native North American mythologies
  Changing Woman, 244
  Cherokee Corn Mother, 253
  Corn Mother, 253
  Coyote, 247–48, 248 (ill.)
  creation myth, 249–52
  definition, 239–40
  earth-diver creation, 249–50
  emergence creation, 250–53,
    251 (ill.)
  flood myths, 252
  Grandmother Sun, 242–43
  Great Goddess deities, 242–46
  Great Spirit, 241
  hero myths, 252–55
  kachinas, 240, 241 (ill.)
  kinaalda, 244
  Monster Slayer, 255
  Navajo emergence myth,
    251–52
  Oneida creation myth, 250
  pantheon, 240
  Penobscot Corn Mother, 253
  Raven, 248–49
  Sedna, 246
  Spider Woman, 243 (ill.), 243–44
  Thinking Woman, 245

  tricksters, 246–49
  Water Pot Boy, 254–55
  White Buffalo Woman, 245–46,
    246 (ill.)
  world-parent deities, 241–42
  yeii, 240
Naunet, 40
Nausicaa/Nausikaa, 60, 62, 63, 324,
  325–26, 327, 328
Nausithous, 324
Nautsiti, 245
Navajo, 240, 243–44, 250
Navajo emergence myth, 251–52
Neanderthals, 3
Near East, 11
Nebuchadnezzar I, 19
Nebuchadnezzar II, 19
Nefertiti, 48
Neith, 38, 41, 267, 275
Nemean Lion, 82, 280
Nemed, 128
Nemedians, 128–29
Nennius, 135, 140
Neo-Babylonians, 19
Neolithic Age, 3
Nephtys, 38, 40, 41, 43, 45, 46
Neptune, 110, 324, 328, 329
Nerthus, 146
Nestor, 59
Nethuns, 110
New Stone Age, 3
Ngai, 217
Nidavellir, 145
Niflheim, 147
Night Journey to Jerusalem, 30
  (ill.), 30–31
Nihon shoki, 190, 191
Ninhursag, 14, 267
Ninigi, 193
Ninigi-no-Mikoto, 193
Ninlil, 13–14
Ninsun, 22
Ninurta, 310, 312
Njambi, 219, 275
Njord, 146, 149
Noah
  al-ilah, 28
  Cesair, 127, 128
  flood, 24, 27, 31, 212, 275,
    318–20
  Gilgamesh, 23
  Ham, 25
  Islamic mythology, 29
  Shem, 18
Nokhubulwane, 219
Norse cosmology, 145
Norse end-of-the-world myth,
  152–53
Norse mythology
  Aesir, 146–47
  Baldr, 149–50

definition, 144
Fenrir, 151
Germanic mythology, 145–46
human heroes, 153
Loki, 151, 151 (ill.)
myth-makers, 143
Norse cosmology, 145
Norse creation myth, 147
Norse end-of-the-world myth, 152–53
Norse flood myth, 148
Norse people, 143
Norse war in heaven, 148–49
Odin, 152
pantheon, 146
Poetic Edda (Snorri), 144, 145
Prose Edda (Snorri), 144–45, 145 (ill.)
Ragnarok, 152–53
relationship to other mythologies, 155
Sigmund, 153 (ill.), 153–54
Sigurd, 154–55
Snorri Sturluson, 144–45
tricksters, 149
Vanir, 146
Vikings, 143
Volsunga Saga, 153–55
Yggdrasill, 152
Nuada, 130
Nuh, 29
Num, 198
Numitor, 111
Nummo, 217, 218, 218 (ill.)
Nummu twins, 272
Nun, 40
Nut
  birth of, 42
  creation myth, 271
  devours sun god, 44
  Egyptian pantheon, 40–41
  Hesiod, 64
  Pyramid Texts, 38
  separation of Heaven and Earth, 183
  separation of world parents, 43, 272
Nuwa, 181, 182, 183, 184, 186, 269
Nyambe, 217
Nyame, 217, 221–22, 336–37, 339, 340
Nyami, 222

O

O no Yasumaro, 190
Obatala, 218–19
Oceanic mythologies, 205. *See also* Australian Aborigine mythology; Polynesian mythology
Octavian, 108, 114
Oddudua, 219
Odin
  Aesir, 146–47
  death of Baldr, 149–50, 150 (ill.)
  dismemberment, 273
  Eddas, 144–45
  hanging, 152
  Loki, 151
  Norse cosmology, 145
  Norse creation myth, 147
  Norse war in heaven, 148–49
  Sigmund, 153
  Sigurd, 154
  Supreme Being, 267
  trickster qualities, 149
  Words of Odin the High One, 334–40
Odlek, 198
Odysseus, 60 (ill.), 117 (ill.)
  Aeneid, 115–17
  Athene, 74
  Circe, 89
  Gilgamesh, 24
  hero myths, 7, 89
  hero's call, 279
  Iliad, 57
  Mycenaean Greeks, 50
  Odyssey, 4, 56, 57, 58–63, 324
  Polyphemos, 86, 91
  Poseidon, 72
  religious hero, 9
  Underworld, 32, 280
Odyssey (Homer)
  Aeneid, 115, 116, 117
  appeal of, 63
  Athene, 74
  background, 58–59
  Book VI, 324–29
  Calypso and Circe, 22
  hero controlled by gods, 62
  hero myth, 89
  Homer, 55–56
  House of Atreus, 97
  myth-maker, 4
  Odysseus, 57, 61–62
  Odysseus and Polyphemos, 91
  plot, 59–61
  quest epic, 24
  taught in school, 70
  Trojan War, 50
  vs. *Iliad,* 62–63
Oedipus, 8, 9, 93, 99 (ill.), 111, 260
Oedipus at Colonus (Sophocles), 96
Oedipus Complex, 260
Oedipus Cycle, 96–100
Oedipus the King (Sophocles), 96, 97, 98–99
Ogboinba, 217
Ogdoad, 7, 40
Ogma, 129
Oisin, 133, 134
Ojibwa, 252
Olmec, 226, 226 (ill.)
Olokun, 218–19
Olorun, 216, 218–19
Olympians, 7, 65, 71–76, 270, 271
Omecihuatl, 231, 275
Ometecuhtli, 231
Ometeotl, 231
Omoikane, 194
Ona, 235
Oneida creation myth, 250
Onini, 337
Ops, 110
The Oresteia, 93, 97
Orestes, 95–96, 100, 101
orishas, 274
Orpheus, 88, 114, 119, 280, 329–34
Orphism, 103–4
Orthus, 83
Orunmila, 219
Osebo, 338
Osiris
  Anubis, 41
  Baldr myth, 150
  Book of the Dead, 39, 320–24
  Coffin Texts, 38
  death of, 46
  descent myth, 16
  Dionysian mysteries, 80
  Dionysos, 79
  duality of the universe, 270
  Egyptian funeral ceremonies, 1
  fertility deity, 268
  Geb and Nut, 43
  heroic quest, 281
  Heryshef, 40
  Horus, 36
  Imperial Rome, 122, 123
  Isis, 48, 276
  myth of Isis, Osiris, and Horus, 44–47, 45 (ill.)
  pantheon of Heliopolis, 40
  Pyramid Texts, 38
  resurrection, 46
  Solar Barque myth, 43, 44
  Underworld, 280
Osiris Khenti-Amenti, 321, 322
Osiris Nu, 321, 322, 323
Ossianic Cycle, 130
Otsirvani, 202
Ovid, 4, 51, 71, 72, 118–22, 262, 329–34
Owatatsumi, 194

P

Pachacamac, 235, 236–37
Pachacuti, 235
Pageantry, 66

Paikea, 212
Pajawone, 53
Paleolithic Period, 3
Pandava brothers, 164, 170–71, 278
Pandora, 67
Pangu, 182–83, 183 (ill.), 272, 273
pantheons, 300–301
　　Assyrian, 18
　　Australian, 206–7
　　Aztec, 231
　　Babylonian, 19
　　Buddhist, 176
　　Canaanite, 25
　　Chinese, 180–81
　　Classical Greek, 71
　　Continental Celts, 126–27
　　deity myths, 7
　　Egyptian, 40–42
　　Heliopolis, 40
　　Hindu, 165–66
　　Inca, 236
　　Japanese, 193–94
　　Japanese Buddhist, 194
　　Japanese Shinto, 193–94
　　Maya, 227–28
　　Minoan, 53–54
　　Native North American, 240
　　Norse, 145, 146
　　Polynesian, 210
　　Shinto, 193–94
　　Sumerian, 13–14
　　Welsh, 136
Papa, 210, 210 (ill.), 211–12, 271
Papa Legba, 220
Papago Coyote, 252
Pappas, 34
Papsukal, 308
Parade of Ants, 166
Parashara, 161
Parasu-Rama, 168
Paris, 57, 58, 62
Parry, Milman, 56
Parsifal, 141
Parthenon, 74, 75 (ill.)
Pārvatī, 165 (ill.), 165–66, 171–72, 174
Pasiphae, Queen, 51, 52, 53, 82
Passion of Jesus, 32
Path of Life, 245
Patrick, Saint, 133, 134 (ill.)
Patroclus, 55 (ill.), 57–58, 78
Paul, Saint, 32, 123
Paul of Tarsus, 32
Pegasus, 85 (ill.), 87
Pele, 210–11, 211 (ill.)
Peleus, 88
Pelias, 87
Peloponnesian War, 70
Pelops, King, 97
Penarddun, 136
Penelope, 58, 59, 61, 62, 89

Penobscot Corn Mother, 253
Pentheus, King, 103
Percival, 141
Perdix, 51
Perdur, 141
Persephone
　　changing seasons, 1
　　descent myth, 16
　　Eleusinian mysteries, 80
　　Hades, 73, 119
　　Homeric Hymns, 56
　　Orphism, 104
　　Theseus, 85
　　Zeus, 66
Perseus, 85 (ill.), 85–87
　　abandonment, 278
　　Athene, 74
　　Classical hero, 81–82
　　Danaë, 72
　　hero myth, 89, 90
　　Medusa, 86–87, 119, 262
　　monomyth, 31
　　monster-slaying myth, 154, 280
　　myth, 85
　　quest, 279
　　world hero, 276, 277
Phaedra, 52, 84
Phaiakia, 62
Phidias, 69, 70
Philip II of Macedonia, 70
Philomela, 119, 121
philosophical myths, 104, 105
Phineus, 88
Phoebe, 64
Phoebus, 74
Phoenicia, 54
Phoenicians, 25
Phorcys/Phorkys, 65, 86
Phrixus, 87
Phrygians, 33–34
Pindar, 70, 71
Pirithoüs, 85
Pisistratus, 69, 70
Pizarro, Francisco, 236
Plains Indians, 247
Plato, 2, 69, 70, 104, 105
Plutarch, 41, 45
Po, 210, 211
Poetic Edda (Snorri), 144, 145
politics, 263
Pollux, 88, 109
Polydektes, King, 85
Polydeuces, 88, 109
Polynesian mythology
　　creation myths, 211–12
　　definition, 209
　　flood myths, 212
　　heroes, 212
　　Maui, 212–14, 213 (ill.)
　　myth of Pele, 210–11, 211 (ill.)
　　origin of, 209

pantheons, 210
Polynesians, 209
　　war in heaven, 212
Polynices, 99
Polyphemos, 60, 86, 91, 91 (ill.)
Popol Vuh, 226–27
popular culture, 263
Posedaone, 53
Poseidon, 73 (ill.)
　　Aeneid, 114, 116
　　Amycus, 88
　　animal deity, 268
　　Athene, 74, 86, 87
　　Classical Greek pantheon, 72
　　Cyclades, 49
　　Great White Bull, 53
　　Herakles, 82
　　Hestia, 73
　　Iliad, 57
　　Medusa, 262
　　Minos, 51–52
　　Odyssey, 59, 60, 61, 324, 328
　　Rhea, 65
　　Theseus, 83, 84, 276
　　Zeus, 66, 67
post-Vedic Hinduism, 161–62
Prajapati, 163, 165, 167, 271
Praxiteles, 70
prehistoric mythologies, 11–12
pre-Indo-European period, 158
Priam, King, 57, 93, 101, 116
Priapus, 74
primordial waters, 301
Prithvi, 163, 165, 172, 272
Prithvi Mata, 160
Procne, 119, 121
Procrustes, 84
Proetus, 85
Prolegomena on the Study of Greek Religion (Harrison), 5
Prometheus, 66, 67, 185
Prose Edda (Snorri), 4, 144–45, 145 (ill.), 152
Proserpina, 119
Pryderi, 138–40
psychology, 259–60
Ptah, 39, 39 (ill.), 42, 274
Ptesan-Wi, 245
puberty, 244
Publius Ovidius Naso, 71, 118
Publius Vergilius Maro, 114
Pueblo, 243, 245, 250
Puranas, 161
Purusha, 163, 183, 273
Puzuramurri, 312
Pwyll, 138
Pygmalion, 119, 121
Pylades, 95
Pyramid Texts, 38, 42
pyramids, 37
Pyrrha, 120

Python, 75, 155
Pyyrha, 275

Q

Qebhsenuf, 321
Qi, 182, 184, 185
Qingu, 20
Qu Yuan, 180
Quetzalcoatl, 233 (ill.)
　animal deity, 269
　Aztec creation myth, 231–32
　Aztec pantheon, 231
　Maya pantheon, 227
　myth, 233
　Toltec, 230
　world hero, 277
　Zapotec, 229
Quirinus, 109, 111, 127
Qur'an, 30

R

Ra
　Book of the Dead, 39, 321
　Egyptian creation myth, 42
　Egyptian flood myth, 47
　eye of, 44
　Heliopolis, 40
　Pyramid Texts, 38
　Supreme Being, 267
Rackham, Arthur, 153 (ill.)
Radha, 169, 174
Ragnarok, 152–53, 270, 275
Raijin, 194
Raine, Lauren, 243 (ill.)
Rama, 164, 172–73, 175, 276
Ra⁻ma⁻yana, 4
Ramey, Étienne-Jules, 52 (ill.)
Rangi, 210, 210 (ill.), 211–12, 213,
　214, 271
Rattlesnake, 247, 248
Ravana, 172, 173
Raven, 7, 247, 248–49, 252, 269, 274
rebirth, 298
Red Book of Hergest, 135
Red Branch Cycle, 130
red god, 270
Red Water Snake, 255
Red Xipe-Totec, 231
Regin, 154–55
Remus, 109, 111 (ill.), 111–12, 113,
　116, 270, 278
Reni, Guido, 91 (ill.)
Rerir, 153
resurrection, 32, 298
revelatory acts, 279
Rhea, 20, 64, 65–66, 74, 267, 333
Rhea Silvia, 111
Rhiannon, 138–40

Rhodope, 333
Rigveda, 159–60
Road Runner, 247
Robert-Jones, Ivor, 136 (ill.)
Roman mythology
　Aeneas, 114
　Aeneid, 115–18
　Archaic Rome, 110–11
　definition, 107
　emperor-god cult, 122–23
　Etruscan gods, 109–10
　Etruscans, 109
　flood myth, 119–20
　Greco-Roman mythology, 119
　Greek mythology, 107–8, 113
　Imperial period, 113
　Indo-Europeans, 108–9
　Latins, 109, 110
　Metamorphoses (Ovid), 118–22
　mythographers, 114
　Ovid, 118–22
　Roman Republic mythology,
　　112–13
　Romulus and Remus, 111 (ill.),
　　111–12
　Virgil, 114 (ill.), 114–18
Romulus, 109, 113, 116, 122, 270,
　278
Rosebud Sioux, 248
Rosetta Stone, 36, 36 (ill.)
Ruatapu, 212
Rudra, 165

S

Sabines, 111
The Sacred and the Profane (Eli-
　ade), 5
Sacred Hoop, 245
sacred texts, 302
Sadb, 134
Sahadeva, 171
Salmon, 134
Samhat, 22
Saoshyants, 33
Sappho of Lesbos, 70
Sarai/Sarah, 27–28
Sarasvati, 165, 167
Sargon I, 13, 18, 276, 278
Satan, 29, 269, 270, 280
Satyavati, 161
The Savage Mind (Lévi-Strauss), 6
Schrödinger, Erwin, 258
Schrödinger's Cat, 258
scientific myths, 258–59
Scylla, 61, 116, 117 (ill.)
Sedna, 242, 246
Sekhmet, 41, 42, 44, 47, 268
Self, 261
Selu, 253

Semele, 67, 76, 102–3, 104
Semites, 18
Sentata, 132
separation of the world parents,
　272–73, 286
Serpent, 247, 269 (ill.), 270
Sesha, 155
Set, 45
Seth, 37, 38, 40, 43, 45, 46–47, 278
Seveki, 199–200
Shakespeare, William, 108
Shakti, 166, 173, 174
Shakyamuni, 175, 176
shamanism, 189
Shamash, 19, 21, 22, 312
Shang Di, 180
Shanhaijing, 180
Shem, 18, 318
Shennong, 184
Shesha, 163
Shiktur, 201
Shinto, 190 (ill.), 190–91
Shinto pantheon, 193–94
Shipibo, 234
Shiva, 165 (ill.), 167–68, 173
　Ganesha, 171, 172
　Hindu pantheon, 165–66
　Indo-European mythology, 109
　Kali, 174
　Mahishi, 175
　Pa⁻rvatı⁻, 174
　pre-Indo-European period, 158
　Puranas, 161
　Shakti, 174
　Shiva myth, 173–74
　Supreme Being, 267
Sholmo, 202
Shu, 40, 42, 43, 44, 187–88, 272
Shullat, 312
Shun, 182
Siberian creation myths, 202–3
Sibyl, 117–18
Sibylline Books, 109
Siddhartha Gautama, 175, 176, 176
　(ill.), 176–77
Siduri, 23
Siegfried, 8, 9
Siggeir, 153, 154
Sigi, 153
Sigmund, 153 (ill.), 153–54
Signy, 153, 154
Sigurd, 134, 135, 153, 154–55, 277,
　278, 280
Simonides, 70
Sin, 19, 305, 308
sipapu, 251 (ill.), 252
Sirens, 63
Sisiphus, 331
Sita, 164, 172–73, 175, 276
Skaldskaparmal, 145
Skoll, 152

Sky Father, 202, 242, 272
Sky Woman, 250, 273
Snorri Sturluson, 4, 144–45, 147
Socrates, 69, 70, 104, 105
Solar Barque myth, 43–44
solar deities, 301–2
Solomon, King, 29
Sombov, 201
Sophocles, 97 (ill.)
    Dionysia festival, 69, 71, 80, 90
    hero's call, 279
    Oedipus Complex, 260
    Oedipus cycle, 96–100
    Ovid, 119
Soushenji, 180
South American mythologies. *See
    also* Mesoamerican mythologies
    apocalyptic and flood myths,
        235
    creation myths, 234–35
    definition, 225
    heroes, 237
    Inca, 235–37
    Inca creation myth, 236–37
    Inca flood myth, 237
    Inca pantheon, 236
    Inca religion, 236
    indigenous people, 234
    origin myths, 235
    themes, 234
Sparta, 70
Special Relativity theory, 258
Sphinx, 37
Spider, 7
Spider Woman, 242, 243 (ill.),
    243–44, 251, 274
Sri-Lakshmi, 168, 171
Sri-Rama, 168
Standing Hollow Horn, 245
Star Wars, 263
stories, 1–2
storm/weather gods, 301
Stygian nymphs, 86
Stymphalian Birds, 82
Suijin, 194
Sulis, 126
Sumerian mythology. *See also* Mid-
    dle Eastern mythologies
    creation of the world, 14
    deities, 13–14
    deity mythology, 15–16
    flood myths, 17
    heroes, 17–18
    Inanna, 16–17
    real life in Sumer, 17
    sexuality, 14–15
    Sumerians, 13
superego, 260
Superman, 263
Supreme Beings, 216–17, 266–67,
    298–99

Surt, 152, 153
Surya, 160, 160 (ill.), 165, 167, 171
Susanowa, 192–93, 194, 269, 270
Svartalfheim, 145
Swallow people, 251
Swamp Hawk, 207
Swimme, Brian, 258
Sybil of Cumae, 109

T

Ta'aroa, 210
Tages, 109
T'ai, 181, 184
t'ai chi, 184
Tain Bo Cuailnge (The Cattle Raid
    of Cooley), 130, 131–32
Taliesin, 4, 135, 135 (ill.), 137, 277
Talking God, 244
Tammuz, 19, 21, 79, 309
Tane, 210, 211, 212
Tangaroa, 210, 211
Tantalus, 93, 331
Tantrism, 176
Taoism, 187–88
Tara, 131, 177, 188, 194
Taranis, 126 (ill.), 126–27
Tarquin, 109
Ta-Tchesert, 320
Taulipa, 235
Tawa, 267
Tawhiri, 210, 212, 267
Te Tuna, 213–14
Tefnut, 40, 42, 44
Teilhard de Chardin, 261
Telemachos, 58, 59, 61
Temmu, Emperor, 189
Tengri, 198
tengri, 200
Tengri ülgen, 201
Tenjin, 194
Teotihuacan people, 229–30, 230
    (ill.)
Tepeu, 227, 228
Terah, 27
Tereus, 119, 121
Tessup, 78
Tesub, 26
Tethys, 64
Teutates, 126–27
Tewa Indians, 254
Tezcatlipoca, 231, 233
Thebes, 39, 47, 81, 98, 103
Themis, 64, 66
Theodosius, 122
Theogony (Hesiod), 4
Theravada, 176
Theseus, 52 (ill.)
    Aegeus, 101
    Classical Greek hero, 80–81

hero, 8, 32, 89, 90
hero's quest, 279
killing of Minotaur, 84–85
Metamorphoses, 119
Minoan palaces, 49, 50
miraculous conception, 276
monster-slayer, 280
myth of, 52, 53, 83–84
Oedipus, 96
Ovid, 72
twelve labors of Herakles, 82, 83
world hero, 277, 278
Thinking Woman, 242, 245, 251,
    267, 271, 274
Thoosa, 86
Thor, 145, 146, 152, 155, 267
Thoth, 38, 41, 46, 322
Thucydides, 69, 70
Thunor, 146
Thunr, 146
Tiamat, 273 (ill.)
    Apsu, 19, 20
    dismemberment, 273
    Enuma Elish, 22
    Marduk, 1, 20, 21, 147, 270, 271,
        280
    personification of water, 272
    Yamm, 26
Tian, 272
Tian Di, 180, 185, 272
Tibetan Buddhism, 176
Tiger Snake, 208
Tillich, Paul, 261
Tinia, 110
Tiresias, 99, 103, 119, 120 (ill.),
    120–21
Titan, 83
Titans, 64, 65–66, 270
Tlaloc, 231, 233, 267
Toltec, 231
Tonacacihuatl, 231
Tonacatecuhtli, 231
Tonatiuh, 232
Toneri, Prince, 190
Torah, 27
Tō¯sho¯-gu¯ Shinto shrine, 190 (ill.)
tragedy, 91–93
tree, 304
tricksters, 287, 302–3
    Aborigine, 207
    African, 215, 216, 219–20,
        222–23
    Ananse, 221, 222, 336
    animal shapes, 269
    Aonghus, 129
    Central Asian, 198, 199
    Coyote, 247, 248 (ill.)
    deity myth, 7
    devil-tricksters, 200, 202
    Enki, 14, 15, 15 (ill.)
    Hermes, 75

Krishna, 169, 169 (ill.)
Loki, 147, 149, 151, 151 (ill.)
Maui, 212, 213
Native North American, 9, 240, 246–49, 252
Norse, 149
Odin, 149, 152
sexuality, 214
shamans, 200
war in heaven, 270
world myth, 266, 269–70, 282
tripartization, 108–9
Tristan, 139 (ill.), 140
Trojan War, 55 (ill.), 57–58
Troy Hosea, 246 (ill.)
Troyes, Chrétien de, 140
Tsichtinako, 245
Tsui-[click]-Goab, 217
Tsukuyomi, 192–93, 194
Tu, 210, 211
Tuamutef, 321
Tuat, 322
Tuatha de Danann, 129–31, 136, 155, 270
Tu-chai-pai, 241–42
Tumatauenga, 210, 211
Tuminikar, 235
Tuna the Eel, 213–14
Tungus, 200
Tungus creation myth, 201
Túpac Amaru, 236
Túpac Inca Yupanqui, 236
Turan, 110, 110 (ill.)
Turkic creation myth, 200–201
Turms, 110
Turnus, 118
Turtle, 247
Turum, 198
Tushanshi, 185
Tutankhaten/Tutankamun, 48
Twelve Labors, 82–83
Twin Paradox, 258–59
twins, 109, 303
Typhon, 45
Tyr, 147, 151, 152

U

Ubartutu, 310
Ulgen, 198
Ulgen Tenger, 202
Ullikummi, 26
Ulster Cycle, 130
Ulysses, 116, 324, 326, 327, 328, 329
Umai, 198
Unas, 38
Underworld, 32, 227, 229, 252, 254, 280–81, 281 (ill.), 298
underworld deity, 303–4
Uni, 110

Uni-Astarte, 113
Unkulunkulu, 217, 273
Unnut, 322
Upanishads, 160–61
Uranos
    Aphrodite, 74
    Classical Greek pantheon, 71
    Enuma Elish, 20
    Hesiod's creation myth, 64, 65
    separation of Heaven and Earth, 183
    world parent creation, 272
Urshanabi, 24, 316, 317
Ushas, 165
Utanapishtim, 310, 314–16
Uther Pendragon, 141
Utnapishtim, 23–24, 275
Uttu, 14
Utu, 13, 19, 21
Uzume, 193

V

Vac, 165
Vajrayana, 176, 177
Valmiki, 4, 162, 172, 173
Vamana, 168
Vanir, 146, 148–49, 270
Varaha, 168
Varuna, 159, 165
Vasudeva, 168
Vasuki, 163
Vayu, 171
Ve, 147
Vedanta, 160–61
Vedas, 159–60
Vedic culture, 159–61
Ventris, Michael, 50
Venus, 9, 110, 113, 114, 116, 119, 121
Venus Erycina, 112
Venus of Laussel, 3
Vesta, 111, 113
Vidar, 153
Vikings, 143
Vili, 147
Viracocha, 236–37, 237 (ill.), 267
Virgil, 4, 113, 114 (ill.), 114–18, 116, 118, 121
Virgin Nana, 34
Vishnu, 164 (ill.), 165 (ill.), 167–68
    avatar, 164, 168, 269
    Brahman, 198
    creation from chaos, 272
    Durga, 175
    earth-diver creation, 274
    ex nihilo creation, 271
    Hindu creation myth, 163
    Hindu pantheon, 165–66
    Hinduism, 157

Indo-European mythology, 109
Krishna, 169, 170
Mahabharata, 170–71
Norse mythology, 155
Parade of Ants, 166
Puranas, 161
Ra¯ma¯yana, 172–73
Shakti, 174
Supreme Being, 267
Vedas, 159
Vishvakarman, 166
Volsung, 153, 277
Volsunga Saga, 153–55
Voluspa (Snorri), 144, 147
Vritra, 160, 163, 166
Vucub-Caquix, 229
Vulcan, 118, 328
Vulcan of Romano-Gaul, 129
Vyasa, 4, 161–62, 170

W

Wace, Maistre, 140
Wagner, Richard, 153
Wakan Tanka, 245
Wala, 206
Wandelaar, Jan, 268 (ill.)
Wanjiru, 223, 277, 280, 281
war among gods, 304
war in heaven myths
    African, 217
    Chinese, 181, 182
    Hesiod, 65–66
    Hindu, 166
    Japanese, 192–93
    Norse, 148–49, 155
    Olympian, 78
    Polynesian, 211, 212
    world myth, 270–71, 271 (ill.)
Waramurungundi, 207
warrior hero, 109
Warrunna, 209
Washington, George, 1, 9
waste, 274, 285
Water Monster, 252
Water Pot Boy, 254–55, 277, 279
Waterhouse, John William, 102 (ill.)
Wawalag Sisters, 207
weather gods, 301
Welsh mythology. *See also* Celtic mythology
    Arthur, King, 140–42, 142 (ill.)
    Blodeuwedd and Lleu, 137
    Bran and Branwen, 136–37
    Celts of Wales, 134–35
    heroes, 138
    Mabinogion, 135
    Math, 137–38
    pantheon, 136–38
    Pryderi, 138–40

Pwyll, 138
sources, 135
Taliesin, 135
Tristan and Iseult, 139 (ill.), 140
Weni, King, 38
White Bead Woman, 244
White Book of Rhydderch, 135
White Buffalo Woman, 242, 245–46,
246 (ill.)
White Doe, 203
"White Master Creator," 198
White Quetzalcoatl, 231
White Shell Woman, 244
Wind Sucker, 255
Woden, 146
Words of Odin the High One,
334–40
world center (tree/mountain), 304
world myth
animal deities, 268–69
animistic creation, 273
birth, 277
chaos, 272
components, 265–66
creation, 271–75
creation myths, 276
definition, 265, 282
deities, 266
dismemberment, 274
duality of the universe, 270
earth-diver creation, 274
emergence creation, 274
ex nihilo creation, 271–72
femme fatale trial, 280
fertility deities, 268
flood myths, 275 (ill.), 275–76
Great Goddess, 267–68, 268 (ill.)
hero, 276–82
hero's call, 279
hero's quest, 279–80
incest, 275
miraculous conception, 277
monster-slayer, 280
primary deity archetypes,
266–67
revelatory acts, 279
separation of the world parents,
272–73
threat and abandonment in
childhood, 278
tricksters, 269–70
Underworld, 280–81, 281 (ill.)

war in heaven, 270–71, 271 (ill.)
waste, 274
world-parent creation, 272
world-parent creation, 272, 286
world-parent deities, 241–42
Wotan, 146
Woyengi, 217, 219, 275
Wulbari, 219, 221
Wunzh, 252
Wuriupranili, 206
Wurugag, 207

X

Xbalanque, 228
Xibalba, 227
Xihe, 185
Ximenez, Francisco, 227
Xipe-Totec, 231
Xirang, 185
Xiuhtecuhtli, 232
Xquic, 228

Y

Yaghan, 235
Yahweh, 27–28, 29, 266, 271
Yakamama, 236
Yama, 112
Yamm, 26
Yang, 272, 273
Yao, 185
Yaxché, 227
yeii, 240, 274
Yellow Emperor, 181, 181 (ill.), 182,
185
Yggdrasill, 145, 152, 153, 162, 198
Yhi, 207–8
Yi, 184, 185
Yin, 272, 273
yin and yang, 184
Yinglong, 182, 185, 186
Ymir, 147, 148, 148 (ill.), 183, 271,
273, 276
Ynakhsyt, 198
Yoruga, 217
Yu, 180, 181, 182, 183, 184, 185,
275
Yu Di, 181
Yudhishthira, 171

Yum Cimil, 228
Yumil Kaxob, 227 (ill.), 228
Yurlunger, 207

Z

Z, 186
Zagreus, 104
Zambe, 215–16
Zapotec, 229
Zarathustra, 32–33, 33 (ill.)
Zephyrus, 78
Zeus, 72 (ill.)
Alkmene, 81
animal deity, 268–69
Aphrodite, 74
Athene, 74, 86
Bacchae, 102–3
bull, 51, 53
Classical Greek pantheon, 71–72
Clytemnestra, 96
deity myth, 7
Demeter, 73
Dionysos, 76
Gaia, 83
Ganymede, 77, 77 (ill.)
Greco-Roman mythology, 119
Hera, 76
Hesiod's stories, 63, 65–67
Hindu pantheon, 165
Iliad, 57
Jupiter, 110
miraculous conception, 276
Odyssey, 59, 61, 324, 326
Olympian deities, 78
Orphism, 104
Perseus, 85, 86
Phrixus, 88
Roman mythology, 113
Supreme Being, 266, 267
Thor, 155
Zhong, 183
Zhuangzi, 187
Zhuanxu, 181, 182, 270
Zhulong, 186
Zhurong, 181, 185
Ziusudra, 17, 23, 275
Zoroaster, 31, 32–33, 33 (ill.), 46, 90
Zoroastrianism, 32–33
Zulus, 1
Zuni, 249